# Sailing Alone

# Sailing Alone

*A History*

RICHARD J. KING

**PARTICULAR BOOKS**
*an imprint of*
PENGUIN BOOKS

PARTICULAR BOOKS

UK | USA | Canada | Ireland | Australia
India | New Zealand | South Africa

Penguin Books is part of the Penguin Random House group of companies
whose addresses can be found at global.penguinrandomhouse.com

First published in Great Britain by Particular Books 2023

001

Text copyright © Richard J. King, 2023

The moral right of the author has been asserted

Set in 13.5/16pt Garamond MT Std
Typeset by Jouve (UK), Milton Keynes
Printed and bound in Great Britain by Clays Ltd, Elcograf S.p.A.

The authorized representative in the EEA is Penguin Random House Ireland,
Morrison Chambers, 32 Nassau Street, Dublin D02 YH68

A CIP catalogue record for this book is available from the British Library

ISBN: 978-0-241-64226-9

To Hoss, Lenny, and Munro

"And where we had thought to be alone, we will be with all the world."

Joseph Campbell

# Contents

## CONTENTS

# List of Figures

# Preface

My own solo crossing was not an exceptional feat of seamanship. This is not false modesty. I'm quite proud of the voyage in terms of endurance and my will and energy to make the whole adventure happen, but the passage across the Atlantic took longer than projected, I did not sail efficiently, and the skills that I lacked the most were exposed in embarrassing fashion. By the time I arrived off Cascais my engine was dead. I navigated at that point with only a torn-out cruising guide map of the Portuguese coast, since I never expected to end up this far south. That final morning, after one of the hardest nights of the trip, I saw mountain peaks above the haze. Elated, I shouted to escorts of surfing dolphins and careening brown seabirds. Even as I sailed beside a string of puzzling yellow buoys, conjuring dangerous possibilities of getting tangled in fishing gear or drifting into a military testing zone, I still knew it was over: I had completed my single-handed passage across the Atlantic Ocean. Without a working engine, though, I had to short-tack up to the marina where two men who zoomed out in an inflatable boat tolerated my few words of Spanish (since I knew no Portuguese) before briskly towing me inside the high walls and around to a berth at the dock, after five weeks at sea by myself.

I was physically exhausted, emotionally spent, and paralytically rattled from the entire experience. I rationalized that I had to get back home to my job. I did not have any difficulty going out on the ocean again, even within a year, but I returned only to larger ships. I have not been on the water sailing by myself since. I sold my boat.

Now over fifteen years later, either at sea or ashore, there is sometimes a particular level of wind, a decibel or tone of wind, a specific sound and volume of angry, grasping, howling, relentless wind through a boat's rigging, or through trees or even across the clapboards of my house, that sucks me back to being aboard my twenty-eight-foot sloop in one of those gales in the North Atlantic. When I hear that particular level of wind, I am again looking out of my porthole aboard *Fox*. I feel afraid again. I start going over scenarios again: what to do if $x$ breaks or $y$ happens. I think of that tiny black storm-petrel veering sidelong across my wake, either in its element or also entirely terrified and out of control—I couldn't tell which. It takes several hours for my fear of that certain sound of wind to fade. I've never talked out loud about this fear of wind, never mentioned this lingering emotion to anyone, even to my family.

In other words, this book is not the story of individual excellence, nor is it a compendium of sailing records or a practical manual on how to do it if you're considering a solo voyage yourself.

*Sailing Alone* is the exploration, firstly, of *why go*. I wanted to find out why other people have committed, exiled themselves into small boats alone on the surface of the open ocean. Among those of Western backgrounds, single-handed ocean sailing began in the late 1800s. Individual and collective motivations to cross an ocean alone have shifted over time as solo sailors responded to social, political, and environmental movements; and telling the history of human reasoning for doing this sort of thing requires a parade of wonderfully compelling and surprisingly different characters, who inevitably raise universal questions for all of us ashore about the choice of an adventure of any kind, about legacy, individualism, and the choice of solitude.

Secondly, *Sailing Alone* is the story of *what they saw*. I wanted to know what other solo sailors observed out there in their small slow boats so close to the surface, tracing their transects across the sea. Although their observations are inevitably anecdotal, and they as witnesses are not always reliable, single-handed sailors have provided useful glimpses into the changing global ocean: the most inaccessible, most unknown, yet most influential set of ecosystems on our planet. Sailors alone at single locations and times have recorded snapshots of the sea, for example, from under the shadow of a blue iceberg or while skimming over a coral reef or when gazing over the rail at night upon milky seas of bioluminescence. Solo sailors have described at different locations and times sailing through schools of flying squid, watching ribbons of thousands of shearwaters, or feeling the bumps of great white sharks rubbing their backs on the bottoms of their boats. The motivations of single-handed sailors and their previous reading shaped what they saw, felt, what they heard, what they smelled, tasted, and how they decided to write about the open ocean environment when they came home. The observations of these sailors— of seabirds, sharks, fish, turtles, and whales—have in turn influenced our cultural perceptions of groups of these animals, as well as more broadly in terms of our relationship with the ocean. Meanwhile, technological developments, such as the marine engine, self-steering, photography, and GPS, have in turn influenced the single-handed mariner's observations. Solo sailors stand as channel markers for our larger marine conservation movements, although their shift to environmental activism happened later than you might expect.

Thirdly, this study, this history titled *Sailing Alone*, is about my own relatively minor voyage within those two terms of enquiry, the *why-go* and the *what-they-saw*, which leads directly—physically, chronologically, and metaphorically—back to that singular moment when I rolled out of my bunk and climbed into the cockpit to the greatest shock of my life. I'm trying here to parse the facts and the meanings from what exactly happened on that windy overcast afternoon in the Canary Current at approximately 16:05 local time: when I stared up at that rumbling wall of red.

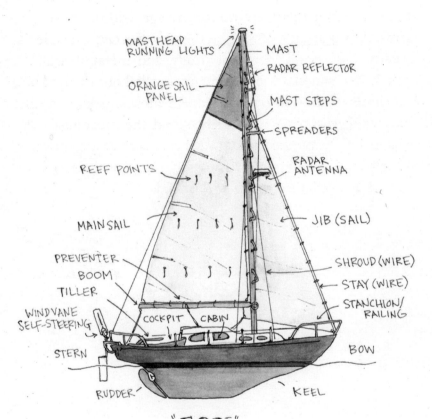

MASTHEAD RUNNING LIGHTS — MAST

ORANGE SAIL PANEL

RADAR REFLECTOR

MAST STEPS

SPREADERS

REEF POINTS

RADAR ANTENNA

MAINSAIL

JIB (SAIL)

PREVENTER

SHROUD (WIRE)

BOOM

STAY (WIRE)

TILLER

WINDVANE SELF-STEERING

STANCHION/ RAILING

COCKPIT   CABIN

STERN

BOW

RUDDER

KEEL

"FOX"

PEARSON TRITON 28.5' (8.7 m)

# 1. Ann Davison and the Meaning of Life

Ann Davison had been a pilot of small airplanes, lived on a small island on a lake, and then with her husband Frank bought an old boat to cruise the world. Aboard this vessel, after two years of devoted but incomplete restoration, they hurried outbound from England in May of 1949 to escape creditors. What followed was a nightmare of two weeks of sleepless days, engine trouble, relentlessly foul winds, and inexperienced navigation. They wrecked on the rocks of Portland Bill, an outcrop into a whirlpool of the English Channel. Abandoning the boat in the middle of the night, they tried to get ashore, shouting to each other to be heard over the gusts and steep seas as the tidal race sucked them away from the coast. Their life raft—an open Carley float rigged with canvas and rope—capsized several times. They endured through the night, through the morning, and then the waves grew still taller and took them farther from land. Frank succumbed to the cold and a particularly violent wave and drowned. After Ann watched this, she numbly drifted in the raft until a shift in the tide and wind enabled her with a makeshift oar to paddle close enough to swim and scrabble ashore. She scaled up the rocks and found help. Inexplicably, despite that horror and fatigue, she knew even then that she would have to go back out to sea. She wrote that her relationship with the ocean could not end there.

A couple of years later, Davison bought a wooden sailboat named previously, by coincidence or fate, the *Felicity Ann*.

She wanted to be the first known woman to attempt to sail across a major ocean alone. Frank had sailed by himself across the Gulf of St Lawrence before they'd met, but Davison's trip was not to better his, nor was it a stunt, an intentional feminist statement, or a bucket-list adventure. Davison's attempt was nothing less than a search for a new meaning in life.

She must have had a certain magnetism, because Ann Davison received enthusiastic help finding and fitting out *Felicity Ann*. Her project remained on the straight rails of activity for a few months until there she was, thirty-eight years old, her brown hair snipped straight across her forehead as if quickly done herself, and now sailing out of Plymouth on the morning of 18 May 1952, three years and a day after she had sailed outbound with Frank.

In the hubbub of this departure day, she nearly crashed into one of her escort boats, but then the press corps and those vessels filled with friends peeled away. The sun went down. She attempted to relax. She watched for ships. She tried to find a more comfortable way to sit in the cockpit with her hand on the tiller. Now she was westbound again near the same waters that she had floated on that life raft, alone this time in a boat of her own, with the intention to sail directly to the island of Madeira, a passage of some 1,500 nautical miles. (I'll be using nautical miles for distances at sea: 10 nautical miles = 11.5 statute miles = 18.5 kilometers; so 1,500 nautical miles is the equivalent to 1,725 statute or land miles.)

Davison was the first to admit that her knowledge of her engine was minimal, her sailing experience still less. She had only taken a brief course in celestial navigation, which she said she found befuddling, but in her self-deprecation she surely undersold this a bit, because from her experience as a pilot of small planes she knew how to read a chart (a map used for navigating at sea), and she understood compass bearings and navigation by dead reckoning (using your speed over the water and the compass course to estimate where you are). She had a radio receiver, so she could often hear the BBC and check her clock on their time signals, but she could not broadcast out to anyone, even to a passing vessel. Local and long-distance radios for two-way conversations, radar for detecting ships and coastlines, and sonar for detecting depth underneath the boat were all instruments in their infancy, technologies beyond the reach of most small boat sailors at the time. More significantly, Davison had no electrical and barely any mechanical means for *Felicity Ann* to steer itself. She wearily sat at the tiller hour after hour, day after day. Sometimes as the voyage went on and conditions were favorable, she was able to tie the tiller in place temporarily or adjust the sails and tie the tiller to guy-lines so the boat could steer itself. More often, though, when she needed to eat or sleep, she resorted to "heaving-to" or "lying-to," meaning she adjusted her sails to stay as stable and stationary in the water as possible. Or she just took down the sails. When lying-to she was forced to content herself with making little progress toward her destination—or even sometimes going backwards.

As *Felicity Ann* was a wooden boat, it would often let in at least a little water at the start of a voyage, even if the planks had already swelled, since the wood was adjusting to open-ocean movement. So by the fifth day, Davison's bilge pumps were clogged with sawdust and other muck from the shipyard work. She was too emotionally exhausted to clear these pumps, "too stupid with fatigue," as she described it. As her

Ann Davison departs from Plymouth, England, on her boat *Felicity Ann* (1952).

boat began to slump in the water, she got herself towed into Douarnenez on the western tip of Brittany by a group of over-eager French fishermen. From here she did what she had not planned, hop-scotching down the coast, sailing south to Vigo, then to Gibraltar, and then south to Casablanca. This unplanned route turned out to be prudent, becoming a shakedown cruise in which Davison was able to gain experience, learn what supplies she did and did not need, and make her mistakes with the boat on shorter passages.

Along the coasts of Spain and Portugal, because of the busy ports and the strong southbound Canary Current, she and *Felicity Ann* regularly had to be mindful of the shipping lanes. In a thick fog off Finisterre, Davison resorted to banging on her frying pan because she had forgotten a horn or any other means of making noise. One night on the way to Gibraltar, she was nearly run down by a merchant ship.

"The seas were fierce and we were lying to without any canvas," she explained, "when suddenly a steamer appeared on the crest of a wave, a triangle of lights, port, starboard and masthead, coming straight for us."

Davison did not have enough time or enough wind to raise a sail to move out of the way, so she hurried down to her engine. Inboard engines had been installed in small boats for a few decades by the time Davison set out, but her little five-horsepower diesel still had to be started by hand cranking. She squeezed her body down below and heaved around the starting handle—"with strength borrowed from fear"— until the pistons began to thump. She leaped back into the cockpit and shifted the engine to forward. The propeller began to spin. Just barely, she scooted her boat out of the way of the freighter, which likely never even saw her.

"After that," she wrote, "there was no more sleep."

Ann Davison's account of her trans-Atlantic passage, titled *My Ship Is So Small* (1956), is in my opinion one of the most artistic and most thoughtful, funny, and surreptitiously poetic narratives ever penned by a solo sailor after their return home.

Sea stories published in English for public entertainment go back at least to the likes of pirate-explorer William Dampier's *New Voyage Round the World*, published in 1697. First-person sea narratives seem to have always been and continue today to be an unapologetic mish-mash of sailing logistics and navigation, of drive-by anthropology, marine biology, and maritime history, with easy blending between fact and fiction. Authors spinning sea stories for publication have usually been eager to tell readers about the creative chores that went into the making of their books, even as they proudly declare that they don't have the authorial gifts to describe the scenes as they sit down later writing with calloused fingers, their foul-weather jackets seemingly still dripping seawater from a hook behind them.

Sailing a boat, historically and today, is in large portion a literary endeavor. Sailors tend to do a lot of reading, turning to reference books for information and to stories to pass the time. They nearly all keep a daily, sometimes hourly, logbook for weather and navigation. And they often keep a personal journal, as well as writing and receiving letters (now emails and texts). When sailor-authors return ashore to write their stories, following the tradition, they often quote directly from their own logbooks, journals, blogs, letters, and from what they were reading on board, sometimes going as far as Sir Francis Chichester in the 1960s, who treated himself sailing alone at sea as a sort of separate on-the-scene reporter, inserting within his books long quotations from his daily log to expound on a given adventure. He transitioned from his past-tense prose to his at-sea writings with phrases such as "My log takes up the tale." Chichester's final words to conclude his *Gipsy Moth Circles the World* (1967) detailed his written output during the voyage: "with eight log books filled up, I had also written more than 200,000 words."

In short, the study of human life on recreational boats, especially those of single-handers, is as much literary analysis as it is history and sociology.

Sailor-writers have consistently been inspired and informed by their predecessors who were able to publish their stories, and sailors who went out alone are particularly blessed when it comes to storytelling on the return because they have no witnesses to hinder the tale. Yet it was not until the mid-twentieth century that solo-sailing authors, all of whom had been men, began to feel open enough to describe their journeys in more personal, emotional terms. In *Sailing Alone Around the World* (1900), Joshua Slocum—the dean of single-handed sailing and the author of what is still the most popular and influential story of them all—is self-effacing at times and shares moments of emotion, but he barely reveals his inner self. Ann Davison, a half-century later, is one of the earliest if not *the* first single-handed sailor to admit candidly and describe in detail her genuine fear, loneliness, and self-doubt.

Sea narratives, single-handed or otherwise, used to spend little time ashore before casting off the dock lines. Before the 1960s or so, sailor-authors usually gave only a slight background as to their internal motivation for the voyage, resting on tough tropes along the lines of "Why not?," "Because I wanted to," and "I ran out of other things to do." Davison, however, delved deeply and mindfully into her reasoning, including her thinking after the drowning of her husband. In setting the stage for her trans-Atlantic attempt in *My Ship Is So Small*, she wrote something that is worth quoting in full:

> The only way to live is to have a dream green and growing in your life, anything else is just existing and a waste of breath . . . Adventure, some people call it, or romance, or when they are really frustrated, escapism. If anyone asked me and I was unguarded enough to reply, I would call it the pursuit of beauty, or truth, and if I was honest I would admit it was largely curiosity, the urge to find out the why, the what and the how at first hand, without simply taking someone else's word for it . . . I know by now that the glitter of romance as seen from afar often turns out to be pretty shoddy at close quarters, and what appears to be a romantic life is invariably an uncomfortable one, but I know, too, that the values in such living are usually sound. They have to be, or you don't survive. And occasionally you are rewarded by an insight into living so splendid, so wholly magnificent, you can be satisfied with nothing less ever after, so that you go on hoping and searching for another glimpse for the rest of your life. The dream-boat business came up three years before I actually set out because I had a life going spare and wanted to use it, and the notion of sailing a small boat about the world appealed because it offered freedom, independence, travel and a home into the bargain.

Davison laid out here much of what has driven people to go to sea for the last two centuries. Certain individuals, by some mixture of nature and nurture, usually spurred by social factors or personal trauma or spiritual ennui or too much reading, have throughout human history rejected the materialism of their day and sought simpler lives as they desired physical adventure and challenge, even if that might put their life in danger. These traits and reasons, however, do not speak precisely to the desire to go by oneself. Davison's single-handed trip for "freedom, independence, travel" was, in many ways, an anti-social, self-centered, and seriously selfish act. But then again, if Davison wanted to go to sea alone again, perhaps the potential of losing someone else might have been too traumatic to imagine.

Single-handed sailor-authors rarely admit that they embark on a trip like this for something to write about, yet Davison explained that "it would surely provide unlimited copy with which to feed the typewriter and incidentally me, for I had degenerated into a writer of sorts through the years." The fact is, a solo voyage across an ocean alone for anyone has a significant, even primary aspect of social and artistic performance. Most sailors, reading others, have envisioned writing about their voyage even before they cast off. Once out at sea, they're reading others' accounts, sending out articles and long letters and writing journal entries, and then after they have survived and returned to shore, they have almost always wanted to write and publish about it, rendering the reader, author, and mariner experience inextricably entwined. Although by today there have been surely hundreds of single-handed sailors who have been truly hermits, shunned all publicity, and written nothing and never had any desire to do so, the solo sailor without literary aspirations seems to be more the exception than the rule. Many, due to lack of writing skills or racism or misogyny in the book business, have been unable to publish their narratives. This often left their voyage feeling incomplete. Decades after her own circumnavigation, single-hander Tania Aebi wrote that the writing of her story directly after her trip, "performing the expected duties—compiling a book," was a necessity for her to provide full closure before she could move on with her life. Sailor-writer John Rousmaniere put it this way: "Equally respected is the tradition of returned solo sailors telling as many people as possible how they did it. This marriage of monastic retreat and public confession may seem contrary, but there it is." Ann Davison laid this all out there in *My Ship Is So Small*.

Davison's *why-go* paragraphs present, most importantly, the genuine, unabashedly aspirational belief that a sail across an ocean is a passage of greater significance, a vision quest, a morality tale for how we each should spend our time on Earth. Voyages alone out to sea, taken so intensely and seriously by their sailor-authors, represent one of the nearest and clearest of metaphors of any single human life spent on Earth. A copy-editor for a newspaper in Ohio named Robert Manry, who sailed a 13.5-foot boat across the Atlantic in 1965, wrote that he tried to craft his voyage "into something nearer to a work of art than my life on land had been." This is perhaps why the single-handed voyage story is so compelling to so many of us—in its madness, pluck, pride, and in its "do not go gentle" journey of solitude before existential unknowns. No one on the planet is more often reminded of one's meaninglessness in time than the solo sailor in a little boat bobbing about on the eternal indifferent deep.

One of the few aspects that Davison did not explore in her explanation of her *why-go* in *My Ship Is So Small*, although she alludes to this with her admission of "escapism," was the state of the world in which she lived in the early 1950s.

Davison had written in her previous book, *Last Voyage* (1951), that "thousands of people, blasted out of their calm by war, found it difficult to settle in their peacetime niches." These people were called escapists, she said, who "turned their eyes to distant lands across the sea, and a broader vista of living."

Both of the world wars had reminded us of our collective human capacity for hatred and violence toward one another, cruelties enabled by our tribalisms, racisms, and our clever inventions such as aircraft, machine guns, lethal gases, and then the development of the atomic bomb. In response to the wars, Western cultures—an imperfect broad grouping that I'll use for lack of a better one—turned toward the ocean for visions of peace and escape. The New Zealand historian Harold Kidd described the rise of a "sea gypsy culture" that began in the 1920s in response to the madness of World War I: "People from England and other places began this move to get the Great War behind them and get the hell out of the place. They sailed all over the world."

After the two world wars, with the atrocities fully revealed and the dead tallied, the floodgates of the world's ports seemed to empty out again to sea dreamers. Frank and Ann Davison, for example, began their search for their own boat immediately after peace was declared in 1945. The sea had emerged as a respite from humanity, finding thousands of survivors seeking new lives, a "Ulysses generation" as Rousmaniere put it: people who perceived the ocean as the last place on Earth that remained wild and untouched by war, still seemingly clean and free without national borders and government authorities.

In 1949, two years before Davison's trip, fellow Englishman Edward Allcard also crossed the Atlantic alone in a wooden boat. He published *Single-Handed Passage* (1950), which is full of small moments of boastful joy, his naked self monkeying around dangerously over the side, and his explanations of nautical strategies in rigging and engine work. Allcard provides a window into the period as he rants regularly about capitalism, paperwork in ports, petty burglary on the docks, lack of respect for the yachtsmen who helped during the war, and most of all how the ocean provides respite from all this. As he approached New York, and the fame for which he declared disinterest, he wrote in *Single-Handed Passage*: "What was there to celebrate? Getting near to the artificialities and impurities of civilization, where money was god? Giving up the glorious freedom of the sea? . . . How many have said to me 'You are doing just what I have always dreamed of doing.'"

Sailors and writers, like Davison and Allcard, as well as marine biologists, oceanographers, anthropologists, artists, and filmmakers, developed and mirrored this cultural interest in the sea in the decades around the world wars. They influenced a flood of Western public interest in the ocean as a representation of a simpler life, a saltwater horizon full of meaning and purpose, a place as yet undiscovered and unspoiled and beyond the influence of people. Scholars refer to this as post-war primitivism. For example, Ernest Hemingway's *The Old Man and the Sea* (1952), which would win him the Pulitzer Prize, had just been published when Davison set out to cross the Atlantic. In the novel an aging poor Cuban fisherman rows out into the Florida Straits alone, then sets his sails and uses a handline, shunning the new motorized technologies of the younger fishermen in the harbor. Hemingway's old man feels a romanticized brotherhood with the animals of the sea, even the ones he kills and eats. By the time of Davison's voyage, Thor Heyerdahl and his war buddies had completed their passage on a raft from Peru to French Polynesia. The expedition, their best-selling book, *Kon-Tiki* (1950), and their Oscar-winning documentary of the same name continued to send escapist, ocean-centric, tiki-themed waves throughout Europe and across North America. Frenchman Jacques Cousteau and his colleague Émile Gagnan had invented the aqualung and were beginning to make their underwater films. American ichthyologist Eugenie Clark had published the international bestseller *Lady with a Spear* (1951), the first mainstream memoir by a woman marine biologist. And Rachel Carson had an unprecedented two books, *Under the Sea-Wind* (1941) and *The Sea Around Us* (1951), both measured, scientifically researched natural histories of the ocean, sitting comfortably at the same time in the top ten of the *New York Times* bestseller list. In the 1953 issue of *Life* magazine in which Davison first told the story of her ocean-crossing, her feature is sandwiched between horrific black and white photographs from the Korean War—soldiers walking past dead bodies and pointing guns at seemingly groveling North Korean "Red" soldiers—and a full-color advertisement for the Hollywood film *Return to Paradise* (1953), featuring scantily clad women in Hibiscus-print dresses, smooching sailors, and being rescued on the beach by Gary Cooper as a turquoise ocean horizon plays placidly in the background.

So it was within this rising tide of public interest in the ocean that on 20 November 1952, Ann Davison aboard *Felicity Ann* nosed her way out alone beyond the island of Gran Canaria to attempt to sail across the Atlantic. Only a few days after she left, the world learned that the United States had weeks earlier detonated the world's first thermonuclear bomb in the Marshall Islands. This weapon exploded a radioactive mushroom cloud over the North Pacific ten miles high.

Davison faced a 2,600-mile passage. Starting off with black clouds and rain, but a mostly auspicious breeze, she knew that already out there was a French physician named Alain Bombard who had set out a month before in a fifteen-foot rubber raft. Bombard had a single sail, a sextant, a fine-mesh net, and two cameras supplied by *Life* magazine. He carried barely any food, which was part of his declared mission. Young Dr. Bombard stowed only sealed emergency rations so he might prove that the ocean could offer a person enough water and enough food in the form of fish, to be supplemented by, as *Life* explained, "the nutritive qualities of plankton." Bombard made it to Barbados in a little over two months. Having proved his point, he published his book *Histoire du Naufragé Volontaire (Story of a Voluntary Castaway)* the following year.

Davison, for her part, had packed her *Felicity Ann* with water and food such as eggs, fruit, potatoes, pre-cooked corn flour, and bread rusks, enough for a possible sixty days, which she believed to be "an excess of caution," because she reasonably anticipated an actual passage of some thirty to forty days. The steady, favorable trade winds are legendary for smooth westbound passages across to the Caribbean. In early November 1952 a new friend in the Canary Islands had given her a canned Christmas pudding, saying, "Not that I don't think you'll make it across before then, but you never know." Even though she got a late start, Davison assumed that by Christmas she would be comfortably drinking cocktails in English Harbour, Antigua—or at least quite close.

She did not even pack a nautical almanac for the following year, an essential book for celestial navigation.

On Christmas morning, Ann Davison floated, crazed, in the latitudes of where all had told her to expect the trade winds. She had not found them. For the entirety of the passage so far she had experienced only occasional days of favorable wind. She saw only teasing glimpses, hours here, a day there, of the characteristic trade-wind clouds, those long low lines of puffy cumulus that have propelled sailors from Europe to the Caribbean for centuries. On this December 25th, however, Davison calculated that she was still only about halfway across the ocean. She could not be entirely sure, because she was not confident about her celestial calculations and sextant work.

The cabin of her boat was like a sauna, the sea like molten lead. Each day of calm she ran the engine for two hours, just to move and feel the breeze on her face. She worried about the barnacles and algae growing along the hull of *Felicity Ann*, making her progress still slower. When there were not calms, there had been winds from the west. Small traditionally rigged boats can at best make fifty or sixty degrees toward the direction of the wind. This meant to go westbound with a west wind she had to aim more toward the north-northwest and then tack, alter course, and sail back toward the south-southwest. On the open ocean, with no long-range weather forecasts, it's terribly hard to calculate when it's best to make these tacks, these long zig-zags, and when to expect wind shifts, how to consider currents, and how to maximize miles and angles toward an eventual direction, especially when you're new at long passages. And if this were not enough to obsess about, Davison worried about hurricanes. She was statistically safe from hurricane season, but this unsettled weather made her doubt if a massive storm was not on the way. Sometimes she suffered aggressive squalls coming out of nowhere. She had no one to consult. She was even having difficulty getting any of the BBC broadcasts on her radio receiver. On the subject of ocean weather in the Atlantic, she read every book that she had aboard, over and over again, yet she could make no sense of her predicament. It's difficult for most of us to imagine the emotional strain and doubt, exacerbated by lack of sleep, that spun a perpetual gauze around Davison's thinking as she endured life aboard her tiny boat, just twenty-three foot long, surrounded by a water horizon for day after day after day.

Davison decided to open her friend's Christmas pudding. When she bit into the sweet dense cake, the dried fruit did not go down well. Another insult. She surely hurled that pudding and its can as far over the side as she could, only to have to watch it bobbing there on the flat sea in sight for the rest of the day. Unless, mercifully, it sank.

Perhaps the only silver lining to traveling so maddeningly slowly is that Davison, like the fanatical Dr. Bombard, had an unprecedented amount of quiet, close-to-the-surface time to observe the open-ocean environment of the temperate Atlantic. Although a rainbow one day lifted her spirits mightily, Davison was not exactly smitten with the blue environmentalism that was beginning to permeate Western cultural perceptions of the sea in the 1950s. She did not see her voyage in those terms. She did not include in her explanation of *why-go*, or surprisingly anywhere in *My Ship Is So Small*, what it is about the ocean itself, about saltwater, this call to the sea, that magnetizes so many Ishmaels to the foot of the harbor or to exile themselves out alone across oceans. Why, for example, did Davison not set off for a long hike in the Alps or the Rockies? She did not wax poetic about the ocean as boundless and free and healing or a space that we need to protect. She did not carefully write down what she saw in terms of species, abundance, or behavior. Davison's ocean was a purgatory with stagnant calms or foul winds. Her ocean was also the environment in which she had watched her husband drown. She flicked her cigarette butts over the side and dumped her daily garbage in the sea. When she came upon a couple of cans floating on the surface, Davison was not disgusted by the litter so far from land. She saw floating trash as a comfort, helping to ease her loneliness, reassuring her that other people were out there.

Ocean-going field guides were in their publishing infancy at the time, and, as far as I can tell, these were not the sort of books Davison brought along anyway. Beyond perhaps one illustrated "fish book," she seemed to prefer volumes on navigation or collections of English verse. She did not look over the rail and envision squeaky dolphins as her personal friends. Even with some mental distance after the trip, when Davison sat down to write *My Ship Is So Small*, she did not relay any spiritual connection to marine mammals or really any open-ocean life.

At most, Davison mentioned some companionship derived from the fish that schooled in the shade of *Felicity Ann*, such as the smaller ones that nibbled at the invertebrate growth on the boat's bottom. Although she never put out a line to catch fish— she said she would have felt badly about killing them—she did eat the occasional flying fish that ended up dead on deck. This started when she had felt "honor bound" to eat one, since she'd read about this so often. After she fried a flying fish in butter and found she liked it, she did so several times more. One day she also recorded "baby cuttlefish" on deck, which were likely unfortunates from a school of flying squid.

Davison's imagery of fish and squid seem mere moments, like curious clouds or, if she had been traveling on land, a mention of an attractive perennial on a front yard in a foreign country. The marine life gave some local flavor to her story, but it carried no moral for humans or messages about ocean health.

More emblematic of Davison's relationship with the sea was an encounter later, in mid-January. As she continued her grueling passage westbound, three large sharks arranged themselves in formation around *Felicity Ann*, one on each side and one astern. "Unspeakably sinister," the sharks swam so close that she could have reached over the rail and touched them. They served only to emphasize the menace of the ocean: what Davison described as the "ceaseless, tireless, lonely, loveless sea."

In other words, Ann Davison felt that people cannot love the ocean any more than anyone can love the sky or outer space. Her sea of the 1950s was a wilderness in which to prove oneself, in the wake of Joseph Conrad, far from the forming eddies of Rachel Carson and Jacques Cousteau. Love of the ocean for Davison was the love of seafaring, the "illusion of mastery."

Eventually, after an anxious slog of sixty-five days alone at sea, which included a troubling stye in one of her eyes and "sea boils," Ann Davison dropped anchor in a small harbor of Dominica in the late afternoon of 24 January 1953, becoming indeed the first woman documented to have crossed an ocean alone. Davison's final words of *My Ship Is So Small* are about courage, which she defined as resilience, going forward, and openly learning from mistakes.

My own personal copy of the book is by chance a used first edition in which the only markings anywhere from a previous reader are on the last page. They are timid, precise lines penciled carefully with a straight edge under the very last words of the book: "I had to sail across thousands of miles of ocean to find out that courage is the key to living."

# 2. Seabirds

I spent my last day on land, my thirty-seventh birthday, in Port-land, Maine. It was a summer downpour. I walked in the rain to the market and then walked home in the rain with bags in both hands. I had to stop often because it was a long walk to the docks, and I had impulsively purchased a lot of last-minute supplies and more food. Into my boat's deck I through-bolted two new shrouds for extra safety, then I walked back through the rain to buy the Sunday *New York Times*. I made a few calls in a phone booth, talking loudly over the rain, and I had my last supper alone at a bar watching the rain out of the window.

I left at dawn the next morning under a clear sky, but with little wind, which puffed ever so slightly from the wrong direction. I used my engine to stay away from the breakwater, because I was continually sloshed toward the rocks and the smell of seaweed by the wakes of a roaring parade of out-going lobster boats. Big-eyed seals poked up their heads and watched me as I sailed slowly, back and forth all morning, in clear view of the city. In the afternoon I was able to edge out into the Gulf of Maine. A dolphin appeared off the star-board side. I heard it exhale first. This dolphin's arrival felt good, because I was grasping for good omens. The gloomy last day ashore and this windless first morning did not bode well for my trans-Atlantic.

I sailed across the Gulf of Maine. By midnight on the second day, at about the longitude of the mouth of the Bay of Fundy, I slid under a blanket of thick fog.

I turned on the radar. I set an alarm on this radar to warn me if a vessel came within a certain distance, but I didn't trust this, so I slept only in short stints. I saw the blue blips of fishing vessels on my radar screen and occasionally heard their engines. Once a vessel came within several hundred yards of me. It was so dark and the fog was so thick that I couldn't see the boat. They didn't answer their radio. I thought about using my air horn, but I knew their engine was far too loud to hear something like that. So I just waited on deck and listened. I stared into the black, continually checking the radar as the boat kept coming closer. Absurdly in retrospect, I brought up my red neoprene survival suit to have at hand in the cockpit. I turned my engine on. I considered tacking. The boat came within a few hundred yards of running me down, but even then I could not see its lights. It was as if I had my ear to a tiled wall of fog when a subway train chugged past.

Meanwhile, I was seasick. I didn't vomit over the side, which might have felt better actually. This was more the kind of seasickness where you're listless, lazy, and wool-brained. Where it's only a few hours into it that you realize, *oh, I'm seasick*. In retrospect, the seasickness probably numbed my anxiety, forcing me to take naps when I otherwise would have been too wired and worried to do so.

Come daylight it was still thick fog, but the wind had died. *Fox* rolled in the flat, green-gray seas and the little red wind indicator at the top of the mast spun in confused circles. Water dripped in rivulets off the sails. While I was trying to figure out how to manage these conditions, a brown shearwater and a couple of white fulmars glided out of the fog and fluttered onto the water's surface beside *Fox*, within my fuzzy cone of visibility. The birds paddled to the stern, pivoting their heads, asking, it seemed, to speak with the commanding officer.

The pair of fulmars stuck with me for the entire morning, pittering around inquisitively as I stood alternating between watching them, checking the radar, and observing silvery drops of water unite together under the stainless-steel railing and blip onto the deck. Northern fulmars (*Fulmarus glacialis*), a seabird you rarely see near shore in New England, are stockier and thicker than a herring gull but with the same white head and body and grayish wings. They have thick, stubby tube-noses, like petrels, and their eyes are dark with some black feathering around them, which makes their eyes look larger and darker with a stern-looking brow.

The fulmars lightened things up a bit. Maybe they had learned to scavenge offal from fishing vessels in the area. Occasionally one bird would look up as if to say: "Having some trouble, Mac? Relax. Got any haddock?"

I kept a daily logbook as mariners do, recording weather observations, barometric pressure, my GPS position, and so forth. I wrote down small bits of observations, kept track of my boat maintenance, and all sail and course changes. Despite my intentions, I rarely at this point sat down with a journal to record my thoughts more broadly. I also rarely took the time to key out a species of animal, to figure out, say, if that was an adult or juvenile northern fulmar or which species of shearwater that might be. I took photographs when I could (from these it looked like they were adult fulmars and a Manx shearwater, *Puffinus puffinus*), but I was usually just too tired and worried to be journaling or paging through field guides, especially early on when sluggish with seasickness.

That foggy morning at the outer edge of the Gulf of Maine,

however, thanks to the fulmars, I had my first moment to smile a little bit. With a towel over most of the page to keep the logbook dry from my dripping jacket, I wrote in the logbook: "11:15. Still becalmed. Followed closely by a Northern Fulmar, paddling faster than me. It sampled both a piece of Cracklin' Oat Bran cereal and a bit of banana peel. Didn't like either."

Seabirds are the most visible marine life for sailors. And especially for the solitary mariner, they are the most relatable. With their eyes, nose-like beaks, and two legs, they are easily anthropomorphized. For tens of thousands of years, early Indigenous wayfinders and fishers and mariners all around the world have used seabirds as guides to land, to sea routes, and as indicators of fish. Sailors of earlier ages from a range of cultures also ate seabirds if they could catch them, and mariners have seemingly always collected seabirds as trophies and created art and tools from their feathers, bones, and webbed feet. Some mariners have imagined the souls of dead sailors in the bodies of birds at sea, a belief that continues among some people today. In 2006 solo circumnavigator Bill Pinkney wrote that one day after sailing past Cape Horn the reincarnation of a friend seemed to appear in an albatross that landed in the sea behind his boat, assuring him the storms were over, that now "you'll be okay."

Sometimes observations by mariners out in the deep sea

give us anecdotal and occasionally quite useful data points about the ecology of different parts of the ocean, the ranges of species, their pelagic behavior, and how, more qualitatively, human actions and our understanding and attitudes around and about the ocean's animals have shifted or remained the same. Single-handed sailors, attentive in their small, quiet boats, have observed seabirds closely and featured them in their stories.

In *My Ship Is So Small*, for example, Ann Davison wrote occasionally of seabirds to paint the setting of the part of the Atlantic on which she traveled and also because these birds offered her the most substantial connection to other living things. Only days out from the Canary Islands, she commented that when she was cleaning out her stores of rotten fruit, she was amazed at how quickly groups of gulls and petrels arrived. She ascribed their ability to find her boat to a sensitivity to physical movement, rather than, as we understand this today, to the birds' superior sense of smell. Later in her trans-Atlantic crossing, Davison identified a pair of "bosun birds," now more commonly called tropicbirds (*Phaethon spp.*), known for their long thin tail feathers. She described their flight and their "shrieking ornithological oaths at one another." Several days later she saw another tropicbird, eastbound. Davison was surprised that this bird was traveling alone and did not stop to observe her boat. She whistled loudly. The tropicbird turned, flapped back to her boat, then "dives and stalls about three feet from my head, looks sharply at me, decides against whatever he had in mind to do and flies smartly away again."

Ann Davison went no further into this meeting in her story, this not being her way, but is telling, because you would think this might have been a profound moment. She had been alone at sea at that point for nearly a month, several hundred miles and weeks of travel from any land, floating in an environment in which humans as individuals are not equipped to live for any length of time. Now here she was, at her urging from her whistle, trying to speak the bird's language, face to face with this representative from another species who very much *did* belong here. Here was another animal fluttering above her that was comfortable living and navigating across this open ocean. Tropicbirds spend the majority of their lives out at sea, usually alone. They have large black eyes, which blend into a thick streak of black plumage that grows across and below, even more dramatically than fulmars, presumably evolved to help with glare while spotting prey below. December can be a time for breeding for tropicbirds in this part of the world. Maybe this was a female tropicbird, a few days out foraging while her mate sat on their single egg. Whoever this wild bird was, whatever their thoughts, their history, their destination, this one tropicbird responded to Davison's sound and paused to consider her: eye to eye.

A half-century earlier, Joshua Slocum wrote more often about seabirds. As a lifelong mariner and navigator, Slocum was especially tuned to notice the difference between coastal versus pelagic species in helping him find safe harbors. On three separate occasions in *Sailing Alone Around the World*, the first known solo circumnavigator described using seabirds to navigate. One afternoon in the Canary Current, after his initial crossing of the Atlantic from Nova Scotia as he approached the Mediterranean (the same current in which Davison would almost be run down), Slocum watched the birds "all flying in one direction" toward shore, confirming his navigation and leading him to joke, "I discovered Spain."

A white-tailed tropicbird flying near the masthead as observed by sailor
Ellen Massey Leonard on the way from Antigua to Bermuda (2010).

On his way home, after a three-week passage in the Indian
Ocean, Slocum's first indication of the low-lying Cocos
Keeling Islands was a coastal bird: "The first unmistakable
sign of the land was a visit one morning from a white tern
that fluttered very knowingly about the vessel, and then took
itself off westward with a businesslike air in its wing." Slocum explained that on these islands this tern, likely what we
call today the white tern or common fairy tern (*Gygis alba*), is
known as the "pilot of the Keeling Cocos." Then, toward
the end of his circumnavigation, in the open South Atlantic,
Slocum "was awakened by that rare bird, the booby, with its
harsh quack, which I recognized at once as a call to go on
deck; it was as much as to say, 'Skipper, there's land in sight.'
I tumbled out quickly, and sure enough, away ahead in the
dim twilight, about twenty miles off, was St. Helena."

Slocum identified coastal seabirds, such as terns and boobies in their general groupings, and he had spent enough years on deck at sea to recognize the latitudinal ranges of different seabirds in the open sea. After passing through the region of Cape Horn and into the South Pacific, he explained, "New species of birds came around; albatrosses fell back and became scarcer and scarcer; lighter gulls [likely petrels, as known today] came in their stead, and pecked for crumbs in the sloop's wake."

Every once in a while a solo sailor will find a bird landed on the boat in mid-ocean. Sometimes these are land birds that have been blown off their migrations or are ill or injured. Seabirds occasionally also suffer the same or land on a sailboat seemingly just to take a break from migrating or foraging. Seabirds who breed in burrows on their island rookeries will at times seek unexpected holes on a boat. Howard Blackburn—a former fisherman who one horrific night when adrift in a fishing dory on the Grand Banks watched his shipmate die from exposure and then lost his own fingers and half his toes to frostbite—was years later in 1899 sailing along on the first of his two solo transAtlantic crossings. Blackburn had left a dirty pan from a supper of stew on the floor of his cabin. In the morning he heard a rustling inside the pan, under the lid that he had left askew. Inside he found a storm-petrel. The bird had likely not flown into the pan for the food, but for the sense of security. Blackburn picked up the tiny dark gray bird. "I took it in my hands," he wrote, "went on deck and threw it up into the air. It flew a short distance and then fell into the water, where I hoped after freeing itself from the stew it would be able to fly again."

As I sailed farther east into the Grand Banks, I came out of the fog. The sky cleared. I made progress. Whenever I saw a sea-bird I found myself welcoming it in a way specific to its type. Spotting a fulmar flying toward the boat, soaring flat-winged like a mini-albatross, I shouted as would a stadium announcer introducing the home-run hitter: "Fuuullll-Maaaar!" as if the name meant, indeed, full ocean. When I saw a shearwater gliding on the scant updraft at the lip of a swell, I found myself whispering: "Sssssshhheearwater," trying to match its effort-less flight. When into view flew a solitary gray skua, a faded leather rugby ball with wings, I chanted like at a war dance: "Aaah, skoo-ah—skoo-ah—skoo-aah!"

The most common and consistent birds that I saw during my passage, especially from the fogs of the Gulf of Maine up until the far outer edges of the Grand Banks, were storm-petrels, the smallest of all open-ocean seabirds. Although none of them tried to hide in one of my cooking pots, by their geographic range I knew they were either Leach's or Wilson's storm-petrels (*Hydrobates leucorhous* or *Oceanites oce-anicus*). They look similar and the differentiation was beyond my skills and attention at the time. Storm-petrels are tiny, ashy gray birds with black tube-nosed beaks. They're so small you can't believe they're all the way out there. Storm-petrels are famous for their thin webbed feet just barely pattering across the surface of the sea, a behavior from which their name is likely derived, as they appear to walk like St Peter over the surface. Some people even call them "Jesus petrels," and they've long been a favorite of solo sailors. Vito Dumas, an Argentinian who in a little wooden boat sailed around the world in the 1940s via the storms of the Southern Ocean, had a special sympathy for the tiny storm-petrels, for what appeared to be their struggles in such high winds and steep troughs. He pondered if they ever rested, if a single storm-petrel might have "sometimes settled in this immensity without my noticing it." When Dr. David Lewis wrote of his solo trans-Atlantic crossing in 1960 he portrayed the storm-petrels as dainty as kittens, "too fragile to live on the face of the ocean."

Before this crossing I once had a moment with a storm-petrel that has always remained with me. I was working on a sail-training ship in the Caribbean when one rough night we heard a thwappy sound in the small boat hung off our stern. A crew member named Sean, who knew a lot about birds, followed the noise and picked up the storm-petrel that had

Wilson's storm-petrels, *Oceanites oceanicus.*

landed in the boat. Due to the slippery bulwarks, it appeared unable to take off again. Sean opened up his hands and showed us this tiny, lightly breathing ball of gray, its little black eye looking terrified—or at least we projected this emotion. We had to shout through the wind to hear each other. When it was my turn to hold the bird in my hand, I was stunned at how light it was. I've since learned that even the larger of the North Atlantic storm-petrels weigh less than a child's handful of paperclips. Sean took the bird down to the leeward rail, faced the wind, and opened his palm. After a pause, the storm-petrel felt a gust of wind and flew off into the dark. It was like a bee finding an open window, as if the storm-petrel suddenly relaxed, relieved to be back into that dark blustery gale at sea, as if thinking "Thank God, now I am safe."

For my North Atlantic passage I had no idea that I'd see so many storm-petrels. When I did, I kept thinking about that one in the Caribbean. Here up north, I saw them almost daily, from the longitude of the Fundian Channel to beyond the Grand Banks until I was over 450 miles away from any land.

Storm-petrels appeared most often around my boat after sunset, which was usually off *Fox*'s stern. Perhaps the hull of the boat stirred up nocturnal zooplankton that the storm-petrels wanted to eat. The dark birds wheeled and fluttered around like bats. I had some spooky, unnerving moments in the fog and dark when I first heard their cackling sounds, before I realized that it was the storm-petrels. I had never heard the call of these birds before, since on the ships I had worked on previously it had never been that quiet on deck, or maybe we had never stopped to really listen. Their creepy call in the dark is part of the folklore of storm-petrels, often referred to as evil hags, cackling creators of storms, or, conversely, sometimes as good witches, as helpful harbingers warning sailors of heavy weather. Anglophone mariners since at least the 1700s have also known these birds as "Mother Carey's Chickens." I had thought this came from how they pecked their beaks in the water, but after my solo ocean passage I think it was because of their chirping, too.

For the first couple of weeks across the North Atlantic, I heard those storm-petrels, in both calm and heavy winds, usually at dusk, but I saw and heard them throughout the night—alone, in pairs, or even in flocks as large as a dozen. Sometimes I saw them during the day. But I don't recall them making any noise when the sun was up. By mid-ocean that early August I saw only shearwaters and an occasional large skua. There were a few different species of shearwaters, or at least varieties of males and females and a range of ages, but I was not able to identify them all. Then in the middle of the third gale, closer to the coast of Europe, I saw one final storm-petrel, eye to eye, which I'll tell you about later.

# 3. Shackford, "Rob Roy," and "Centennial" Set the Stage

Recognizing millennia of human mariners and their comfort and skill out at sea—from the Aleutian paddlers of the far North Pacific to the Kawésqar of Tierra del Fuego, from the Vietnamese navigators of Southeast Asia to the Incas of Peru, from the Taino people of the Caribbean to the ancient Sumerians of the Middle East, from the ancient mariners of Mogadishu to the early deep-water tuna fishermen of the Maldives, and on and on and on—it is certain that previous long-distance voyages of weeks out of sight of land, if not entire ocean-crossings, were undertaken by Indigenous solo sailors many centuries ago. For example, "There seems little doubt that the first single-handed transatlantic voyages were accomplished by Eskimos [Inuit]," declared the historian of sailing D. H. Clarke, because over multiple centuries several kayaks and their lone Inuit mariners had been recorded arriving in the Azores, in Spain, and on the coast of Scotland. The Māori historian Sir Peter Buck wrote of a man named Ipo who sometime in the 1300s sailed alone from what was likely Pitcairn Island to Mangareva, a distance of about 350 miles at sea.

I am confident that people have crossed an ocean by themselves before modern written records—or at least those beyond my limited Anglophone research efforts. Just maybe Pytheas of Massalia from Ancient Greece sailed by himself in his exploration of coastal Britain and perhaps farther north, about which he wrote *On the Ocean* (c. 320 BCE), which is now lost. An artist in Ancient Greece painted "The Wondrous Sea Voyage of Dionysus" in c. 530 BCE, which shows the god of pleasure himself, sailing alone, surrounded by dolphins. A couple of stories of early single-handed sailors have been published in English-language texts and told to a global audience, such as the legends of Irish monks, notably Brendan the Navigator, who in some versions left Ireland c. 520 on solitary or collective voyages into the open Atlantic in small skin boats in search of a metaphorical or literal land of paradise. In Witi Ihimaera's *Whale Rider* (1987) the narrator describes an early Kupe-like explorer traveling alone across the entire sea c. 1200 to discover Aotearoa (New Zealand) on board a metaphoric or literal whale.

Legendary and actual single-handed voyages were surely

"The Wondrous Sea Voyage of Dionysus," perhaps one of the earliest depictions of a single-handed voyager, by Exekias (c. 530 BCE).

also accomplished in previous centuries out of desperation or due to the death or incapacitation of shipmates. People who were shipwrecked have crossed large bodies of water alone on small boats or rafts. After living alone on one of the Galápagos Islands and selling vegetables to passing ships, a surly, drunken man named Patrick Watkins managed in 1809 to steal a whaleboat and sail toward mainland Ecuador with a few men, who he reportedly killed along the way, arriving alone at Guayaquil after an open-sea passage of roughly 700 miles. Watkins then sailed by himself down the coast to Paita in Peru—where he was thrown in jail. In about 1870, two men who had been part of a small group lured into slavery from an island in the Santa Cruz group at the eastern edge of the Solomon Islands, escaped in a boat and found their way home from Fiji, a distance of nearly 1,000 miles of open water. And I find it hard to believe that not a single African person, millions of whom had grown up in seafaring cultures back home, did not sail off alone up north or back across the Atlantic to escape slavery in the Americas.

My point here is simply that we will never know who was the first person to cross an ocean alone, and how many have done so. But surely this feat was not first accomplished by someone of Anglo-European descent.

The first ocean-crossing solo sailor documented by Western historians writing in English seems to have been a man named Josiah Shackford, who was born in Portsmouth, New

Hampshire, in 1745. The history of his voyage is sparse, but as we set the stage, opening the curtain for the likes of Joshua Slocum and all those to follow, the evolution of the yarn about Shackford's voyage is as relevant as the hard truth.

The documented story begins with a short article published on 2 May 1787 in *The Essex Journal & New-Hampshire Packet*, which read in full:

NEWBURY-PORT, *May 2*

A gentleman at New-York relates the following account for fact, he having it from such authority as puts the truth of it quite out of dispute.

*"A Mr. Shackford some time since from Piscataqua, having the misfortune of discontent with his wife, left that place for Surinam; on his arrival there, he left the vessel he first sailed in, and took the command of one for Europe; he performed his voyage and gave such satisfaction to his owners, that they gave him a cutter-built sloop of about 15 tons; with her he returned to Surinam ALONE after a passage of 35 days; when he arrived Suspicions prevailed of his having dealt unfairly by the people who were supposed to have come out with him; but he produced his papers and journal, and proved his integrity so far to the satisfaction of his examiners, that they permitted him to take another man on board and proceed to St Bartholomew's, where he arrived in safety, and now follows the coasting business from that Island."*

The story was reprinted verbatim in a few other newspapers along the East Coast of America in the following weeks. Some newspapers kept the "alone" in caps or italics, while others dropped the emphasis altogether. At least as reported from a source that heard it from another, Shackford's *why-go* was an impulsive stubbornness along the lines of the

Scotsman Alexander Selkirk, the inspiration for *Robinson Crusoe* (1719). (Selkirk ended up an island castaway in the South Pacific because he said in essence 'Let's get off this lousy ship! Who's with me?' When no one was, he said, 'Ach, fine then. I'll stay alone.')

Josiah Shackford was a real person, a known captain of a merchant ship and a former officer in the Revolutionary War. John Singleton Copley painted his portrait in 1776. Shackford's marriage to Deborah, a daughter of his father's second wife, has been reliably documented, as has his re-emergence in later merchant voyages and then during his life in Ohio, where he would live until he died of old age in 1829. You can visit Captain Shackford's grave in the town of Portsmouth, Ohio.

Shackford left no account of his solo trans-Atlantic voyage, however, or of any of his travels. In 1823 in *The New York Gazette*, amid a report of an unnamed sailor proposing his own solo trans-Atlantic crossing, an author discussed what Shackford had accomplished, yet in this brief recounting, Shackford now had a dog (who died en route), his boat was larger, the passage took him longer, and it occurred a few years later. In this version Shackford, the "eccentric character," later sailed alone up to the Caribbean and then later still from Pittsburgh, Pennsylvania, down and around to New Orleans. A reprinting of this story a couple of weeks later in the newspaper of his previous home town of Portsmouth, New Hampshire, unaware if he was still alive, added at the end: "We may be permitted to relate the following from among a number of anecdotes, which have been related to us.—On one occasion, among other interrogations, a countryman asked him how he slept on the voyage? He replied, 'With my eyes shut.'"

Josiah Shackford as painted by John Singleton Copley, with the USS *Raleigh* in the background (1776).

Another strand of this yarn, printed at least as early as 1832 in *The Sailor's Magazine*, but then reprinted in multiple other publications over the years, is Josiah Shackford's meeting with none other than Sir Joseph Banks. By this account, Shackford has sailed both back and forth alone across the Atlantic, from America to England. In his alleged interview with the famous English naturalist at his home in London, Shackford comes across as dry, sarcastic, and matter-of-fact about his voyage. For example, when Banks asks him about his navigation, Shackford replies, "I guessed I was right, as I steered east when I got pretty well up to the north, and that I knew would take me to England, or somewhere thereabouts, and that was right enough for one whose time was his own, and who owned the craft he was in, and had plenty of provision on board." In this likely fictional account, smacking of the age-old conflict of sailor smart over the lubberly scholar—not to mention a young American's sense of pragmatic patriotism over dusty English intellectualism— Shackford explains that he brought the Bible, a collection of psalms and hymns, and a copy of *Robinson Crusoe*. When not reading, "I looked around and read the book of nature." Shackford reportedly schools Banks about American alligators, stumps the naturalist with a riddle about frogs, and by the end "Sir Joseph was glad to get rid of the maniac, who had crossed the Atlantic alone in a boat—something more than Cook had done."

The story of the first solo sailor really grew legs, however, in the early 1860s, when a newspaper editor named Charles Brewster of Portsmouth, New Hampshire, wrote the most detailed account that remains, including more detail of Shackford's life and the voyage sketched more thoroughly and romantically. Brewster, a lifelong historian of the town, wrote that "the misfortune of discontent" stemmed from when Shackford asked his wife Deborah to move to New York City, from where he regularly shipped out. She refused on account of her sick mother. So Shackford sailed out as usual and ended up in Surinam, then skippered the ship to France, where he was given the sailboat as a personal gift. A little over forty years old at that point, Shackford did have a dog and a crew member on board to sail his new boat back to Surinam, but the man became afraid once they put out to sea and jumped aboard a pilot boat to go back ashore. The dog apparently stayed on board. (An account by another author years later said the dog's name was Bruno.)

"He was a man of too stern materials to turn about," Brewster wrote. In his description of this first American solo sailor, Brewster helped lay the foundations for the imaginative figure of the rugged, self-sufficient individual out at sea on the briny deep: "so he undertook the voyage of three thousand miles alone. What a resolute spirit! See him on the boisterous mid-ocean alone in his little bark a thousand miles from any land—without a human being to consult when awake, or to aid in keeping watch while he slept; without a hand to aid when the storm beat about him, and his little boat is hid between the mountain swells!" Writing two decades before the popular paintings of Winslow Homer and Michael Ancher, which depicted heroic, nostalgic scenes of working fishermen on both sides of the Atlantic, Brewster's imagery of this solitary individual out at sea, whether historically accurate or only somewhat, is significant to the crafting of the Western cultural idea that to go out and try to cross an ocean alone is an admirable, even heroic thing to do.

According to Brewster, when Josiah Shackford arrived in Surinam, officials made him sail out and back alone to prove that he could handle the boat by himself. Shackford returned to Portsmouth, New Hampshire, for his wife Deborah at one point, but the meeting did not go well. He then moved out west where he helped found and name the town of Portsmouth, Ohio, where he stayed and reportedly built a house with a second-floor hatch and a rope ladder that he pulled up after him each night. When his wife's mother died, Deborah reportedly asked to come out and join him, but he said no. As Deborah sold property to try to make ends meet, the local newspaper spoke of Josiah as having "gone abroad in a disordered melancholy state of mind." A story out of Ohio reports that old Captain Shackford would allow no women in his home whatsoever.

Charles Brewster's lines in the 1860s about Josiah Shackford's heroic self-reliance upon the great waters of the deep were reflecting a movement, a perception of life at sea, that had been building for at least a generation, a *why-go* for both escape and personal challenge, before those artistic appreciations of working mariners and long before Ann Davison's surge of post-war wanderers. The author Jonathan Raban, a solo sailor himself, explained that small-boat sailing and the flood of Western writers and poets who wanted to go to sea traced their inspiration back to England and to the Romantic poets, such as Lord Byron, who wrote of a solitary urban figure finding inspiration and soul-cleansing in nature, especially at sea. England was the logical place for this to take off, since without any kind of American West the island nation, for better or worse, sent its people out to sea and to distant lands and back. Britain's home ports were a nexus of the Industrial Revolution, bristling with factories and mills and the advancements of steel and steam that smoked out scores of young people who wanted to go to the seashore and into the bracing, healing water or float out in small boats and test themselves in tall waves. (The Romantic poet Percy Shelley drowned off the coast of Italy with two others, his small boat foundering with too much sail up in heavy weather.) Recreational boating on either side of the Atlantic, just going out sailing for the sport of it, had not been common practice in the West until the nineteenth century. Boats were generally considered tools, for fishing, for travel, not as objects for fun or personal trial by choice.

As "yachting" began to find wider and wider audiences, several long-distance voyages followed, usually with small crews and boats sailing back and forth across the Atlantic Ocean. Perhaps Brewster's image of Shackford, "that resolute spirit," even influenced, for example, John Hudson and Frank Fitch in 1866, who with their pet dog Fanny sailed from New York to London in the *Red, White, and Blue*, a twenty-six-foot miniature iron sailing ship with "INGERSOLL'S IMPROVED METALLIC LIFE BOAT" painted on the sides. The two men exhibited the boat in England, Scotland, and France for still more advertising for the maker of the lifeboat.

The next year, a British writer, philanthropist, and self-promoter named John "Rob Roy" MacGregor sailed across the English Channel. MacGregor was independently wealthy. He hired craftsmen to build a custom twenty-one-foot wooden boat, the *Rob Roy*, aboard which he sailed alone to the French coast. He continued up the Seine to Paris, and then back across to England and home, after which he made sure the newspapers recognized his achievement. He soon published *The Voyage Alone in the Yawl Rob Roy* (1867), which included his own lovely illustrations of his galley and his labor-savers on deck. He wrote of the ship-shape, tea-sipping, independent joy of traveling and sailing by oneself. He survived his near misses and terrible tempests. Throughout the harbors and canals of France, MacGregor passed around religious pamphlets to try to spread Protestantism to Catholics. He gave lectures about his voyage and his boat, while he sold copies of his three previous books about traveling in a canoe, which had proven exceptionally popular throughout Europe, inspiring voyages and narratives by several others, including Robert Louis Stevenson's *An Inland Voyage* (1878). Years later, Arthur Ransome wrote of "Rob Roy" MacGregor: "I do not suppose any man ever sent so many of his countrymen to find their pleasure on the water." MacGregor's adventures and books inspired regattas, canoe clubs, and small-boat building throughout Europe.

In his wake, other British single-handed small-boat voyages were soon achieved and books about them written, notably by R.T. McMullen, who turned up his nose at garish, profit-driven stunts by Americans, and by Empson Edward Middleton, who circumnavigated Great Britain alone with his sailboat *The Kate*. McMullen and Middleton, like MacGregor before them, saw their monastic voyages and their boats as models toward a moral English society. (If you'd like to keep all these characters straight, by the way, there is a *dramatis personae* at the end.)

In the summer of 1876, Alfred Johnson, a Danish-born fisherman in his thirties who wore a huge moustache like a pair of bird's wings, was living in Gloucester, Massachusetts.

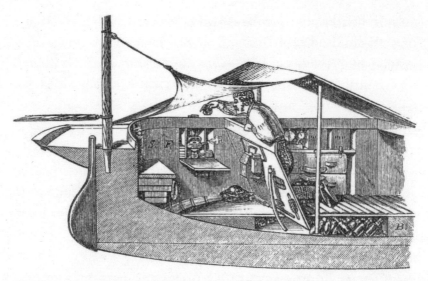

"Cooking in the Rain," an illustration by John "Rob Roy" MacGregor for his *The Voyage Alone in the Yawl Rob Roy* (1867).

Illustration of E. E. Middleton calmly sailing alone at the brink of pitchpoling in heavy weather in the English Channel in *The Cruise of "The Kate"* (1870).

Part of his declared *why-go* was that he wanted to celebrate the one hundredth birthday of the United States by sailing a custom-built twenty-foot wooden dory, decked over, across the Atlantic by himself. He and his boat, *Centennial*, survived gales, a capsizing, and were fortunate to speak to a couple officers on large sailing ships who confirmed his position and resupplied him with food after his had been spoiled by seawater. At one point, when he was pumping out after the capsize, a large shark came lurking nearby. Johnson lashed a knife to an oar and stabbed at the shark, which seems to have scared the animal off. After a little over two months, Johnson arrived in England. The London *Daily News* reported that when asked if he wanted to undertake another solo voyage, Johnson said that he "thought he had about enough of it." Thousands of people came to see his red, white, and blue boat on exhibit in Liverpool, then he put the dory on a steamship for its journey home. "Centennial" Johnson went back to fishing and lived into old age. The little boat is on exhibit today at the Cape Ann Museum in Massachusetts.

Crossing the Atlantic in a tiny boat became a new fad for a select crowd of adventurers. In 1877, Thomas and Joanna Crapo, a married couple, crossed successfully from America. In 1878 the brothers William and Walter Andrews made the same trans-Atlantic journey. William, a Civil War veteran and a piano maker, and his brother, who had some experience at sea, talked to other sailors on thirty-seven different ships along the way to help with their navigation—which gives a sense of the amount of sailing-ship traffic in the North Atlantic at the time.

Inspired by Alfred Johnson, a man from Buffalo, New York, a veteran of the US Navy named Bernard Gilboy sailed out of California in 1882 in a nineteen-foot

PROCTER BROTHERS, 192 Front St. Gloucester, Mass.

CAPE ANN SCENERY.

Dory " Centennial," Capt. Alfred Johnsen.

Stereograph of Alfred "Centennial" Johnson in his boat in Gloucester, MA, likely the first ever photograph of a solo sailor (1876).

custom-built boat that he named the *Pacific*. He was picked up, exhausted and near-starving, only 160 miles short of the coast of Australia after an eventful passage alone with various calamities that lasted 162 days during which he never anchored once. Near starving, he captured and ate seabirds that landed on his head. He suffered from sharks ramming the hull. In February of 1883 a heroic poem about Gilboy's voyage, echoing the image of Josiah Shackford, was printed in *Sydney Punch*, beginning:

> Alone on the raging ocean, alone in my craft I ride,
> Alone on the foaming billows, in all their crested pride,
> No man before hath ventured, alone, so far to sail;
> Nor mind hath yet conceived a ship so small, so frail.

Gilboy had a portion of his logbook published in the San Francisco *Evening Bulletin* as early as 22 March 1883, and the full story printed in Sydney and for sale for one shilling by the end of April.

Back in the Atlantic, William Andrews in 1888 decided to cross the ocean again, this time by himself, as his brother had since died. After two months in the mid-Atlantic in his thirteen-foot boat, Andrews asked to be rescued by a passing vessel, but that same summer another man from America named Josiah "Si" Lawlor, a sailor and the son of a boatbuilder, managed to complete his own small-boat trans-Atlantic crossing. Andrews and Lawlor then teamed up to stage a single-handed race in fifteen-foot boats out of Boston in 1891. This received enormous public attention, including tens of thousands of people lining the docks to wave them goodbye. Lawlor made it across the Atlantic again and Andrews had to be rescued a second time, but this time he got much closer to Europe. The two men raced one final time in the summer of 1892. On this crossing Andrews made it to Spain, now in a collapsible canvas-sided boat sponsored by a soap manufacturer. With a stop in the Azores, it took him sixty-nine days. Si Lawlor in his *Christopher Columbus* was never seen again. Neither his body nor the boat was ever found.

In sum, by the time Joshua Slocum was finding few opportunities in the midst of his midlife crisis, twirling the last bits of hair on his balding head and pottering around in a field rebuilding an old fishing boat, several well-publicized characters had adventured on small-boat voyages across oceans, men with far less blue-water experience than him, as they claimed various firsts and turned over a few dimes and newspaper clippings in the process. Those ashore wrote of them more often as heroes, rather than maniacs. It was now Slocum's turn to stage an entirely new, revolutionary performance.

# 4. Wind, Ships, Sleep, Engines, Wind

After I made it through the fog and first met my fulmars, shear-waters, and storm-petrels, I next made it through my first rough weather. This was my first taste of challenging open-water conditions with steep seas and winds over twenty-five knots. (A "knot" for speed of the wind, current, or the boat, is short for nautical miles per hour; 10 knots = 11.5 mph = 18.5 kmh.) This wind speed is classified technically as a "near gale." I was over Browns Bank below Nova Scotia. The wind was blowing hard with whitecaps everywhere, yet the sun was bright, and I was pleased to get this early test to see how the boat and I would do. Tilted at a steep angle, trying not to fall off the slippery deck, I reefed the mainsail, backed the jib, and tried heaving to, or "lying to" as Ann Davison called it. It's a way to avoid too much bashing or heeling. I adjusted the sails to stabilize the boat, to counteract the direction of the rudder, putting on the brakes to reduce my boat speeding forward, trying to keep the rail from digging half under the water. Heaving to is a bit like treading water. I could not accomplish this entirely, but even with the boat forereaching, meaning it was pitching and thumping forward into the waves far more slowly, it felt sustainable, with far less heel and lurching, crashing speed. Holding the wood coaming and assessing things, I wore my full foul-weather gear because of the spray and splash. As I'd done from the start whenever I was on deck, regardless of weather conditions, I clipped in with my harness on the windward side to a flat strap of yellow nylon webbing, a jackline, which I'd secured from the bow to the stern on both sides of the mast.

So I stood in the cockpit that day, my sunglasses spotted with salt drops, seeing how the boat and I handled these bigger winds and seas. I had given myself a lot of space to back out of this trip. I barely told anyone about my full plans so that I could more easily decide to just head home or be satisfied with a trip to Halifax or something. But after that near gale over Browns Bank, with the self-steering gear working and *Fox* and me weathering the blow without too much chaos, I decided to truly commit to sailing across the Atlantic. When the near-gale abated, I set my course to the east.

At eleven days out, just beyond the longitude of Newfoundland, I sailed across the region known as the Tail of the Banks. I sat in the cockpit and stitched on a little patch where I'd seen some daylight through an older sail. *Fox* was moving nicely, pointing more northerly than I wanted, but otherwise smoothly underway. The sun had come up about a half hour earlier, but it was behind a cloud bank so the sky kept some of that gentle pink of dawn. I had made easy-mix pancakes, and I'd treated myself to some canned peaches over the top and drank the peach juice out of the can.

Maybe I could do this after all, I thought.

For me, the choice to sail by myself was the opposite of confidence. I wanted to make my own mistakes, to figure stuff out slowly without someone looking over my shoulder, without feeling any more thick and slow than I usually do. The reason I renamed this boat *Fox*, other than I like boats named after animals, was that this was the name of a dory that two fishermen from Gloucester, Massachusetts, George Harbo and Frank Samuelson, had rowed across the Atlantic in 1896. As Ann Davison drew strength considering Alain

Bombard and other single-handers, relying on the precedent of others who have done something similar, I too tried to scrape some courage from far more impressive experiences, or at least ocean passages with far more masochism.

Avoiding getting run down by a ship while you sleep is a major concern for people sailing by themselves. My plan that morning, after the sail repair, was to go to sleep for two hours. I was settling into the routine I had planned of staying awake at night to watch for ships and changes in the weather. After breakfast and perhaps an easy chore, I slept in chunks of an hour or two during the day when I hoped I was more visible. I woke myself up with a brutally loud kitchen timer, sometimes just for a moment to look around on deck and then go right back to sleep. To increase the chances a ship might see me in daylight while I slept, I had hired a sailmaker to stitch a large bright orange triangle into the head of *Fox*'s mainsail.

*Fox* was a 28.5-foot (8.7 m) boat with a full keel. It had been constructed of thick fiberglass in 1966, before I was born. A hull like this is not easily picked up by the radar of large ships, but it did have at least an aluminum mast with aluminum mast steps and an aluminum boom. To increase my visibility to the radar of larger ships, I had lashed as high as possible a long cylindrical-type radar reflector, and when I was in Portland, Maine, I had also lashed an octahedral-type reflector on the opposite side. Because I knew I'd be sailing in the Gulf of Maine and across the Grand Banks in the summer, an area known for fog, I purchased radar, despite the expense. I like radar not only for collision avoidance, but because I trusted it more than GPS for coastal navigation, especially in limited visibility. My radar set had a case like a large white cake cover that protected the rotating antennae inside. This case was mounted on the forward side of the mast, then wired down through it and the cabin to an LED screen display that I screwed into a piece of wood on an old door hinge, so that I could see the radar screen in the cabin or swing the screen out when I was at the tiller in the cockpit.

Radar is a wonderful tool to avoid ship collisions on any size of boat, but it requires a lot of energy, way too much power to keep it on at all times during long passages. At the start of the trip, I used radar about every twenty minutes in the fog of the Grand Banks. If there was nearby traffic, if I anticipated a possible collision, I would turn on my VHF and make a call. There are alarm features on the radar that I could have used, which will start beeping if a target enters a radius you set, say, of five miles, but these require the radar to be on and for you to put a lot of faith into an electronic device. Mostly in the fog, when I just had to get some sleep, I left my fate in Neptune's hands, napped for only short stints, and tried to trust that the reflectors I'd lashed into the mast would help me be seen. Considering that one all-too-close fishing boat in the fog, I was fortunate to get through the area unscathed. Besides the several fishing boats I saw, I did not actually lay my eyes on a merchant ship until about a week into the voyage, though I had seen, identifiable by the size of the targets, a couple on radar. One merchant mariner on the Grand Banks told me that I was a clear target on his radar, which was comforting.

In addition to the orange patch on the mainsail and the radar set and reflectors, on the masthead I also had a high-end bright LED tricolor—these lights help other boats and ships know that you're a sailboat and which direction you're going. I carried, too, a hand-held spotlight that I could use to light up my sails or flash at an oncoming vessel. In short, given my budget and supply of electricity, I thought I was as ready as I could be for ship traffic.

*Fox*, like any sailboat, was most quiet when there was a steady, mid-range wind. Too much wind and you hear whistling and moaning at different pitches as it blows through the rig, as if some of the wind is on top of you and other winds are dangerous phantoms gathering forces over the horizon. Another type of loud noise comes from the wind of these gales whipping up waves that thwack and whump against the hull, often in unpredictable patterns and with forces that sound like your boat has run into a wall. Because you've read about all these calamities happening to others, you worry in heavy winds that the boat is going to flip over, the portholes will smash open, or the hull will split apart at the joints. The bludgeon of a wave on the hull is often followed, a long second later, by a slosh or crash of spray across the cockpit.

Yet when there is no wind at all, counter-intuitively, the noises can be still worse. In preparation for my crossing, I had spent countless hours considering and preparing for heavy weather. I made the mistake of not preparing for calms. On the open ocean, even with no wind at all or no lobster boats roaring past you, if your boat is not super wide and beamy, your hull usually bobs and rolls in swells. The movement is especially bad for a sailboat on a windless day because the fabric of the sails, built to billow outward, instead slaps and chafes on the wire supports of the mast. When there is no wind, ropes clank on the mast and they whip themselves raw or saw themselves thin against burrs of wire. Steel, plastic, and bronze shackles, hanks, and pins lazily rotate to odd angles and then suddenly jerk and jolt back the wrong way: wearing, breaking, snapping, and shearing themselves. Your own body is thrown in the same fashion, standing still and calm at one moment and then abruptly with the boat's roll you are flung foolishly from one side of your cabin to the other. Unexpectedly, unevenly, you're sent sideways, banging elbows, spraining wrists, spilling drinks, and frustrating even the simplest tasks.

Sometimes I tried to set the spinnaker, a silky, ballooning sail for very light air and downwind sailing. I only was able to set this once by myself, after two hours of effort. Often in calm conditions I would try to steer for the tiniest wind in case I could just get the hull moving a little bit. With these tasks I wasted barrels of physical and mental energy accomplishing nothing except getting more tired, frustrated, and learning the lessons one more time. You would think that you could just give up in light winds, take all the sails down, and go to sleep for a few hours. But sometimes when there was no wind, I tried this, furled all the sails, but this often made the situation worse and louder, because then *Fox* rolled even more steeply from side to side. I felt like a bobble head doll. I endured these conditions for several days on multiple occasions during the crossing. I was forced to listen to the no-wind sounds of the rig, which are like a rat nibbling the wires up in your attic in the middle of the night, with no way to make it stop unless you want to take the pillow off your head and peel yourself out of your bunk and try something futile and at best temporary—again.

Sleep is the most important thing on a single-handed passage. You can't steer for twenty-four hours a day, which is why, if you don't want to heave-to your boat for hours at a time, making little or negative progress, as Davison and so many others have been forced to do, it's crucial to figure out how to get the boat to steer itself. Nor can you stay awake all the time to stand lookout for unexpected bad weather, wind shifts, big ships, or floating matter that might be dangerous to your hull. This is why sailing alone is technically illegal by the letter of domestic and international regulations. Although not enforced on recreational sailboats, every vessel is required to post a lookout at all times.

In heavy weather, unless the motions of the vessel are too terrific and your concerns too terrifying, you can usually sleep a little bit if your self-steering system is working. (More on self-steering later.) But in an idle wind, when self-steering doesn't matter, it can be downright impossible to sleep. Ann Davison explained the frustration well, but she did not describe the kind where you stand in the cockpit and scream at the top of your lungs and tear out chunks of your hair from the sleep-deprived hysteria that exploded out of me during the lowest moments of hot, flat, rat-scraping windless rolling. A sailor named Dodge Morgan, who at one time in the 1980s held the record for the fastest non-stop solo circumnavigation, said of the calms he experienced in the Southern Ocean, "I am just about ready to lose my mind. It is devastating." Sailor-historian Richard Henderson wrote that for the single-hander "perhaps the ultimate frustration may be day after day of calm weather."

I have never been any kind of competitive small-boat sailor or racer, so I was not good at getting *Fox* to move in really light wind, and, because I had not adequately prepared in this department, I did not have the proper gear either. In my case, as with Ann Davison, I could occasionally turn on the engine and motor for a couple of hours. I did not have solar panels or a wind-powered generator, so I used the engine foremost and primarily to charge my two batteries, which in turn ran technologies that Davison did not have, such as my electric navigation lights, GPS, and radar. I needed to run the engine a couple of hours now and then. But I also did not want to run the motor too often, because I only had so much fuel with me and because of an irrational, self-imposed, anti-machine feeling that if I used the engine a lot, then my trans-Atlantic *sail* was somehow less valid.

The small-boat engine is a compelling object on a couple of levels. People have been used to engines on little boats now for over a century, which has resulted in much less patience and understanding about how to row or skull or paddle or dock a boat, as well as, unless you race sailboats, how to coax your vessel to move in really light winds. As our collective and individual daily patience in Western cultures has in all things diminished by the decade, so has followed life on boats at sea.

An engine on a boat has a deep influence on our relationship with the ocean. The majority of single-handed sailors want to go to sea to simplify their lives. An engine adds a piece of technology that can be crucial to safety—Ann Davison survived being run down by a freighter in the Canary Current with the use of her engine in the 1950s—but the machine also adds an entire other matrix of knowledge, not to mention expense, weight, space, and noise. Smoke and fuel have their own specific potential hazards, too, notably fumes, fire, and explosions. Engines also require a specific level of expertise and training. Mechanization and fossil fuels had different meanings for Davison in the 1950s than they do for many of us in the twenty-first century. Yet I suspect even though she had been a pilot, Davison would affirm my overall feeling that while I might not know how to fix a sail or splice a line expertly or how to bolt on standing rigging to the deck, I understood the general gist and felt comfortable giving it a try. Those were tasks that fit in a branch of knowledge that was within my grasp, that I could muddle through or read up further on if necessary. Engines, radios, and now marine electronics, all add entirely other areas of knowledge, micro-electrical worlds screwed inside boxes and forged into steel and plastic casings, of all of which I have little understanding at all.

In his *South Sea Vagabonds* (1939), Johnny Wray personified a boat engine that he named "Methuselah," a motor that he and a couple friends rejuvenated after it had been left rusting in an old field in Aotearoa New Zealand. Methuselah seemed to function only occasionally and seemingly on his own schedule. So began a long tradition of the cranky engine in sea narratives: motorized characters that often stood as metaphors for modernity, the technologies of war, and the new impersonal machines and appliances of supposed convenience.

Davison's relationship with her engine aboard *Felicity Ann*, written on the other side of World War II, is also funny and relatable. She recounted a half-dozen failures of the engine at just the wrong times. One day she wrote that the motor seized up entirely: "I did optimistic things with oil cans on visible moving parts acting with more valor than hope. However, next day it consented to work."

My own experiences with the motor on *Fox* fit right in with this history. I had an old gasoline engine, a 1960s design the manufacturer called the "Atomic 4." This engine is legendary in small-boat circles, like how specific old Volkswagen engines are to a certain antique automobile crowd. There are a pocket of skilled enthusiasts with beards and suspenders who believe the Atomic 4 to be the perfect engine. They cannot wait for something to break so they can set their stopwatch, fix it, and then write about it in the Atomic 4 online forum. The rest of us are left with Davison's optimistic valor and spare parts passed down from the previous owner and, more importantly, an anchor we can throw overboard to keep from drifting onto the rocks.

After functioning fine on the way up the New England coast and for the first two weeks in the North Atlantic, my Atomic 4 engine inside *Fox* began to overheat and then boil over green coolant. The first signs of this failure actually began the day after the lovely pink morning when I was stitching the sail. I even remember wiping a little peach juice off the engine's temperature gauge in the cockpit as I watched the temperature rise.

My trip exemplified that an engine on ocean voyages is a blessing and a curse. This has been true since the 1920s when Harry Pidgeon, a man who built his own boat from scratch, wrote simply: "a motor never functions properly when left alone with me." Pidgeon brought an outboard engine with him, but he barely used it, managing to sail alone around the world without one. There are people who still do so.

To emphasize the obvious then, for sailors at sea in deep water it is the wind that is the essential factor in moving your boat, both from hour to hour, but also in planning the weeks and months of a given path. Sailors are constantly attentive to the wind's direction and its strength and consistency. Like they say about farmers and the weather, sailors are never satisfied with the wind: it is too light or too much or too variable or too firmly in the wrong direction.

Joshua Slocum at the turn of the twentieth century was similar to the early navigators of the Pacific in that he had a life's worth of experience watching and maneuvering and planning within local and open-ocean wind conditions. Throughout his voyage, without an engine, he observed and quantified the "great palpitations of sea-winds and of the sea itself." He understood trends in clouds, wind-shifts, sea states: a sort of knowledge that one simply does not get from reading or classroom instruction, only from decades of first-hand personal experience. Slocum advised future single-handers, slipping into the voice of a professor: "To know the laws that govern the winds, and to know that you know them, will give you an easy mind on your voyage round the world; otherwise you may tremble at the appearance of every cloud. What is true of this in the trade-winds is much more so in the variables, where changes run more to extremes."

Although my eastbound trip across the North Atlantic, a

drop in Slocum's bucket, was in the band of ocean known as the variables, the regular march of gales and calms proved to be predictable, common, and not extreme during the summer I crossed. In general, because of the massive clockwise North Atlantic gyre of winds and currents, going from America to Europe eastbound is easier to the north, while going westbound from Europe to the Caribbean is usually easier when sailing a more southerly route. By far the most lovely sailing experience I've ever had was a downwind westbound run from the Canaries to the Windward Islands, when the trade winds blew cleanly and consistently. I was a watch officer on a small schooner for that passage. About the only thing we needed to do for our rapid seventeen-day run was to gybe now and again and adjust the way the rope was sitting in the halyard blocks so the lines didn't chafe through. Davison's trans-Atlantic crossing was such a brutal trial because of the inexplicable lack of the trade winds that year.

Consistent wind, not too much and not too little, moving your boat in the right direction at a safe, steady clip, is the height of a sailor's bliss, especially when you are on your own. A fair wind allows some sleep, and it feels as if a higher force is favoring your mission. Similar to how a surfer or skier is willing to try five hundred times for one good run, nearly every single-handed narrative has a paragraph or two recounting a perfect moment or day of sailing that implies or states outright a deeper connection to the Earth's natural forces. Davison wrote of how she was overcome the first time she sailed well by herself with a full breeze on a clear night, the hull stirring up bioluminescence under a spray of stars. This was an "ecstasy of being so pure," she wrote, a moment that was "an exquisite distillation of the meaning of life."

For my small part on that soft pink morning, I had my

own little ecstasy-so-pure sailing moment of emotional peace. I looked up at my sails drawing the rare steady breeze that slid *Fox* speedily eastward across that bit of the North Atlantic. My boat, with its small but mighty blue-gray hull that I had painted myself, with a royal blue boot stripe, slid through the dark Atlantic. Miming the clouds, the jib stood curved and motionless, backlit a peach-pink by the light of the sunrise ahead. The full mainsail proudly flew its orange triangle at the peak above a black triton stitched on the white sail. I grew to love that orange triangle for its steadfast spirit; it had a certain "hell, yeah" that I found gave me strength. Like when you see an older person walking down the street with bright red running shoes.

That morning I looked down at my hands holding the needle, my sailor's palm, and the waxed thread. A section of the sail was spread across my lap while I had the rest loosely furled in the cockpit around me like a gown, using my knee against a bunch of it in case there was an unexpected puff of wind.

Here was my boat, *Fox*, moving so silently in the right direction. The self-steering gear kept the vessel on course on its own, also in response to the wind. I had opened up the forward hatch that morning to air out the cabin. The breeze flowed through down below, drying out the bulkheads from the fogs. I'd be in my bunk for a morning nap in a short time, right after the 0800 navigation fix.

*Fox* drove along steadily and safely across the sea. It was all so lovely. I began to think that I could really do this thing. After the Atlantic, why not the whole world? Every sixth or seventh wave, the hull rolled just enough further that I needed to brace my elbow against the wood coaming while the water on the sea's surface beside me sizzled a little foam, sliding a sweet white fold over the surface.

# 5. The First Solo Circumnavigator: Joshua Slocum

Joshua Slocum was not just another green Ishmael pacing the docks to escape from urban life. The stage had been set in the 1890s for this sort of first, to sail alone around the world, but it is hard to imagine many other people better up for the role, especially with the scant material and financial resources Slocum had at hand. His career of over three decades leading up to his single-handed circumnavigation seems impossibly crammed with saltwater adventure, personal successes and failures at sea, and the building, commanding, and navigating of ships, crews, and boats. All of this equipped Slocum with the skills and perhaps the emotional state needed not only to aspire to the endeavor, but to see it through and then bring his story home.

Slocum was born in 1844 on a farm in Nova Scotia, the fifth of eleven children. He once told an interviewer that when he was a boy he built a raft of fence rails and rigged a sail to drift across his mill pond. When the family's efforts on the farm failed, they moved into a town, to Westport on tiny Brier Island at the turbid mouth of the Bay of Fundy. Here his father, a stern Bible-thumper, ran a shop beside the harbor to make leather fishermen's boots, a trade in which Joshua was put to work at age ten. In the shop's basement when he was twelve, as Slocum told it later, he had built a model ship that his father discovered and smashed to the ground in front of his son, believing this kind of crafting to be a blasphemous waste of time. At fourteen Slocum got a job as a cook on a fishing schooner, a position at which he said he failed miserably. Around the age of sixteen, after his mother died, he ran off to find work in Yarmouth and then Massachusetts, where he likely worked at a shoe factory. A couple of years later he signed aboard a lumber ship bound for Ireland. He would not return to Brier Island or anywhere in Nova Scotia until thirty-five years later on his way outbound for the solo circumnavigation.

On one passage during his years working in the Atlantic, he survived a fall from aloft, hitting a lower yard on the way down and landing on deck with only minor injuries but a lifelong scar over his left eye. Soon he sailed to Asia, where he was part of a poorly treated crew and was eventually disabled with a fever that forced him ashore in Jakarta. As he recovered, young Slocum was taken under the wing of a captain who helped him learn navigation, then recommended him to be second mate for a voyage from San Francisco to Liverpool. That completed, Slocum returned to the Pacific Coast and after some time fishing, hunting sea otters, and building boats for gill-netting salmon at the mouth of the Columbia River, at about twenty-five years old he earned his first command, a schooner along the coast of California.

After the coasting gig, he was given his first ocean-crossing command. On his first major stop in Sydney, Australia, he met a young American expat named Virginia Walker, who was part Native American from the Leni-Lenape tribe. They married after only a couple of weeks of courting. She sailed back to San Francisco in the aft cabin. By the accounts that remain, their marriage seems to have been a loving match. They never had a permanent home on shore, only at sea or in short-term lodging by the water or with Slocum's extended family. Virginia raised four children at sea and lost in infancy three more: a baby daughter and a set of twins. She taught the children school lessons on the ship, played piano, assisted with navigation, and joined her husband through years of adventures and often excruciating circumstances, including soon after they were married when Slocum commanded a ship that fished for salmon off the coast of Alaska but ran aground in the newly American territory. Slocum led the construction of a smaller boat to get the fish to port while Virginia escaped aboard a US Coast Guard cutter to meet up with him later. At one point years afterwards in the Philippines, Virginia and Joshua with their three young kids lived in a raised nipa hut beside the rainforest where Slocum had been hired to build a coastal steamboat out of local timber. At one point while Slocum was away in Manila, a rival group of Chinese men tried to burn down the hut and the boat, but Virginia and the family were protected by the local Tagalog workers.

Throughout his career Slocum sailed mostly on what were known as tramp freighters, merchant ships that focused on bulk cargoes and moved around the world following supply and demand. Over the course of his professional years, approximately five full times around the world, Slocum carried cargoes such as lumber, sugar, salt, grain, cans of food, and, though he commanded sailing ships exclusively, his holds were often transporting cargoes of coal or containers of mineral and petroleum oils.

Slocum's professional and filial peak came in 1882 with his

command and part-ownership of an enormous ship named the *Northern Light*. In New York City, as workers were putting the finishing touches on the Brooklyn Bridge, Slocum paid to have his father come to visit and be reconciled with him, to see his success. The *New York Tribune* wrote a feature on the captain and his family, describing their palatial cabin, replete with a piano, a large library, oil paintings on the bulkheads, and sweetly mannered children cleaning and sketching.

By this point in American history, if you weren't in the aft cabin as captain, jobs aboard ships in the merchant marine were unappealing. It had become harder and harder for owners to find willing and capable crew. The *Northern Light* itself was not in the prime of life either. On the way outbound from New York City the ship had rudder problems, requiring a stop in New London, Connecticut, where at anchor a mutiny broke out. Virginia stood behind Slocum with a revolver to protect him. With a knife one mutineer killed the first mate. Once the mutineer was bound for prison, Slocum found a new chief officer and supervised repairs to the rudder. They carried on with their voyage to Asia and around the world. Off South Africa and homeward bound they had rudder problems again. The ship lost steerage in rough seas, which resulted in waves over the decks and seawater leaking into the holds to the point that the crew had to heave some of the cargo overboard to stabilize the vessel. Slocum managed to bring the *Northern Light* to port for repairs, where he found a new second mate who proved inept and mutinous. Slocum clapped the man in irons, imprisoning him for over fifty days. Once back in New York City, vastly different reports about what had actually happened made the newspapers and into the courtroom, including one claim that the man was kept in an unbearably hot pen the entire time, having to sleep beside his own feces. Slocum was fined. He sold his part ownership of the *Northern Light*.

After some time staying with his family and licking their wounds, the Slocums bought a smaller ship, the *Aquidneck*. On the way to trade in Australia, in part to visit with her family, Virginia became ill, perhaps of heart failure. Still in her mid-thirties, she died in Slocum's arms at anchor off Buenos Aires. Their four children were aboard, aged three to twelve.

A few days after burying her, Slocum accidentally ran his ship aground on the way out of port. He wrote a pained letter to his mother-in-law explaining what had happened. Their youngest son Garfield said later that he understood his father was now like "a ship with a broken rudder."

A year and a half later, Slocum married a much younger cousin of his from Nova Scotia named Henrietta "Hettie" Elliott. The two middle children stayed home with other family members while Slocum, Hettie, Garfield, and the oldest son Victor, serving as first mate, set sail on the *Aquidneck* bound back to South America to deliver cargo. After a storm in New England waters with the ship leaking, they made it to South America where Slocum quelled yet another mutiny, this time injuring one man and shooting another dead. Slocum was jailed for a month, but was then pardoned in local courts. After further months of diplomatic issues, quarantines, changes of cargo, and crew illness and death from cholera and smallpox, Slocum with a short-handed crew and bad weather was unable to keep the *Aquidneck* from running aground off the coast of southern Brazil. As the *Aquidneck* broke up, shipwrecked and uninsured with a cargo of lumber, he could sell his ship only for salvage.

Slocum was now practically bankrupt. This had been

Hettie's first voyage at sea, her "honeymoon." Yet instead of taking a loan to book a passage back to Boston, Slocum crafted himself a funky thirty-five-foot wooden boat with sails rigged like a Chinese sampan. They sailed this vessel, the *Liberdade*, not without incident but with some fame, all the way back to New England.

Once home, the captain, despite his experience and skills, was no longer trusted with a ship to command after so many groundings and crew troubles. There were also not many American vessels under sail by the late 1800s. Nearly all merchant ships by that point had shifted to iron hulls and had installed steam engines. Most had abandoned masts and canvas altogether. Entire populations of wood-and-canvas sailors, if they did not decide to work ashore, were reduced to helping to shovel coal below decks, steering and handling cargo up above, and then getting ready to put the fenders over the side when the ship belched smoke and chugged up to the dock. It was now the engineers who possessed the essential knowledge that made the ships run. Joseph Conrad, who had been a career mariner himself, lamented this transition in his novella *Typhoon* (1902)—a story in which the ship's survival in a monster storm is not in the hands of Captain MacWhirr (note the name), who has lost the imagination to read the weather signs of the open ocean, but instead the crew is dependent on Solomon Rout, a slipper-shod engineer who scuffles down below in the hold managing the gauges and coal shovelers. In the same year another mariner-turned-author named John Masefield published nostalgic verse to the days of sail, most famously his poem "Sea-Fever" (1902), which remains popular today: "I must go down to the seas again, to the lonely sea and the sky, / And all I ask is a tall ship and a star to steer her by."

In other words, the nostalgia and the specific longing for sailing ships and quiet wind-driven passages out at sea began at the turn of the twentieth century, even before all of the sailing merchant ships were retired.

In *Sailing Alone Around the World*, Slocum regularly contrasts the beauty of the sailing ship to the smoky, linear steamship. "There are no poetry-enshrined freighters on the sea now," Slocum wrote. Although he had once directed the building of a steamship himself (out of wood) and relied on steamships regularly as a merchant trader, especially going in and out of harbors, and even a few times conceding a short tow during his single-handed circumnavigation, Slocum wanted no part of commanding these vessels or learning to build with iron or steel.

So after returning from South America on the little *Liberdade*, Slocum, in his late forties, had now lost the love of his life, his ship, and his career. Having been a captain for so long, he surely did not like being ordered around in a boat yard. He didn't really want these new jobs ashore, anyway. He was apparently offered the command of a White Star Line steam-packet ship at one point, but he told his youngest son Garfield, "I would have to get used to steamships and I do not like steamships." In *Sailing Alone Around the World* Slocum explained his *why-go* in a lighter tone that surely belied his personal and professional desperation before setting off for his circumnavigation: "And so when times for [sailing] freighters got bad, as at last they did, and I tried to quit the sea, what was there for an old sailor to do? I was born in the breezes, and I had studied the sea as perhaps few men have studied it, neglecting all else."

Slocum continued trying to network for a job that he liked until the winter of 1891, when he caught up with a friend, a retired captain named Eben Pierce, a man who had made his fortune by manufacturing an explosive lance and gun for killing whales. Slocum wrote that Pierce said: "Come to Fairhaven and I'll give you a ship. But she wants some repairs."

In *Sailing Alone Around the World*, Slocum probably played up the perfidy of Captain Pierce offering a ship, but *Spray* was certainly a rotten hulk when he found it. Since he had nothing else on the horizon, Slocum stayed at Pierce's house and rebuilt the old boat entirely on his own. By the summer of 1891, when William Andrews and Si Lawlor staged their solo trans-Atlantic race, Slocum had moved down to Fairhaven to work on *Spray*. But maybe he was back in Boston in the crowd the day they left, or he read about it in the newspaper, or he heard it from old salts deriding the stunt in the shipyard? Just maybe it started him thinking? Meanwhile, Hettie and the kids visited him in Fairhaven occasionally, and once Slocum had finished the restoration, with nearly every timber replaced and modified to his liking, he tried doing some charters for tourists and even did some fishing aboard *Spray*. And at some point the idea to sail alone around the world came to dominate his mind.

Joshua Slocum was an indefatigable trader, an entrepreneur in pursuit of a dollar. He had learned, as one biographer Geoffrey Wolff assessed, to make lemonade whenever and wherever he found lemons. On the back half of his circumnavigation, for example, he emptied about three tons of cement ballast from his hold to load up with some thirty gigantic tridacna clam shells to sell as curios back in New England. At first his writing tracked within this entrepreneurial *modus operandi*. Although he'd had only a few years of formal education, Slocum had always been a devoted reader and was eager to write his own sea stories. He wrote and self-published *Voyage of the "Liberdade"* in 1890, his story of their sail home from Brazil in his home-made boat. This did not sell well, but he received at least one major positive review. He self-published a pamphlet titled *Voyage of the "Destroyer"* in 1894, which was his account of a curious military delivery job he had after rebuilding the *Spray*. Neither narrative made him much money, but they gave him some experience in writing and provided him with contacts and something to shop around as he appealed to newspapers to pay for the letters he would send home during his world voyage. Slocum hoped the fame of being the first to sail single-handed around the world was a way to make some money and fund the adventure.

In other words, Slocum's *why-go* was not primarily to publish a book, but writing down his yarns to help support the expedition was part of his plan from the start. He had an advance agreement with the *Boston Globe* and a couple of other newspapers. Certainly, too, an element of Slocum's *why-go* involved his attempt to escape domestic responsibilities, his financial and professional failures, and as a way to cope with the loss of Virginia and the degradation of his career and self-worth. He told the newspapers that he had asked Hettie and the kids if they wanted to go, but it's fair to assume this was a half-mumbled invitation. Hettie was clear, anyway, even with journalists, that she wasn't interested in life at sea after the *Liberdade* odyssey. Of the kids, Garfield was fourteen at that point and the other three were twenty or older and living their own lives. Slocum wished, needed to get back out to sea, and what better way to do so than by yourself, with no one else to be concerned about? In *Sailing Alone Around the World* he regularly quipped about the satisfaction of his own company, "There was never a ship's crew so well agreed." Aboard *Spray* at last, Slocum enjoyed a voyage free from mutiny, domestic life, and living under the roof of another family member. At sea he could avoid any interpersonal conflict at all.

Slocum likely did not see his voyage in terms of a Byronic escape from urbanization or from Western civilization. He certainly wanted out of steamship travel and liked the simplicity of his way of life, but he stuck almost entirely to English-speaking ports. In *Sailing Alone Around the World* he wrote about the Pacific Islanders of Samoa rejecting Western money-chasing materialism, but then, even in his text, Slocum quickly forgot this lesson by the next port of call. Capitalism was too ingrained in his core. In practice, he sought no island paradises away from Western civilization. What Slocum craved foremost was the open sea and time with his boat—and a bit of money, respect for his seamanship, and maybe even some appreciation for his storytelling.

Captain Slocum left Boston alone aboard *Spray* on 24 April 1895. He stopped first in the fishing port of Gloucester, Massachusetts, then visited for about a month with family in his home town in Nova Scotia before he set off to cross his first ocean. He stopped at the Azores and "discovered Spain" on the way to Gibraltar, where Slocum was toasted by the Royal Navy and the English yachtsmen at the port. His dispatches to American newspapers quickly fizzled out because he could not meet predictable deadlines or write copy engaging enough in the short term. Before

Joshua Slocum aboard *Spray* early in the first recorded solo circumnavigation, docked in a port on the east coast of South America (1895).

continuing, the officials in Gibraltar convinced him that pirates were too dangerous on the eastbound route by way of the Suez Canal, so he changed his plan and aimed to sail around the world westbound, sailing toward Brazil and south to the Strait of Magellan, the craggy storm-ravaged channel above Cape Horn, in order to cross into the South Pacific. The Panama Canal still seemed a failed project at that point.

As Slocum approached the Strait of Magellan from the Atlantic, a rogue wave engulfed him from astern. The single wave was so steep and tall that he had to leap into the rigging to escape being swept overboard. *Spray* was a wide thirty-seven-foot wooden sloop, originally designed for tonging oysters in shallow water, but it was a reliable fishing boat design that he had beefed up further. In the hands of an expert like Slocum, the boat proved an ideal cruising boat, even in heavy open-ocean seas or when overtopped by a freak wave.

Once in the relative safety of the Strait in the austral summer of 1896, the westerly work was a different kind of sailing. He anchored nearly every night. To keep his boat secure in case of williwaws, the downdraft winds that can reach hurricane force and could blow *Spray* to shipwreck on the rocks, the captain surely needed his heaviest anchor, which weighed about 180 pounds. Each morning, with no one else to mind the helm, Slocum, in his early fifties, cranked a hand windlass to get the anchor off the bottom. Then with block and tackle he hauled the anchor in place on the rail so that he could lash the stock firmly enough to sail safely again before the next blow. To set sail, though he knew how to use his thin 5' 9" frame, he had to raise the heavy canvas mainsail and the gaff, a stout wooden spar, with two different halyards: first heave down on one, or both at the same time, make one fast, then haul down on the other to finish it up. On his way through the Strait, Slocum regularly checked his depth with some rope and a sounding lead. He had good charts, but no engine and no electricity aboard *Spray*. When possible, he went ashore with a hatchet to gather wood for his stove. After weaving through the desolate fjords for nearly a month, Slocum succeeded in passing through into the Pacific Ocean. Alone under dark clouds, he tacked out of the frigid passage at Cabo Pilar.

Any feelings of pride and relief were promptly blasted. A severe northwesterly gale charged down so aggressively that Slocum had to spin the wheel to run south ahead of the wind and seas. His mainsail in tatters, he precariously surfed under bare poles for four days down toward Cape Horn itself, until, intensely sleep-deprived and confused as to where he was exactly, he was able—in the dark—to sail back into a channel, threading through a maze of white-water breakers known as the Milky Way, scudding past a terrifying rockpile named Fury Island. In his telling of this in *Sailing Alone Around the World*, Slocum roughly quotes "the great naturalist" Charles Darwin, who when visiting the region in the 1830s aboard HMS *Beagle*, wrote: "Any landsman seeing the Milky Way would have nightmare [sic] for a week." Once through, at daybreak, Slocum now had a bitter sail back into the Strait of Magellan, about halfway in, meaning he was forced to loop around to get west again from where he had been weeks ago. Anchorage after anchorage, he cranked and hauled and sounded his way back through the Strait once more, often in danger from night-time raids by small local bands of "Fuegians," which included people perhaps of the Yaghan or Alacaluf tribes. The groups that Slocum described were led by a foreign outlaw nicknamed Black Pedro. When finally back at the western mouth, Slocum wrote that it took him seven attempts to stick his boat's nose out and weather this exit and Cabo Pilar again, allowing him to enter, this time for good, into the proper South Pacific. That is, not before he paused to load some cargo: Slocum could not resist salvaging a shipwreck, spending the better part of a day towing and hauling aboard barrels of tallow and wine, thinking—correctly as it turned out—that he would be able to make some money several months later, even if the new cargo weighed down his boat.

Slocum had needed two brutal months to pass through the Strait of Magellan. At last he shouted goodbye to the penguins, gulls, and seals, praised his *Spray*, and set all sail under a clear sky. One final wave broke over the stern, which seemed to bookend the rogue wave in the Atlantic and wash clean that experience of the passage.

"Then was the time to uncover my head, for I sailed alone with God," Slocum wrote. "The vast ocean was again around me, and the horizon was unbroken by land."

The captain now sailed northwesterly to the Juan Fernández Islands, anchoring in Robinson Crusoe Bay, where he "of course made a pilgrimage to [Alexander Selkirk's] old lookout place." Slocum then coasted into the ocean world of the trade winds. Here he found his true stride, his satisfaction with life at sea and a personal glory. Slocum occasionally wrote of the marine life and the encounters he had with birds, fish, and whales, but he saw his connections with the ocean more often and more truly in the relationship between his wooden boat and himself and in his ability to navigate celestially in spite of and often in direct opposition to the emerging technologies and materials of his time. Earlier in the voyage when still in the Atlantic, Slocum proudly personified his boat within the wind and seas, one of his ecstasy-so-pure sailing moments: "Her mast now bent under a strong, steady pressure, and her bellying sail swept the sea as she rolled scuppers under, curtseying to the waves. These rolling waves thrilled me as they tossed my ship, passing quickly under her keel. This was grand sailing."

In the South Pacific trade winds Slocum found affirmation in this voyage alone, with a brand of love for the sea that Ann Davison would come to understand a half-century later: an ocean adoration that was about humble mastery of seamanship and navigation. In other words, Slocum's *what-they-saw* was woven primarily into his brotherhood with his boat navigating blue water. He wrote of his westbound passage in the South Pacific trades this way:

For one whole month my vessel held her course true; I had not, the while, so much as a light in the binnacle. The Southern Cross I saw every night abeam. The sun every morning came up astern; every evening it went down ahead. I wished for no other compass to guide me, for these were true. If I doubted my reckoning after a long time at sea I verified it by reading the clock aloft made by the Great Architect, and it was right ... it was my ship on her course, sailing as no other ship had ever sailed before in the world.

Slocum wrote here of a oneness with the universe, navigating with only the stars and sun, his sextant, and with the method of dead reckoning by feel, compass, and taffrail log. One of his running jokes in *Sailing Alone Around the World* is his reference to his rickety tin clock, which he said he purchased before leaving instead of fixing his professional chronometer. He could not afford to fix the chronometer, even though it was a piece of technology, like GPS today, that in his era was considered essential for navigation by nearly all Western deep-water sailors. With nineteenth-century tools and a knowledge of the lunar-distance method to calculate longitude regardless of accurate time, Slocum and *Spray* sailed across the surface of the Pacific with a type of reckoning and celestial navigation that, although Slocum did not mention this if he knew anything at all about it, tilted closer to that of the Pacific Islanders, especially when added to his knowledge of seabirds.

Slocum sailed all the way across the South Pacific to Samoa, after a passage of over seventy-two days. In Samoa he paid a visit to the widow of Robert Louis Stevenson, one of his literary heroes.

Slocum's love of life at sea, his mastery of navigation, was intertwined with his personal faith, which he held through a philosophy like that of an earlier pre-Darwinian era, notably the theories of Bishop Paley's clockwork universe designed by the "Great Architect." Of the trade winds of the South Pacific, Slocum wrote: "I was *en rapport* now with my surroundings, and was carried on a vast stream where I felt the buoyancy of His hand who made all the worlds. I realized the mathematical truth of their motions, so well-known that astronomers compile tables of their positions."

Slocum sailed into Sydney harbor, then down to Tasmania, and back up past the Great Barrier Reef, west through the Torres Strait and across the Timor Sea. After an exceptionally long open-water passage, he arrived at the Cocos Keeling Islands (where he was greeted by fairy terns as he approached). Here Slocum admitted to being moved to tears in his ability to find this tiny atoll in the vast Indian Ocean. In this way his time at sea by himself was deeply spiritual. After he returned to the United States, he wrote to a clergyman cousin: "Old Sailors may have odd ways of showing their religious feeling but there are no infidels at sea."

This is not to suggest that Slocum observed the Sabbath aboard *Spray* or delivered religious tracts for the missionaries in the South Pacific like "Rob Roy" MacGregor in France. And though he sailed with a library and read constantly while at sea, there is no indication he sailed with a Bible. It's just that Slocum, sailing by himself for so many days, felt connected and small before a deep-sea natural environment that he saw as the creation and realm of the Christian God, which included everything from the movement of the stars and planets in the universe and all the way down to the behavior of fish. For example, Slocum wrote that small fish seemed to know they were made to be eaten, as if "they knew they were created for the larger fishes," schooling tightly as if to render it easier for their predators.

After navigating across the Indian Ocean and around the Cape of Good Hope, stopping in Cape Town, *Spray* sailed back up the South Atlantic, punctuated by port stops and anchorages in St Helena, Ascension Island, and Grenada, before he returned to the United States and made landfall in Newport, Rhode Island, on 27 June 1898, completing his world voyage in about three years and two months. No one was there to greet him.

News of Slocum's circumnavigation was overshadowed by the Spanish-American War. He was immediately eager to serve, writing in a public letter about his desire to help the war effort with all his knowledge of the islands in the Pacific: "I burn to be of some use now of all times."

The US Navy did not take him up on the offer, though, and Joshua Slocum's life after his world voyage appears on the whole a sad one, in part because he felt he never got the type of credit he deserved, and because he never could quite get a handle on what to do with the rest of his life.

First he worked on *Sailing Alone Around the World*. As Slocum's circumnavigation had progressed along friendly harbors, he had begun to earn money for lectures, which he illustrated with lantern slides. Although he never mentioned this in his narrative, he apparently had a camera with him on the voyage. None of this material has survived. Slocum honed his stories and smoothed his delivery in his latter port stops, which prepared him well for when he sat down to write after his return. He often wrote his narrative while at anchor aboard *Spray* in various New England ports, sending in drafts for editorial help. The articles first appeared serially in *Century Illustrated Monthly Magazine* with the now famous drawings by Thomas Fogarty and George Varian. The articles did well, as did the book, receiving good reviews in America, and then a British edition, about which the poet and journalist Edwin Arnold extolled the story's true, plain, salty style, "yet full of touches which show what hidden poetry and passionate love of Nature were in the soul of this 'blue-nose' skipper."

*Sailing Alone Around the World* made Slocum enough money to buy an old house and some land for Hettie and himself on Martha's Vineyard, near other retired sea captains and one of his brothers. He tried farming for a couple of seasons, but he did not stick with it. Meanwhile, he and Hettie seemed never to share any real connection. Soon he was barely living there. Instead he sailed alone again on *Spray* around New England and even seasonally down to the Caribbean collecting shells, selling his books, and giving tours of the boat. His old friend Captain Pierce, who had given him *Spray*, was run over and killed by an electric trolley. His old ship the *Northern Light* ended up as a coal barge.

After taking the *Spray* up the Hudson River with Hettie and Garfield to exhibit it at the Pan-American Exposition in Buffalo, and after proposing various endeavors such as starting a university program on a sailing ship and offering himself as a second mate aboard a dirigible, Slocum sailed alone in 1906 aboard *Spray* back down to the Caribbean where he collected wild orchids and other goods to sell back home. On the way back he stopped to give a lecture in Riverton, New

Jersey, where he was thrown in jail for indecency toward a twelve-year-old girl who came aboard with a friend to tour the boat. Historians aren't certain what happened here exactly. There's not much information or testimony besides a doctor reporting afterwards that this was not physical assault, because there appeared to be no evidence of physical contact, about which the girl's parents seem to have agreed. Slocum did not have money for bail and the story made the newspapers. After he was jailed for forty-two days, Slocum was respectfully reprimanded by the judge who told him he was banned from Riverton, by land or sea.

One week later, as if nothing had happened, Slocum delivered his last surviving orchid to the Long Island home of Theodore Roosevelt, whose twelve-year-old son Archibald invited him to dinner with the president, after which the son and a US Navy sailor went cruising with Slocum for a week in Long Island Sound aboard *Spray*. The president wrote to Slocum about his book: "I entirely sympathize with your feeling of delight in the sheer loneliness and vastness of the ocean. It was just my feeling in the wilderness of the west." This was perhaps in response to a line that Slocum wrote of his long passage across the South Pacific, which "brings you for many days close on nature, and you realize the vastness of the sea."

Despite earning the respect of Roosevelt, both Slocum and *Spray* had been deteriorating. Archibald and others left accounts of how the boat appeared to be in a shambles. In 1907 a reporter visiting Jamaica met Slocum there and reported that he told her: "I can patch up the *Spray*, but who will patch up Captain Slocum?"

In early 1908, now sixty-four years old, he got a commission to sail a two-ton piece of coral from the Bahamas to the American Museum of Natural History in New York. After he returned, Slocum sailed *Spray* out of Martha's Vineyard, perhaps bound for an adventure up the Amazon. He was never heard from again. Some historians speculate that Slocum did not get far and sank in heavy weather due to the state of his boat. Decades later, the historian Edward Rowe Snowe found an account that suggests convincingly that Slocum was run down by a 125-foot inter-island steamship ferry, somewhere near the north coast of Haiti. The officers had been afraid to report the incident. Snowe's source was a professional mariner traveling on board who noticed damage on the bow and asked the captain of the ferry about what had happened. The captain said that it was a local fishing boat. The second mate who had been on watch, however, told the source that he knew immediately it was *not* a local boat and that no one was at the wheel. Snowe put events together: Slocum's boat and the timing would have been exactly along this route.

Slocum's death at sea, perhaps while he slept, run down by a steamship as *Spray* steered itself, seems the most probable explanation. It is by far the most poetically fitting: that the first single-handed circumnavigator Joshua Slocum was, as Geoffrey Wolff phrased it, "murdered by modernity."

Slocum's first biographer was his oldest son Victor, who became a sailor-writer himself. Victor argued the case, well before the Caribbean steamship account came to light, that his father's death at the bow of a merchant ship was the only likely scenario.

Since then, Slocum has been the subject of at least five

other book-length biographies and hundreds of popular and scholarly articles. The first major scholarly biography, by Walter Teller, was published during the 1950s boom in ocean interest. Teller was able to interview Hettie, Slocum's children, and others who knew them. Slocum's boat *Spray* has been the topic of multiple studies, experiments, two entire books, and the model for more than eight hundred known replicas, several of which have crossed oceans. *Sailing Alone Around the World* has never gone out of print. It's been translated into at least nine languages. Excerpts have been anthologized in nearly every nautical compendium, as well as works that commemorate American literature.

In other words, Joshua Slocum is the original gangster. Among modern mariners, he is the furling founding father, and the most daring double-reefed Davey Jones among all solo sailors in history. Slocum's circumnavigation, his seamanship, his highly readable Twain-like account of the voyage, and the near-mythical self-steering abilities of his *Spray* have continued to influence and inspire generation after generation, not just on tactics and boat design, but on his view of the sea and the possibilities of an ocean-crossing endeavor for everyone. Although rarely considered as such, and for all of his personal flaws, Slocum's voyage should appear on the same shelf as accounts of the greatest individual achievements in modern human history. He had no support team and barely a whiff of assistance at any point, before or during his voyages, anywhere.

"The sea has been much maligned," Slocum concluded in *Sailing Alone Around the World*, writing directly to each aspiring adventurer: "To young men contemplating a voyage, I would say go. The tales of rough usage are for the most part exaggerations, as also are the stories of sea danger."

# 6. Sharks

One day early in my trans-Atlantic crossing I was leaning over the stern to clear some seaweed off the self-steering gear with a boat hook when I saw a large dorsal fin speeding up to the stern. I hustled down below to the cabin. This was partly to get my camera, but I was also half-imagining that Jaws himself was going to leap out of the water into the cockpit and eat me up.

I look at my photographs now and can barely see the fin. In retrospect, I don't even know confidently that it was a shark. Maybe it was a killer whale or a Risso's dolphin or some other medium-sized whale with a tall falcate fin. Regardless, I was terrified of the real or imagined shark.

The hull of *Fox* was low in the water. When sailing hard and sitting on the leeward side, I could reach over and touch the sea with my fingers, so I could not help imagining an enormous shark surging right onto the boat and bursting across like a truck with teeth plowing through a wicker fence. I clutched my little retractable boat hook as if I could some-how beat the monster off—or poke it in the eye.

Solo sailors have demonized sharks from the first voyages. Their stories and behaviors have perpetuated fears of the man-eating cruelty of sharks, well before Peter Benchley's novel *Jaws* (1974) and Steven Spielberg's iconic film that followed the year after.

The newspaper account of Alfred "Centennial" Johnson's 1876 crossing devoted a full section titled "Peril from a Shark," even though nothing really happened. One night in the summer of 1891, while Si Lawlor was sailing alone, racing William Andrews across the Atlantic for the first time, a shark woke Lawlor by chewing and crunching at the bow of his tiny open boat. Lawlor yarned that he wrapped an exploding flare in paper, lit the bundle, and threw the flare at the shark's head. He claimed the shark snatched it up just before the flare exploded in its mouth. The animal sank and disappeared into the dark.

Joshua Slocum had a particular hatred of sharks throughout his life. For family sport, his first wife Virginia would lean over the rail to kill sharks with a revolver as their son Benjamin attracted them over with a shiny can on a string. In *Voyage of the "Liberdade"*, Slocum wrote of how these "monsters" are the sea's greatest terror, and how he knew the story of a second mate who went for a swim off the coast of Cuba and was torn in half by a shark, who then swallowed the two parts and when later captured still had some of the body's remains in his gullet. In *Voyage of the "Destroyer"*, Slocum told more stories of men swimming off the ship and being nearly torn apart by twenty-foot sharks, one of which ate instead a plank of wood. (The longest carnivorous shark ever reliably recorded in Western records, by the way, was 19.5 feet long.) In *Sailing Alone Around the World*, Slocum described the shark as both the wolf and the tiger of the sea: "nothing is more dreadful to the mind of a sailor" than the hungry shark. When sharks approached the *Spray* at anchor, he shot at them. Off the coast of Chile he harpooned a shark, killed it, and removed its "ugly jaws," presumably as a keepsake or an object to sell. "I had not till then felt inclined to take the life of any animal," Slocum wrote, explaining that the Strait of Magellan was so desolate and lonely that he could not bear to kill even a duck for food, "but when John Shark hove in sight my sympathy flew to the winds." Later in Australia, Slocum caught a twelve-and-a-half-foot shark and charged sixpence for people to see the dead animal, as well as her twenty-six babies that he kept alive and swimming in a canoe. Slocum had found these fetal sharks, each about two feet long, when he slit open the mother shark's belly. Later he stuffed the adult shark with hay and brought it with him to his next port at Tasmania where he exhibited the carcass before he gave it to the local museum.

"The Shark on the Deck of the 'Spray'," original illustration for *Sailing Alone Around the World*, by Thomas Fogarty (1900).

When Harry Pidgeon was first sailing by himself on his boat *Islander* in the South Pacific toward Tahiti in 1921, he went over the side one flat calm day to swim laps around the boat. At the start of his second lap, he had a "sudden apprehension" and turned back, clambering back aboard just as a shark slalomed over toward the hull. The shark had pilot fish swimming around its mouth and remoras attached. It rubbed its back on the hull of *Islander*.

"He followed the boat all day," Pidgeon wrote, "and only left off after I had wounded him twice with the boat hook."

Thus, Pidgeon continued to strike fear in every sailor-reader who thought they might want to take a dip over the side.

A generation later, in addition to her description of sinister, menacing sharks in formation as the representation of the loveless, dangerous sea, Ann Davison wrote of them again when sailing alone in the Bahamas. Here she said sharks, at first appearing like dark shadows rising up toward the surface, rubbed up against the hull of *Felicity Ann* and turned to look directly at her with their "cold, calculating, pig-like eyes."

In 1962 a young Japanese sailor named Kenichi Horie described dozens of sharks six to ten feet long bumping into his tiny boat's wooden hull during his solo crossing of the North Pacific. He wrote: "They looked more like some kind of ominous weapon than fish—steely colored with cold, heartless faces. Eyes half-closed, dorsal fin protruding into the sunshine, they cut through the water giving me and the *Mermaid* cold, dirty looks." Horie tried to take photographs, with inevitably unimpressive results when they were later developed.

Perhaps the scariest of single-hander shark stories was that of Bill King, a former World War II submarine commander.

King was on his second attempt to sail alone around the world in 1971 when off the southwest coast of Australia, a few days out of port in the Southern Ocean, he was down below in his cabin when he saw the timbers of his hull punched in by some enormous beast, the planking split and hammered inwards. The sea flooded in as he leaped out on deck and saw blood in the water and the swimming animal astern, later identified by experts ashore, due to the behavior, region, and shape of the impact on the boat, as a great white shark (*Carcharodon carcharias*). King was able to tack his boat around and keep the busted hole enough out of the water to stay afloat. He endured a couple of horrific days trying to patch it up and sail back to port, which he managed to do without sinking because of a nearly miraculous shift in the wind that allowed him to keep the hole tilted mostly out of the water.

Every single-handed sailing story, it seems, needs to have some yarn about a shark, second only to at least one storm, one ecstasy-so-pure moment of sailing, one clever repair, and one near miss by a passing ship. If the solo mariner did not see a shark directly, they will talk about how they imagined sharks when they had to dive into the water to fix something or when they dared to indulge in a mid-ocean swim. Today nearly every boat, from the tiniest cruising craft to the largest naval destroyers, posts some sort of "shark watch" when crew are going over the side for a swim mid-ocean. Swimmers and surfers occasionally get gashed by curious sharks along the coast, and even occasionally killed from loss of blood—but this rarely if ever happens out at sea if the person isn't already bleeding or wounded.

For example, in 2022 an Australian single-hander named John Deer fell off his stern while setting his fishing gear. He watched his boat sail away. Treading water about ten miles off the coast of Panama, the closest town being Cabo Tiburon, meaning Cape Shark, he felt some nibbling at his legs at dusk from something, but to his amazement nothing ever broke the skin. He managed to swim the whole way, aided by adrenalin and the current, to an isolated shore. From here he was rescued by a passing boat within a day.

# 7. Just Cruisin' with Harry Pidgeon

He was not only a person who calmly reported sharks snuffling at his toes as he climbed out of the water, but Harry Pidgeon seems by all accounts to have been a remarkably capable man who might fell a patch of forest, build himself a log cabin, and then later softly mention that he'd been studying origami so he'd like to fold you a pink crane or two. Joshua Slocum had a curmudgeonly side; you'd want to learn from him, but you get the sense that he'd make you feel a fool in the process, maybe even on purpose now and again. Pidgeon, by contrast, his hands just as rough and chipped, perhaps because he had never served as a ship's master, seems to have had an easy-going, non-judgmental competence that would put you at ease. Pidgeon's two solo circumnavigations, beginning in the 1920s, represent a new trend in *why-go* and *what-they-saw* because primarily he wanted to visit the islands of the South Pacific—then once underway he fell in love with life at sea. As a relative amateur, Pidgeon did all this on a boat that he built himself from a plan published by a weekend-warrior boating magazine called *The Rudder*, which had started in the 1890s.

Born in 1869, a quarter-century after Slocum, Harry Pidgeon grew up as part of a large family working a farm in Iowa.

When he was eighteen he found a job on a ranch in California, and then spent a summer up north where he built a boat with a friend and ran the rapids of the Yukon River. In southeast Alaska he owned his first boat and cruised along the coast. From here he continued his lifelong walkabout, building a raft and sailing down the Mississippi. Pidgeon then traveled overland back to California, where, now in his late forties, he decided to build his own boat for blue-water sailing. He bought the plans through the mail and constructed from scratch a thirty-four-foot ketch out of plywood and other timbers, using hand tools, on a vacant lot beside Los Angeles Harbor. Another man nearby was building a multi-storied ark in anticipation of The Flood.

As Pidgeon was completing his boat, which he named *Islander*, a friend invited him and two others for a sail to Hawai'i. On the first day out, the weather was rough. They all got seasick, vomiting plums over the side. Pidgeon found himself steeled to the expedition, though, even as the others were down below incapacitated. He was disappointed when his friend directed the boat to head back home.

"I returned to the *Islander* with a feeling," Pidgeon wrote, "that the problems of a single-handed sailor were comparatively simple." In other words, if you go it alone on a boat (or in life), you don't have to worry about other people's schedules or needs.

Having taught himself navigation at the public library, Pidgeon decided to sail his new boat to Hawai'i from Los Angeles, a distance that is only a few days shorter than an entire trans-Atlantic crossing. Once underway, Pidgeon stopped bothering with dead reckoning and multiple sun sights, since working with the mathematical tables down below made him seasick. With an accurate chronometer—more advanced and

reliable than Slocum's tin clock—he obtained his daily latitude with a single sun sight at local apparent noon each
day—when the sun is at its highest point. He compared this
timing to that of Greenwich, with his tables, and thus roughly
estimated his longitude, too. A fix once a day was all he
needed on this passage, as he sailed for three weeks with
favorable trade winds along a latitude, more or less straight
across over to Hawai'i. He saw only one other vessel during
the whole trip, a long four-masted schooner piled high with
lumber. He followed it for as long as he could, which, com-
bined with the mountain peaks of Hawai'i in the coming
days, helped him navigate the final leg with relative ease.

Pidgeon was not yet convinced that sailing alone was for
him, though. He made a friend with whom he sailed back to
Los Angeles, but once there, after getting no firm commit-
ments from anybody to join him for a sail to the South Pacific,
Pidgeon just figured it best to go alone or the trip would never
happen. He had read Slocum's *Sailing Alone Around the World*
and had spoken to a few cruisers, but completing a circumnavigation was not in his plans at first. Pidgeon just wanted
to travel and to have a cheap floating home.

If escaping modern civilization was on Pidgeon's mind,
he did not share this in his account of the voyage, titled
*Around the World Single-Handed* (1928), although there was
plenty from which to flee in 1921. The city of Los Angeles
had been entirely shut down to try and stop the spread of
the Spanish Flu, a horrific pandemic that killed whole groups
of young people who bled out of their eyes and ears. The
quarantine of the city began in the harbor where Pidgeon
built his boat and the pandemic lasted into 1919, while the
local government closed schools and businesses. Los Angeles
fared better than most other American cities, but it still lost

nearly 500 people for every 100,000. Meanwhile, the legacy of World War I remained raw. Too old to enlist and having been raised a Quaker, Pidgeon had not served in the military.

When Pidgeon first sailed to Hawai'i on his shakedown cruise, he was fifty-one. This was the same age as Joshua Slocum when he left Boston. (That's my age, too, as I write this.) Fifty-one was also the same age as Don Quixote, one of Slocum's favorite fictional characters, that soft-handed Spanish gentleman who is so entranced by his books that he hoists on some old knight's armor and saddles up an aging horse named Rocinante to walk out his back gate to try to achieve fame and fortune by behaving in the old ways as a knight savant. Don Quixote lives in his imagination and yearns to serve a world that has long since moved on. Go to nearly any marina today anywhere in the world and you'll find a Don Quixote, half-mystic and half-fool, applying another coat of varnish to the rail of his old, beloved Rocinante.

Harry Pidgeon sailed without any significant incident to the South Pacific. As he traveled from place to place, he began to grow more confident.

"I had found the sea to be a great highway leading to wherever I wished to go," he wrote. Pidgeon learned to balance *Islander*'s steering with the sails, and if his boat "did run off course a bit, what of it?"

He tightened up his navigation when he needed to, now tracing through the low island atolls. He rarely traveled with an extensive collection of updated charts, nor did he have any previous experience in these places. No one wore safety harnesses back then and his boat had an even lower rail than Slocum's *Spray*. Yet Pidgeon cruised throughout the South Pacific, with the most exciting event, as he tells it, being when some Americans took him for an automobile ride around Papeete, on Tahiti, and their car flipped over at a sharp turn.

Pidgeon continued on to cruise aboard *Islander* from anchorage to anchorage. He took photographs of topless women in Samoa. He photographed Melanesian men in loincloths with huge heads of hair. He photographed tattoos, traditional craftwork, a curly-tusked pig bred for sacrifice, and he climbed hills and took photographs of his boat in tropical bays and harbors. He wrote of customs and quarantine procedures, shifts in the historical diet of Pacific Islanders in the wake of colonial epidemics, the landing sites of Herman Melville and Robert Louis Stevenson, and the taste and effects of kava and the betel nut. By the way Pidgeon told it, he was on a long Sunday amble across exotic Oceania.

After nearly two years, he sailed *Islander* north of Australia where he joined the "route of Captain Joshua Slocum," the westbound path to follow into the Indian Ocean, South Atlantic, and the Caribbean. Pidgeon decided, aw shucks, that he intended to be the second person to circumnavigate the world alone, and that he would be the first to do so via the Panama Canal.

After the automobile crash in Tahiti, Pidgeon wrote of only two more significant brushes with danger, both of which occurred at sea after rounding the Cape of Good Hope.

The first happened after a long, lovely stay in Cape Town. He began his sail north along the coast, but the wind was light, so he wasn't able to get much rest being too close to shore. By the third night he was able to get a little farther out to sea, so he lashed his tiller, checked his sails, and went below to sleep. He woke up to *Islander* scraping on the beach, thrashing in turbid white water. The wind had shifted and his boat had sailed itself into danger. Looking over the rail at two in the morning, Pidgeon thought this was the end of his trip. *Islander* washed helplessly higher and harder on the beach. By daylight it was low tide. He jumped off the boat into the surf to go search for help, looking back at his home heeled perilously on its side as it suffered, thumped and lifted by incoming waves.

Pidgeon would learn in the coming days, the glass-half-full news story in the local press, that he had been almost supernaturally fortunate. This was the only sandy beach along a ten-mile coastline of rock cliffs and ledges, and, even here, if there had not been a favorable high tide at the moment *Islander* sailed in, the outer rocky reef would have ripped out its keel as it steered itself into the bay.

With *Islander* restored, Pidgeon sailed into the South Atlantic and westward to the mid-ocean island of St Helena. Here he met a Mr. R. A. Clark, who remembered hosting Joshua Slocum twenty years earlier. When writing about this amble around St Helena with Clark, Pidgeon waxed nostalgic in a fashion that Slocum would have appreciated: "In the days when the commerce of the world was carried on in sailing ships, St Helena lay right in the track of the home-ward bound East Indiamen ... Then it was a prosperous place, but steamships and the Suez Canal have left it only an island of romance." By the 1920s steam vessels had taken over nearly every trade and route. Masts and canvas remained only on coastal boats sailing among island nations and on a few enormous old sailing ships with iron hulls that carried huge bulk cargoes, such as grain and guano.

Pidgeon's second near-disaster came at the hands of a steamship captain off the coast of Brazil. This happened near the equator in the shipping lanes. Pidgeon watched a steamship with a load of lumber on deck. "In all my voyage I had never met a vessel within hailing distance," he wrote, which speaks to both his route and the lack of global shipping in the 1920s. He was curious as to what people on a large ship would think of meeting his little boat out at sea. He would be sorry what he had wished for, because in heavy seas the following evening, a full moon, when all looked clear enough for him to go below for a rest, he woke up to a crash:

> I sprang up to see the dark hull of a steamer looming along-side. My first thought was that she had run into my vessel, but she was going on the same course as the *Islander*, and at the same speed. If the crew had seen my boat in time to slow down, why had they not kept away? I threw the tiller over and tried to bring my boat up into the wind, but she was in too close contact. There I was with my boat on the windward side of the steamer, and every sea washing her up and down the iron side. In one of her upward rushes the foremast speared the steamer's bridge. In the bright moonlight I saw a row of faces lined up along the steamer's waist and peering down at me.

As Pidgeon desperately tried to reduce the damage, *Islander* heaving up and down with the seas that washed him violently against the tanker's hull, the chief mate threw a heavy rope down that hit the solo sailor on the head. They were trying to rescue him.

Now the Quaker farm boy began to get angry.

"I was somewhat excited, so my answer was not polite! *What do I want with your rope?*"

The whole matter with this ship only lasted about five minutes, but before returning to its course towards Buenos Aires, the vessel, which he would later learn was the oil tanker *San Quirino*, rolled steeply toward *Islander*. The backwash sent Pidgeon's boat clear, but not before a final collision broke parts of his mizzen boom, bowsprit, and damaged the foremast and jib stay.

In the morning, as he sawed off two-thirds of the remaining bowsprit and re-rigged the boat, a shark patrolled just underneath him. "As a species that I had not seen before, he interested me greatly," Pidgeon wrote, "but if he was expecting me to furnish him his dinner, he was disappointed." By the end of the day, under shortened sail, Pidgeon was able to continue on to the Caribbean.

In Trinidad, as he repaired and repainted his boat, Captain Pidgeon received a tour of a visiting cruise ship as an honored guest. He walked the stairways, looked upon the shipboard pool and the shipboard golf course, and he marveled at all the windows. But the view from so far up on the bridge made him lonely. "I liked my way of seeing the world best, and sometimes one of the tourists confided that he envied me my independent way of voyaging."

Pidgeon sailed on to the Panama Canal and took *Islander* through, despite his outboard engine not working for the one time he really could have used it. Once safely on the Pacific side, planning an inland photography trip, he had a chance meeting of sacred significance in single-handers' lore. On 12 May 1925, Pidgeon gammed with the famous Frenchman Alain Gerbault, who was bound alone for the South Pacific aboard his own boat. Gerbault would in a couple of years succeed with his own single-handed circumnavigation, the third person to do so.

Gerbault and Pidgeon could not have been more different. Gerbault had come to sailing as a veteran, a disaffected fighter pilot who sought the sea for solace in the boat he had planned to cruise with two of his friends who had died in World War I. Before entering the war, Gerbault had been a champion tennis player. He was young, handsome, dynamic, and his sailboat was tender, uncomfortable, and wet—a racing yacht built for speed but not for cruising comfort. He'd already done a trans-Atlantic crossing with this boat, during which he had endured an epic passage of over one hundred days with rotting rigging, threadbare sails, a rogue wave that broke his bowsprit, and a barrel of spoiled water. Yet Gerbault survived that first crossing and was crowned a hero on his arrival in New York City in 1923, garnering more fame for himself, even as Harry Pidgeon, lesser known, smoothly skimmed ever westward around the world. Gerbault—who carefully described the books with which he sailed, his favorite poet being John Masefield, and Joshua Slocum's book at the top of his list of sea narratives—had sailed from New York with the intention to go around the world. Now he had transited through the Panama Canal. Gerbault wore on his sleeve a passion for adventure at the edge of survival, his rail seemingly always in white foam, sailing for poetry. Pidgeon sailed as calmly as he could, and if he carried any strain of anti-establishment angst, post-traumatic stress, or a desire for thrills for art, he kept these emotions under his buttoned narrative.

Pidgeon wrote briefly of the meeting in his book, but Alain Gerbault chose not to mention it in his *In Quest of the Sun* (1929). Gerbault at the time was not dawdling in Panama, and surely seeing Pidgeon on the back end of his own dream must have fired his need to keep moving. The two took a photograph together on Gerbault's boat. They both wear white shirts and trousers, but Pidgeon has on leather shoes, a tie, a cap, and, with his arm leaning against the rigging behind Gerbault, there's the confidence of a square-jawed older brother, maybe even a teacher from church. Gerbault has his collar open, his shoes off, and he is slumped a bit. He is eager to sail to the South Pacific alone and fall in love with an ideal of Polynesian life.

Although the two never met, another solo sailing contemporary of Harry Pidgeon was Vito Dumas, an Argentinian whose *why-go* tilted far more strongly toward Gerbault's passion for adventure and artistic expression. In 1931, Dumas, after attempting to swim across the English Channel, sailed a small wooden boat alone from Arcachon in southwestern France back home across the Atlantic to Buenos Aires. A decade later, in the middle of World War II, Dumas was eager to get to sea again. He, too, wrote of how Masefield's "Sea-Fever" poem was a good expression of his feelings. At the age of forty-one Dumas sold his cattle and repurchased

UN BEL EXEMPLE D'ÉNERGIE

Seul sur son bateau, le "Fire-Crest", Alain Gerbault achève son voyage autour du monde.

*Le Petit Journal* cover illustration of Alain Gerbault aboard *Firecrest* after completing his solo circumnavigation (1929).

a boat that he had commissioned years earlier. He set out to become the first person to sail around the world by way of the Southern Ocean, along the high tempestuous latitudes known as the Roaring Forties and the Furious Fifties. With no engine, nothing electronic, nothing but wool, cotton, and leather for clothing, he sailed through the storms and towering seas common to this region of the globe. To be a sailor was to suffer, he declared. Once early on, during his first crossing from Buenos Aires toward the Cape of Good Hope, one arm became so infected and swollen and began to smell of decay, presumably because of wounds sustained while he was repairing a leak in the hull, that he thought his only option would be to amputate, at least at the elbow. After praying to Saint Teresa of Lisieux, he passed out. As he slept, the abscess burst a hole in his forearm that poured out so much pus that when he awoke he thought he had been drenched by a wave that swept into the cabin.

After stops in Cape Town, Wellington, and Valparaiso, Dumas returned to the docks of Buenos Aires where throngs of people had assembled to see the man who had spent 272 days alone, almost entirely on the Southern Ocean. He was the first known single-hander to sail around Cape Horn and survive. (In 1934 the Norwegian mariner Alfon Hansen had sailed alone around Cape Horn in the other direction, but died soon after, his boat shipwrecked off the coast of Chile; Hansen, his pet dog and cat were never found.)

Over the course of his trip, which he called "the impossible voyage," Dumas depicted a world in dramatic contrast to Pidgeon's. The Southern Ocean weather along with the war filtered Dumas' *what-they-saw.* Over the rail of his little ketch, Dumas observed submarines, warships, bombers, and in Cape Town he watched the military dead brought home

by ship. In Dumas' narrative, *Alone Through the Roaring Forties*
(1944), the only time he spoke to a merchant ship on his voyage, the British officers aboard were unable to give him a
proper position because of wartime regulations; they could
only hint and wink that he was making the progress he had
hoped. He depicted his voyage as a constant battle—always
cold, tired, injured, and soaked to the bone. In a storm of
waves over sixty feet high, half-hallucinating due to stress
and lack of sleep, he envisioned himself as a man falling
from scaffolding in a scene like a bombed city: "fantastic
shapes of ruined buildings flickered ahead."

When Dumas watched a shark swim under his boat he
could not resist the temptation to shoot the animal in the back,
yet he wrote with loving care of the seabirds in the Southern
Ocean, such as his description of storm-petrels. As he watched
birds soar and glide, he had moments of reflection during his
unprecedented time alone. At one point, after explaining in his
narrative how he never got bored, he wrote a passage as if
straight out of Henry David Thoreau's *Walden* (1854):

> It is said that solitude is best shared with another. These seas
> offer joys to anyone who is capable of loving and understand-
> ing nature. Are there not people who can spend hours
> watching the rain as it falls? I once read somewhere that three
> things could never be boring: passing clouds, dancing flames
> and running water. They are not the only ones. I should add
> in the first place, work. The self-sufficient man acquires a
> peculiar state of mind which may be reflected in these pages.

Although he had not grown up in a fishing port or spent a lifetime as a mariner, Harry Pidgeon's depiction of the ocean, his *what-they-saw*, was far closer to that of Joshua Slocum than to that of Dumas. Because he had the benefit of the Panama Canal and sailed in more temperate latitudes, Pidgeon's sea from his peaceful platform was a setting of even less peril and contest than the voyage of Slocum's *Spray*. By design, Pidgeon never had to beat his way through the Strait of Magellan or surf perilously around Cape Horn. He wrote of no dramatic storms or rogue waves, not even adverse currents or sudden squalls. Once off the Cape of Good Hope he encountered winds fierce enough that he required a storm drogue to maintain some steerage and safety—yet even of this he wrote in a tone that matches how we might complain today about having to pull over in the car because of a hard rain.

Pidgeon first came to deep-water sailing as a middle-aged man of the fields, of woods and rivers, with an eye for a photograph. He once had a job photo-documenting the large trees of California. During this trip aboard *Islander* he took photographs of colonies of penguins and frigatebirds. On the last leg of his circumnavigation, on the way north from Panama, Pidgeon watched two seabirds alight on his boat. He named them Blue Bill and Yellow Bill. By his descriptions and this part of the ocean, these were likely a juvenile and an adult brown booby (*Sula leucogaster*). Pidgeon reasonably assumed because of its dusky feathers that Blue Bill was an old bird, when it was almost certainly the opposite. The juvenile, Blue Bill, arrived first, then the adult bird, Yellow Bill, slapped its wide webbed feet aboard *Islander* a couple of days later. Pidgeon tried to poke them off certain parts of the boat, to reduce their droppings on his deck, but he enjoyed the birds' company and watched their behaviors. The two birds occasionally scuffled but otherwise claimed opposite ends of the *Islander*. Pidgeon fed a dead flying fish to Yellow Bill by hand. Blue Bill wasn't interested. The pair of seabirds usually left several times during the day to forage, then returned to the deck for the night. Yellow Bill, the elder, left after a couple weeks. Blue Bill stayed longer, took Yellow Bill's spot on the aft deck, and remained a resident on *Islander* for nearly a month as the boat sailed on toward California.

Pidgeon ends his narrative *Around the World Single-Handed* in a similar tone to Slocum's: "I avoided adventure as much as possible."

When he returned to Los Angeles after his four-year circumnavigation, Pidgeon, like Slocum, said he had never felt healthier. "Those days were the freest and happiest of my life. The *Islander* is seaworthy as ever," Pidgeon wrote, by which he meant himself, too: "and the future may find her sailing over seas as beautiful as did the past."

Pidgeon's *Around the World Single-Handed* never received the same reception as Slocum's story, perhaps because he was the second to circumnavigate the world alone or maybe because he made it all sound too calm and boring. Pidgeon's voyage did, however, earn a full-length feature in *National Geographic* magazine, loaded with his photographs, and his account had a sneakily powerful influence that propelled generations of small-boat sailors who dreamed of casting off. Pidgeon showed that it could be done, even if you were not a master mariner beforehand. Amateur sailors and boatbuilders in the 1930s and 1940s, working desk jobs or inland labor jobs, nostalgic for the days of sail and inspired by the smell of wood chips and varnish, could not see themselves quite like Slocum, but they could flip through the pages of

Harry Pidgeon in front of *Islander*, after sailing solo around the world for the first time (1926).

*The Rudder* magazine and see the plywood design used to make the *Islander* and imagine themselves as a Harry Pidgeon, at anchor on their own boat in a tropical harbor of the South Pacific.

After Pidgeon completed a second and also uneventful entire circumnavigation, dawdling along for an extra year this time, he returned home in 1937. A sailor-writer colleague of mine named Steve Jones remembers when he was eight years old and his father rowed him out to see the *Islander* and the man himself in Long Island Sound. Pidgeon's boat was anchored at the outer edge of a harbor, because the officers of the yacht club kept it out there since they thought his boat too scrappy and the sailor too lowbrow to be given an expensive dockside berth or even a mooring. Jones explained to me that they had stuck the famous sailor out to anchor in the current because he did not dress like the yachtsmen at the club, his boat "looked exactly like she had been doing what she had been doing," and they wordlessly resented this easy-going solo circumnavigator who threatened their self-esteem and view of themselves as sailors.

At the age of seventy-four, Pidgeon married Margaret Dexter Gardner, who was twenty-five years younger. She had been born at sea, the daughter of a ship's captain. After some time, waiting out World War II, Harry and Margaret sailed out of Los Angeles aboard *Islander*. At anchor at Vanuatu in the South Pacific, nearly halfway around a third circumnavigation, the boat ran aground during a hurricane and was destroyed beyond repair. Before the worst of it occurred, the two were able to climb safely ashore and unhurt with their belongings. They returned home. When Pidgeon was in his eighties they rebuilt a smaller version of *Islander* and made a few trips over to Catalina.

"It's curious that this man," assessed the French writer and sailing scholar Eric Vibart, "who preferred photographing sheep in Alaska over the frenetic search for gold, whose 19th-century simplicity echoed that of poet and philosopher Henry David Thoreau, who refused honors and the footlights, who lived in opposition to the society of greedy consumption that was coming into being before his eyes, should be so overlooked."

But Harry Pidgeon seemed to die content at age eighty-five with what Slocum never had, a grave on dry land next to his wife, who would be laid to rest beside him years later. Pidgeon's grave is an ordinary square-edged stone, outlined with carved leaves, sitting flush with the grass. It's up in the hills of Los Angeles on a plot beside a cemetery road named "Ocean View." I've stood there to pay my respects, looking out on the open Pacific towards Hawai'i. Flat on the stone is a bronze plaque that reads simply:

*Harry Pidgeon*
*Skipper of the "Islander"*
*1869–1954.*

# 8. Sea Turtles, Fish, Squid

After I survived the voracious shark attack, I sailed beyond the Continental Shelf over a deep-water region known as the Newfoundland Basin. I was two weeks into my trip by then, sailing southeasterly at over five knots, which was speedy for *Fox*. I stood over water that was about 15,700 feet deep.

In the mid-afternoon at approximately 41° 30' west longitude, I spotted an enormous sea turtle swimming beside the hull going in the opposite direction. It was off to port, my left, paddling gently, if warily. I see in my mold-stained logbook that I had spotted another sea turtle a few days earlier, but it is this second one that has remained in my mind. I remember watching this turtle as if it were a stray dog walking by me on a sidewalk. The turtle had a particular somewhere to go, toward Nova Scotia, just as I had a particular somewhere to go, toward Falmouth, England.

My first response to this sea turtle was to stop the boat: should I sail back around to check it out, to identify it, maybe even pick it up? Was it okay—so far out here? Maybe the turtle was lost and in trouble?

At that stage of the trip, though, in a slot between calms and gales, I was anxious about making miles in the right direction. Quickly calculating the logistics, I dismissed the idea as not worth the energy or the time lost. I just stood in the cockpit and watched that turtle swim astern until its paddling wake was no longer visible. What was I really going to do anyway, I thought. Harpoon it? Haul it aboard with the main halyard, as Slocum had once done with a turtle, to cut it up for steaks?

I've since learned that I probably saw a loggerhead turtle (*Caretta caretta*), an endangered species that spends on average a dozen years of its life in the open ocean. My sighting was at the outer edges of its known range. I was about 600 miles from the nearest land.

This mid-ocean sea turtle sighting turned out to be my closest encounter during the entire crossing with any reptile, cephalopod, or even fish. Occasionally during the trip I tried to catch fish with a line and a goggle-eyed plastic lure dragged astern. On the morning I saw the first turtle, along with dolphins and plenty of storm-petrels, I had the lures snapped clean off, twice in a matter of hours. Something big and strong nabbed the lure and swam off too powerfully each time, despite the thick gauge line and my bungee cord at the rail to reduce the shock. I heard the snaps from inside the cabin. After that I mostly gave up fishing, because I imagined the remaining line spinning around the propeller somehow. And once I had that image in my head I became paranoid about it. Later in the trip, one cool dawn, I tried fishing again. While leaning over the side to secure the lure my warm hat and only headlamp slid off my head and into the water, both significant losses for my day-to-day work. As I watched my possessions float away in the water, berating myself, I knocked the back of my head on a stanchion. I took the hint to stop fishing for a while.

Regardless of my experience, because of their slow and quiet sailing speed, undivided attention, and desire for fresh food, single-handed mariners crossing oceans have usually returned home with some of the most wondrous of fish stories.

Since I sailed over the cool waters of the North Atlantic that summer, I only on two occasions saw flying fish, the most iconic of creatures that seem to move even the saltiest mariners to poetry. Flying fish symbolize an arrival to warmer weather, and when sailors haven't written about the graceful glides of flying fish over the surface, they have, like Davison, extolled their flavor as a convenient breakfast when found freshly dead on deck in the morning. I saw one flying fish early on when I seemed to have entered the Gulf Stream, that day of the first turtle and snapped lures. The second I saw was not until the end of the passage when I entered warmer waters near Portugal. Both of these sightings were simply of one single flying fish coming out of the water for a glide, but they served as clear indicators of a rise in water temperature in a productive current.

My trans-Atlantic track was also just north of the range of dolphinfish, another renowned species that's been regularly described by sailors for centuries. Known for their brilliant bright green-yellow bodies, carmine yellow tailfins, and long iridescent royal blue dorsal fins, dolphinfish, known also as mahi-mahi, dorado, or pompano (*Coryphaena hippurus* and *C. equiselis*), are more common in temperate and tropical waters. When dolphinfish are not trying to capture flying fish, they like shady, slow floating objects to follow, which is why they're often reported by small-boat sailors. Slocum described a particular dolphinfish that he recognized by "its scars." The fish stayed with him for about 1,000 miles in the South Atlantic. Dolphinfish were the one species that Davison confidently identified and that sparked the most interest for her. She, too, found one individual fish coming to her hull every morning. This dolphinfish became so familiar that she could lower a canvas bucket on to the fish's nose without it swimming away. "Gorgeous creatures," she wrote, sizing them up at between four and five feet long. These were the fish that she had found "too friendly and trusting" to catch.

The larger predator fish, such as billfish, tarpon, and tuna, if less commonly seen from the rail of a boat, certainly provide dramatic single-hander yarns. While sailing across the South Pacific in 1882, for example, Bernard Gilboy reported that his tiny wooden boat was rammed by a swordfish, causing a leak that had everything floating in his cabin. He was able to stop the leak by stuffing some rags into the piercing. Twenty years later, while crossing the North Atlantic, Howard Blackburn said he was surrounded by schools of swordfish so close that for hours he kept throwing a coil of line on top of them to scare them off because he was afraid that their bills would stab into his hull, too. Later during that same passage Blackburn's boat smacked right into a *Mola mola*, an ocean sunfish, which was bobbing flat on the surface.

In the 1920s, Alain Gerbault wrote of the "many marvels of the sea" with a belief and tone that his voyages had something genuine to offer the scientific community ashore. He recorded observations such as this: "The day after my departure from Galapagos a bonito (*Thynnus pelamys*) made an extraordinary leap out of the water and, striking the mainsail about twelve feet up, fell with a thud on the deck. The creature weighed nearly thirty-five pounds."

Gerbault was not the only early single-hander to have taken pride in the value of their experience to the scientific community. Edward Allcard, the Englishman who crossed

Teenage single-hander Robin Lee Graham holds up a dolphinfish that he caught aboard *Dove*, featured on the cover of *National Geographic School Bulletin* (1970). Note the wind-vane self-steering sail behind him and his right hand pulling a string to take the photograph.

the Atlantic a few years before Davison, refuted earlier theories of pilot-fish behavior in relation to sharks, ideas held
by, he believed, Irishmen. In his *Single-Handed Passage*, Allcard
tallied his observations of fish and marine life as an ongoing
contest with other single-handers. He disputed Gerbault's
observations of Portuguese man-of-war and how they
moved, correcting (incorrectly), that these sea jellies swam
over the surface by using "chiefly auxiliary power below."
(These colonial sea jellies primarily use their sail-like gelatin-
ous peaks above the water to propel themselves.) Allcard
boasted of how quickly he became skilled at harpooning
bonito, using a piece of newspaper as a lure. He speared
dolphinfish with their "dazzling" colors, "an incarnation of
the Tropical Ocean." He ate one for his most celebratory meal
at sea. Allcard also cooked and ate the flying fish and flying
squid that landed on his boat's deck, but he didn't like the
taste of either. One of the squid, "the little beasts," even
exploded in his pan, spattering the cooking fat all over his
galley. Allcard saw his ocean-crossing mission as part marine
biologist, seeking "heavy debunking material," or at least as
top-notch adventure-naturalist. For example, he tested the
effect of his lantern on deck at night, lit versus running dark,
to quantify how many flying fish landed aboard. "If a steamer
cut me down," he joked with machismo, "it would not matter, as it would all be in the interests of science."

In *Around the World Single-Handed*, Harry Pidgeon wrote of
a range of fish and turtles, as well as seabirds, bioluminescence, barnacles, sea snakes, sea jellies, and even fish-eating
bats. His observations were closer to a correspondent's wonder than to Allcard's brand of competitive marine ecology.
As Pidgeon completed his first world voyage in 1925, he
sailed his longest passage on the final homeward-bound leg

from Panama to Los Angeles, hosting the two brown boobies, Yellow Bill and Blue Bill. He sailed for over eighty quiet
days alone at sea in light winds.

"No part of the sea was so full of life as this," Pidgeon
wrote in this final section of his narrative, in which he
described marine life, especially the prolific schools of tuna,
dolphinfish, flying fish, and seabirds of several species:

> For more than a month a vast school of albacore [tuna] and
> dolphins [dolphinfish] accompanied *Islander* on her course.
> At night they appeared as great luminous wings stretching
> far on either side of the boat. In calm weather great num-
> bers of turtles were seen floating lazily on the surface.
> There was a continuous flight of flying fishes striving to
> escape from the dolphins and albacore, often to be caught
> by the gannets [boobies] and man-of-war [frigate]birds that
> were always circling about.

Pidgeon wrote that a tuna nipped a strip of flying fish right
out of his hands when he dipped the meat into the water to
rinse it off. One day his boat startled a school of flying fish
"numbering thousands," all taking to the air in one "gleam-
ing silvery band spread out across the course of the *Islander*."
Another day he stood on deck and watched whales. On
another, he watched a dead sea turtle floating, upon which a
frigatebird swooped down to snatch small fish that had frantically skittered up on top of the shell as they were trying to
escape the larger fish preying under the turtle's rotting belly.

Throughout his story of his first circumnavigation, Pidgeon was far more focused on the characteristics of his boat
and the places and people he met in the harbors he visited—
yet as he wrote of these last weeks before completing his
world voyage, he began to slip into the tone of the gentleman

naturalist, savoring his extended time at sea. He described the differences in the way a shark and a tuna ate the fish he threw over the side. As Allcard would decades later, Pidgeon wondered about the relationship between the pilot fish and the sharks. He wrote carefully about his brown boobies, Blue Bill and Yellow Bill, including the details of their preening behaviors and the physical hints they gave to warn him about the presence of sharks.

At one point Pidgeon devoted some time to a small squid that ended up on deck, which he believed similar to the flying-squid species he had observed in the Indian Ocean. He recognized squid's importance within the local food web, noting that when he tossed one of these back into the ocean it sparked more attention from the thrashing, hungry albacore than when he threw back a flying fish. Pidgeon placed one squid in a water basin to watch how it propelled itself and how it ejected its murky brown fluid. The squid's ink, he suggested accurately, serves as a smokescreen to defend itself against predators. Pidgeon wrote of the squid's bioluminescence at night. In all, here were this sailor's most careful observations of sea life from a four-year voyage.

Reading this today, it's worth considering if these were the most prolific seas that Harry Pidgeon ever experienced, or whether he now, at last, was able to open up the mental space to really observe them since he was not as worried about trying to survive, less focused on watching the weather and no longer pacing about thinking of all the things that could go wrong. There's a larger metaphor here, of course, a lesson for our twenty-first-century beehived screen-eyed lives, how we don't take the time or have the mental space to pause to, say, watch a turtle, because we are too busy trying to get somewhere.

Did my thin transect observation of fish scarcity on the

surface in the summer North Atlantic of 2007 mean anything at all from the perspective of environmental history? Or was I, regardless of how slowly I sailed, just a poor observer? I'd have done well to take a few samples of zooplankton density and to have really quantified the numbers of birds and marine mammals that I saw, which might have given a sense of general activity beneath the surface. I didn't have the mental energy for that kind of thing at the time.

Consider, too, that Harry Pidgeon described an area of the ocean that American whalemen in the previous century had called "lively grounds." *Islander* sailed this part of the tropical and subtropical eastern Pacific in the months of September and October 1925. Scientists report now that the biology of the region is dramatically affected by seasonal fluctuations in water temperature and winds, as well as annual variations, such as the El Niño and La Niña phases, trends not yet identified by Western oceanographers, but well known to Indigenous cultures. Pidgeon did not know that his fall 1925 was *not* during an El Niño phase, which meant that fish populations should have indeed been especially healthy that year. Pidgeon also observed this region decades before the crash of the sardine and anchoveta fisheries due to overfishing along the Californian and then Peruvian coasts. Studies today confirm that yes, the ocean in this part of the Pacific in Pidgeon's time, a century ago, was unequivocally healthier with more marine life than it is now, by biomass and by diversity. For example, after analyzing the accounts of sport fishermen and naturalists of the 1920s to 1950s who observed the Gulf of California and this eastern part of the Pacific, environmental historian Callum Roberts wrote of this region: "The seas they described tumbled, roiled, and thrashed with fish in such immense numbers that today they seem the stuff of fiction, not reportage. But the destruction of life that has happened since is far from mythical."

When I saw a solitary sea turtle in the distant reaches of the North Atlantic, my twenty-first-century thoughts were curious as to how this animal could be so far out here, which really meant what was I doing so far out there. I was the one gasping for air. And, for better or worse, what was in my mind's eye as I watched that deliberately paddling reptile recede toward the horizon were plastic rings from soda bottles, license plates with a "Save the Turtles" logo, and the Disney film *Finding Nemo* (2003), in which animated-cartoon surfer-dude sea turtles soar acrobatically, careening along underwater with the currents.

# 9. Florentino Das: For Family

Born in 1918 of Visayan descent, Florentino Resulta Das grew up in the town of Allen on the island of Samar in the Philippines, the son of a man who ran a local sixty-foot ferry. Years later, after his solo odyssey, Das told the journalist Nick Joaquin:

> Much of what I know about the sea I learned from my father. I was already a sailor when I was still a baby, for my father and mother took me along on the *parao* whenever they went on a trip. I am the fourth of five children, but my other brothers have never been interested in boats. Me, I have loved them since I was a kid. Whenever my father was building a new boat, I was sure to be there beside him, even when I was very little, watching him eagerly and trying to help. My fingers are scarred from the cuts I got from knives and chisels while making my own small boats—boats that I sent sailing on the Allen beach.

Das grew up sailing with his father, marveling at his ability to predict landfalls based on the wind and the stars. He wanted to be as observant as his father, so he practiced by lying on the beach at night and tracing the stars, even tracking their distance and time using sticks in the sand.

His parents identified Florentino as being bright so they enrolled him in school, where he was doing very well, but one day when he was twelve and they were out of town he was expelled from school over an altercation with a teacher.

Das was so embarrassed, afraid to face his mother, that he ran away from home with a friend. The boys made their way to working the docks of Manila, with Das working as a cabin boy on ferries and then as a stevedore. His parents tracked him down and wrote to him to come home, but he "had tasted adventure," and he wanted to return home having accomplished something. So at sixteen, Das and another friend stowed away on an English freighter to go to America. While his friend continued on to California, Das chose to stay in Hawai'i, which was still recovering from the Great Depression at the time. Das found work where he could, including as a professional boxer. Soon he met and married a woman named Gloria Lorita Espartino, also of Filipino ancestry, and the couple raised a family of eight children, living through the attack on Pearl Harbor in December 1941 and the resulting war in the Pacific. The family did reasonably well for themselves, renting a small property. Das had a reputation as a hard-working jack-of-all-trades. He worked as a fishing-boat captain, carpenter, ceramicist, and at the shipyard at Pearl Harbor. He repaired boats and cars, and his children have explained that he was a great reader, even though he never had schooling beyond the seventh grade. He loved to take his kids fishing out on the boat. At their house he kept the jaws of all the sharks he had caught, lined up from smallest to largest. At one point he sailed out, trapped, and finished off the shark believed to have been the one that killed one of his daughter's classmates.

Yet after some twenty years in Hawai'i, Das grew increasingly more entranced in the early 1950s, driven to return home to the Philippines. Not only was he finding Honolulu growing too quickly and becoming too urbanized, but his parents had been robbed and murdered back in Samar over money that he had sent home for them. He could not afford a passage by ship or plane, so he resolved to take a small boat, with the hopes of establishing a profitable fishing or ferry business in Samar and then bringing his Hawai'i family back there, too. Das' *why-go* was rooted in family and ethnic pride. Driven by poverty, one of his brothers back in Samar had turned to piracy and been killed. Florentino wanted to restore honor to the Das name. And he wanted to do something for Filipino pride internationally. He had seen what Charles Lindbergh had achieved with his solo flight non-stop from New York to Paris in 1927. Maybe he had learned, too, about historic Polynesian navigation or read about or even met Harry Pidgeon when he visited Hawai'i, or perhaps he read about Alain Bombard or Ann Davison in *Life* magazine. "During the war," Das recounted, "I was fishing captain on a boat that made expeditions to the South Seas. The navigation captain on this boat was one of the men who had sailed on a double-canoe from Hawai'i to France, and he taught me how to read a chart and how to use a sextant." This navigator was the French sailor and boatbuilder Éric de Bisschop, who had sailed around the Pacific, back and forth to France, and written books about his adventures.

With the help of his children over three years in his backyard, Das built a boat using a navy surplus hull. He replaced structural parts with spare timbers, added a mast and a centerboard, and scavenged parts of other vessels, resulting in a new twenty-four-foot seaworthy wooden boat with four watertight compartments. It had a self-bailing cockpit and was built so he could dog himself into the cabin in any weather. Das set up the boat with two twenty-five-horsepower outboard engines and a single mast. His project generated some local excitement and even some sponsorship from the Timarau Club of Honolulu, a group of Filipino businessmen who had done well economically. He named the boat *Lady Timarau* and in exchange for some start-up funds he agreed to return fifty percent of any lecture fees, book contracts, or any other profits from the adventure. The Timarau Club also offered betting odds if he would make it—all proceeds going to scholarships for Filipino students to the University of Hawai'i.

Das' eldest son Junior, who had helped the most with the building of the boat, wanted to join his father for the trip, which Florentino considered seriously, but in the end he was convinced it would be better for the family if he went by himself. An officer from the local US Coast Guard came and sat down with Das to dissuade him from going, explaining that he could not prevent a person going alone, but if Das took a passenger, then he said, "We need assurance that a life is not endangered through equipment or navigational preparation. Junior could be more useful at home helping his mother with the family while Das was gone. Honolulu officials were not all doom and gloom, however. Officers at the US Navy Hydrographic Office suggested the best route for him, estimating a sailing time of forty-five to fifty-five days with stops at Johnston Island and the Marshall Islands on the way to cover the approximately 4,700-mile trip. They wanted him to clear in at Johnston, to make sure there were no new nuclear tests planned.

One of the things I'm trying to explore is why in the modern era single-handed voyaging is more often practiced and

valued in wealthy, Western countries, yet not among Pacific
Island or Southeast Asian communities, nor in so many of
the other maritime communities around the world with
millennia-long traditions of seafaring? You have to dig pretty
deep to find the story of Florentino Das, and there are surely
more Southeast Asian and Pacific Island single-handers that
are less known. Perhaps they did not want their voyages to
be publicized or maybe they were unable to publish books or
articles about them. Maybe, though, there is something
deeper here, crudely summarized, in terms of social values
in modern Pacific Island cultures: an emphasis on family,
serving the community, and decentering the individual?
Maybe, for mariners in some communities over the last two
centuries, to go off alone would be to shirk your filial and
local responsibilities?

Maybe there could be something, too, in the overly sim-
plistic, perhaps unfair generalization that non-Western,
non-white cultures tend to value collective adaptation over
individual manipulation. The social-science researcher Peter
Belmi, a Filipino immigrant and professor in the business
program at the University of Virginia, has found that people
from wealthier backgrounds end up focusing more on themselves, whereas people from communities with fewer
resources seek power or success to benefit others, since they
have been raised relying on their communities to survive.
"We don't need others as much in order to survive," said
Belmi, referring to the thinking of those in power, "and so
what it means to be a good person is to pursue your own
identity, to figure out how you are unique, compared to
others."

Larry Raigetal, a master boatbuilder and navigator from
Yap in Micronesia, put it this way in 2021: "The day you

are born until the day you die, you are to give back to the community."

"In the year of our Lord, 1955—departed Kewalo Basin, Honolulu, May 14, Saturday, with the blessings from family, friends, and the good people of Honolulu, that I may reach my destination, the Philippines, swiftly and safely."

So wrote Florentino Das in his journal, which was later published in excerpts in the *Honolulu Star-Bulletin* (which said he wrote like a modern-day Robinson Crusoe). Das departed with letters from the mayor of Honolulu and the governor of Hawai'i that were addressed on his behalf to the mayor of Manila and to the president of the Philippines. The docks were crowded with people, photographers, and journalists. A reverend blessed the voyage, a six-piece band played, and he sailed away wearing multiple leis around his neck, an enormous flag of the Philippines flying from his mast, and "Spirit of Hawaii Filipinos Aloha" painted on the port and starboard rail. He was thirty-seven years old.

The first days did not start auspiciously. His main boom broke only a couple of hours out of the harbor. He was able to replace this with an oar. As he caught up on sleep from the last three weeks of dashing around to get ready, he realized he had forgotten some key parts for his outboards. He had also forgotten a mirror, "sunburn oil," a sea anchor, a regular anchor, nets for fishing, and spare batteries for his radio— for which he depended on the time signal for navigation and from which he planned to get weather reports, news, and music for company. Regardless, each morning he began with prayer. He decided that going back at this point to get those supplies would send the wrong message; he did not want to seem afraid.

In early rough weather, Das wrote that he was "shaken like a dice in a cup." He wished he had a hammock. The darkness of the early nights out at sea reminded him of the wartime blackouts in Hawai'i. His *Lady Timarau* held up, though, which gave him confidence. He caught a large male dolphinfish, but the leader snapped, and he lost the fish and his lure before he could get the animal on board.

Soon Das began to settle in, ever westbound. He had a sextant, a compass, a watch, and he knew the stars well. He was handy working on his engines, which needed constant maintenance due to the waves and spray. He had a mainsail, a staysail, and it appears he used a lateen rig with parachute material, setting this like a spinnaker for sailing in light air downwind. He had a small stove to make coffee and to warm the canned food, of which he had packed supplies to last him ninety days. He had loaded thirty-five gallons of water, four gallons of wine, four quarts of whiskey, and 150 gallons of gasoline. He had a motorcycle stored in the hold for when he reached the Philippines.

A friend had given him a safety helmet, which he was actually wearing one day while taking a sextant sight. His foot was on the tiller easing the boat over, so he could get the sun in view, when the boom swung across and bashed him on the back of his head, knocking him to the deck and sending the helmet into the water. Das figured that the helmet had saved his voyage, if not his life. He resolved to always use a boom preventer from now on.

"I happened to think of my wife and children and felt so

Das driving the outboard engine on his boat in Manila (c. 1957). He sent this photograph to his oldest daughter Louisa, with a note on the back, which included: "I'll always love you and the rest of your brothers and sisters for as long as I live and even beyond."

lonesome," he wrote on the ninth day out. "Wondering how they are. If they only know what their daddy is going through. Out here, with only the skies and the horizons around you, you feel so lost. I never feel lonely before in all my life till only now. You never know how much I prayed to the good Lord, to bring me carefully and safely to my destination."

Without a method of self-steering, Das became terribly sleep-deprived. He hung a rosary above the tiller, "with the hope that the Almighty will take care of the boat and me while I go to sleep."

Das continued west, watching the sky for Hawai'i-bound aircraft to confirm his bearings. He took angles on the sun, its height above the horizon, and used his compass. On one day of high seas a jar in his cabin tumbled over and broke. He accidentally stepped on it with his bare feet, then had to use his knife to cut into his foot to remove the glass. Although the sea was rough, the winds had been largely favorable, yet there had not yet been as much rain as he had expected in order to resupply his drinking water and take a proper shower. He was finally able to land dolphinfish, some of which he ate and some he dried for eating later. In calms, he constructed a higher bracket for the motors, because they were getting too wet when not in use. He rebuilt one of the ignitions. His watch, which he had set to Greenwich Mean Time for his celestial navigation, stopped, but he still felt he had a reasonable sense of where he was, so he decided to steer north of west, to stay above the Marshall Islands, since he did not trust his motors if he ended up being blown onto the reefs. As his fresh food ran out, he ate canned kidney beans, canned mangoes, and with his dried fish he often ate poi, a traditional Hawaiian paste made from taro root.

As the winds continued to blow favorably, Das got the

idea to rig up an old car radio that he had aboard to his battery. He managed to make this work, using the mast stays as an antenna. Sixteen days out from Oahu he tuned in to a radio station from Japan, then one from Hawai'i, from which he was able to reset his watch on their time signal and calculate his local time and his longitude. Das and *Lady Timarau* had sailed 1,350 miles. Ever since he had left, his boat had been leaking around the centerboard trunk, requiring regular repairs to his bilge pump to keep ahead of it. Fair winds continued, though, and he finally figured out a system of how to get the boat to steer itself. Once while sitting down with a can of chilli con carne, he caught two more large dolphinfish in a matter of minutes. All was well.

The short on-board journal of Florentino Das that he sent in to the newspaper finishes about there. His final published entry, on 3 June 1955, ends: "I have been a good boy all my life, so I guess the good Lord will not leave me in the lurch. I am not a bit worried. I know somehow, that the good Lord is watching over me. For all these things that is happening, he must have some reason. I dare not question His decision."

While Florentino Das was traveling alone, sailing for his family and for Filipino pride, for the legacy of his name and the stories his children could tell their descendants, Western stories about Pacific Islander relationships to the sea were growing in popularity, which would in turn continue to influence sailors from around the world to go out to sea—as well as how people saw themselves out there alone.

For example, in 1940 an American writer and illustrator named Armstrong Sperry created a young adult novel titled *Call It Courage*. This became a bestseller in the United States, was given the Newbery Medal for children's literature, and was soon taught in schools and read by millions of early teenagers. *Call It Courage* remained a mainstay in American school curricula up into the 1990s. The story is about a fictional teenager, Mafatu, who lives on the island atoll of Hikueru in the Tuamotus. The son of the chief, Mafatu, is ostracized by his community because he is afraid of the ocean—the sounds, the animals, the act of fishing—a terror that began when as a toddler he and his mother were swept out to sea. His mother saved him, kept him alive out at sea all night, but after managing eventually to float him to safety on the beach, she died of exhaustion. Years later, life with this fear of the ocean becomes so unbearable and shameful that Mafatu steals out in a boat alone with the *why-go* to conquer his personal horrors and make his father proud. He sails out past the reef with his pet dog and an albatross flying above. Mafatu finds another island where he shipwrecks, losing his boat to the coral on the way in. On this new island he is forced to slowly build his confidence and his self-sufficiency. He fishes for his food. He kills a large shark. Then he slays a large octopus. He makes tools out of whale bones, constructs a new boat, and launches it by himself, sailing out toward the barrier reef: "The reef thunder no longer filled Mafatu with unease. He had lived too close to it these past weeks. Out here, half a mile from shore, detached from all security of the land, he had come to believe that at last he had established a truce with Moana, the Sea God. His skill against the ocean's might."

Mafatu has a mastery of the sea now, but he recognizes a

personified ocean of which full knowledge is impossible and safe passage requires utmost preparation—and also luck, appeasement, and blessings. On the way home, his dog and albatross with him, Mafatu barely manages to escape the "black eaters-of-men" who chase after him in six "black canoes." He survives by endurance, his sailing skills, and the blessing of Moana, a male ocean deity who gives him enough of a breeze at the crucial moment to escape the cannibals. Mafatu finds his way home with the help of the stars, knowledge of the currents, and the albatross. On his return, his father recognizes his son's courage and Mafatu collapses on the beach. His voyage and heroic return will now be fixed in the chants and stories of his island.

Less than a decade after the publication of *Call It Courage* and a few years before the voyage of Florentino Das, the cultural theorist Joseph Campbell published his seminal study of myth and heroism, *The Hero with a Thousand Faces* (1949), which outlines an archetypal storyline that has existed across cultures and across millennia. It goes like this: there is an isolated hero who is different in some way and forced to leave home for some reason, going on a vision-quest by choice or by force; the hero finds a friend or two along the journey, conquers his fears, slays a dragon or two (or some equivalent); the hero then returns home a changed, wiser, more mature person, bringing something new or significant to his community. "You leave the world that you're in and go into a depth or into a distance or up to a height," wrote Campbell. "There you come to what was missing in your consciousness in the world you formerly inhabited." From here you return home with "that boon." Campbell identifies this mythical story structure in various forms in cultures all around the world and in humanity's major religions, such as Moses climbing Mt Sinai, Buddha sitting in solitude under the bo tree, and Jesus off in the desert alone for forty days.

*Call It Courage* fits right into this universal hero's journey story structure, which has been embraced in so many modern Western stories. You can see it in epics like *Star Wars* and *Harry Potter*. Fitting particularly well into Campbell's hero's journey, too, is the sea story, especially that of the single-handed sailor—both on paper and in that person's perception of their own experience, their voyage on Earth. *Call It Courage* is a Western story using Pacific Island characters, but if Campbell is right, then maybe this rare need to adventure alone for physical trial in environments distant from human influence is a desire intrinsic to certain people everywhere and has been always? In the 1960s historian and writer J. R. L. Anderson argued the universality of the need, even the genetic selection in certain individuals, to strive for this sort of adventure, what he called the "Ulysses Factor."

With all this in mind, did Florentino Das see himself in these terms when he was out there, getting thrown around inside his cabin among big seas? Did he see himself as a conquering hero who sought challenge and wisdom, returning with a boon to share when he returned home?

On 19 June 1955, Das signaled a passing Japanese fishing boat with a foghorn and by raising and lowering his upside-down American flag, showed he was in distress. The *Lady Timarau*'s engines were now entirely out of commission and his hull was leaking so badly that he was having to pump

continuously. The captain of the *Daisan Shinsei Maru No. 3* agreed to tow Florentino Das for about 500 miles, for three days, to a harbor on the island of Pohnpei in Micronesia, which was in the direction they were heading anyway.

Safely ashore on Pohnpei, Das wrote to his wife in Hawai'i about how much he loved her, how much he missed her and the children, how he felt like a championship prize-fighter who had been knocked out for a round. When word got back to his sponsors in Hawai'i with his request for money for repairs, some tried to raise funds, while others, including the Philippine Consulate in Hawai'i, asked him to abandon the voyage. Das felt obligated to continue. He said in a radio interview at the time that he had been away from home for so long already, and that more than the voyage was at stake at that point. "The world was waiting how I would fare," he said. "I wanted to prove that Filipinos are not only good boxers but also good boat builders and sailors."

Das spent eight months in Pohnpei, repairing his boat and waiting out the typhoon season. Then he continued on, his departure making international news. During the second half of his voyage, over 2,000 more miles, Das stopped in the Chuuk Islands in Micronesia for a couple of weeks. On his way to his next landfall, a passage of several hundred more miles, he decided to do some fishing for sharks. He later explained that he sailed into a school of sharks that were about eight feet long: "Whenever they grabbed my line, I would pull them in, kill them with my knife and take my hook out. Sometimes I cut off their fins. Late in the afternoon, I hooked a really monstrous shark—about twelve feet long— and it almost dragged me into the water and I hurt my leg in the struggle to save myself. I cut my line and let the shark go. My leg was badly bruised. I was limping when I arrived in Yap."

He stayed in Yap for a few weeks, healing himself, then made his final approach to the Philippines. He managed to scoot south away from the path of Typhoon Thelma, but still he and *Lady Timarau* were battered by winds and seas until, knowing he had neared land because of the approach of dolphins, Das arrived safely on a beach at Siargao Island on 25 April 1956, a 346-day odyssey since he had left Honolulu.

Das continued on to his home in Samar, reuniting with his siblings and extended family. From here he was escorted by the Philippine Navy and Coast Guard to Manila, where he was paraded around, met by President Ramon Magsaysay, and celebrated as a hero throughout the country. The local newspapers declared his voyage more significant than Heyerdahl's *Kon-Tiki*. He was awarded the Legion of Honor, named an honorary Commodore of the Philippine Navy, and he was given the keys to the City of Manila. Back in Hawai'i there was a large banquet for his wife, Gloria, who was named "Mother of the Year" and presented with formal gifts from several local societies and clubs. A fund was set up to raise money to send the whole family to Manila to be with their father.

Florentino Das never claimed to be, nor did it seem that he thought of himself as a master navigator in any traditional sense, like the early wayfinders, but he did safely sail across a massive swath of the central Pacific, the length of more than one and a half trans-Atlantic crossings, in a boat he built from scrap—with no electronics, extraordinary ingenuity and grit, and a great deal of faith in himself and a higher power.

The celebrations of Florentino Das in the Philippines fizzled out far too quickly. Das was never able to gain any financial footing. The fund in Hawai'i to bring his family over never raised enough to send the entire family. Gloria, understandably, would only go if she could bring all the children. Das struggled to find money at his end, even enough to fly when he decided he would try to go back to Oahu to be with them. He even toyed with the idea of sailing back to Honolulu in *Lady Timarau*. A fishing or ferry business never got going. At first he worked as a shipyard caretaker, then at the Philippine tourism and travel agency, since his English was so good. But this also did not earn him enough to get himself back to Hawai'i. In 1957, Gloria requested a divorce so she could remarry and have someone to help raise the children. He agreed.

In 1962, after doing some tourist sails and some survey work with *Lady Timarau*, his boat sank at the dock during a typhoon. He had no money to raise the boat himself. Das had recently remarried himself, to a widowed school principal with four children of her own, but he remained poor, and he began to lose his eyesight from complications of diabetes and high blood pressure. He was unable to work. Until he was completely blind, he wrote regular letters and called his children on the phone when he could afford it. Recent interviews with the Das children reveal that they never felt abandoned by their father, that he so clearly loved them always and deeply. Das' new wife kept up the correspondence with his children in Hawai'i. In 1964, at only forty-six years old, he died of organ failure in a hospital in Manila.

Florentino R. Das left no autobiography other than the as-told-to story by journalist Nick Joaquin and the short at-sea entries published in the *Honolulu Star-Bulletin*. His original journal is lost. We have no further record of his observations and thoughts on birds, marine mammals, the sea more specifically, his *what-they-saw* of his voyage. Largely due to efforts beginning in the 1980s, however, there are now two monuments to his voyage in the Philippines; one monument in Honolulu; and at the Philippine Consulate in Hawai'i, after a group sent an unsuccessful delegation to try to recover the boat, is a scale model of *Lady Timarau* on display. The day of Das' arrival is now celebrated each year as "Lone Voyagers Day" on Siargao Island. A loving biography, *Bold Dream, Uncommon Valor: The Florentino Das Story*, was published in 2013, and it is filled with color photographs of his descendants and crafted as a book for schools, with each chapter ending with reflective questions and activities with the intention that Das' story will build Filipino pride, identity, values, and encourage students to "take social action." The authors explain that the heroism of his solo voyage is "by all means, a personal success, a fulfillment of a personal dream. But it was also an achievement of a people and, most of all, a triumph of faith and the human spirit."

In his argument for including this solo sailing story in school curricula, as well as the importance of properly maintaining and interpreting the monuments to the voyage, Professor Jonas Robert L. Miranda explained in 2014: "Florentino Das' entire life epitomizes the ambivalent nature of Filipino values. His undaunting spirit to begin the unthinkable journey can only be understood by considering the paradigm regarding Filipino values of *Bahala na* and Love for Family."

# 10. Pets, Companionship over the Rail

After a couple of weeks I noticed a gooseneck barnacle fixed on the hull below the transom. I named the barnacle "Charles," I assume because Darwin was into barnacles. That was as close as I came to any kind of pet on board. For the long-distance solo cruisers, though, animal life within or outside the rails of their boats can be a genuine emotional comfort—not to mention a welcome new character to a single-hander's story.

"Yes, I was often frightened. Yes, I was often lonely," wrote Ann Davison. "Once I had thought if only there was a rabbit to stroke . . . something reassuringly alive on board." In other words, caring for some other living thing can provide a welcome distraction from one's own fears.

After Josiah Shackford's dog Bruno allegedly sailed aboard in 1787, several other pets have gone to sea with solo sailors. In 1999, for example, American David Clark, in his sixties and sailing alone around the world for a second time, was in his sinking boat off South Africa with his dog, Mickey, a West Highland terrier. The two were rescued by a Russian freighter. Mickey was nearly on board the ship after being hoisted over five stories high—but at the final moment, upon seeing the merchant seamen on deck, he frantically wriggled out of the sling and fell to his death between the boat and the freighter.

The truth is, it almost inevitably ends badly for the animal, who has of course no say in its *why-go*. The moment some kind of pet appears on board in a solo sea story, be ready for tragedy.

Joshua Slocum had no interest in having a pet on *Spray*, although in the Strait of Magellan he found a spider that he believed had been on board since Boston. He developed a great affection for the creature, proud of it as a tough survivor. Later in the voyage he was convinced to ship a goat, an animal that ate through its rope leash and then through his charts and his sun hat. Disgusted, he left the animal at the next island he visited. There is something to the fact that he did not simply kill the goat and eat it. He had no problem hacking up a sea turtle on deck or shooting sharks, but as the voyage went on he explained that he had begun to dread killing any animal companions on board. Slocum became a near vegetarian, he said, not even wanting to kill or eat a chicken.

On the way to Hawai'i out of San Diego in 1965, her first big single-handed passage, Sharon Sites Adams sailed with her pet turtle, named Sarah Beth-Ann. Adams equipped the turtle with a little harness so she could walk on deck. But Sarah Beth-Ann lost her appetite, had no energy, and then died about ten days out. Adams gave the turtle a sea burial and a prayer, and, as she told the story decades later without humor or irony, her pet's death was "a jarring loss."

Cats in particular have become popular shipmates for sailors, in the belief they might be the most adaptable pet for life at sea and they could also help with mice, cockroaches, and other pests. Robin Lee Graham, a teenager who circumnavigated the world alone over five years in the late 1960s, began with two sister kittens on board: one jumped ship in American Samoa and the other, Joliette, was impregnated there, but her kittens were stillborn. Joliette was later run over by a truck in Fiji. After a waiter informed him, Graham locked himself in his boat and cried, drinking a bottle of vodka by himself: "I had not felt lonelier five hundred miles from land." Graham shipped another cat in Tonga, a mean one who hated being at sea. This cat occasionally ambushed Graham, scratched him, tore up his charts, and eventually the sailor gave up and left it on the Cocos Keeling Islands. He learned later that the animal had died the very next day and was found floating in the surf. Yet too fond of feline companionship while at sea, Graham received a gift of two kittens in Cape Town, naming them Kili and Fili after the dwarves from *The Hobbit*. Fili was practically blind, but both lived well on his boat. Fili later got pregnant during one of the shore visits and gave birth to two kittens. Sailing from the Galápagos back home and through the doldrums to California (with two skinned goats hanging in the rigging for his food), Graham had four cats aboard his little boat, two of which were only just being litter-trained. Not long after Fili vomited some bad goat meat, she disappeared, falling overboard somehow. Kili seemed to adopt the kittens and the remaining three survived to make it back to Graham's home in California.

I could go on with tortuous cat stories, but there is at least one that ends reasonably well. A decade after Robin Graham, a young American sailor named Tania Aebi, the first American woman to sail around the world alone and the youngest at the time at twenty years old when she finished, also had cats on her solo circumnavigation. Her first, "Dinghy," was an adult black cat with white paws that she rescued from a shelter in New York City. He became "my closest companion for half the world . . . my only comfort," but then the cat died of kidney cancer under the care of a veterinarian in Vanuatu. Within days Aebi got a young tabby, who

Solo circumnavigator Naomi James early in her voyage with her cat Boris (1977).

she named Tarzoon. After getting seasick and vomiting in Aebi's bunk, Tarzoon was fun, adventurous, and seemed to love boat life. Tarzoon survived the rest of voyage—through the Indian Ocean, the Mediterranean, and across the Atlantic—even after going overboard one day (Aebi was on deck and was able to turn the boat around and scoop him up), falling overboard a second time (he managed to clamber back up himself while Aebi slept below, reporting himself back aboard by standing over her sopping wet), and then horrifying his owner when he killed and ate a wild canary that had landed on deck. Tarzoon returned with Aebi to New York and was her companion while she wrote up her account of the circumnavigation. Aebi thanked Tarzoon prominently and genuinely in the acknowledgments.

Sometimes wild hitchhikers or regular visitors near the boat become companions as familiar as domestic pets, such as Harry Pidgeon's Yellow Bill and Blue Bill. During his Southern Ocean circumnavigation, Vito Dumas watched a single "cape pigeon," known more often now as a cape petrel (*Daption capense*), visit him regularly all the way across the Indian Ocean and even up until landfall in Wellington. He fed the bird, and it regularly reappeared, sometimes after several days away. "He was a great friend," Dumas wrote, "I awaited him anxiously and he must have felt as I did." In the far Indian Ocean, Dumas even found companionship with a fly that must have hatched on board, his "traveling companion," whom he fed sugar until the fly was blown away in heavy weather.

Not to be outdone by Slocum's spider or Dumas' fly, South African Neal Petersen, sailing alone in the 1990s in a technological age in which he could communicate with schoolchildren from his boat out at sea, befriended a cockroach on board. He had difficulty killing it because the kids got behind "Cockie." That is until Cockie had babies and the lot were heaved overboard as an equatorial tribute to Neptune.

Slocum in 1900 and Pidgeon in 1928 wrote about loneliness in their way, but after their first crossings it did not, they said, seem to bother them. They found companionship in books and the marine life around them over the rail. One day on the open South Atlantic, on a day filled with flying fish, Slocum wrote, "One could not be lonely in a sea like this."

Tania Aebi in the 1980s, with her first cat safely on board, began to feel a spiritual connection in the eastern Pacific, too, echoing the feeling of Hemingway's fictional lone fisherman, Santiago, who on seeing birds overhead thinks that "no man was ever alone on the sea." Aebi wrote of sailing over a "sapphire-blue seaway," with more than a mile of deep ocean beneath her keel. She was humbled by the feelings of the sea itself, of seabirds, and of bioluminescent plankton. She praised the pilot fish and the dolphinfish following in her wake, her boat a pied piper that "pulled along" soaring flying fish. Pods of dolphins followed her boat so actively and playfully that Aebi was moved to tears. The dolphins stayed with her boat for ten hours. "On the ocean, I never feel lonely," Aebi wrote, "There's too much beauty— the sea, the wind, the sky, the animals and fish."

At one point on this long passage in the eastern Pacific, an enormous sea turtle floated by Aebi's boat, which elicited a still more significant connection. Aebi saw the sea turtle as female, anthropomorphized: "her horny head straining for air as her stubby legs paddled away, a thousand miles from land."

"What is she doing here?" Aebi wondered. "How long will it take for her to get where she wants to go? I marveled that she didn't need to carry around a sextant and chart. On her back would rest tired sea birds, hitchhikers on the seaway."

# 11. Kenichi Horie Against the North Pacific

To catch the tide and to avoid prying eyes who might report him to the Japanese Coast Guard or to customs, Kenichi Horie left in the dark on the night of 12 May 1962. The calm water of the harbor of Nishinomiya, a suburb of Osaka, reflected a mirror image of the street lights onshore. A tiny craft at only nineteen feet long, Horie's boat design was never intended for deep-ocean cruising. The shipwrights had constructed the mast a little shorter for stability, but the boat still had no safety lines or stanchions, and, even though Horie was at most 5'3" tall, it barely staged any decking forward to allow work with sails. Painted black with a white band of upper planking that tilted in toward the centerline, his boat looked a bit like a water beetle. He named it *Mermaid* after the logo of a textile company that had donated the sails.

Horie believed his boat was sound and seaworthy enough, though, and he did what he could to prepare for the passage. In the months before his departure, he practiced with a range of sea trials and coastal trips. He agonized over the specifics and amounts of his cargo, since weight for such a long trip in a small boat is crucial. He stowed fresh water in vinyl bags, but tried not to bring too much, calculating his daily hydration stores to include cans and bottles of beer, the juice in his cans of fruit, and his estimate for the capture of rainwater.

Horie left the harbor that night with a compass, a sextant, a barometer, and a radio direction finder, which used radio waves from devoted towers on coastlines to give bearings to help sailors find their positions. Horie brought along one life jacket, which he used as a pillow. He brought one anchor. Among his stores of clothing, tools, medical supplies, and food stuffs, he packed the following: 276 cans food (including salmon, tuna, boiled octopus, boiled whale meat, and boiled beef), 6 can openers, 11 lbs. ham, 4 cans *nori*, 2 jars pickled onion, 50 bags instant soybean soup, 10 packages chewing gum, 60 boxes matches, 1 bottle antibiotics, 3 screwdrivers, 50 screws, 1 pair of a new product called "vicegrips," 2 umbrellas (for sun protection), 3 hand spears with bamboo handles, 1 ukulele, 10 notebooks, 1 pad-style calendar, and "a good supply of toilet paper." Horie also packed: 1 set foul-weather gear, 1 pair rain boots, and 2 pairs rubber *zori* (what most Americans now call flip-flops). Where he splurged was with 80 pairs of undershorts, because he didn't want to bother too often with laundry and cotton underwear was so cheap; he planned to drop the dirty ones over the side.

Horie published his packing list in his narrative of his crossing, which was translated and published in the United States in 1964 with the title *Kodoku: Sailing Alone Across the Pacific*. The word *kodoku* means solitude. The American publishers, still surfing the post-war best-selling wave of ocean stories, placed *Kodoku* solidly in the tradition. The endpapers map shows Horie's passage on the Pacific Ocean alongside the dotted cruise tracks and illustrations of Slocum's *Spray*, Pidgeon's *Islander*, and Heyerdahl's *Kon-Tiki*. For scale and to emphasize his crossing's historical importance, inside *Kodoku* is a two-page spread with a diagram of Horie's boat in comparison to those and other famous sailing vessels.

Horie, as much as his publishers, saw himself and his voyage within this global history of seafaring. The "light reading" that he brought aboard included Kyosuke Fukunaga's *Stories of Ocean Explorers* and Japanese translations of Hemingway's *The Old Man and the Sea* and Alain Bombard's *Naufragé Volontaire*. Horie brought back issues of yachting magazines in both English and Japanese. He intended along the voyage to spend some time with his dictionaries and language books, too, to try to learn some more conversational English in preparation for his arrival and his need to explain why he lacked any documentation. He found in practice, though, that the act of reading below in the cabin, as it had done for Harry Pidgeon, often gave him a headache. Sometimes in the middle of the ocean he just flipped through his sailing magazines.

How Kenichi Horie, born in 1938, arrived at this point of assembling a packing list for a solo sail across the North Pacific is somehow at once random and inevitable. His father was an auto-parts salesman and his mother did most of the raising of Kenichi and his sister. Horie picked up sailing in high school, joining the club on a whim. He became enthralled with the hard work and the discipline the sport demanded, as well as the challenge of sailing a small boat. He rose through the ranks in the club until he was the senior skipper. In his spare time he started to collect maps and books and guides on navigation, cruising, and the Pacific Ocean. In particular, two books were the most inspiring: the account by Joshua Slocum, "a man of amazing, almost supernatural, accomplishment," and that of Bombard, who "proved that man can survive on the sea." Horie's dreams of crossing the Pacific continued to grow.

After graduating from high school, Horie decided not to attend college but work with his father. To save money for his own boat, he lived at home and barely went out socially. When members of the club chipped in for a boat together, he did, too, yet he found that he got seasick on longer passages, hated working in the galley, and bristled at the age hierarchy among his co-owners, who too often told him what to do. As he continued to save money, he worked part-time at a travel agency hoping this would help him obtain a visa to leave Japan legally for the United States. He had no romantic partner.

By the age of twenty-three, Horie had funds enough to commission the building of his own boat, although he had to watch every yen to stay on budget. When the best season for departure came around, his visa application had still gone nowhere, and he knew that his father would not approve of this ocean-crossing endeavor. This is why Horie slipped away in the dark after saying goodbye only to his mother and sister and a couple of friends.

Kenichi Horie's *Kodoku* opens immediately with the questions: "What made you want to cross the Pacific? Why did you do it? What did you expect to get out of it?"

He was asked these questions over and again by the press and his new acquaintances once he sailed under the Golden Gate Bridge into San Francisco. He explained that there was nothing more to his reasoning beyond "I crossed it just because I wanted to." Horie made the finer point that this was very much not a "because it was there" explorer scenario. He desired the challenge of the open ocean, not the conquering of the ocean itself. Nearly every sailor, he said, wants to cross oceans. He was just someone who made it happen.

Horie wrote that the press could not accept this. Some reporter always said, "you *must* have had a *reason*, you know, something special that made you set out to sea in a tiny sail-boat." People began coming up with their own explanations and trying to prove their theories as to his *why-go*. Horie explained that cruising off the coast of Japan is difficult. The North Pacific is the big ocean for Japanese people, their horizon, thus this trans-Pacific endeavor is simply the ultimate desire of so many sailors along the coast of Japan.

He punctuated his protest against deeper motives with a bashful, almost sly postscript: "Maybe I had a craving for the fame of being the first Japanese yachtsman to cross the Pacific single-handed, but I don't know."

Perhaps Horie knew that a few years earlier, Brian Platt had become the first known person to sail alone eastbound across the North Pacific. Platt had actually met with Florentino Das in the Philippines before he left. An Englishman born in Hong Kong, Platt sailed alone from China to Japan then across to Humboldt Bay, California, in a custom-built Chinese junk, along the precedent set by Éric de Bisschop. "One cannot make a trip like that without making some interesting discoveries," Platt said, "but all I wanted to do was to sail across the Pacific in a small boat—a desire that doesn't have to be explained to yachtsmen."

On the night of Kenichi Horie's departure, the two sails of *Mermaid* hung damp and flat. With absolutely no wind, the boat sat limp in the water. Unable to move, Horie missed the tide. It took him two days just to get out of Osaka Bay and down Kii Strait.

Once Horie reached the open North Pacific, he got hammered with heavy weather, a full gale. Violently seasick, he barely slept. Even at the time, however, he appreciated the early pounding as a chance to test the boat while still within reach of the coast. The heavy weather also meant fewer vessels were out there who might report him to the Coast Guard. He and his boat struggled, but nothing broke.

After the gale, Horie continued his eastward progress until the wind died down completely again. It was as if the North Pacific was taunting him. The boat now had no steerage, while the big seas from the heavy weather remained, rolling the boat unmercifully. "I had a good, solid cry," he wrote, explaining that the outburst did him a lot of good. He wondered if he would have cried so easily and cathartically if he weren't sailing alone.

Horie kept seeing steamships. When he had some wind, he tacked north to avoid being seen, even if that wasted precious miles. He wanted all the ships to think he was just heading north along the coast, to avoid any "helpful" rescuers who might report him to authorities or try to pick him up.

A few days later the barometer's needle plummeted. He was engulfed by a second low-pressure system, this time an even stronger gale with, he estimated, winds of over forty knots. He took all his sails down and tied his anchor to 270 feet of line, trailing it behind *Mermaid* to slow down his boat so it wouldn't surf too fast and then pitchpole, flip end over end, and to keep his stern facing the oncoming waves so the boat didn't broach and roll over sideways. This type of sea anchor, also referred to as a drogue, is a long-practiced heavy-weather strategy for survival in small boats—Slocum did the same—and it mostly worked for Horie, yet the immense seas still violently flung *Mermaid* around as the waves towered in from two different directions. His boat jerked so violently that Horie could not even put on his foul-weather pants. One wave smashed in a porthole, sending shards of glass into the cabin. He managed to screw a piece of wood over the opening, but meanwhile other seas filled the cockpit, flooded the cabin, opened leaks, and forced him to constantly bail with buckets.

"It was impossible to stand or sit," Horie wrote. "The only way to take it was lying—lying on the quarter berth using hands, head, shoulders, elbows, knees, feet to brace in *all* directions. And the fingernails came in handy for clawing into the berth sides."

This was the worst weather that he had ever experienced.

"The pitch and toss was so bad," he wrote, "that I couldn't tell whether I was lying on my back, side, or stomach. At times I felt as if I was standing on my head, and the cabin sole [floor] looked as if it were a bulkhead [wall]. Gravity didn't mean a thing—I was like an astronaut on the loose."

During a lull in this chaos, Horie somehow managed to get out his camera. Like all still images of heavy weather, without the sound of wind or the motion of the boat or much sense of scale, the blurry black and white photographs do little to convey the true power of the storm. But the amount of white water and foam on the surface of the waves give some sense of the stunning scene.

Horie and *Mermaid* survived this weather, and though he would see more gales and still larger waves mid-ocean, some he estimated at over fifty feet high, this would turn out to be the worst weather that he would encounter for the entirety of the passage. *Mermaid*, like a glass bottle on the surface, held together with wood planking that was only 1/3-inch thick.

Not that an engine would have helped him in the rough weather, but Horie had refused to bring an outboard or install any kind of inboard motor, both of which he saw as a "nuisance" and "kind of cheating." Nor did *Mermaid* have any wiring for electricity. He carried only batteries for flashlights and his radio direction finder. He used kerosene for his navigation lights and for his little stove, which was not gimballed, meaning his cooking source heeled and rolled (and spilled) at the same angle as the boat.

As he progressed across the North Pacific, after avoiding coastal waters "infested with steamships," Horie recorded a couple of interactions with big commercial vessels even though his route was largely, consciously, out of the main trans-Pacific shipping lanes. With no engine, no two-way radio, only his kerosene lamp to hang in the rigging at night and a wood hull with wood spars, the boat would have shown as barely a blip of wave clutter on a large ship's radar screen. Before leaving Japan, Horie had tried to fabricate some radar reflectors with foil or thin metal, but he found these to be unmanageable and unrealistic, hanging awkwardly in his tiny rig, so he took them down.

On the night of his thirty-third day at sea, he saw a ship that he estimated to be two to three miles away, the brightness of its lights glaring suddenly, intensely, after he had spent so much time watching darkness. He usually kept his kerosene lamp unlit at night. Like Vito Dumas who did not want to be shot at sea as a wartime spy, Horie was in the rare contradictory position among single-handers in history (at least those not doing so as emigrants or smugglers) in that he wanted a ship to see him to avoid a collision yet did not want that ship to notice him too carefully—since he lacked documentation.

Two days after that brightly lit ship, he saw another

freighter. This one was during the day, and the ship saw *Mermaid*, too, and slowed down. The watch officer appeared to be observing Horie take a sun sight with a sextant. This seemed enough reassurance for the officer that Horie was not in distress, so he ordered the ship to return to full speed, continuing on its way, which left Horie admitting mixed feelings: "How could he have been so sure at that distance that I really wasn't in need of anything?"

On the morning of his seventy-fifth day out, now beyond the longitude of Anchorage, Alaska, Horie woke up to the horn blast of an eastbound steamship that had slowed from twenty-two knots and was now making a full circle to come to a stop near *Mermaid*. This, he would learn, was the SS *Pioneer Minx*, about 560 feet long, bound for New York via the Panama Canal. Horie sailed safely around to the stern, below the officer cabins. Through some broken English, broken Japanese, and made-up sign language, the crew asked if he needed food or water, or anything else. Horie communicated that he was fine, on his way to San Francisco. He got a position from one of the crew (which turned out to be inaccurate and would be a source of daily confusion for Horie until he sighted Pt. Reyes, California). The crew took photographs of him. He took photographs of them. As the *Pioneer Minx* departed, the captain sent a cable to the US Coast Guard in San Francisco, which included:

SIGHTED SLOOP MERMAID BLACK HULL DEPARTED OSAKA JAPAN ON MAY 12 1962 BOUND SAN FRANCISCO REQUIRED NO ASSISTANCE ONE PERSON ONBOARD NAMED HORIE AGE 23 YEARS IN GOOD HEALTH. – MASTER

One of the crew on board the ship, named F. T. Soule, later sent a description of the encounter to *The Rudder* magazine, explaining that at first they thought the tiny boat had a dead body on the deck. As they steamed closer they realized that what they thought was a body was just a furled sail. Soule explained that it took Horie a half hour to safely sail up to the stern of their ship. He described the boat in detail, one "fit for coastwise cruising but hardly one in which to cross the Pacific." He concluded his letter to the editor: "In minutes we were out of sight. If you happen to read of his successful arrival in the United States, I'd appreciate hearing about it."

Horie continued slowly eastward and finally passed under the Golden Gate Bridge, after which, in his joy, he began

Kenichi Horie on arrival in San Francisco Bay, his hand on his local yacht club flag, with members of the US Coast Guard behind him (1962). Note the plywood over the porthole.

looking for a suitable place to dock. By chance he sailed beside a yacht whose owner happened to be involved in television. The man radioed the US Coast Guard, who towed *Mermaid* to a berth. By the time he reached the dock, the press were already there. Horie—healthy, proud, and an instant celebrity—passed out his remaining cans of beer to anybody who would take one. After contacting his family—who had been tortured with lack of information—and some initial concern over the legality of his visit among officials from both countries, Horie was given the welcome of a hero-adventurer. He was granted a special thirty-day visa. Officials celebrated him in the Bay Area, especially since, as Horie had strategized from the start, San Francisco had recently been named a sister city to Osaka, as part of a post-war reconciliation campaign. Horie was feted at Disneyland, honored by the mayor of Los Angeles, given plaques and certificates from various yacht clubs and societies in California, and then flown home for free. The return journey took thirteen hours across the North Pacific by plane, after his ninety-four days crossing Earth's largest ocean alone in his little sailboat.

In *Kodoku*, Horie does not comment on the flight home. But I have experienced this often after voyages at sea, collective ones and after my solo trip when I flew out of Lisbon. It is the mariner's feeling of quietly flying in the air over water you recently knew. You are now flying inconceivably fast, imperceptibly, hundreds of miles per hour (although you can only barely sense this speed), over an ocean so very far down there, looking out the window and down toward the sea's surface, the same ocean on which you had been sailing in a small boat, maybe averaging three to five knots, the speed of a slow jog. Recently you were unable in your boat even to see the curvature of the horizon on the flattest of days, and now here you are in a steel and plastic chair in the sky, belted beside dozens of others, encased by the sound of the fans, holding a cold drink, the smell of vinyl and cranberry juice. You're in the care of some other captain who doesn't know you, doesn't know where you've been, what you have just done. You are now looking *down* on the clouds, seeing in between them a glimpse of raspy sea so far beneath, thin spatula lines of swells, miles upon miles long, the same which rolled your hull and sprayed saltwater across the cockpit, across your sun-warmed cheeks and lips. All the way down there on the surface. You spend the start of the plane ride transfixed, remembering the heat on the back of your neck when you sat in the boat, feeling now like there is something you should be doing, something to check or monitor, looking out the window before you fall asleep, astounded that no one else is looking out the window, too: because you are scanning for a boat, a ship, a splash of a whale, wondering how you could possibly have been all the way down there, so small, so tiny and alone under the clouds: a speck on all that blue immensity.

In his early twenties, the youngest known person to cross an ocean alone at the time, Kenichi Horie's views on the sea and marine life, his *what-they-saw*, aligned closer with those of

Davison and Dumas than those of Pidgeon or Slocum. Horie's ocean in *Kodoku* was a proving ground. "No matter how you look at it, it's a battle with the sea," he wrote, "the sailor had to be able to achieve his victory." The Japanese feature film about Horie's crossing, released soon after, was titled *Alone Against the Pacific* or *My Enemy, the Sea* (1963).

It is not that Horie did not have his moments to revel in natural beauty. Similar to Davison's ecstasy-so-pure moment, Horie described one night during which he identified the constellations above and wrote of the "lyric beauty of the sea and sky—breathtaking and mystic almost." But these moments seem almost distractions from his larger issue at hand of survival and contest. Horie wrote of a strange incident when an albatross swooped down and appeared to kill a shark that looked to be four times its size. One day Horie managed to catch a half dozen fish, about five to six inches long. He scooped them right up from astern with only his hands and took a photograph of his catch in a bucket. He couldn't identify the fish species, though, so to play it safe he did not eat them.

At one point during his trans-Pacific crossing, Horie sailed for hours through miles of a "huge armada" of sea jellies, which by his description seem to have been a prolific population of by-the-wind sailors (*Velella velella*), small colorful sea jellies with little translucent triangular sails, close relatives to man-of-war (*Physalia physalis*). By-the-wind sailors are the same animals that Edward Allcard wrote about in the Atlantic with his competitive ecology. As one example of a shift in how sailor-authors depicted marine life over time, sailor-author Peter Nichols wrote in *Sea Change: Alone Across the Atlantic in a Wooden Boat* (1997), three decades after Horie, that sea jellies were a metaphoric version of his small boat in a big ocean, and even a symbol of himself, a human sailor alone, who felt so small compared to the forces of wind, waves, space, and time. Horie in *Kodoku* simply relayed the measurements of the jellies' anatomy, the dizzying numbers of them, and left his observation at that.

Horie's most compelling sight beyond his boat was not marine life at all, but a stunning bright flash one night that he first took for lightning. He then realized thunder never followed.

"It was an awesome sight," he wrote, "the blazing clouds spreading across the sky."

When Horie returned to shore, he confirmed his intuition by checking the timing against the testing of a thermonuclear bomb over Johnston Island, over 2,000 miles away from his position, to the southwest of the Hawaiian Islands. Horie had witnessed from his boat mid-ocean the launching of a 1.4 megaton bomb named "Starfish Prime," which was launched and detonated 250 miles up in the sky with one hundred times the power of the nuclear bombs that the United States had dropped on Hiroshima and Nagasaki in 1945. Horie had been six years old when these bombs killed somewhere near 200,000 people, mostly civilians, about half of whom perished on the first day, while the other half died later of burns and radiation sickness and other complications. In *Kodoku*, Horie stayed away from any judgment of Starfish Prime, at least in the English translation, other than to say he had read about the test before he left and thought it had already happened.

The next day at sea his radio reception was only static. He understood the implications: "The only flash that could kick all the radio waves out of the air was a nuclear explosion. I got the chills thinking about it. If things went bad, I would be covered by the deadly radioactive fallout. And if that happened, with me sailing out there in the middle of nowhere, there would be little chance my surviving it. I decided not to use any rain water."

Horie got his radio reception back the next day. It was hot. He sailed slowly. He stopped worrying about the nuclear fallout. It was no coincidence that on the next night he wrote that entry about the beauty of the stars. He drank tea in his cockpit that evening and enjoyed the realization of his dream to sail alone across an ocean. As if plucked out of Davison's *why-go*, Horie wrote: "Life is well worth living for moments like this."

Kenichi Horie's career as a solo sailor had only just begun. After his crossing of the North Pacific in 1962, which he saw mostly as a contest between man and sea, Horie became a figurehead for ocean environmentalism through a series of high-profile voyages. In 1974 he circumnavigated the world non-stop via Cape Horn. Horie, by then, had stopped throwing his underwear and other trash overboard. Next he sailed around the globe from north to south, meaning he sailed around Cape Horn again and then up the Atlantic and through the Northwest Passage. This took him four years because of various setbacks, including being rolled over twice when sailing through the Aleutian Islands chain. At age forty-six, Horie began to cross oceans for conservation awareness, beginning in 1985 with a passage from Hawai'i to Japan in a solar-powered boat—no sails at all—just solar panels that charged batteries to power a propeller. Horie then crossed the Pacific in a pedal-powered boat. He crossed in a boat made of recycled aluminum. He sailed around the world non-stop a second time.

Kenichi Horie is today a national hero in Japan and to

ocean environmentalists around the world. In the summer of 2022 he completed yet another crossing of the North Pacific at eighty-three years old. His boat, *Mermaid III*, was the same size as the original, only nineteen feet long, but this time it was made of aluminum and expertly designed and built for the single-hander with wind-vane self-steering and double-headsails, a suite of electronics and satellite connections, and a hard dodger under which Horie kept sheltered from spray and sun. This new boat was designed by the son of the man who designed the original wooden *Mermaid*.

I was honored to meet with Horie, through an interpreter at a yacht club in San Francisco before he left. With a mop of white hair, he was easy-going, unassuming, and he seemed most interested to speak about self-steering gear. It turns out that Horie has never seen writing or public speaking or environmental activism or even the voyages themselves as a form of public outreach. He told me that he does not see himself as an environmentalist at all. He is a sailor first. His *why-go* is mostly centered around his enjoyment in planning new voyages, his fascination with the technical challenges and the fastidious preparation. If his passages reveal the possibilities of alternative fuels or a public desire to protect the ocean, then this is a fortunate secondary benefit.

Since the 1960s, even as portions of the general public throughout the world began to really consider anthropogenic threats to the open-ocean environment, this has proven more the exception than the rule among single-handed mariners and the narratives they created: the sailing and adventure came first and then—often, but definitely not always—the environmental advocacy follows.

# 12. Extrasensory Perception

I never had any moments of extrasensory perception on my trip across the Atlantic—although it would have proved useful, to put it mildly, considering what happened to me in the end. But I had not earned anything like this. Several single-handed sailors, however, have written of moments when they woke up suddenly—had a sixth sense, a Spiderman tingling, that alerted them that something was off. It was an intuition that shook their shoulder, waking them up or alerting them to look around.

For example, in 1931 a Latvian man who had changed his name to Fred Rebell sailed in a tiny boat alone from Australia to Los Angeles. At one point he hallucinated that he levitated, floated above his boat, during which he spotted a ship perhaps over a hundred miles away. Later when he returned to his rational senses, Rebell actually saw the ship nearby. In 1946 a man named Hans de Meiss-Teuffen was crossing the Atlantic alone and woke up inexplicably at 0300 "with the urge to have a quick look on deck, and there, only 300 yards off, a fishing motor vessel." Perhaps in his sleep he heard the boat, smelled the diesel, or felt the vibrations? The sailor-writer H. E. Ross, a US Army veteran and a historian of Black mariners and Caribbean turtlers, told me how once he was sailing alone off San Pedro, California, soon after sunset, when he just felt something odd while he was down below cooking. He came on deck and saw the stern of an unlit vessel in front of him. Something in the dusky early evening told him to get out of there. He wasn't sure why. "Pure luck or dumb luck," he said. As he tacked the boat away he saw that he had been only eight or nine yards from the tow line of the barge that the vessel was towing—this cable would have cut him down and sunk his boat. English solo sailor Michael Richey, a World War II veteran who crossed the Atlantic alone thirteen times up until he was eighty years old, once said that "the experience of waking up mysteriously at the right time seems to be a common one."

Solo circumnavigator Bill King wrote in the early 1970s of developing "some sort of ESP" during his years as a submarine commander in World War II. It was on his second attempt to circumnavigate the world that the great white shark holed his boat off southwestern Australia. One of the notable details about this event was that he remembered staring a split second before at the exact spot inside his boat that the animal hit. A couple of years later Bill King was sailing with author Stuart Woods from England to the Azores as Woods was preparing for a solo trans-Atlantic crossing. The two were napping below while they were underway, when King suddenly woke up, knowing he had to get on deck. He tacked the boat because it was on a collision course with a merchant ship. As Woods saw the large ship steaming too closely astern, he reflected, "I wondered if I would ever become that attuned to what was happening around the boat."

In *Sailing Alone Around the World*, Joshua Slocum wrote of a similar intuition. Once as he was entering the Strait of Magellan he was down below napping when "the very air I breathed seemed to warn me of danger. My senses heard '*Spray* ahoy!' shouted in warning." He jumped on to the deck and was just able to take in sail and lash everything in place before a white squall exploded across the water and attacked the *Spray*.

When I asked Kenichi Horie if he had ever experienced extrasensory perception, any special warning in all his years of solo sailing, he said, "No. But that sure would be nice."

## 13. Sharon Sites Adams Had the Right to Sail Alone

It is a cool, foggy morning in 1969. Sharon Sites Adams looks over the rail at waters so lively that she feels compelled to whisper into her tape recorder so that she will not disturb the whale whose spout she just heard. Soon she is able to see its dark back emerge close to her boat. She smells its fishy, mossy breath in the fog.

Around 1:45 p.m. she makes out Point Arguello, California. In relief and celebration, she raises two colorful windsocks with a Japanese carp design to decorate her rig and to honor her two children. A little over an hour later, she finds a northbound fishing vessel named the *Little Swede*. She waves her arms. The boat alters course and motors over. Its engine thumps loudly and echoes across the surface of the gray water.

"Did you want something?" the captain asks.

"I've just sailed from Japan," Adams states, unfamiliar with the sound of her own voice and unable to contain her thrill and pride.

The *Little Swede* is a salmon boat bound for Oregon with two men aboard. The captain tries to use their radio to make contact with her people in Los Angeles, which does not work, so they radio a fisherman buddy in Morro Bay, who says he will walk up the dock and make the call for her.

"You sure have a lot of friends with you," the mate says, nodding down toward the water where two dolphins swim off the bow of Adams' boat and a large seal paddles off her stern.

*Little Swede* spends about forty-five minutes floating beside her, then motors off, having done what they could do. Adams watches them suddenly spin back around.

"We forgot to ask if there's anything you need."

"What I needed most," she wrote later, "to be found— had already been taken care of."

After the meeting with the fishing boat, Adams continues sailing south down the California coast, knowing she has realized her dream—yet still anxious. She gropes in the fog and sometimes drifts too close to the shore in calms. *Sea Sharp II*, unlike Horie's *Mermaid*, was equipped with both an engine and kerosene running lights, but both had failed by the end of the first week off Japan, so she had no auxiliary power at that point and had to run dark every night of the crossing. Hoping her news has gone through, she tries to find a boat sailed by her friends, who she anticipates are sailing up to meet her. She hears the train on shore. She inhales the smell of the cedar trees and the dunes and the kelp. On her radio the next morning, she listens to the announcement of her own arrival. Later a small plane flies overhead with a cameraman filming her boat. She looks up and waves. To try to stay awake and focused, she takes a Ritalin pill, as she had done occasionally while in the middle of the Pacific.

On the afternoon of the next day, something extraordinary happens, an event that Adams mostly brushes aside (but I cannot). She is napping with her self-steering gear engaged, but then wakes up abruptly after about forty-five minutes, sensing something wrong.

"We had just slipped past an oil rig on the starboard side," she writes. "Not ten feet from our stern was a black mooring can used by the tenders. The men on board looked startled to see us, but their expression didn't compare with mine when I realized *Sea Sharp II*, all on her own, had steered us safely through the maze. Another angel at the helm."

When her friends find her, the two vessels sail south in company. They pass her fresh fruit over the rail. So she can sleep occasionally, they keep her boat lit at night or blare their horn to wake her up if there is danger. At 5:15 a.m. on the morning of 23 July 1969, wearing the same flamingo pink pantsuit that she had worn when she left Yokohama, Sharon Sites Adams sails *Sea Sharp II* into San Diego Bay.

Although she would be a national celebrity for a time, including as the *Los Angeles Times* Woman of the Year, Sharon Sites Adams could not find a publisher for her story, even with multiple agents. She was told there wasn't enough interest in her voyage. She gave it multiple tries over the years with different agents and editors.

"Women weren't supposed to be out there doing those things," she told me.

Forty years later her book was finally printed by a small landlocked academic press at the University of Nebraska, co-written with Karen J. Oates, with the title *Pacific Lady: The First Woman to Sail Solo Across the World's Largest Ocean* (2008). Adams was now living in a tidy trailer home in Oregon, retired from a range of jobs that included stints in banking, property management, owning a coffee shop, and for many years serving hot dogs at a stand on the campus of California State University at Hayward.

Wearing her pink pantsuit, Sharon Sites Adams left Tokyo Bay seven years to the day after the departure of Kenichi Horie, which, she said, was a coincidence. She sailed across in seventy-four days, the fastest non-stop single-handed passage of the North Pacific at the time and as only the third known person to have done so.

Adams' passage across to San Diego was a longer distance overall than Horie's and Platt's, nearly 7,000 miles as the albatross flies, and she covered the passage in nearly three weeks less time. To be fair, her boat *Sea Sharp II* was a full third larger than *Mermaid*. (Marine architects explain that a boat's maximum speed through the water is mostly a direct function of its length.) Built of fiberglass, with a larger suite of sails, *Sea Sharp II* was also equipped with a wind-vane self-steering system.

Similar to how Horie had strategized regarding public relations, so too Adams had planned ahead. She connected with an American builder who already had a company in Yokohama that built boats for export. Yokohama was the sister city of San Diego. The American designer donated the boat for her trip, knowing that if she were successful *Sea Sharp II* would be both easily sold after she arrived in California and tremendous advertising for his company. All of which proved true when Adams gave the boat back after she arrived safely. Adams was, however, allowed to customize the boat, which she did with extra rigging, larger winches, a beefier bow pulpit, more substantial safety lines, the self-steering system, and a unique plexiglass dome that stuck up from the cabin, which she conceptualized herself so that she could see outside without having to open the hatch in rough, wet weather. She had the deck painted a pastel pink, a pink stripe painted on the topsides, and a hot-pink stripe stitched into her sails.

Once the passage was all arranged and boat construction nearly complete, Adams rewrote her will, had her appendix removed, then flew to Tokyo to meet the new vessel. She tried to go on several sea trials, but was often stymied with press obligations and other impediments. So after only a couple of days of sailing *Sea Sharp II*, she stuck to her depart-ure date with the hope that she would figure it all out once she was underway.

At sea she began reading Horie's *Kodoku*. Adams felt for-tunate when compared to how much rough weather he had had at the start. Although she did not experience difficult weather conditions at first, she needed to cope with a brand-new vessel, aboard which parts kept breaking and systems failed in maddening succession. Much of this, she believes, was due to hasty, even shoddy work by her soon-to-be ex-husband, her first sailing instructor, who had flown over to Japan to rig the boat. Sawdust and oil clogged a bilge pump. A radar reflector blew off in the first gale. A backstay dis-connected. Two halyard blocks broke. Winches, topping lifts, a string of hardware malfunctioned. At one point, though, in a gale of over forty knots she ran ahead of the weather with only a small rolled staysail and still made one hundred miles over twenty-four hours. That's a fast, dramatic run in a small boat, especially with rigging you haven't yet learned to trust.

Adams got help figuring out the self-steering before she left Yokohama, but she never had it quite mastered in Tokyo Bay. Sailing eastbound into the open Pacific, she soon began to get the hang of how to adjust it properly, but she, like all single-handers, could never turn over the helm with entire confidence. Once during a gale, when she happened to be awake and on deck during the day, she watched a full-sized log, "like a torpedo," speed down a steep wave and just miss her bow. This would have sunk her boat in seconds.

With merchant shipping, Adams' experiences were similar to those of Horie and Pidgeon. She could count on one hand the number of times she saw large ships. About three weeks out, early in the morning, a large freighter named the SS *President McKinley* scared the wits out of her. The ship powered slowly up while she was sleeping and blasted the horn. She peeked through the hatch, realized she was naked, and then returned below while the ship kept blasting the horn as she struggled to pull on damp sweatpants and a shirt. Once back in her cockpit and presentable, looking up at the captain and trying to shout to be heard, she found she had little to say. The conversation was brief. She said she did not need anything. They offered her the latitude and longitude.

"It was nice seeing you," the captain of the bulk carrier said. A few of the passengers and crew looked down at her over the rail, taking pictures. Then they powered away. Adams took a photograph of the ship's stern. She felt shattered and confused, suddenly launched out of her rhythm and

Sharon Sites Adams taking a sun sight aboard her first boat, *Sea Sharp*, on her solo voyage to Hawai'i (1965).

profoundly alone at sea, having lost the opportunity for at least some conversation.

Especially in contrast with Horie's *Kodoku*, Sharon Sites Adams' *what-they-saw* and her perspective on the ocean seem to represent the start of a turn among single-handers who began to tell their stories with more environmental concerns in mind. Adams noted human impact on ocean ecosystems and considered marine life as meaningful in and of itself: animals were no longer just resources for humans to exploit. Her narrative *Pacific Lady* is complicated, however, in that it was published forty years later. Less interested in writing while at sea, Adams had spoken her daily journal into a tape recorder. She finished with seventy-five hours of tape, which she revisited over the years to write her account. Her published story, she told me, was barely influenced by her co-author, who mostly served to copy-edit and organize it, but the final revision did happen after four decades of distance and dramatic cultural shifts in American perspectives on ocean spaces and marine life.

For example, like Horie, Adams wrote in *Pacific Lady* that she was not interested in washing her clothes on her first solo passage, from California to Hawai'i a few years earlier, so she had thrown her dirty garments over the side. "I know, I know, I was a litterbug!" she wrote. "But everything went overboard in those pre-eco days."

In *Pacific Lady* a sunset bathed her in pink. Dolphins swam "gracefully." Squid that washed up on her deck had "pretty faces." Like her predecessors, Adams saw sharks as ravenous and dangerous—one shark developed a red stripe on its back from bottom paint it rubbed off her hull (Johnny Wray witnessed the exact same thing in the 1930s). Yet another time a shark was graceful, and when she threw overboard a red plaid shirt, she did not imagine the shark rushing after a patch of blood, but instead swimming into the shirt, a Disney image, making it "the best-dressed shark at sea."

Adams loved "her friends" the albatrosses, which she called gooney birds, a nickname often used by earlier sailors. Adams wrote that she loved these goofy and funny seabirds. Her favorite seabirds were "sea swallows," which by her description and distance from land perhaps were a species of tern, veering around her rigging and playing games with her.

One night Adams watched a green flash after the sunset, a phenomenon almost unique to life at sea. You need a clean long horizon and a clear sky. The exact moment after the sun has gone down, if you look a bit obliquely, you can often see a quick plume of green glow in your peripheral vision. "I don't have the ability or the words," Adams wrote of the green flash and the sunset scene, "to convey the beauty of what I saw."

Environmentalism or simply the desire to connect with a beautiful ocean world had not been part of Adams' initial *why-go*. Her motivation to cross an ocean alone began abruptly after she learned how to sail at the age of thirty-four. Adams had left her first husband and two children in Oregon, realizing that she was too young and never wanted that sort of domestic life. Then, over a decade later, after losing her second husband to cancer and working for many years managing a dentist's office in San Diego, she decided to try sailing. She had spent almost no time on the water. Less than eight months after her first sailing lessons, she embarked on a solo sail to Hawai'i, the trip that would give her the confidence to attempt the full North Pacific eastbound crossing.

Like Davison and Horie, in *Pacific Lady* Adams was candid about pangs of loneliness at sea; but in her telling, the sea was less about competition and more about companionship. Her love of the ocean and its inhabitants comes across not solely as garnish but as the main meal, foregrounding her adventure in the introduction to her narrative:

> But you know, we sailors have this: Even in the worst of times, we see the best of nature's beauty. On calm seas, the water acted like mirrors beneath my boat, in the center of an ocean, an utter silence broken only by the faint sound of a sail crinkling in the air. I drifted with sleek sharks that circled me and scratched their backs on the bottom of the boat. I watched the boat's wake spread like a silver lace fan behind me. Many times I witnessed the disappearance of horizon as sky melded with water to form a belly that ate me whole. And I drifted in that misty tomb, wet and tired and often too annoyed to appreciate the magnificence of it all.
>
> Other times, I relished the wonder of the universe ... God has blessed me with these things.

As Adams completed her voyage, navigating by sextant and dead reckoning in the summer of 1969, Rachel Carson's *Silent Spring* had been out for several years. *National Geographic* magazine was sponsoring the voyage and publishing features about the solo circumnavigation of Robin Lee Graham, the golden-haired, big-smiling, barefooted sixteen-year-old who had left San Pedro, California, in 1965 and was now on the verge of returning (see p. 113). Jacques Cousteau and Émile

Gagnan's self-contained underwater breathing apparatus (SCUBA) had continued to improve, delivering through television new vistas and access under the surface to the broadest of audiences. Cousteau's underwater film documentary *The Silent World* (1956) had won an Oscar, and by the time of Adams' trans-Pacific crossing in 1969 his American television series *The Undersea World of Jacques Cousteau* was in its third of ten seasons. The popular show *Flipper* had finished its run on television and crafted in the American imagination a dolphin that was as loving and loyal as a Labrador retriever.

Preparations were also underway to mark the first Earth Day the following spring, in 1970. Shortly to follow in 1972, from public pressure in the United States, were the Marine Mammal Protection Act, the Clean Water Act, the Migratory Bird Treaty Act, the Endangered Species Act, and the Marine Protection, Research, and Sanctuaries Act.

In *Pacific Lady* Adams did not mention this rising tide of American environmentalism, nor nuclear testing in the Pacific. She did not mention the Santa Barbara oil spill, either, the largest oil spill in American history at the time and still the largest ever in California waters—a disaster that soiled beaches and coated bays in January and February of 1969, a couple of months before she flew to Japan to begin her passage. It would have been easy to strike a cynical or metaphorical note as *Sea Sharp II* steered around the oil rigs in the final days of her trip. The Santa Barbara spill was one of the key catalysts, a visual crisis for the television set, that boosted further momentum for those environmental regulations of the early 1970s.

What Adams did choose to explore in *Pacific Lady* was that on the very day she chatted with the men of the *Little Swede*, Neil Armstrong walked on the moon. Mixed with the emotions of completing her record-setting passage, Adams sat in the cockpit of her boat that night, looking up at the moon and listening on her radio as Walter Cronkite on CBS news announced the human steps walking on its surface. She wished then, like Slocum who returned home burning to be of use, that her passage had made some contribution to science or something helpful to humanity.

"I hadn't done anything but bring an idea to fruition," she wrote. "The journey fulfilled my own wishes, and maybe I'd be setting a world record. But I wasn't charting new worlds. Or was I?"

What Sharon Sites Adams charted were new routes and further precedents that led to the continued expansion of women's roles and expectations in Western society. She did not refer to any specific previous solo sailors in *Pacific Lady* other than Slocum ("one of the greatest sailors to have lived") and Horie ("I felt that we had some kind of connection"), but she had, Adams told me, read Pidgeon's account and Davison's, too. In *Pacific Lady*, she explained that her decision to embark on her first big solo trip, the one to Hawai'i, had come somewhat out of nowhere, rooted only in her reading: "The idea plagued me, day and night, for two weeks. I couldn't wipe it way, couldn't sleep, couldn't think of anything else. Men had done it; I had read about them. I didn't know that no woman had, and that had nothing to do with my fixation anyway."

Although her name has largely been forgotten among American feminist heroes, Sharon Sites Adams became an inspiring figure for people ashore and especially for a new wave of solo single-handed sailors. Slocum, as you likely noticed, had encouraged only young men to go on a voyage like his. But one year before Adams' solo sail to Hawai'i,

Edith Baumann of West Germany became the first woman entrant in the OSTAR, a single-handed trans-Atlantic race. Baumann had to be rescued off the Azores when her boat broke up in heavy weather, but hers was hardly the only one to founder that summer, as other sailors also ran into storms and wind of over sixty knots: only eighteen of thirty-five entrants made it across.

A few months after Adams became the first woman to cross the North Pacific alone, a woman named Ingeborg von Heister, in her mid-forties, became the second known woman (after Davison) to cross the Atlantic, as well as the first German sailor of any gender to cross an ocean alone. After the crossing, von Heister cruised the Caribbean alone on her trimaran and returned alone in the other direction. Von Heister once wrote in her logbook: "I believe that it's better to sail alone than with a crew you can't get along with. And who should I take with me? Another woman? Not sure a woman can make a good comrade. A married couple? Out of the question. A man you are not in love with? That will definitely cause big problems. And I can't find or haven't found someone with whom I'm in mutual love and also enjoys sailing. Either he has no money, no inclination to sail or he's too old."

In 1971 a young British woman named Nicolette Milnes Walker sailed across the Atlantic from Wales to Rhode Island. Largely new to sailing, like Adams, Walker completed a steady, safe passage. Although she did not further feminist movements—stating in her first chapter, titled "Why," that "like most women I wanted to impress men"—her narrative *When I Put Out to Sea* (1972) was one of the first solo-sailor narratives that began to lean toward an environmentalist perspective. Walker wrote of her relationship with the sea as partly to test oneself—the ocean, with a male pronoun, is "a child of immense power and quick temper," yet at the same time she explained that "one of the pleasures of ocean voyaging is the enjoyment of natural things, of the abundant life of the sea, from the smallest plankton, visible only when it lights up with fear, to the great whales, to the birds that live on the open ocean and rarely touch down on land." At another point during her crossing Walker wrote how she let herself down in the way she was careless with plastic trash, throwing it overboard. She found it too hard to motivate herself when she knew that "the ocean liners discharge all their waste into the sea." As she approached the coast of Rhode Island, she was surprised to see a whale, because she had heard that these waters would be too polluted. So Walker was pleased that "the great whaling fleets of New England had not completely wiped out their victims."

Still more women made notable solo voyages in the 1970s after Sharon Sites Adams. In 1975 Noriko Kobayashi from Japan finished with six others in a single-handed trans-Pacific race from California to Japan. In 1976, Krystyna Chojnowska-Liskiewicz from Poland, in her boat *Mazurek*, became the first woman to sail solo around the world, departing from the Canary Islands in March 1976 and returning there in April 1978. Also that year, three other women sailing independently of each other completed single-handed circumnavigations. Naomi James (see p. 140) and Brigitte Oudry, from New Zealand and France respectively, each completed their voyages months later by going in opposite directions around Cape Horn.

In 2020 a man who lived on his boat at the harbor in Oakland, California, found *Sea Sharp II* sunk at the dock. He began to research its provenance and found the connection to Sharon Sites Adams, which was confirmed when he identified the custom Plexiglas dome on the cabin. Adams had not seen the boat in fifty years, since she gave it up after the crossing. The man extracted the wheel and brought it up to Adams' Oregon home. Holding the wheel with her ninety-year-old hands, she began to cry. Now it leans against the window, resting on a doily. "I look at it every day," she told me.

Adams said that despite what the world sees today as a powerful feminist act of being the first woman to sail the Pacific alone, she did not identify as a feminist then or now. Her *why-go* was not to prove anything about women. Adams feels as she always had, that this trip was simply something she wanted to do—and could. Her friend and fellow single-handed sailor Carol Baker, who herself in her late seventies still sails alone along the coast of the Pacific Northwest, told me that Adams has never had any axe to grind and "never had any patience at all with the feminist movement." Nor has Adams ever thought of herself as an environmentalist. She had always just wanted to be an adventurer.

"Critics have accused me of being too independent, and I'm sure that's true," Adams wrote in *Pacific Lady*. "They called me a foolish housewife. They psychoanalyzed me. Some asked who gave me the right to sail the ocean alone."

# 14. Self-Steering

After the fog and the fulmars, after my first gales and flat calms, after the twenty-foot-long great white shark gnawed at my main boom, after the indifferent sea turtle, I was now more than halfway to England at about the longitude of the Azores and Iceland with less than one thousand miles to go. The wind was perfect, unexpectedly from the south, so I had my full mainsail and my largest jib set and was making excellent time in the right direction. Down below in the cabin that afternoon, I pinned up a Union Jack. Also on that bulkhead, beside the barometer, I had tacked a photograph of Lisa (my girlfriend, now spouse) and our dog in the snow. I also had a curious old postcard of four young men sitting and looking at the camera. It is an image from where I don't know, maybe the 1930s, but I have always found it oddly moving: the young men from another generation, each of whom seemed to look at the camera yearning with aspirations that I found motivating somehow. I still have the postcard.

By that point in the trip the only reason I was able to sit below in the cabin of *Fox* and fart around with the bulkhead décor or page through books and manuals to try to fix my overheating engine was because the self-steering gear was working so well. I had learned by that point how to adjust it properly. It had worked for short periods before I left when I sailed with friends along the coast of New England for the shakedown trip, but I still felt like I did not have a clear feel for it when I sailed out of Portland. I'd been unreasonably fortunate that a man named Sandy Van Zandt, a retired sail-maker and a former world cruiser who with his wife became nationally recognized environmental advocates for public lands, had one day walked by my boat when it was still hauled out on the stands at the boatyard in Noank, Connecticut, at the mouth of the Mystic River. Sandy and I struck up a conversation. I can't remember how we got started on my hope to sail across the North Atlantic by myself, because I told very few people about this. I must have trusted him immediately—or he just asked me outright. I can't remember exactly how it got started. Sandy took some interest in my endeavor. He helped me set up the steering gear before I left, cutting me some chain and fabricating a hard plastic piece to clamp around the tiller. Without him I would have been lost in terms of this gear. I bought the self-steering device by mail from a company in California. I took the stainless-steel bars to an auto company to drill the holes I needed, and then I drilled the holes through the fiberglass transom of *Fox* myself and bolted the thing to the stern of the boat. But even as I corresponded with the company and other owners with my same boat design and also regularly checked in with Sandy, I still felt like I was making too much of this up as I was going along.

Sir Francis Chichester, who in 1960 was about to sail alone across his first ocean, designed his own self-steering gear, which he named "Miranda" after the character in Shakespeare's *The Tempest* who delivers the famous line, "O brave new world."

Self-steering mechanisms and strategies have likely done more to enable single-handed voyaging than any other factor, more than the use of fiberglass production hulls or the small-boat engine or even GPS. Self-steering has allowed more sailors to get out there and given them more time and mental space to look over the side for sea turtles, coral reefs, or icebergs. Thus a brief technical digression here is useful for the larger story, as well as my small one.

Part of the reason boat designs like Slocum's *Spray* and Pidgeon's *Islander* could sail thousands of miles without a helmsperson was because they were larger, heavier hulls with full keels under the water (helping to keep the boat on a straight line track), wide initial stability (less tippy and rolly), and these boats supported a range of different sails from one all the way in the back (a mizzen) to a sail all the way out front on a bowsprit (a jib). These boat characteristics allowed these experienced sailors several options to balance their hull with the amount and orientation of canvas set on a given day. In most conditions Slocum and Pidgeon were able to adjust their sails and tie their wheel or tiller in place before going below to nap, read, or make some coffee.

Self-steering mechanisms for crossing oceans in modern boats, ones not blessed with the magic dust and design of *Spray* and *Islander*, began as early as 1936, credited to French sailor and artist Marin-Marie, who crafted and tested his wind-powered self-steering system on a motorboat going trans-Atlantic. At least three different British and French sailors then further designed and advanced the use of vane systems in the 1950s.

The devices were not well known or cheap enough for boaters like Davison to install on *Felicity Ann* in the early 1950s. Horie's *Mermaid* in 1962 was meant to have a system, but he wasn't able to finish it before he left Japan. Soon, however, homemade and production self-steering gear became accessible and tested enough that by the time Sharon Sites Adams crossed the North Pacific in the 1960s and Nicolette Milnes Walker crossed the North Atlantic in 1971, they each had multiple brands from which to choose and were able to use their self-steering with little previous experience.

In general, these wind-powered self-steering systems start with a wood, fabric, or fiberglass wind vane on a vertical post that is at the very back of the boat, the stern. As an oversimplified explanation, imagine, like at the top of a house, a weather vane shaped like a sperm whale. The top of the vertical post is attached to the whale's forehead. When you've got your boat sailing well in the direction you want, you adjust the whale to face into the direction from which the wind comes (not in the direction the boat itself is heading) and connect the system to the tiller or wheel. If the boat starts to turn in one direction or the other, the wind puts pressure on the whale's tail on one side or the other, forcing the rotation of the whale's head and hence the post. The bottom of the post is attached to a little auxiliary rudder in the water or to the back edge of the main rudder or through pulleys and lines that lead directly to the tiller or wheel. Regardless of the exact system, the wind moving the tail turns the post, which eventually steers the boat until it is back on track, until the boat is sailing in the direction in which the vane, the whale's forehead, is again pointed directly into the wind with no pressure on its tail. In small increments this carries on constantly in the same way you can stick your hand out of the car window and angle it to keep it straight with as little resistance to the wind as possible.

That's oversimplified, but hopefully you get the idea. I've included in the chapter notes a link to a video that demonstrates this well.

Most budget ocean cruisers today use, as I did, a self-steering design called a servo-pendulum vane system. This employs both the wind and its own small rudder in the water, utilizing both forces to adjust the tiller or wheel via pulleys and ropes. This wind vane works vertically in that the "whale" is diving down toward the water, so its tail tilts from left to right, which then, in my case, turned a small rudder in the water which rotated a rod that swung like a pendulum as it was connected to the lines leading into the cockpit and to the tiller, moving it to the right or left, to starboard or port (see p. 313). The early systems in the 1960s, like on Chichester's "Miranda," had blanket-sized wind vanes, little sails really (see p. 113), whereas by the twenty-first century, thanks in part to the new systems, the vanes were now down to the size of skinny skateboards. My self-steering system was a beautiful contraption. It had a transparent plastic vane that acted on a mechanism of thick shiny stainless-steel bars and bolts, smooth bearings and gears, and a counterbalance weight. It was also nonsensical-looking. The lines made a spider's web in the cockpit. Even as I watched it tilting from one side to the other, moving lines that moved through the pulleys that I'd installed and led to a bit of chain and Sandy Van Zandt's custom collar around the end of the tiller, I remained only on the edge of understanding how it all worked.

With friends on the coastal shakedown trip north we experimented a bit more with the vane, which I'll call Sandy. Once alone during the first days of the trans-Atlantic crossing, I learned how to adjust the direction and the tension of the lines and when to use either the larger or the smaller of the paddle-shaped vanes, depending on the force of the wind. These vanes were switched out with little wing nuts that I prayed I would not drop into the water when I leaned over the rail at the stern. I had two back-up vanes of each size and several spare nuts, but it was a finite supply for such crucial equipment.

Once Sandy was set for a time, I could sit in the cockpit as *Fox* rolled and sloshed across the blue waves. I would usually sit with my back to the cabin on the windward, higher side of the boat, looking aft and watching the wake, marveling how the steering gear did his thing, converting the wind and my boat's direction to rotating pulleys and ropes that moved the tiller as if by the hands of a ghost. Sandy was gimballed in his way, too, staying vertical to the horizon from where he was fastened off the stern, so even as the boat heeled in one direction or the other the rotating part of the mechanism stayed vertical. The whole silent system was miraculous and mesmerizing, a modern-art mobile. Once in motion Sandy ran entirely on his own, like one of those metal sculptures where you push a counterweight to get it started and then the bicyclist rides and rocks back and forth on a wire endlessly.

Wind-vane self-steering systems work best in steady wind and when the wind is coming from angles forward or from the side of the boat. Wind-vane self-steering gear does not work as well with light, fluky winds or when you're sailing directly downwind, meaning when the wind is behind the boat. Each boat is unique, though, and the sea and wind conditions vary from day to day. Besides the fact that they generally do not work as well in light breezes or in winds from directly astern, there are two other facts about these self-steering systems that are perhaps obvious but important to clarify, including to inform later events in this story.

First: if you fall off the boat, the self-steering gear does not care about you and will just keep sailing ahead. In 1979, Yukio Hasebe fell overboard while sailing alone off the Great Barrier Reef with his wind-vane gear engaged. He was still connected by his harness, which dragged him astern, but the boat was sailing too fast for him to be able to climb back aboard. Beaten and bloody, he held on until his boat grounded into a reef. (Hasebe later bought another boat and made it nearly all the way around the world, but then died somewhere in the middle of the North Pacific; neither he nor his boat were ever found.) Some single-handers stream a line astern from their self-steering to which they might desperately grab if they fall overboard in order to disengage the gear and allow the boat to round up into the wind, luff the sails, and stop itself. I chose not to send a rope astern, because I didn't want a random line getting tangled with fishing gear or getting wrapped up in the propeller or around the self-steering rudder.

Second: since wind-powered self-steering systems are beholden to the direction of the wind, when the wind shifts from, say, northerly to easterly, and you're down below sleeping, cooking, or engrossed in reading your Ann Davison, the boat will quietly just turn along with the wind without telling you about the course change. Self-steering based on the wind maintains the boat's *relative position* to the wind. This is how Pidgeon's *Islander*, with the sails adjusted and the tiller lashed, ended up on the beach while he slept. For another example, one night when Horie had been at sea for nearly a month, he went below with the tiller tied in place so he could sleep. The wind slowly shifted clockwise without him sensing any change in speed or heel. When he woke up he had sailed about twenty miles in entirely the wrong direction. Angry at the loss of perhaps half a day, Horie wrote: "From here on I set myself two rules: 'Keep an eye on the compass as often as possible' and 'Do not let "feeling" be your guide under any circumstances.'" And so it seemed indeed an "angel at the helm" that steered Adams' boat past that oil-rig buoy, seemingly changing the course on its own, while she slept during the last couple of days of her North Pacific crossing.

Electrically powered compass alarms do exist; they were in place in the 1960s, but many of the early single-handers found them too loud or too sensitive or too cumbersome. To be honest, I'm not sure why I didn't think to get one in 2007 or why I anticipated it wasn't necessary. Today's off-course alarms are now easily integrated into GPS and radar units if you want to enable them.

In addition to the wind-driven self-steering systems, there are also now electronic self-steering mechanisms, known as autopilots. The earlier of these devices were set to a compass course rather than a relative wind position. Autopilots adjust the tiller or wheel via electronic signals to gears, pistons, or belts. This technology was just being developed in the 1960s for smaller boats, and Chichester, Horie, or Adams did not want to waste the money for new technology like that, nor did they have the power supply to support it. Today these electronic self-steering devices still require a lot of electricity, but there are some smaller types for on-deck use that are affordable enough that even low-budget sailors can have one of these electronic "tiller pilots." Once a marine technician (or you, if you have the skill) has cued it up to your compass, you just connect the little robotic piston and key in a course into the box as easily as setting the temperature on your home thermostat. The advantage of the autopilot is that you can use it in any weather, in really light wind, coming from any wind direction, and just as well when motoring. More recently, modern sophisticated autopilots try to manage the best of both worlds, wiring an apparent wind indicator on the mast to this electronic self-steering, meaning the device can steer a course with the relative wind at, say, the boat's beam, 90 degrees to your hull. Some budget single-handed sailors who can't afford a reliable autopilot set-up below will embark on a long voyage with a few tiller pilots available for using on deck, knowing they'll likely fail after a long time in the sun and saltwater. Tiller pilots and autopilots can be difficult to repair on your own.

Thus, wind-vane self-steering systems have the advantage over autopilots in that they require no electricity and are visibly mechanical. They can be used for the majority of the sailing miles out on open water. But there were times when I was changing a sail up forward, for example, and I wanted to keep the boat on a compass course. In those situations I would stand down Sandy and set up the tiller pilot for a short time. Almost all of the time, though, the tiller pilot lived in a waterproof bag down below. It worked great the couple of times I used it. It never had a name.

Many believe the greatest sailing movie ever made was *With Jean-du-Sud Around the World* (1984), created by Yves Gélinas, a French-Canadian single-hander. Gélinas filmed himself, produced the movie, and innovated several cinematic methods, decades before waterproof smart phones and

GoPro cameras and selfie-sticks and drones. He was likely the first person from a boat to use a kite to hold up a camera and film down on his vessel under sail (and himself in his birthday suit), and he was also likely the first on a boat to use a camera mounted on a helmet. Gélinas, with an earnest respect for the sailing and writing of Bernard Moitessier, left a career in acting and theatre to become a sailor, funding his early trip learning about aluminum and steel work in ship-yards in France.

After the circumnavigation, his film and book did not make enough money to support his daughters at home in Quebec. Gélinas said that his book was never translated into English because the anglophone Canadian publishers did not like his outspoken stance on independence for Quebec. So to make a living he turned to fabricating a wind-vane self-steering gear similar to the one that he had made for his own boat. He made each unit by hand at first, learning how to use a lathe and how to weld. He named his company CapeHorn. His device was quickly successful, even as electronic auto-pilots were arriving on the scene, so he was able to scale up and make it a family business. CapeHorn wind vanes are still available. His design is widely known as one of the most aes-thetically pleasing, along with its simplicity and durability. Gélinas once explained: "I am an artist basically . . . When I made the film I attempted to make it a work of art. And I had the same attitude with the self-steering gear. I was very conscious [that] to claim the title of 'work of art' it did not only have to look good, it also had to work perfectly."

Gélinas added that he felt you couldn't be an artist in one part of your life and not in others: "A [sea] passage well made, without any mishap, without any problems, can also be considered a work of art."

After I pinned up the Union Jack on the bulkhead and marked less than one thousand miles to go in my logbook, with multiple exclamation points, I wrote down the barometric pressure. I poked my head out of the companionway to look at the altocumulus clouds, piled and balled on top of each other in colossal castles stretching impossibly high, clouds crafted as if by children, accented a creamy yellow by the sun behind me. I noted the wind direction and scanned 360 degrees for ships. All looked good. Sandy faithfully held the course. I updated these weather details, too, in the logbook.

The barometer was dropping slowly, but I was making 4.5 knots at 100 degrees by the compass. All of this was just fine. I spread out my books on the leeward settee to calculate my noon sextant fix and found that it was within five miles of my GPS position, which was plenty good enough for me. I checked my wristwatch again, ate my daily power bar, and got ready to tune in my multi-band radio receiver to see if I could hear a weather forecast. I thought of the first beer I'd order at the pub in Falmouth.

# 15. Bernard Moitessier and a Sea of Spiritual Solitude

As Horie and Adams were crossing the North Pacific in the 1960s, still more people around the world were setting out alone in their own small boats to cruise across oceans. They set out with a cabin bookshelf that reverentially held a well-worn copy of Slocum's *Sailing Alone Around the World* and a growing library of other single-handed sea stories. They flipped though the articles about teenager Robin Lee Graham and *Dove* in *National Geographic* and read technical developments about small engines or rolling furl systems in magazines such as *The Rudder* or *Yachting*. As their little home heeled and proudly passed over the waves, the bindings of the books and magazines they carried clicked against the wooden fiddles that were slotted across the shelves so the volumes didn't tumble out into the cabin. Some people set sail in their boats primarily to challenge themselves or to escape constricting personal circumstances or to flee choking post-war modernity or materialism. Others went to sea primarily for the dream of slurping fresh mangoes and snorkeling off their floating house in warm, turquoise water. Still others chased a vision of gazing up at the Milky Way as their cozy little craft glided gently through blue-green bioluminescence.

The blossoming number of small-boat voyages in the 1960s was enabled by advances in self-steering devices, improved electronics, and technologies developed initially for the military that made navigation and communication at sea safer and easier. Boat designers continued to experiment with multihulls, constructing with materials like fiberglass, aluminum, steel, and even cement, building the vessels more cheaply, while also aiming for more stability, speed, and better abilities to sail closer to the direction of the wind. (A "monohull" means just that, one hull, a traditional Western boat; i.e. not a catamaran or trimaran, called a "multihull," which had been perfected, likely invented, by Pacific cultures centuries earlier. Catamarans and trimarans almost always sail faster, but usually far less safely if pushed to maximum speed.)

A further spark for the expansion of small-boat cruising was the reintroduction of solo races across oceans, reignited some seventy years after the first stunts across the Atlantic by Si Lawlor and William Andrews in the 1890s. For the first public race of this new era, five middle-aged men in 1960 sailed alone from Plymouth, England, over to New York City, aiming across a route largely against the prevailing winds. They convinced the *Observer* newspaper to sponsor them, so it was first known as the Observer Singlehanded Transatlantic Race, or the OSTAR, which has continued roughly every four years since with a variety of sponsors and different names.

This organized, competitive racing alone under sail across the Atlantic Ocean, along with voyages like Horie's and Adams' across the North Pacific, and the enduring legacy of Slocum, Pidgeon, Gerbault, Dumas, Davison, and others, led to the ultimate challenge of sailing alone around the world non-stop, a voyage of nearly a full year alone without stepping on land or even anchoring. The first of these non-stop circumnavigation races in 1968 thrust into the Western imagination a court of truly extraordinary and varied characters. Perhaps the most remarkable was a French sailor named

Bernard Moitessier. An explorer-hippy-poet of the sea, Moitessier was a generationally unique blend of Edmund Hillary, Henry David Thoreau, John Lennon, and Jacques Cousteau: a spiritual, ocean-adoring anti-capitalist who had endless energy and we-can-change-the-world aspirations. He and a British sailor named Robin Knox-Johnston accomplished, and I mean this without hyperbole, one of the most astounding and difficult individual feats of physical and mental endurance and skill in modern history. Moitessier returned to shore after his voyage to then craft a work of transcendent sea literature, a narrative of nature writing delivered from a deep-ocean physical and emotional space that few humans have or will ever visit.

Bernard Moitessier published his first book, *Vagabond des mers du sud* (*Vagabond of the Southern Seas*, published in English as *Sailing to the Reefs*) in 1959. This was a memoir about his youthful sailing adventures. A bestseller in France, the book earned him enough money and inspired enough fame and generosity from others to commission the construction of a tank-tough ketch made of steel, which he painted bright red and named *Joshua*, after Slocum. Moitessier used this bare-bones vessel as a sailing school for a couple of years in the coastal Atlantic and the Mediterranean. In 1963, the year after Horie's trans-Pacific crossing, Moitessier and his wife Françoise sailed from France to the South Pacific via the Panama Canal, leaving behind their three young children in boarding schools and with family. They returned around

Cape Horn and back up to Europe, not only weathering a six-day trial of hurricane-force winds and seas in the Southern Ocean, but also, in part due to their haste to get back to see the children, setting a new record at the time for the longest-known non-stop voyage in a small sailboat, landing in Spain after cruising over 14,200 miles in 126 days.

Meanwhile, the first OSTAR race had been completed. Of the five competitors, in third place was Dr. David Lewis, who would go on to research traditional Pacific navigation and sail alone to Antarctica. In second place was an English war veteran named Blondie Hasler, who had organized the race and would become influential in single-handed boat design, including inventing a popular self-steering servo-pendulum device. The winner of this first OSTAR in 1960 was Francis Chichester, the oldest among them and the owner of that wind vane he designed and called Miranda. To put Bernard Moitessier in context, it's necessary to tack over for a bit to learn about Chichester.

By 1960, Francis Chichester had thick bottle glasses, large ears, and was nearly bald. Born in 1901, the year after the publication of Slocum's *Sailing Alone Around the World*, Chichester was raised in a church rectory. Beginning at the age of six, he attended British boarding schools. After shipping out to the then British dominion of New Zealand at eighteen, he made his fortune there in the business of lumber and other natural resources. Chichester's fascination with solitary adventure began with airplanes. He flew small aircraft alone

across oceans in the pursuit of various firsts, some successful, others nearly so. One solo crash nearly killed him. By the
time Britain's involvement in World War II became inevitable, he was too old and his eyesight too poor to be an active
pilot, so he served as an instructor. After the war, as his
fellow-pilot Ann Davison was sailing across the Atlantic in
*Felicity Ann*, Chichester and his wife Sheila started a cartogra-
phy business, writing books on navigation and aircraft. It
was around this time that Chichester got seriously interested
in sailboats.

After winning that first OSTAR with a passage of forty
days, Chichester sailed back across with his wife Sheila and
designed a new boat for the next OSTAR in 1964. This time
he came in second, now among fourteen participants. Over
this time he wrote three sailing memoirs, but growing older
(now sixty-four) he wanted a still bigger challenge. In September of 1966, after over two years of preparation and with
a custom-designed boat, he set out to sail around the world
with only one stop. He sailed eastbound by way of the big
westerly winds and waves of the Southern Ocean, steering
around the three big, famous, scary capes—the Cape of
Good Hope at the edge of South Africa, Cape Leeuwin at
the corner of Western Australia, and then around the most
notorious, Cape Horn at the tip of South America. Not
including a six-week refit in Sydney, he did this all in a bone-
weary nine months and one day. The guiding idea was that he
was recalling the clipper-ship runs that carried bulk cargo,
such as wool or grain, the last of which were underway in
Harry Pidgeon's time. Chichester ceremoniously departed
from London, near the berth of the record-setting square-
rigger *Cutty Sark*, replicating the trip of the clippers down
the Thames before he departed from Plymouth. During all

his preparations Chichester managed to publish an annotated anthology titled *Along the Clipper Way* (1966), which
included a selection from Davison's *My Ship Is So Small.*

This historical tap into the nostalgia of the clipper ships
provided context and motivation for another expedition and
another first. In his best-selling narrative of his one-stop circumnavigation, *Gipsy Moth Circles the World* (1967)—the book
that ends with the number of words written in his
logbooks—Chichester's explanation for his *why-go* (which is
in the first chapter, as nearly all the solo stories of this era
begin) is about achievement and the records remaining.

Chichester gave two major reasons for this solo trip. His
first was that he wanted to sail single-handed around Cape
Horn. Slocum, for example, had chosen the Strait of Magellan, because sailing around open Cape Horn, just to the
south, seemed just too dangerous for *Spray.* "I told myself
for a long time that anyone who tried to round the Horn in a
small yacht must be crazy," Chichester wrote. "Of the eight
yachts I knew to have attempted it, six had been capsized or
somersaulted, before, during or after the passage. I hate
being frightened, but, even more, I detest being prevented by
fright. At the same time the Horn had a fearsome fascination, and it offered one of the greatest challenges left in the
world." Chichester explained in his narrative, as an aside, that
one other small boat had made it around Cape Horn that he
did not know about before he left. This was the voyage
undertaken by Bernard and Françoise Moitessier aboard
*Joshua.* They had arrived home in Europe only a few months
before Chichester left England, and Chichester was halfway
around the world by the time Moitessier actually published
his account, his second book, *Cap Horn à la Voile* (*Cape Horn:
The Logical Route,* 1967).

Chichester's second *why-go* was simply about speed, believing he could set the record for the fastest solo circumnavigation and compare a modern yacht's run to that of the big ships of old. He accomplished both of these goals, the fastest single-handed circumnavigation by far and a passage safely around Cape Horn. In the process, Chichester set a half dozen other more specific speed records, such as the farthest week's run for a solo sailor, and he more than doubled the miles previously traveled by a single-hander without stopping in port.

The voyage from the start was a high-profile, big-budget, public event. Chichester became a national hero. An airplane of journalists and a Royal Navy ice-patrol ship photographed him off Cape Horn in the Sir Francis Drake passage. As he began the homeward-bound trip north in the Atlantic, other planes and ships were dispatched to view him, reporting on his progress. On the return to the English Channel in May of 1967, a flotilla of personal and official boats and five large naval ships came out to escort the solo yachtsman back into Plymouth and to a quarter of a million people lining the docks. It was covered on the radio, on television, and on the front of the newspapers. He was knighted by Queen Elizabeth II with the same sword that the first Queen Elizabeth had held to knight Sir Francis Drake, 386 years earlier. The English public seized upon the person and the idea of Sir Francis Chichester, a man arriving home when the country felt spiritually and economically depressed in the wake of the convulsive loss of its empire around the world. Chichester provided a throwback sort of heroism, especially for a sector of the British populace that could not quite feel the same patriotic pride about the Beatles or even from the more Tory fictional heroisms of James Bond. Chichester's solo

Sir Francis Chichester waves to the crowds while raising a commemorative medallion of *Gipsy Moth IV* given to him by the Lord Mayor of London (1967).

circumnavigation, while most men his age were comparing pruning shears with their neighbors, managed to strike a cultural nerve. He inspired millions of people in Britain, as well as around the world.

Chichester loved his country and his queen. All clean shaves and collared shirts, he presented himself as a man of precision, decimals, half-degrees, and careful record-keeping, yet he still had time for a cocktail or a beer. He loved his wife and his tea and his toast. In his writings and radio dispatches from the boat, he kept his emotions to himself. In *Gipsy Moth Circles the World* he recounted all his setbacks with "it could have been worse," revealing only low points that feel performed, such as when he quotes from his own journal as he celebrated his wedding anniversary alone: "A very remarkable exceptional woman is Sheila. I did what is supposed to be un-British, shed a tear. Life seems such a slender thread in these circumstances here, and they make one see the true values in life."

Chichester spent most of the narrative of his monumental voyage talking about his yacht, *Gipsy Moth IV*, which he hated because it was too large and in many ways all wrong for the job. Yet he made it work against all odds. He described how much he disliked having to think about a motor at all on a sailboat. In his era before solar panels or wind generators, he needed his motor to work for a few hours now and again to charge his batteries. He managed to keep it chugging along thanks to his clever repairs, scrunching his body and bracing himself upside down in rough seas with tools in his teeth. In other words, Chichester presented his trip around the world as a series of technical challenges to be overcome by intellect, proper preparation, and moral fortitude.

Like Davison, his descriptions of marine life seem almost obligatory, to give his reader a sense of the different locales at sea. His flying-fish breakfasts were often detailed. He offered an intriguing account of albatross cries sounding like human screams. At another point he approached a poetic moment when a storm-petrel landed on deck. The tiny bird offered a touch of soft warmth, something alive after months of only cold on the inanimate boat, but Chichester quickly pulled back from this emotional connection in his prose. The bird died the next day.

Another small telling moment revealed how driven Chichester was by competition, by records, by an English boarding-school childhood, which even shaped his relationship with *what-he-saw* in these lonely open-water spaces. Of his outbound passage in the South Atlantic, he wrote: "Those

rainless days had compensations, for they were mostly pleasant weather, with clear skies and calm seas . . . I saw lots of
birds, and always enjoyed watching them. I appointed myself
a judge at a birds' sports day, and awarded first prize for
graceful flight to the Cape Pigeons."

A full generation younger than Chichester, Bernard Moitessier was born in 1925 in French-colonial Vietnam, then known
as Indochina, the oldest of five children. His parents were
French, his father a successful businessman, his mother an
artist. Bernard grew up in French schools, and when young
had an influential nurse of Chinese descent whose teachings
stuck with him. His childhood in Saigon was rural and coastal
enough that he spent much of his time in the rainforests and
along the coasts, where he first learned how to fish and sail a
boat. He spoke Vietnamese fluently.

Toward the end of World War II, the invading Japanese
military imprisoned French expats. After Hiroshima, with
his father imprisoned because he was a reserve officer, Bernard, now aged twenty, brazenly flew the French flag out of
their apartment window. This got his family all thrown in jail.
Moitessier often recounted the time when a soldier came
into his cell intending to kill him, but with a wordless
exchange of eyes, the Japanese man decided to lower his gun
and walk back out. It was a moment that would stick with
Moitessier for the rest of his life, sowing his distaste for killing anything if not for food, even rats.

After he and his family were released, amidst bloody

conflicts between communists and French colonizers, Moitessier (and his two brothers) joined a volunteer anti-communist military patrol, serving on a gunboat as an armed seaman and interpreter. One day when Moitessier's brother, Françou, was on a different patrol, he gunned down a man who had once been their close friend as children. A few days later, tortured by remorse, Françou killed himself.

When these conflicts cooled, still mourning for his brother, Moitessier tried to work for his father, but then decided to return to the water, working a business under sail on the Gulf of Siam, delivering rice and returning with wood or sugar. This lasted six months, until he was accused of smuggling arms. So he went to France and hitchhiked and biked around Europe for a while. This was not satisfying, either. He took a ship home to Saigon.

Now in his mid-twenties, Moitessier, with his thin beak nose and sharp chin, began his voyaging years by sailing off with a friend to Singapore and back in a roughly built boat. Moitessier then purchased another old wooden sailboat, which he named the *Marie Thérèse* after a woman he loved but to whom he could not commit. Moitessier departed alone westbound through Indonesia and the gulfs of Siam and Bengal until he ran hard aground on the coral reefs of the Chagos Bank in the Indian Ocean. The boat was lost. By other means he made it to Madagascar where he spent a couple of years building a new boat, which he later sailed across the Atlantic and then wrecked in the Caribbean. All of these events proved fodder for that first book in France that earned him, perhaps ironically, the supporters and money to build a new boat.

Moitessier loved his steel boat *Joshua* and the trials with his wife Françoise on their sail to the Southern Ocean and around Cape Horn. But he loathed *Cap Horn à la Voile*, the book he wrote about the voyage. He had allowed himself to be pressured, to write it too quickly to meet his publisher's desire to get it printed before a big boat show. This sense of creating a rushed, poor piece of work slumped Moitessier into a depression. Back living a domestic life in France, pacing the streets like a Byron, an Ishmael, a Paul Gauguin, he devolved to near madness, according to his biographer and friend Jean-Michel Barrault. Moitessier felt trapped, self-loathing, and he still mourned the tragedy of his brother.

Moitessier wrote later that the idea of a new book, one of true quality and sincerity, and the idea to circumnavigate the Earth aboard *Joshua* alone without a single port stop, came to him in a eureka moment as one glorious thing together with the *why-go* desire to create a work of literary art:

> I must have been on the point of suicide when the Child hurled the lightning bolt that paralyzed the Monster. In one blinding flash, an entire part of my future appeared before my eyes, and I saw how I could redeem myself. Since I had been a traitor by knocking off my book, what I had to do was write another one to erase the first and lift that curse weighing on my soul.
>
> A fresh, brand-new book about a new journey . . . a gigantic passage . . .
>
> Drunk with joy, full of life, I was flying among the stars now. Together, my heart and hands held the only solution, and it was so luminous, so obvious, so enormous, too, that it became transcendent: a non-stop sail around the world by the three capes!

This was toward the end of 1967, only a few months after the knighting of Sir Francis.

Even before Chichester completed his one-stop circumnavigation via the three capes, others besides Moitessier were fantasizing and even planning a non-stop world voyage, what now seemed the remaining pinnacle of sailing alone. Getting wind of these disparate plans and wanting to get in on the publicity in the wake of Chichester's phenomenal success, staff at the *Sunday Times* newspaper in London conjured up the Golden Globe race. Within a given set of dates for departure, they would award a prize for the first person home and then another prize for the fastest time. Although the captain need not enter the race officially and no trials or inspections were necessary, a representative from the newspaper did go to France to speak with Moitessier, in the hopes that he would enter. Disdainfully, Moitessier agreed to sail out of Plymouth to be a part of the race, but he would not be sponsored nor would he take a radio to send updates. He told the newspaper and race committee that if he won he would take the money without a thank you.

Between June and October of 1968 nine men sailed out of the ports of England and Ireland, choosing their time to leave based on their readiness, personal schedules, and own strategies as to the best projected weather to round the three capes. Of these men, only one, a young English merchant mariner named Robin Knox-Johnston, completed the voyage. Like the proverbial tortoise beating the hare, through

Robin Knox-Johnston returning home, just off the Isles of Scilly, aboard his 32-foot boat *Suahili*, as the first person to sail alone around the world without a single port stop (1969).

seamanship, preparation, experience, and sheer grit, he sailed home triumphantly in his rust-streaked, copper-patched wooden boat after 312 days at sea. Although forty years younger, Knox-Johnston was forged out of a similar patriotic English mold as Chichester. He too received a national welcome as he stepped back on to the stone quay, bearded and bedraggled but beaming from ear to ear.

Of the other seven entrants, leaving Moitessier aside for now, five were unable to sail beyond the Cape of Good Hope, dropping out at different distances due to some variation of gear failure and bad weather. Some of them had departed in small fiberglass boats that simply were not built for a world voyage like this. Nigel Tetley, a British lieutenant commander who grew up in South Africa, competed in his cruising trimaran and managed to pass the three capes, circumnavigate the world, and come within a couple weeks of arriving home in Plymouth with a far faster time than Knox-Johnston—but his boat broke up underneath him in heavy weather off the Azores. Tetley was pushing his vessel too hard to try to better the voyage of an English electronics engineer named Donald Crowhurst, who apparently also was making excellent speed himself in a similar trimaran. Tetley's boat sank. He had to be rescued from his life raft.

The tragic, stranger-than-fiction irony of this was that Crowhurst, suffering early structural failure of his boat and a chaotic lack of preparation, had been so afraid of the shame and the financial ruin of pulling out of the race that he began to fake his times and distances. He created a false logbook and never left the Atlantic. After a disqualifying stop in Argentina for repairs and supplies and then a sail down to the Falkland Islands for video footage to suggest he had come around Cape Horn, Crowhurst slowly sailed back north toward England in the hopes that with Knox-Johnston and Tetley claiming the prizes, his voyage would be highly honored but not too closely scrutinized. The stress of the voyage, his guilt, his mental state deteriorating, and the information over the radio that Tetley was out of the race—meaning that he would now win the fastest time and his treachery would surely be exposed in the most public fashion—proved to be too much. Crowhurst almost certainly took his own life by walking off his deck on a calm, sunny day in the middle of the North Atlantic, likely on 1 July 1969. His boat was found a week later by a passing merchant ship whose crew found nothing disturbed inside Crowhurst's cabin. There was no evidence of any substantial wave action or bad weather. Dishes were piled in the sink and a can-opener on the counter hadn't even rolled off. Although Crowhurst's falsified logbook seems to have been taken with him into the sea, the logbook of his true progress was left on board, as were all of his audiotapes and film footage. The writings and film show him in an increasingly psychotic state. Donald Crowhurst left behind his wife, Clare, and four young children.

After the boat was discovered, Robin Knox-Johnston gave his prize money to Clare Crowhurst. Two journalists pieced together a careful, best-selling exposé, *The Strange Last Voyage of Donald Crowhurst* (1970), explaining what had happened. Nigel Tetley wrote his own book, *Trimaran Solo* (1970) as he tried to get funding for another go around the world alone, yet no one wanted to support him. He had been thoroughly upstaged by Knox-Johnston, Crowhurst, and Moitessier. In early February 1972, wearing women's lingerie, his hands tied behind his back, Tetley was found dead in the woods of Dover, hanging from a tree. Suicide seems most likely, but the coroner could not be certain.

Knox-Johnston wrote his own book, too, of course. In *A World of My Own* (1969) he described how he kept calm and got on with it despite his slow wooden boat and multiple gear failures. Early in the trip, Knox-Johnston had to dive into the ocean to re-caulk and nail copper over seams that were leaking water into the hull from both sides near the keel. While Knox-Johnston was on deck resting, a large shark swam over and began circling his boat. Knox-Johnston wrote that he dispatched the animal with a single bullet to its head. When no other sharks appeared, he resumed his underwater repair.

Another day, after passing the Cape of Good Hope, he was doing some routine maintenance when battery acid splashed into one of his eyes. It didn't come to this—he flushed the eye with water and bandaged it for some time—but he wrote that he was willing to go blind in one eye to achieve this first for England.

*A World of My Own* is like Chichester's narrative in that it was primarily interested in technical descriptions and patriotic heroism. More than a fifth of Knox-Johnston's onboard library, the list of which he published in an appendix, were books about oceanic natural history—field guides on fish, whales, birds, and two books by Rachel Carson—but his story as told was less interested in marine life beyond providing the flavor of his pelagic locations. Divorced at the time (he and his wife would later reunite) and the father of a young child, he did, however, pause with an awareness of giving something else to the larger world. This came out in a moment on Christmas Day in 1968, sailing in the Southern Ocean, during which he lamented that he would not be able to listen to the Queen's speech. As he dined on steak, potatoes, peas, and currant duff, he compared his voyage to that of NASA's *Apollo 8* expedition after hearing about it on the radio, a moment quite similar to that felt by Sharon Sites Adams several months later, as she approached California after crossing the North Pacific. Knox-Johnston felt the space program contributed to scientific knowledge more broadly, something his voyage did not. But then he dismissed this idea of a broader good with the tone of the hero at the pub—with a shot of Davison-like candor:

> True, once Chichester had shown that this trip was possible, I could not accept that anyone but a Briton should be the first to do it, and I wanted to be that Briton. But nevertheless to my mind there was still an element of selfishness in it. My

mother, when asked her opinion of the voyage before I sailed, had replied that she considered it 'totally irresponsible' and on this Christmas Day I began to think she was right. I was sailing round the world simply because I bloody well wanted to—and, I realized, I was thoroughly enjoying myself.

For the record, I do not believe Francis Chichester, Robin Knox-Johnston, or any of these awe-inspiring single-handed mariners fabricated much if any of their major acts of almost ludicrous, stunningly impressive bravery and seamanship. I do believe, however, that they thought to themselves before, say, diving into the water after the shark's blood had dissipated: *this will make a good story.*

Peter Nichols, who wrote the excellent account of this first Golden Globe race, titled *A Voyage for Madmen* (2001), had himself attempted a single-handed trans-Atlantic crossing and then later wrote about it in his narrative *Sea Change.* Nichols was the one who wrote about sea jellies reflecting human existence. Highly capable and experienced, he had nearly made it across, but a few days from Bermuda, swaths of the outer laminate of his wooden hull peeled away and the caulking spilled out. His boat began to leak beyond repair or any human ability to pump. He imagined Knox-Johnston diving to replace his caulking, but this would be ten times the job. As Nichols was choosing what to bring with him from his sinking boat, gathering the pages of the draft of his novel, he wrote: "I yearn to write something great and wonderful." Throughout *Sea Change* his boat is an overt symbol of his relationship with his first true love, his ex-wife with whom he had purchased, repaired, and sailed the boat—but who he had recently abandoned. Both their relationship and their boat had been falling apart over time.

Do I think that Peter Nichols was reflecting on how metaphorically appropriate this was, how sadly perfect his sinking boat was for his future book, even as he was stepping up the ladder onto the merchant ship that had answered his mayday? I do.

I do not think, however, there is anything unethical or false in this. Aren't we all doing this at some level all the time, always imagining an audience? It is part of that fair, old question: can you be a storyteller and be pure of endeavor at the same time? Is an adventurer, athlete, activist, politician, or even a social worker or teacher to be considered compromised, less "true," if they know from the start that they are going to create something from it, craft some form of art or research project or any other form of creative or scholarly expression? Solo sailors present an exceptionally compelling case study in this fluidity of experience and art and story, because there is so long a tradition of the ancient mariner's sea stories. There is no one to confirm the tale. For singlehanders the stakes are often life and death, and the remains and the reality of a death are almost always unrecoverable and unknown. We will never know if Slocum's *Spray* really did steer itself so well, if he did in fact escape pirates, or even how or when he died. "The sea is trackless, the sea is without explanations," wrote the novelist Alessandro Baricco in 1993, lines written and spoken and painted and photographed and sung in slightly different ways by thousands of people over millennia before him and to be expressed for millennia to come. Put another way, it's often quoted that the novelist

Gabriel García Márquez once said: "Fiction was invented the day Jonah arrived home and told his wife that he was three days late because he had been swallowed by a whale."

Donald Crowhurst, the person who entered the 1968 Golden Globe race with minimal offshore experience then faked his voyage and killed himself, seemed to have always been putting on an act since childhood. He was an amateur thespian in his town, performing in several plays. Before he left for the non-stop circumnavigation he was telling sailing stories to reporters that had never happened to him. Once at sea, as the months wore on and he floated alone in the South Atlantic, he steadily grew less and less stable due to the stress and solitude, however self-inflicted. He created in his logbooks and records and films a fictionalized depiction of his voyage, a new reality based on his previous readings of other sailors and what he was living, as he was living it. He went as far as writing a romantic poem to the Southern Ocean even though he was not even sailing in that part of the world. Chichester's *Gipsy Moth Circles the World* was one of the few sailing narratives that Crowhurst brought aboard with him. Nicholas Tomalin and Ron Hall found passages in Crowhurst's journals and recordings that are nearly identical to those of Chichester's, perhaps cribbed unconsciously. The journalists considered the possibility that Crowhurst even play-acted his own madness, but concluded after consulting psychiatrists that it was too well performed to be unreal. The stress and isolation had sent him into a suicidal mania.

Consider the case of Bas Jan Ader. Only a few years after Moitessier's masterpiece, in 1975 the Dutch artist, photographer, and conceptual performer, who had built his reputation using himself as a subject doing physical stunts or emotional displays, cast off from the coast of Massachusetts

Donald Crowhurst posing on board his boat *Teignmouth Electron* months
before leaving for the Golden Globe race (1969).

in a tiny pocket day-sailer that was only 12.5 feet long. Ader
was thirty-three years old: tall, thin, with a big, endearing
smile. He planned to sail alone that summer to Europe to
complete a show scheduled to run in Amsterdam. He had
been putting together a display titled "In Search of Something Miraculous," part of which he had already shown in
Los Angeles. During this first installation some of his art
students wore black and sang sea ballads. "A life on the ocean
wave," they sang, "a home on the rolling deep!" Photographs
from his trip aboard his boat *Ocean Wave* were presumably to
be placed in the center of his show after he arrived.

Ader had had some experience at sea before the trip. Prior
to art school in Los Angeles, he had crossed the Atlantic and
traveled through the Panama Canal as a crew member. His
biographer Alexander Dumbadze saw Ader's voyage this

way: "He wanted to make a masterpiece, desperately. He figured, well, look, I can't lose. Either I cross and I'm in the
Guinness Book of Records, and/or I die—and you know
what, it will be a phenomenal piece of work."

About nine months after Bas Jan Ader cast off, in April
1976, a Spanish trawler near Ireland found *Ocean Wave* floating vertically, covered in gooseneck barnacles, the type that
only grow on floating things at sea after months at very low
speed. The Spanish Navy saw stress on the waterboards,
suggesting, maybe, that Ader had been clipped in and was
thrown out in big seas somewhere. No one knows how far
he got. He did not have a radio with him. Any journal or film
Ader made was never recovered. One of the fishermen
snapped photographs of *Ocean Wave* when it was first found.
Then someone stole the boat from the Spanish captain's
shed before Ader's wife and his brother could see it and con-
duct any further forensics. In Ader's locker at the art school,
friends found a copy of *The Strange Last Voyage of Donald
Crowhurst*.

Ader's widow, Mary Sue Andersen, stated confidently,
painfully, over and again, that Bas Jan never intended to die
as art: he was not staging his death. Still, many clung to this
idea during the years after. Or said that Ader was still alive
somewhere, with secret plans to re-emerge in the ultimate
work of performance art: reincarnation.

Bernard Moitessier left Plymouth, England, in August 1968,
a few months after the assassination of Martin Luther King, Jr.,

after the "May 68" demonstration-strikes in France, and a few months before the release of the Beatles' *White Album*. In 1968, Andy Warhol, the pop artist who so famously mixed celebrity, life, and art, oversaw his first solo show in mainland Europe.

Moitessier's narrative of his non-stop solo trip around the world, *The Long Way* (1971), starts off in a similar fashion to so many of the other single-handed sea stories before his: at his departure from the dock. What Moitessier does uniquely from the first paragraph, however, is that he expresses himself in the present tense. This subtle style choice, a form more common in French literary writing, is a significant representation of his declared mindset as a sailor.

Aboard *Joshua*, Moitessier sails out of Plymouth in a scene in which he sounds, at least to twenty-first-century readers, like a selfish jerk. He speaks with great feeling for his fellow single-handers, but as he is sailing away, he writes that he says to his wife, who is crying: "Don't give me the blues at a time like this." He compares himself to a "tame seagull" who simply needs to go to sea from time to time.

As he sails south toward Madeira, riding in the Canary Current, Moitessier gives some brief back story on his entrance in the Golden Globe race. Implicitly, his identification with a seabird is his *why-go*. He simply needs to be alone on the open sea for parts of his life. Seabirds, as well as dolphins, are major characters in Moitessier's narrative during his voyage. He anthropomorphizes marine life, to be sure: the ocean animals guide him spiritually and directly, but he does not give them human names like Blue Bill or Freddy Flying Fish. In his logbook intended for publication Crowhurst gave his animals storybook names such as "Desmond the Doddery Dorado," a dolphinfish that he wrote was eventually eaten by a shark, and "Peter the Prior," a seabird, perhaps a tern, which ate flying fish off his deck. (Crowhurst later wrote in one of his logbooks a short story titled "The Misfit," about finding a weak land bird on the boat—with overt parallels to his own personal state.) Moitessier in contrast does not name his animals at all, yet as he sails on he describes himself growing more animal-like, seeing himself closer in behavior and intuition to the truly pelagic life of the ocean.

Like Slocum with *Spray*, Moitessier also sails in brotherhood with his beloved vessel, feeling his boat as a living, breathing being. Unlike any Western sailor-writer before him, however, Moitessier depicts himself sailing within, as part of, the very breath of the sea and sky and sun. Regarding the challenge of sailing the Southern Ocean, the most dangerous seas in the most distant inhospitable places for human life, he contrasts sailors with geographers: "A great cape, for us, can't be expressed in longitude and latitude alone. A great cape has a soul, with very soft, very violent shadows and colours. A soul as smooth as a child's, as hard as a criminal's. And that is why we go."

Moitessier makes exceptionally good time heading south in the Atlantic. He knows his boat. He has learned lessons from his last big trip, notably about what to bring and what to leave on the dock. His *Joshua* is prepared to be knocked flat and flipped over. He can steer it from a little steel turret cockpit. His deck is clean of gear and lashings, of nearly any electronics or any bells and whistles, even almost entirely absent of any wood that could rot or need varnish. His self-steering system is simple, hand-built, and long-practiced. Before he leaves, he offloads hundreds of pounds of unnecessary weight. As the voyage progresses he continues to fling things over the side that he deems no longer useful: gear, food, fuel, repair cement (after he clears the region of possible icebergs), anything that he knows he no longer needs in order to help his boat sail more freely, lighter, in better trim. As he flings things merrily overboard, he makes no comment about non-biodegradable garbage.

Continuing south, Moitessier observes the flying fish that signal tropical waters, eats them with gusto, and watches them preyed upon by dolphinfish, which he also captures and eats, drying their flesh in the rigging. He writes of one moment where a barracuda, leaping out of the water, captures a flying fish in mid-air, even adjusting itself above the surface to snatch its prey. Moitessier does not observe marine life in conversation with other sailors—there is no competitive ecology here. His tone is closer to that of Pidgeon at the end of his voyage, but with far more detail and book learning. Moitessier writes not of how he is consulting field guides, but how he is reading more thematic books such as Jean Dorst's *Avant que nature meure* (*Before Nature Dies*, 1965), a global overview of humanity's negative impact on natural systems and species, which Moitessier describes: "All our earth's beauty . . . all the havoc we wreak on it." Moitessier records what he sees on the ocean, lovingly, more often raising questions, occasionally using Darwinian phrases such as when regarding the flying fish and their "struggle for life," but he also writes in the same breath like Slocum, with a near-religious belief in a master spiritual system, wondering about predation and the lives of defenseless prey, the tons of crustaceans killed in one gulp by a whale: this "must have some purpose."

While still writing of his passage outbound in the Atlantic, Moitessier in *The Long Way* further distinguishes himself from previous narratives in his discussions of weather and oceanography. Moitessier uses pilot charts and weather reports, like the others, but he speaks in far more detail about currents, wind patterns, ocean depths, wave directions, and low- and high-pressure systems, all carefully and well explained to his lay audience. His voice is one of long experience, but also humility. In an appendix, Moitessier makes clear that the ocean's weather and sea states are too variable and complex for full human knowledge. "The sea will always remain the great unknown," he says. "It is sometimes enormous without being too vicious; not as high a week or a month later, it can become very dangerous because of either cross-swells, or an unexpected or completely new factor. The person who can write a really good book on the sea is probably not yet born, or else is already senile, because one would have to sail a hundred years to know it well enough."

Arriving off the Cape of Good Hope, Moitessier wants to report himself safe and to send home photographs of his logbook pages and rolls of film. He uses a slingshot—a skill he learned as a boy in Vietnam—to zip messages in cannisters onto the decks of passing ships. As he tells it, he gets too greedy here and the merchant ship steers too close. The collision badly bends *Joshua*'s steel bowsprit. In the following days Moitessier manages to pull the spar back into place by cleverly using a tackle rigged through an outboard block on the staysail boom then led back aft to a winch.

Once clear of Good Hope and his *Joshua* repaired, Moitessier enters the Indian Ocean, which he believes to be the most treacherous in the world. He enters a new phase of connection to the sea.

If Chichester's classic feels at times to modern readers a bit too technical and stiffly performed, Moitessier's masterpiece, in its own way, feels over-acted in its evocation of the author's spiritual relationship with an oceanic natural world. One almost expects Moitessier to move into a discussion of healing crystals and essential oils with language, at least in translation, that would make Ann Davison gag. Moitessier builds this all up slowly in *The Long Way*, increasing, opening, as he travels farther and farther from shore into more desolate seas, physically and metaphorically, with several references to Hemingway's fictional character Santiago, the old man who ventures too far into the ocean and to the limits of his endurance when searching for a big fish that means far more.

"I wonder if my apparent lack of fatigue," Moitessier writes as he scuds eastwards in the Indian Ocean, "could be a kind of hypnotic trance born of contact with this great sea, giving off so many pure forces, rustling with the ghosts of all the beautiful sailing ships that died around here and now escort us. I am full of life, like the sea I contemplate so intensely. I feel it watching me as well, and that we are nonetheless friends."

Heading toward Australia, staying north of any threat of ice and the highest of winds, Moitessier finds weather more temperate than he expected, if at the expense of a loss of speed. He begins to study yoga at sea, sometimes practicing naked on deck and absorbing the sun. Although his hair and beard grow long and matted, he's amazed that he never needs to wash with soap; his skin remains perfectly clear. Between sail changes and light maintenance, he drinks coffee, smokes cigarettes, drinks an occasional glass of wine. He reads books. He watches and watches and watches the ocean and the birds. His self-steering gear is always working well. He shoots video footage, writes and sketches in his journal. He fishes. He takes sun sights for navigation.

Bernard Moitessier's photograph of himself doing yoga aboard *Joshua* during the 1968–9 Golden Globe race.

Although Moitessier presents himself in *The Long Way* as more of a hippie cruiser than a racer, he is traveling far faster than Knox-Johnston and faster even than did Chichester. At his sailing school in the Mediterranean, eager to convey the need to watch the swells and the wind direction, he shunned compasses in his navigation teachings. In *The Long Way* he speaks highly of the traditional navigation of his mentors in Southeast Asia. He is in practice no less exacting and careful than Knox-Johnston or Chichester, nor does he shun most modern technologies. Moitessier has been a devoted reader of previous narratives, such as Slocum, Pidgeon, John Voss, Conor O'Brien, and Vito Dumas, all of whom he credits. Before the trip he corresponded with as many Cape Horn captains as he could, including commercial mariners who had sailed in the Southern Ocean. In his lengthy appendix he includes information that might distract from his present-tense spiritual story, meticulously detailing his choices of rigging, paint, anti-rust systems, different metals, sail-stitching methods, food, types of socks and boots, all of his small and large lessons, which he openly shares without a didactic or definitive tone. Moitessier navigated with celestial navigation and dead reckoning, using a wristwatch and a chronometer that he checked regularly with his one-way radio, everything dutifully written out. When he could hear weather reports over the radio, he recorded them on a tape cassette so he could play them back and work out the long-term trends. He incorporated all this into a more sensory experience of his voyage and his day-to-day practice: "Now I listen for the threat of a gale in the cirrus and the sounds of the sea."

In the relative calms of the Indian Ocean, Moitessier writes of sharks, how he does not fear them exactly, though he is always quick to be ready to get out of the water. Sharks, he explains, are usually just curious, not aggressive—that is, except for the big ones. Moitessier does not pull out a gun to shoot at them.

Moitessier watches albatrosses, cape pigeons, and what he calls "cape robins," a type of petrel he is unable to identify. He writes of the variability in plumage of seabirds and their flight patterns, and how birds in the deep Southern Ocean are less social than those of the temperate or tropical regions, like the tropicbirds and frigatebirds. These Southern Ocean birds, he writes, are constantly seeking, searching, earnest, which he sees as like himself. Moitessier grows especially close to a flock of shearwaters that learn to recognize his call. Each day he feeds the shearwaters butter, paté, and dried dolphinfish. The birds grow so familiar that at the end of his time in light airs before Cape Leeuwin, he feeds a couple of shearwaters out of his hand.

Now into the full wind and waves of the Southern Ocean, continuing under the continent of Australia, Moitessier pauses off the coast of Tasmania to pass letters and a package of film to a few fishermen that he happens to see near port. From here he continues below Aotearoa New Zealand and begins the haul across the broad Southern Ocean of the Pacific on the way to Cape Horn. He writes that he is feeling secrets between his boat and himself, connections that cannot be captured on film: sounds, realizations, and internal expansions in his conversations with the ocean that is leading him to existential, personal truths. He is reading John Steinbeck, Romain Gary, and Antoine de Saint-Exupéry. He writes without any direct reference to Crowhurst—the reality of which he knew by the time he sat down to write *The Long Way*—but Moitessier recognizes that he too sails on the thin edge of sanity.

On his approach to Cape Horn, now having spent over five months alone at sea with only two brief shouted conversations across the rail to other mariners on boats off Good Hope and Tasmania, he witnesses and details a display of the Aurora Australis, the most beautiful thing he says he has ever seen. He is reaching the outer reaches of the sublime. Rounding Cape Horn, *Joshua* sails fast, surfing down large seas, at times at the edge of his control. A full moon lights the evening from behind the clouds, painting the entire sea luminous, its reflection mixing with bioluminescence in the water and the sparkling night-time spray on his sails as the bowsprit plunges ahead. Moitessier forgets himself as he becomes part of the scene, standing on the windward side, clipped in and holding on to his mainmast and the main halyard, like an Odysseus before starry sirens. His story is at a physical climax. The northwest wind whooshes across from Patagonia. He searches to sense the seaweed and the ice. He needs to remind himself not to go stand on the bowsprit, to cinch his hood back on his head so his ears don't freeze. But he wants to feel everything. He wishes he could be barefoot. At one point, standing on deck as *Joshua* hurls down seas that are laced with moonlit froth, his body becomes so relaxed, he feels so out of his physical self, that he does not even notice until afterward that he has urinated down his leg into his boot.

Moitessier loses himself in the dangerous beauty of this passage, describing droplets of sea spray as jewelry on the sails. *Joshua* crashes through mists and surfs down the icy seas around phosphorescent orbs of "plankton colonies" that appear to him like the eyes of giant squids. He admits that he has gone too far. He should reduce sail, but everything is humming. He wants to get beyond Cape Horn as fast as possible. He writes (his punctuation):

A gust. This time *Joshua* luffs with more heel. The bowsprit buries itself and solid water roars across the deck. I grip the stay hard. The little wind vane is still there. It must have been dunked in the sea when we heeled, but did not break. I blow it a kiss.

A sea approaches, fairly high, all light at the summit, black below . . . and vrooouuum . . . the keel hardly wavers in the 20 or 25 yards. A great plume shoots up on either side of the bow, climbs high, filled with swirls which the wind throws down into the staysail, and some into the storm jib.

I listen. One surfing run taken the wrong way in the clear night . . . and my beautiful bird of the capes would go on her way with the ghosts in the foam, guided by a seagull or a porpoise. I am not sure which I would prefer, a gull or a porpoise.

*Joshua* drives toward the Horn under the light of the stars and the somewhat distant tenderness of the moon. Pearls run off the staysail; you want to hold them in your hand, they are real precious stones, that live only in the eyes.

At the height of this glory, Bernard Moitessier and his *Joshua* weather Cape Horn.

In the days to follow, hungover from his last great cape, he sails, spent and fatigued, up to the Falkland Islands in the hopes of leaving film and letters and assuring his family that he is okay. He slows down past the lighthouse there and hopes to encounter a boat or ship of some kind. But it is a

Sunday. He is too tired to risk steering in towards the harbor, so he continues on up north into the South Atlantic.

He is seen, however. The lighthouse-keeper reports him back to London. At this point, Moitessier is only a couple of weeks behind Robin Knox-Johnston and gaining fast. Based on these few positions, reporters in England predict a neck-and-neck finish for the first one home, the claim for the winner's country to be the first person in history to accomplish this Everest-of-the-ocean challenge. All believe that Moitessier is sure to win the money for the fastest time even if he doesn't finish first—unless Tetley and Crowhurst can continue their speeds. Moitessier knows none of this, having only heard from the Tasmanian fishermen something uncertain about an Englishman who had passed by weeks earlier.

As Moitessier sails up into the South Atlantic, toward calmer, safer waters, he finds himself conflicted, even afraid of returning to the materialism of Europe. He wants to see his wife, his stepchildren, his mother who is growing old, but the return to France feels to him like giving up. In *The Long Way*, the story of the voyage, he has been teasing out this longer mission to keep going, to ignore the race and the return to Plymouth, to keep sailing all the way back to the South Pacific, another full two-thirds around the globe, but these hints are only clear if you know already what is going to happen. In a story-telling strategy used by Horie and Chichester to infuse authenticity, in *The Long Way* Moitessier includes a photograph of a page from his onboard journal, in which he scribbles the existential climax of his masterpiece: "I have set course for the Pacific again."

Moitessier admits to benefitting from the technologies of modern society, but he cannot accept the modern world, "the Monster," which is "destroying our earth, and trampling the soul of men." He has been debating, wavering, and then he finally leaves it up to the winds, the seas, to tell him which direction to go. To answer, the winds blow favorably toward South Africa. While Moitessier sits cross-legged and naked in the cockpit, a white fairy tern, the same species of bird that once welcomed Slocum to Cocos Keeling from his passage across the Indian Ocean, lands on Bernard's knee. He writes that with its large black eyes the seabird tells him a fable about how the people on the ship of life have grown fat, have accepted mediocrity and ugliness. The ship of the world is headed for disaster. The people don't heed the word of the barefooted sailors. The captain is just waiting for a miracle, "but he has forgotten that a miracle is only born if men create it themselves, out of their own being."

Moitessier includes his own cartoon of a fairy tern with his boat, the sea, the sun, and an island. This is an illustration motif that he apparently used regularly in his letters and to sign his books. The drawing is etched onto his gravestone.

Bernard Moitessier's drawing of a fairy tern and his boat in his narrative *The Long Way* (1971).

He makes his decision that spring of 1969. In one of the most profound single acts of performance art in recorded history, a couple of months before Neil Armstrong's one step on the moon, from the deck of *Joshua* Bernard Moitessier flings with a slingshot a cannister that lands on the deck of a ship off Cape Town, South Africa, perfectly named *British Argosy*. Addressed to the *Sunday Times* newspaper, the message inside reads: "The Horn was rounded February 5, and today is March 18. I am continuing nonstop towards the Pacific Islands because I am happy at sea, and perhaps also to save my soul."

Off Cape Town, Moitessier also dispatched a jug filled with still and movie film, cassette tapes, and letters—enough he believed to make the book if something happened to him. He continued sailing alone, across the Indian Ocean again, under Australia and Aotearoa New Zealand again, another halfway around the globe and on to French Polynesia, where he tied up at last in Tahiti and set foot on land for the first time in ten months. Meanwhile, the newspapers in Europe had exploded with the news. His wife was mobbed for comment. She told the press that she was pleased that Bernard had his full freedom.

Once in Tahiti, Moitessier began work on writing *The Long Way*. It took him two years to finish. He donated the royalties to the Pope, to distribute as he wished to better the world. Uncharacteristic of most of these solo captain stories, *The Long Way* does not end when he ties up to the dock in Tahiti.

Moitessier's story continues further to explain how his fellow sailors were distressed by the cutting down of trees to make a waterfront highway in Papeete. He wrote of how good it would be if the cities and towns of the world began to plant more fruit trees—for the food, the shade, and the symbolism. From the dock in Tahiti, he wrote of the ailing human race, of "robot-man," the "Corporate State," the machines that must keep making new roads and buildings in order to reproduce, that people are swarming all over the earth on a "suicide tack."

Fruit trees became a major cause for Moitessier for the rest of his life. He wrote hundreds of letters to world leaders, town leaders, and he teamed up with environmentalists when he could. The Vatican never claimed the royalties, so he offered to send funds privately to any community that wanted to plant fruit trees. Only a couple of small towns in France took him up on the offer.

Moitessier mostly remained in French Polynesia at first. He remarried, they had a son, and the family spent three years living and planting on a remote atoll, trying to bring in a new type of sustainable agriculture and to raise their child in a simple way close to nature. Occasionally, French filmmakers came to him wanting to write about his exploits or to make documentaries about him, but Moitessier was particular about his messaging. He demanded that in interviews the topics of fruit trees and nuclear disarmament be the main points of discussion.

When the island experiment fizzled out, he and his young family sailed to San Francisco. But the United States disappointed him. He was not able to make a living there. In 1982, at fifty-seven years old, Moitessier left his second wife and son in San Francisco for a time to head south on *Joshua* again.

Here his boat wrecked in a hurricane while at anchor off the coast of Mexico. He built a new boat, a smaller one, and returned to Polynesia. In 1986, Moitessier returned to France where he worked for several years on a fourth and final book, a memoir, reaching back to his childhood in Vietnam.

Bernard Moitessier died in 1994 in France. He lived to see *Joshua* refurbished and donated to the Maritime Museum of La Rochelle, where it still lives and is sailed by devotees.

# 16. Landlessness, Loneliness, Death Wish

After weeks without seeing any land or any other people, the mental and physical fatigue begins to wear. All told, I have spent well over two full years of my life out at sea before this trip, so I feel comfortable within 360 degrees of water and sky, even crave this when ashore, but I have never been out on the open ocean by myself or even with any real final responsibility on a boat before. So for this crossing aboard *Fox*, daily anxiety is my struggle.

One day I hear a creaking from the joint where the tiller meets the rudder stock. The rudder stock is a long bronze bar that runs from the tiller down through the floor of the cockpit, then when underwater is strapped and fiberglassed to the forward edge of the rudder and connected by bronze hinges to the hull. I put my ear to the tiller, to the cockpit, and it sounds like something might be seriously wrong down there. The rudder on *Fox* is tucked far underneath the boat, so I can't lean over the rail to look. Over the winter before I left, a friend of a friend fiberglassed over the wood rudder for me, but I don't know for sure how good a job she did, and I had hemmed and hawed over whether I should replace it. I had thought, too, about having the metal-shop guy cut and bend me a brand-new rudder stock. One expert thought I should, but it was so expensive, and I was running out of time. When another guy thought the old one should be fine, I just reinstalled it all with new hinges and plenty of underwater adhesive. Because I had done the work myself for the first time, I don't trust it.

As the hours go by, it seems that the creaking sound increases. When I try to sleep I can hear it even louder in the cabin. Is the bronze stock itself cracked? Is it going to snap? Maybe the rudder is separating from the stock. I spend a lot of time, somewhat academically, wondering if the rudder pulls off, will it float or sink? I begin to make plans as to how to rig my harness so I can dive down and look at the rudder underwater, but I worry about sharks. I'm no Robin Knox-Johnston. I read up on emergency rudder systems, how I might use Sandy for emergency steering. The hours wear on. This goes on for two days. I am certain that the creaking is getting louder. When I tack, change course, it feels that the boat is not responding quite as well as before. Or is that my imagination? I check the bilges for rising water. If the screws for the hinges pull out, will the hull leak? I try to remember the length of the screws, the thickness of the fiberglass at the back edge.

It's the dawn of the third day of this, a hot sweaty light-air morning.

I cannot sleep.

I'm lying there listening to the deathly creaking, when inspired out of nowhere, by what I'm not sure, a small idea flickers: I grab a little container of all-purpose A-1 oil. I clip in, step up into the cockpit, and drip the red nozzle into the bolts of the joint where the stock meets the tiller. The creaking stops almost immediately. Everything is fine.

These sorts of moments are funny in retrospect, but I don't recall laughing then. I was too worried. I found something else to stress about immediately after my initial sigh of relief. If I discovered anything about myself on this passage, it was that I can emit truly animal-like sounds of frustration: mental strain that desperately wanted to find an exclamation point of breaking something—but I knew even at the heights of this that I had to hold my fist. Smashing something or a part of myself so far away from shore could only create a much larger problem. Above my portable potty was a cupboard door that didn't yet have a method to latch open, so when I needed to get something inside that cupboard during heavy weather, when I didn't have a free hand with the hull rocking steeply, this wooden door would swing and slam against the bulkhead in such an ear-splitting manner that I once held the little varnished thing with both hands and screamed, raged, so angry that I wanted to rip it off at the hinges, bite it, bash it over my knee, throw it overboard. I shrieked at its wood slat face. It was not a quick flash of profanity, either, but a fist-clenched deranged Jack Nicholson horror-movie red-faced harangue.

It was after spells like this that I empathized with Donald Crowhurst and wondered if stress can indeed induce psychosis. Experts have since explained to me that, yes, of course, this can happen. Consider victims of torture or wartime trauma. My trials, of course, were nothing compared to those. For starters, I had chosen to do this.

Over the five weeks of my Atlantic crossing, at least as I remember it, I was fortunate to never have been truly afraid in any dramatic way, even in the gales and rough weather. I mean, I never had any major gear failure, personal injury, dismasting, rogue wave, knockdown, or flooding, or any sort of

*I'm about to die* moment. In truth, aside from what happened the day before arriving in Portugal, my trip was rather uneventful. This was certainly how I wanted it. My daily anxiety was more a nagging, constant concern, the stress of hyper-vigilance—checking every part of the boat, lubricating, planning for emergency scenarios—perpetual paranoia for too long a period of time and all darkened by deepening sleep deprivation since I rarely slept for more than one or two hours at a time. In retrospect, I totally mismanaged my sleep. This resulted in poor decision-making, dramatic emotional swings, and a fluid dream-like state unlike anything I've ever experienced before or since. On this trans-Atlantic passage I never felt truly suicidal, but I'd be lying if I didn't admit to occasionally fantasizing a final, intentional step over the side at a few points during my crossing—although, to be honest, I do so every time I'm at sea whether I'm alone or not. Sharon Sites Adams admitted in *Pacific Lady* that she felt this, too.

I like to think that if I had stuck with single-handing and gathered the experience of multiple solo passages over the years with *Fox* I would have reduced the anxiety. At the dock in Portugal I met this lovely young couple, English sailors who had been fixing up traditional wooden boats and sailing around Europe. The boats they refurbished were their homes and their business. They invited me to sail in tandem with them up to Cornwall. They said they would help me find a place to store the boat, fix the engine, and so on. I often wonder, sometimes wistfully, even longingly, where I'd be now if I'd taken them up on that. Would I have kept on sailing alone around the world from there?

"Sailing is a compromise between distance covered and mounting fatigue, for both crew and boat," Bernard Moitessier wrote in *The Long Way*, "and fatigue can snowball fast."

The single-hander must relentlessly make decisions about how or whether to fix something that has broken or when to alter course based on weather predictions, how to prioritize what to worry about. For an example of poorly executed planning, as I began to recognize that I was having trouble with my Atomic 4 engine, I thought it would be prudent to head south and stop in the Azores to fix it. So I turned the boat southeast. But I began to read over and again in my books about the Azores High, an enormous high-pressure system where there can be no wind for hundreds of miles. That got me worried, ironically, about being stuck becalmed with no engine, so then the next day I changed my mind abruptly and sailed northeasterly again. I had no one with whom to talk through these things. I often did not think clearly and made illogical decisions.

I did know then and realize now even more since I've been conducting this study, that compared to solo trans-Atlantic passages like Ann Davison's, I could whine about nothing in terms of isolation from human contact.

First of all, I was comfortable in knowing where I was in the world. I had had some experience with celestial navigation beforehand, but I hadn't realized how difficult it is with the motion on a tiny boat. I'm embarrassed to admit that I really only took sextant sights on a few calm days. I have a beautiful sextant that was a generous surprise gift from a group of friends years earlier, but mostly on this trip it lived wedged on a shelf in its lovely varnished box with the little brass dedication plaque near the handle. I did a lot of looking at the GPS. I found that I was staring at this too much, actually—monitoring my distance covered, speed over the ground, and distance still to go—so I made rules with myself about checking only every four hours or so. When I lost engine power and was trying to conserve my batteries, I turned my main GPS off entirely and simply navigated with my handheld GPS, which in 2007 was a pixelated black and white device the size of a boxy phone in a yellow case. Since the 1990s, the technologies of GPS and satellite communications have enabled far more single-handers to go to sea and do so more safely, but the technologies have also encouraged a larger portion of mariners to avoid learning or practicing celestial navigation and wayfinding, which surely reduces their spiritual connections and their deeper awareness of the sea, the clouds, and the movement of the solar system. I used a paper chart, kept track of my dead reckoning, but I relied on that little electronic box far more than I would have liked. Bernard Moitessier would have been disappointed in me.

Second, my perception of helplessness and isolation was greatly reduced because of my ability to hear and contact people ashore. I had a working VHF radio to talk to ships if they came within twenty miles or so and to get weather forecasts when I was in range of the coast. On my portable multi-band radio I listened to long-range weather forecasts when I could dial them in, and on that radio I listened to international stations. Once I could no longer listen to a women's book-club radio show from Nova Scotia, I was able to pick up an English-language news hour from China, even in the very middle of the North Atlantic. As I approached Europe and was standing watch at night, I was thrilled to be able to dial in the BBC, including their coastal weather report, as well as a terrific *classique* rock 'n' roll station from Paris. Because my supply of AA batteries was not bottomless, I couldn't listen to this radio all the time, but the voices provided a great deal of information and companionship, not to mention some necessary perspective. When I was having trouble with things on the boat, they paled in comparison to the deaths of the unlucky victims of the Minneapolis bridge collapse or the lives of HIV/AIDS orphans in Tanzania, two of the major stories on the radio during the summer of my crossing.

In addition to buying the GPS and the radio, I rented at absurd expense in a blur of credit-card delusion a satellite phone on which I got daily forecast texts from a weather service. I could speak to someone at this service with this phone every three to five days if I wanted. On this satellite phone I talked to my partner Lisa nearly every day for around two minutes. We knew that the phone breaking or any kind of missed call could set off unnecessary concerns on either side, but we decided it was worth the risk and the expense. Lisa has never said this, but I know those daily phone calls were a burden on her, both emotionally and logistically. The satellite phone was also there for a real emergency. I could make a call for help.

Beginning in the 1960s, solo-sailing narratives began to include anecdotes recounting difficult or failed attempts to make a radio or phone call while at sea. Francis Chichester is constantly lamenting time, energy, and ship's power wasted trying to make a call, causing anxiety both for him and those ashore. Robin Lee Graham in the late 1960s, deeply in love and regularly torn apart from his new wife, was often crushed under still more intense loneliness while at sea when a radio contact with her failed or was too faint. In 1979, Naomi James wrote a description of trying to reach her new husband from her boat in the distant Southern Ocean. The connection was terrible, she had to shout to be heard, so they agreed to try again in twenty-four hours. "I was frustrated at not being able to say more than a simple hello and good-bye, and for the rest of the day remained restless and worried in case something prevented me from speaking to him the next day." In so many of these stories the single-hander details the technological failures, the timing, and the stress for them and those on land when the connections get dropped or missed. This usually makes for droll reading, but most sailor-writers cannot resist recounting these failed communications for good reason: they often involve their safety, and these calls anchor their mental health and safety. Once anticipated, it can feel crucial to the solo sailor to make contact. The satellite phone and now the internet, both still exceptionally expensive out at sea, provide emotional comfort, safety, weather, anchorage information, and gear assistance. But they also reduce the sailor's focus on the sea and their self-reliant endeavor, which was supposedly why so many went out there in the first place.

Neal Petersen, a solo circumnavigator in the 1990s, put it succinctly: "Modern technology had put an end to the isolation of solo sailing. No longer was I truly alone, and, with no desperate drama to survive, the highlight of every day became my five- to ten-minute telephone chat with [my girlfriend] Gwen."

Every evening after I finished the call with Lisa, I placed the satellite phone back in its black foam, clicking it shut in the yellow waterproof case that I kept beside my red "ditch bag," to grab them both if *Fox* was suddenly sinking. I normally then went back on deck and did dinner dishes, sloshing the single pot over the side. I tried to relax and watch the sunset, the licks of color on the trough of each wave. Once the sun went under the horizon, I would toast the night with two sips of whiskey, one splashed over the side for Neptune and one pull from the bottle for me. I had read somewhere (incorrectly as I learned later) that Robin Knox-Johnston did this, which seemed a reasonable way to take the edge off. I kept up that tradition all the way across. Yet whenever that sun went down I still felt the most lonely and nervous, preparing to stay up for most or all of the night to look for ships, bad weather, floating debris, and to make appropriate sail changes. On calm nights while Sandy steered I sat in the cabin hatch, looking forward, watching the stars, and listening for hours to almost anything I could find on the long-range radio.

Over the course of my trans-Atlantic crossing alone, despite having many more technological and physical comforts than previous generations of single-handers, I still experienced all manner of intensities, facets and feelings of loneliness, helplessness, inadequacy, and missing others, such as when I saw something beautiful and wished that I might be able to share it with someone. I also had a common type of loneliness regarding the regular reminder of being so minuscule in the middle of an indifferent ocean under low dark clouds, a landlessness where I might disappear and no one ashore would know how or why or even when exactly. These thoughts all mixed at different moments with the recognition of just how little my, anyone's, existence matters to anything in the scale of the larger forces of space and time as I watched carefully the relative rotation of the sun, the moon, and each night the counter-clockwise movement of the stars around Polaris, all glimmering over the ancient sea horizon.

In the end, though, I had less time than I expected for such thoughts, since my mind was so occupied with real or perceived problems and safety concerns. When I first left Maine I had contacted nearly every ship or boat that I saw to check in on my visibility on their radar and, I think, just to make contact. As I moved beyond the Grand Banks, I saw a ship only every other day or so.

I remember distinctly one morning, right at sunrise. Underneath the main boom, on the horizon ahead of me, just to starboard, the rising sun, a blade of orange, emerged within the dawn. I reached below to grab my sunglasses from their hook. *Fox* was moving well, but with no spray over the bow. When I looked back up I saw the hull of a merchant ship several miles off to port, steaming in the opposite direction, westbound. I picked up my radio to call them but found myself setting the mic back in the bracket, uninterested in any conversation. This was a turning point, a new level of comfort with my aloneness. I recognized this even in the moment.

I never got drunk at sea, whiskey sips aside, although I know others have done so as a way to celebrate, relax, or cope with the anxiety. Moitessier drank full bottles of champagne at Christmas and to mark each passing of the big capes. Horie, after reeling sleepless in an early gale while crossing the North Pacific on his first voyage, decided to get drunk one day to break the strain. In one sitting he alternated "doses" of whisky, red wine, and sake, which forced him to vomit aggressively and then shut his body down to sleep: "The drunkenness tortured me, but it also relieved some of that awful strain on my mind. For a while the loneliness was gone."

Mealtime is a big deal to sailors, and eating well can do a lot to cure boredom and loneliness along with maintaining physical health. On my passage, though, I did not spend a lot of time preparing food, eating mostly cereal with UHT milk and gobbling up snack bars. I made pasta, ramen, and rice that I ate out of a little pot, or I ate canned foods directly out of the can. For cooking I used a simple one-burner stove that was gimballed and that I powered with a little camping propane tank. Although I stored the tanks in the cockpit in a pvc tube, I remained terrified that I was going to blow myself up every time I lit the stove, perhaps igniting any residual gasoline engine fumes trapped below. I've read a story of this happening—a single-hander who severely burned his face and torso and had to jump over the side to extinguish the flames burning his flesh. In other words, food and cooking did little to deter loneliness for me.

Ann Davison in 1956 seems to be the first single-handed author to open up honestly in her narrative about her true daily anxieties. Her reasons for writing in this way surely were wrapped up in the time period, her personality, her being more of an amateur sailor, and perhaps also cultural formations of gender. Less than a decade later, though, Kenichi Horie too was surprisingly candid about his fears and loneliness, as was Sharon Sites Adams. She took Ritalin pills occasionally to help her stay awake and focused, which a psychiatrist friend explained to me might have unintentionally helped with her anxiety. Adams told me that she played the radio all the time—kept it on always—to keep her company.

Writers, on shore and at sea, have often spoken of how the loneliness among crowds in cities is far more acute than when alone in a more natural setting. Tristan Jones, a single-hander from Ireland, wrote: "Being alone is not the same thing as being lonely. I can feel more alone on the New York streets than I ever would in mid-Atlantic." He explained that his connections to friends and family were not always based on vicinity. He had "felt closer to them, alone in mid-ocean, than I sometimes have while being in the same room with them."

Moitessier wrote in *The Long Way* of a companionship with the sea and marine life as a genuinely felt spiritual connection, a feeling of being within, being a part of a watery universe that welcomed him and kept him company. Moitessier is more the exception than the rule, however, and even among Western single-handers he is unique because of his cultural background, his skill as a sailor, and because he voyaged within a narrow technological slot of human history to which he clung. Moitessier's *Joshua* had a steel hull and a self-steering wind vane that worked well, allowing him to spend so many months offshore safely, yet at the start of the Golden Globe race he and another sailor deliberately declined the use of a radio transmitter because of the cumbersome and heavy gear, the drain on electricity, and the distraction. "Our peace of mind, and thereby our safety, was more important," he wrote. Imagine how different might have been Crowhurst's experience if he had had no radio, could not report false positions, and never heard about the progress of the others.

To cope with landlessness and loneliness, Joshua Slocum and Howard Blackburn, for example, wrote about how they gave orders to themselves on deck to keep their voices active.

I can't imagine there are many single-handers who haven't regularly talked out loud to themselves, whether that was to shout a chantey about Mother Carey's chickens or simply to discuss whether or not to set a sail. While Moitessier was fixing his broken bowsprit after his slow-motion collision with the freighter, he imagined a long-time friend of his working beside him on deck, figuring out the problem together. Adams spoke into her tape recorder for her journal, as did Robin Lee Graham, recording entries regularly, more so than on paper. Horie explained that sometimes he talked with himself as if he were two people, one who was lazy and another who was motivated and responsible; the latter would berate the lazy one.

Several single-handers have reported that sickness, sleeplessness, or stress led to full hallucinations. The most famous vision like this among single-handers is the pilot aboard *Spray*. Early on in his circumnavigation, after leaving the Azores, Slocum was ill and doubled over with cramps from eating cheese and plums. Lying in his cabin in heavy weather he wrote that he looked up and saw a piratical Spanish sailor that was the pilot of Columbus' *Pinta*. This man in historical dress steered the boat all night while Slocum slept off the food poisoning. Letters from the voyage reveal that at the time Slocum had been reading Washington Irving's biography of Columbus. Occasionally throughout *Sailing Alone Around the World*, Slocum refers to this pilot helping out on board *Spray*. This was likely in part a literary device and a fun yarn, but I don't doubt that Slocum did indeed hallucinate a flesh and blood figure on deck that night as he clutched his stomach and fell back asleep, nor that he imagined this pilot over the course of his voyage as a sort of personal mascot, a guardian angel at the helm.

Hallucinations at sea seem to inevitably involve the mind

"The Apparition at the Wheel," original illustration for *Sailing Alone Around the World*, depicting Joshua Slocum's hallucination of the pilot of the *Pinta*, by Thomas Fogarty (1900).

conjuring human company or a setting surrounded by people. On his first solo ocean crossing in 1931, Vito Dumas, only recently departed from France and struggling in a storm in the Bay of Biscay, hallucinated about hearing two men in the bow of his little boat for three full days. In hot weather off Gibraltar two decades later, having not slept for about forty-eight hours, Davison imagined two people aboard her boat, too, except in her case one of them took the tiller, sending her down to the cabin: "Obediently I went below and slept till morning." At one point during foul weather, two weeks into the trip, Kenichi Horie imagined a shipmate on board taking the watch while he dozed below one night. Sharon Sites Adams woke up to a soothing voice saying her name during her first single-handed crossing to Hawai'i. Moitessier once hallucinated, likely induced by fatigue and a celebratory bottle of champagne, a clear vision of a giddy man standing at the stern, mocking the Cape of Good Hope as *Joshua* cleared the region. As he was pumping for his life and severely sleep-deprived in the North Atlantic, Neal Petersen, the South African single-handed racer, clearly saw a dead sailor-friend at the helm.

Aboard his tiny *Tinkerbelle* in the North Atlantic in 1965, Robert Manry reported the longest, most extensive hallucinations of anyone I have read. He endured days of confusion that seemed to have been induced by fatigue, anxiety as to his position, and the "stay-awake" or "pep" pills that he swallowed. Once early in the trip he was awake for over forty-eight hours, trying to stay alert in the shipping lanes, when he fantasized a hitchhiker aboard his boat who demanded that he be put ashore on an island of low, blue rocks, which "they" then spent all day zig-zagging around to find. Manry eventually did locate the imaginary rocks and put the hitchhiker ashore with his waiting family and their blue rock house. Manry had read his Slocum and knew of the account of the pilot of the *Pinta*, but his hallucinations were far more ornate and threatening. Another time, for hours in heavy weather as he was trying to get to an imagined place to help his daughter, a Scottish king and a band of "evil-faced, surplice-clad cutthroats" were trying to knock Manry off *Tinkerbelle* with singing that increased the size of the waves. This led further to a lengthy, fantastical journey, a live-dreaming that involved him falling overboard and quickly hurling himself back into the cockpit. Afterwards he had difficulty parsing out what had actually happened: "No MacGregor, [no] sinister choir ... But what about those duckings? Were they hallucinatory, too? Had I or hadn't I been washed overboard four times?"

For my small part, I sometimes had nightmares, vivid acid-trip dreams in which I was conscious enough to try to reach myself inside the dream, if that makes sense, to tear myself out of the scene with an eye-clenching shout to burst out into consciousness. I've had nightmares like that on land before—perhaps you have, too—but I had never before or since had them as developed or as intense. Once during my crossing I dreamt that *Fox* was on fire and that a Satanic man demanded that I flip the switch of the EPIRB then jump overboard. The EPIRB, which stands for Emergency Position-Indicating Radio Beacon, is a device that can be activated manually or will flip itself on when submerged under a certain amount of water, notifying the Coast Guard of a vessel's distress with a boat-specific satellite signal. If I'd flipped that switch a whole set of emergencies would have been set in motion (or at least I operated on the assumption that they would).

More often, though, I had more benign dreams and semi-delusions, what psychologists refer to as "savior"-type dreams rather than the "destroyer"-type described above. I often have odd dreams at sea; many report this, perhaps because of the wave motion, but more often because when you're working at sea, you are woken at odd hours and awake in the middle of your normal cycles. Aboard *Fox* I often dreamed that I was ashore but needed to get back to my boat because I was in the middle of the Atlantic. In my dreams, friends ashore asked what I was doing there, because I was supposed to be on this trip. Once I dreamt that *Fox* was tied up to a parking meter in New York City; I was going to visit my brother. At least twice I dreamed that an experienced captain with whom I had often sailed in previous years was on board to give me advice.

Sandy Van Zandt, the elderly man who helped me set up the self-steering device, appeared most regularly in my dreams. Sandy, slightly stooped and nobby, could weld, do electrics, anything and everything to do with boats. He was also kind, humble, and generous with his knowledge. In one of the few real journal entries I wrote while at sea, I described the following, transcribed verbatim:

> People ask me what I'm doing, I mean I'm in the dream, conscious that I am in the middle of cruising in the Atlantic, so inevitably at some point in the dream, I think "Wait, how can I be in Maine if I'm trying to cross the Atlantic—have made no progress at all" which leads to me waking up, actually relieved that I'm here, on the boat, indeed very very far far from Maine . . . These things aren't clear in my head just as the dreams have been more open-ended, not quite hallucinations, but with more dialogue with my conscious self. I'm often explaining to people in my dream, "I'm here, I'm doing this, but you should know I'm actually only half-here because I'm in the middle of sailing across the Atlantic right now." I was trying to explain this to Sandy in the dream. I figured he would understand.

A few people have attempted careful studies of single-handed sailors and their psychological states. Just as Alain Bombard sent himself into a raft to study castaway diet at sea in 1952, so military- and space-exploration researchers have been interested in solo sailors as test subjects, for survival tactics and to examine their emotional swings. Before the first OSTAR race in 1960, Dr. David Lewis organized with fellow physicians and researchers ashore a set of daily forms for the five entrants to record their food intake, sleep, and emotional state in as quantitative a way as possible. "The idea of doing some research during the voyage first came to me as a possible excuse for such a long absence," he wrote, speaking in part to his *why-go*. "But before long the prospect of breaking fresh ground in a field that had long interested me became an exciting prospect in its own right." The daily log for each solo sailor included a section titled "How do you feel?" The form had rows with tick-boxes that ranged from "my normal self" to "seeing things"; "lonely" to "completely self-sufficient"; "a new confident mood" to "wish it were all over"; and even "sexy" to "not sexy" and "happy without feminine company" to "would enjoy company of other sex."

Dr. Lewis wrote about how during his crossing, chronic exhaustion forced him to make serious mistakes. Referencing Slocum's pilot, though, he thought that the wind-vane self-steering systems reduced hallucinations, since the fatigue was not mixed with relentless hours at the helm. Observations he made at the time, he found, were the only ones scientifically valid, because he realized, looking back at his notes about being afraid during a gale, that his mind had quickly created memories that saw things more favorably in retrospect than how he really felt them at the time. (Note to self.) All the sailors agreed that solitude and loneliness are not the same thing; Lewis wrote that he certainly never felt lonely. Overall, "A relaxed confidence, a sense of being 'at one' with the ocean and its winds, was our main emotional state, after the period of adjustment had passed."

In 1971, Nicolette Milnes Walker, who had been trained as a laboratory psychologist before her solo Atlantic crossing, monitored her mental state, too. She reported dreams of being ashore and needing to get back to her boat at sea, much as I would.

John C. Lilly, the scientist famous for mind experimentation with LSD and dolphins, was also a sailor. Although he never did a single-handed passage himself, in one of his earlier studies in the 1950s, Lilly and his team used water-submersion tanks to examine the effects on people who experienced reduced stimuli. Lilly tried to learn from single-handers in this same vein, such as analyzing Slocum's report of his pilot hallucination and the accounts by Dr. Alain Bombard from his trans-Atlantic crossing in an inflatable boat. Lilly laid these self-reports beside those of polar explorers and shipwreck survivors. He found that "persons in isolation experience many, if not all, of the symptoms of the mentally ill," but "The symptoms can be reversible. How easily reversible, we do not know. Most survivors report a new inner security and a new integration of themselves on a deep and basic level."

My friend Jon and I pulled into Portland, Maine, aboard *Fox* the day before my thirty-seventh birthday. Jon was the last remaining of my three friends who had joined me on the shakedown trip; the other two had had to peel away earlier to get back to work and family. Jon had built a new hatch cover for me in the cockpit and helped me with a dozen other things. He understood my situation, how to be supportive. We had gone through drills together on the shakedown, trying to sail the boat as aggressively and roughly as possible to test the self-steering and the safety of the rig. He spent hours down below to help me get used to managing the boat by myself, watching me climb the mast in rolling conditions.

"You've already accomplished more than all of us by getting to this point," Jon said. "So if we see you sooner rather than later, I'll be the first to buy the beer."

"Maybe I won't even make it back. Something could happen. A rogue wave or I might go all Donald Crowhurst crazy by myself."

"Maybe. If it happens, it happens."

"And even if something does happen, I mean, it would be hard on my parents, on Lisa, but I, it's not that I feel suicidal, it's just that—"

"—I know, I know, I feel the same. We've had a good life already."

"Exactly. I'm just not that important. I don't see my single life as that important."

"That's the advantage to going alone," he said.

"Exactly."

What I think I'm driving at here is that, like I presume nearly all single-handers, I was not afraid of death itself as a concept. I had no children at the time and was confident Lisa would be fine without me. My parents, however, would be the ones who would be crushed. I did not tell them what I was doing, to spare them the worry—and my own selfish guilt. Certainly, human society did not need me. I did not see my venture as suicidal, but a couple of people I told about it joked that this trip was "a death wish."

In Portland, Maine, that day, having survived on Earth for that long, I was more afraid of being unprepared. And I was afraid of the shame of failure. I was unreasonably afraid, too, of the judgment of the men in the boatyard on the Mystic River, who I did not even know but who I believed were laughing at me behind my back as I was preparing *Fox* and talking with Sandy Van Zandt and quietly planning to attempt something like this. Isn't it astounding the lengths to which we will go to earn the respect of complete strangers, most of whom have not considered us at all? I was afraid of rough weather, yes, but I was more afraid, at least at a distance, that I would in a selfish moment of panic click off that EPIRB and require another person to risk their life to come save me.

Yet perhaps I was most afraid, above all, like Ann Davison, that I had been living "a life going spare." Like her, the planning and this crossing attempt felt as if it were the right thing to give my little life a jumpstart while my physical self was still up for the challenge. I had been raised in a culture that places great value on youth and individual accomplishment, "finding what you're good at." I was approaching forty. I believed my body would soon start to decay. (This has proven to be valid, although it's been slower than I had thought.) In short, *oh, the cliché*, my crossing was a midlife crisis. Again, it is surely no coincidence that most of the early single-handers, Slocum and Pidgeon and Dumas, were in their forties and fifties when they set sail, with Davison being one of the youngest sailing pioneers at thirty-eight. The adventure also, as for Davison and so many others, gave me something to write about—since I had been making a middling career reading, writing, and teaching about the literature of the ocean. I was in the middle of getting a PhD, and I used money from my scholarship and my part-time illustration job to buy a used boat, emptying my savings to fit out the little craft for the crossing.

How many other people sailed alone across the Atlantic that summer? Ten? A hundred? I just have no idea. I've tried to research this from a few different angles, but have been unsuccessful. I asked Herb McCormick, a long-time editor at *Cruising World*. "No clue there," he said. "I wouldn't hazard a guess, it would be wildly speculative." Most of the people he knew who have done solo crossings were either racing or qualifying for a race. McCormick added: "It [is] such a rare and esoteric quest."

I'll tell you something that I have never said out loud or written to anyone, but has borne out to be true as I grow older and my trans-Atlantic sail fades further away: I like having this ocean crossing in my pocket. It's like when you touch your wallet or phone now and again just to make sure it's there. I did not plan for this to be the impact of the passage, but it has remained an ego crutch for me, even though I almost never bring it out. I just put my fingers on it when I'm speaking with someone who I think is a condescending jerk.

My solo ocean-crossing was not pretty, but it is mine. Mostly, anyway. I couldn't have done it without my parents, without Jon and other friends, or without Lisa or Sandy or the self-steering gear, and without luck, or an angel or God or an attentive watch officer, or whatever you want to call it.

# 17. Tevake and the Voyage of No Return

Although there had been a surge in Western public interest in a romanticized Pacific after World War II, it took longer for many to understand and appreciate the excellence of Pacific Islanders out at sea, whether that be the current skills like those of Florentino Das and his father or the millennia-old traditions of long-range migrations across the entire Pacific. The earliest European explorers left records in the late 1700s of the stunning skill of individual Pacific Island navigators, such as Tupaia and Puhoro, and the speed and design of their vessels, but none of these European mariners had an idea of the true extent of Indigenous voyaging over millennia and the range of the pockets of remaining expertise throughout the Pacific and Southeast Asia. As the colonial era continued, many if not most Western naturalists, historians, captains, and anthropologists, all the way into the 1950s and 1960s, suppressed these original reports; or they simply did not believe, with racist undertones, that anyone in the South Pacific or Southeast Asia could have been capable of sailing and settling systematically this vast region with boats of wood and fiber and without compasses, timepieces, and sextants.

One of the benefits of the post-war boom in small-boat cruising, single-handed or otherwise, was that many sailors who were turning away from modern technologies and looking for alternative ways of living took to the sea with an interest in historical boat design, navigational techniques, and anthropology. This led them to the South Pacific as the ultimate destination, and, however clumsily and reductively, to affirm and popularize the histories and expertise of Pacific Island mariners, their knowledge, and their vessels. One of the significant Western researchers in this field, who went to sea with some of the few remaining master navigators in different parts of the South Pacific, was the single-hander, Dr. David Lewis, a New Zealander who served as an airborne medic in World War II, spent over a decade as a doctor ashore in England, and then exploded out for the rest of his life into a tumultuous series of successive ocean adventures that began with his participation in the first OSTAR in 1960 when he sailed alone across the Atlantic against Francis Chichester and led that study of single-hander psychology. In the late 1960s and early 1970s, Dr. Lewis conducted research into traditional techniques. After sailing throughout the central Pacific region and interviewing and learning from master Pacific Island navigators, he wrote scholarly papers and books, including a widely read general audience overview titled *The Voyaging Stars* (1978), which was lauded by the boating community. A reviewer in the American magazine *Cruising World*, for example, in the time just before GPS and radar on small boats, wrote that the book was not only a brilliant work of maritime history, like that of Samuel Eliot Morison, but something to inspire a more connected way of life on the water: "For the cruising sailor, Lewis does something more than Morison by helping us learn to live more comfortably and intimately with the sea."

In the decades after the voyage of Florentino Das, perhaps in small part due to his example (although no one wrote about him in *Cruising World*), as well as the scholarship of Dr. Lewis and others, Indigenous communities throughout the South Pacific raised louder their own voices for social justice and decolonization, aligning with other movements around the world. A large part of this progress among Pacific Islanders involved new celebrations and re-education campaigns within local communities, which included reminders about their ancestral navigational prowess. This included the building of new voyaging boats aboard which Native people crossed oceans along ancestral routes using mostly traditional techniques. The most famous and long-lasting of these endeavors was the founding of the Polynesian Voyaging Society in Hawai'i, which led to the construction of *Hōkūle'a*, a large double-hulled voyaging sailboat in the style of the traditional vessels. Under the guidance of Mau Piailug, a master wayfinder from the Caroline Islands, they sailed *Hōkūle'a* from Hawai'i to Tahiti in 1976 (Lewis was on board for the ride and doing research). Piailug had explained in an interview a couple of years earlier: "I have no fear when I am at sea because I have faith in the words of the ancestors. This faith is what we call courage. With this courage you can travel anywhere in the world and not get lost."

Perhaps the most inspiring and generous person that Dr. Lewis met during his immersive studies of traditional Pacific navigation was a master navigator named Tevake. Tevake grew up on the atoll of Pileni, which is in the Santa Cruz Island group, the eastern edge of the Solomon Islands. Tevake had learned navigation from his father, beginning when he was seven or eight. For most of his life Tevake sailed his own thirty-foot outrigger for trading voyages, going for distances of as much as 320 miles between islands. In his old age, for more than a decade, he continued to sail among the islands in a small canoe without an outrigger. He trained at least two younger navigators, especially his nephew

Bongi from Matema atoll, but when Lewis met Tevake in the late 1960s, he remained in actuality the last true master navigator of the region.

Tevake agreed to take command of Lewis' boat *Isbjorn* for several ocean passages, including one that was a hundred miles from island to island. Once Tevake got used to judging the speed and leeway of Lewis' vessel, he navigated *Isbjorn* perfectly without any clocks, paper charts, compass, or even pencil or paper. Tevake was patient and proud of his skills and tried to teach Lewis, for example, about the three types of swell patterns—which he used more often than the sun during the day—as well as the regular march of star orientations that he had his helmsman steer by over the course of a night. By the time he sailed with Tevake, Lewis had sailed solo across the Atlantic three times and led his family's full circumnavigation of the world, yet in his books his awe of Tevake's perception and skill is irrepressible, even as he tries to keep a scholarly tone. This was especially so when Tevake navigated almost purely by swell and his analysis of speed, currents, and leeway when the sky was overcast and it was pouring rain.

Lewis kept in touch with Tevake, wrote to him about the book, how his photograph would be included. Tevake dictated a letter back to Lewis in early 1970 that said, "Now I am still alive. But you will meet me one day or not? Because I am getting old."

A few months later, Lewis received a letter from the district officer of the Santa Cruz island group, which reported that Tevake had disappeared, lost at sea, during a voyage by himself on a passage that should have been no trouble to him. No trace had been found. Tevake had "made something in the nature of a formal farewell before his departure

Tevake of Pileni navigating David Lewis' boat *Isbjorn* with his traditional skills (c. 1968).

from Nufilole," wrote the district officer to Lewis, either anticipating disaster or planning his own death. This apparently was not uncommon among the people of Tikopia, just to the south, who referred to death at sea as a "sweet burial." Lewis referred to Tevake's last trip as being on a "voyage of no return."

# 18. Animism, the Boat

One day at sea, at about the longitude of Iceland, I was doing dishes after dinner and forgot to take a fork out of a pot before I washed the contents over the side. In a moment of graveyard humor, I wrote in my logbook about "the loss of Fork, he was a good utensil, and that after last rites, tomorrow Knife and Spoon would begin dividing up his stuff."

Probably true in every workplace to some extent, but on every ship I've been on the community has named inanimate objects. This has a function to help with the specificity of language and tasks in a small environment with so many working parts, but also for fun. And among isolated people under stress, companionship and security is not only gleaned from intentional pets or relationships with animals over the rail, but they infuse the physical inanimate objects around them with personalities, feelings, and intentionality, what scholars call "animism."

I talked to, cajoled, bickered with, and regularly thanked Sandy while aboard *Fox*. The self-steering gear's very existence was magical and essential to the success of the passage. Many other single-handers named their self-steering gear, but it seems more often to be the less experienced ones like me. Stuart Woods, for example, a writer who for the first time sailed across the Atlantic in the 1976 OSTAR, named his wind vane "Fred," after his pet dog left ashore. David Lewis named his on his first cruise, calling it "Kiwi," after his native country's bird mascot which he had painted on the wind vane. As far as I can tell, Chichester did not name his self-steering gear after his first one, Miranda. Moitessier did not name his, either. Nor did Adams. Then again, when young Robin Lee Graham got a new wind vane, nearing the end of his circumnavigation, he named it "Gandalf." And during his record-setting non-stop around the world, experienced single-hander Knox-Johnston named his "The Admiral."

Aboard my boat, I found myself naming other things, too, such as the preventer tackle for the main boom. This little rope-and-pulley system often got twisted, and because of the shape of the deck house, I often had to crawl and contort in awkward ways to untangle or move it to the other side of the boat after tacking. I used this preventer tackle to adjust the shape of the mainsail and to keep it from swinging in the wrong direction. I imagined it to be too proud and righteous, like a young waiter in a fancy restaurant who imagines himself superior to his customers because he's an artist. I gave him a name, too: Philip. This allowed some nice alliteration for the angry adjective I most often ascribed to the finicky, frustrating thing.

Then there was the boat as a whole, the sloop *Fox*. I'd worked on *Fox* all winter, doing what were for me very big jobs, such as changing all the running rigging, installing new chain plates, new sea cocks, fiberglassing parts of the deck, repacking the propeller, reinstalling the rudder and bolting on the self-steering. In the spring I'd painted the hull a battleship gray, brushed on an ultramarine blue boot stripe, and rolled the bottom with green anti-fouling paint. I hand-painted the white letters on the transom: "FOX" and underneath "MYSTIC." My Pearson Triton was an antique. With a deep traditional keel, it was graceful, simple, clean, and tough—a design that had made many deep-ocean passages.

A man named James Baldwin has sailed his 1963 Pearson Triton twice around the world alone. He still sails the boat and specializes in repairing the Pearson Tritons of other sailors. I believe quite sincerely that *Fox* took care of me and suffered through many of my mistakes. I regret that I later sold the boat and have lost track of the person who bought it. Every once in a while I search the Internet to see if it is owned somewhere or is for sale. It's hull #646, if you ever see it anywhere.

As I was sailing in the middle of the North Atlantic, I talked to the boat, usually saying thank you. Sometimes I patted it. Although I didn't use the pronoun, "she," I was as steeped in the animism of my boat as any other sailor. I didn't really imagine it as exactly matriarchal or as a lover of any kind, but I understand the sentiment. Many single-handed writers use "we" when talking in their narratives about their progress, referring to themselves and their boat. This makes sense, because it shows humility and the recognition that this couldn't be done without a good boat. It was certainly true for me that *Fox* tolerated its new owner, caring for me far more patiently than I deserved.

There is something magical about propelling your own little home across the water by the power of the fickle, faceless breezes—to travel along while the boat takes care of itself. The *why-go* to sail across an ocean alone in your beloved tidy house by the power of the wind has always seemed to hold a challenge and a magnetism that is quite different from any other sporting event or adventure of any kind at all, even ocean rowing or ice climbing or polar crossings. Richard Hutch, a philosopher of sport and a scholar of single-handed sailing literature, wrote that offshore sailing reaches "outer existential limits" beyond any other sporting activity. Hutch compared the solo sailor to a pearl that is shaped, honed, and crafted by the oyster that is their sailboat.

The soulful relationship between the sailor and boat is eloquently exemplified in the narratives of Slocum, Pidgeon, and Moitessier, those who spent years with their vessels and were intimately responsible for every stage of the building and voyaging. Dumas, even though he did not build his boat himself, wrote of a moment after leaving Valparaiso, his first night alone and back at sea on the way to pass around Cape Horn, when he found himself leaning over and kissing a wood panel down below in "a surge of affection for my 'shipmate.'" At the end of the voyage Dumas wrote that he patted the boat, thanked him—Spanish uses the male pronoun, *el barco*—for how much he had been through, believing that "God must have loved him."

After his first voyage in 1962, Kenichi Horie donated his *Mermaid* to the city of San Francisco. It is now curated and maintained by the San Francisco Maritime Museum and displayed in the welcome center. When Horie donated the boat he gave the museum a commemorative plate, on which is inscribed a letter explaining how he was entrusting this boat to them, this craft who had given him courage and to whom he had given encouragement back. "Please be kind to my tired lover," he wrote as translated: "Will you please speak to her, this lonely heart, when you are moved to do so. And will you please listen to her talk about the stars, the waves and the skies over the Pacific Ocean." A member of the staff who maintains the small boats at the museum told me that she always feels a little guilty when reading this: she said she doesn't speak often enough to *Mermaid*.

One of the best descriptions regarding the importance of the vessel itself was written by Robert Manry in the 1960s, writing about his 13.5-foot sloop *Tinkerbelle*, his companion, his friend, which he had rebuilt himself over many years to make it ocean-safe:

> A voyage made by a solitary person is sometimes called a singlehanded voyage or a solo voyage, but neither of these terms gives proper credit to the most important factor in any voyage, the boat. Far from being solo, a one-man voyage is a kind of a maritime duet in which the boat plays the melody and its skipper plays the harmonic counterpoint. The performances of the boat and the skipper are both important, undeniably, but if it comes to making a choice between the two the decision must be in favor of the boat.

Manry pointed out that boats have floated by themselves over great distances and survived at sea for months at a time on their own. Not the other way around.

# 19. Sailing While Black: Teddy Seymour Plays His *Love Song*

Teddy Seymour was born in 1941 and grew up in Yonkers, New York City, across from the freight yard beside the Hudson River. His father worked at an elevator foundry across the street. Teddy grew up outdoors, moving around the city. He had a paper route, fished on the pier, delivered fish and crabs to houses, and picked up any work he could, playing hooky from school if he needed to. His grandfather, who lived near them in Yonkers, had been a fisherman in Trinidad, and he filled young Teddy's mind with watery adventures. "I never turned down a dare," Seymour wrote when looking back on his childhood. At age thirteen, as the story goes, he and some friends built a raft from scrap wood, in which Teddy floated down the Hudson River and needed to be rescued by the Coast Guard. In 1956, when Seymour was in high school, the same year Davison published *My Ship Is So Small*, a global economic revolution was beginning downriver: the first ship to carry containers departed from the port of Newark, New Jersey. The containers were long steel boxes filled with cargo that could be lifted or driven on and off a ship and right onto a railroad car or a truck. Containerization would enable consumer and economic growth unlike anything our world had ever seen, to the point that today, besides bulk goods like oil and grain, nearly all products travel internationally inside one of these forty-foot boxes before being hoisted onto a truck or a train. Few people at the time saw the significance of this invention, the paradigm-shifting impact of "intermodal shipping" that would grease the skids of globalization.

Seymour likely took no notice of the dawn of containerization. He had no plans to enter the merchant marine, and at that point he had not spent any significant days in boats, under sail or power. He was, however, a skilled and hardworking runner, which earned him a track scholarship to Central State University in Ohio, where he earned All-America honors. During college he got a taste of sailing with two of his older cousins who owned their own boats. After graduating, Seymour joined the US Marines. He served in Vietnam, attaining the rank of captain as he excelled in an amphibious landing force, his unit delivered by Navy ships to clear out a beach. "I loved it," he wrote later. For his tour he was nominated for the Navy Cross for bravery. Later, until 1972, Seymour was stationed as an artillery officer at Camp Pendleton, south of Los Angeles. He served there during the Santa Barbara oil spill, when Sharon Sites Adams returned from her trans-Pacific crossing, and when teenager Robin Lee Graham returned to Los Angeles from his circumnavigation. During his free time, when not running, Seymour learned to sail dinghies while he earned a master's degree in recreation administration. He bought a day-sailer, then a small pocket cruising boat, and then took out a loan for a larger ocean-going boat named *Love Song*, aboard which he lived during graduate school and when he worked a job as a production manager at the American Can Company, in the Dixie Cup division. With larger voyages already on his mind, Seymour did his first solo trip out to Catalina Island, about twenty-five miles away. He never forgot sailing alongside basking sharks, "my friends," with which he sailed in company both there and back.

In 1979, Seymour set out from Los Angeles. He sailed alone down to the Panama Canal and then alone across the Caribbean Sea, a tremendous single-handed passage in itself, finishing in St Croix in the Virgin Islands, where he had previously made friends and secured a job as a primary-school teacher. To fit out *Love Song* for a world voyage, he did additional odd jobs around the island, including working as a night watchman and as a waiter, keeping the goal of a circumnavigation in his sights. All this time, he still kept up with his long-distance running. With a friend from St Croix he hopped on a plane one year and completed the Boston Marathon.

Seymour's *why-go* was not initially to sail around the world by himself. "Originally, I planned the trip with three women, on a different occasion," he said in one interview in St Croix years later. "They [each] backed out. All along, I was getting ready."

By the late 1980s, several hundred, perhaps even over a thousand people, had now sailed alone in their own small boats across one of Earth's oceans. More than people had completed solo circumnavigations, and of that number, at least eighteen, including Robin Knox-Johnston, Bernard Moitessier, Kay Cottee, and Kenichi Horie, had circled the globe without pausing at a single port stop.

Single-handed ocean-crossings had by the 1980s been increasingly bifurcating between the solo "cruisers," sailors like Teddy Seymour who in the wake of Harry Pidgeon mostly wanted to sail on their own schedules in fair winds and visit distant ports as tourists, and the solo "racers," sailors who in the wake of Francis Chichester mostly wanted to compete and challenge themselves on a public stage to set a record or sail with, as put by circumnavigator Naomi James in 1979, a competitive "survival element." Although the cruisers and the racers continued to move philosophically and physically farther apart at marinas and anchorages, the two groups still inspired and informed each other despite their different means and ends. And both solo cruisers and racers kept pushing new boundaries of geography, artistic expression, and the types of people casting off the dock. After his research into traditional navigation in the South Pacific, Dr. Lewis sailed by himself to the Antarctic Peninsula, from which he wrote a bestseller titled *Ice Bird* (1975). In 1987, young Tania Aebi and her cat Tarzoon completed a world voyage, after which she wrote *Maiden Voyage* (1989) from her regular dispatches to *Cruising World* magazine.

The further historical backdrop to Seymour's voyage was that environmental awareness and ocean activism around the world had blossomed, inspired in part by the famous Blue Planet photo from space, that image of Earth reminding us that ours is primarily a saltwater-ocean planet. The image was the symbol of the first Earth Day in 1970 and part of the "Save the Whales" campaigns. By the end of the 1980s, James Hansen had given his foundational report to the US Congress affirming global warming and the impact of the greenhouse effect, with "99 percent confidence" that human activities were the cause. It made the front page of *The New York Times*, but did not really shift public opinion. The international maritime community, meanwhile, had expanded its discharge regulations on ships to mandate that no plastic of any kind could be sent overboard.

Thus it was under the radar of environmental campaigns

and the higher-profile solo voyages like Lewis' and Aebi's that Teddy Seymour breezed along, bound to be the first African American person to sail around the world alone.

Seymour finally just set himself a hard deadline for departure, quit his teaching job, and, after a couple more shakedown trips, sailed toward the sunset, westbound into the Caribbean in February of 1986. He planned to keep in the temperate latitudes and follow the trade winds and the best seasons for the safest weather. Seymour was forty-five, unmarried, and classically handsome with a square jaw, thick moustache, and a runner's physique.

Aboard *Love Song*, Seymour transited the Panama Canal and stopped in Bora Bora and then American Samoa, where, after seeing a doctor about an infection developed at sea, he finished second in a local running race without having trained in months. He sailed on to Papua New Guinea, to Australia, and then, when others convinced him that it would be too dangerous for an African American person to stop in Cape Town during apartheid—he could not be guaranteed diplomatic protection—he decided to sail up through the Red Sea and the Suez Canal. After stopping in Yemen, Israel, and Egypt, Seymour and *Love Song* sailed westbound through the Mediterranean in what would be the worst winter in some forty years—the most challenging weather of his entire voyage. He at last escaped beyond the Strait of Gibraltar, and sailed westbound across the Atlantic, riding the trade winds that had shunned Davison a quarter-century before. After a

Teddy Seymour aboard *Love Song* (c. 1988).

circumnavigation of sixteen months, during which he spent less than $6,000, he returned to the same dock from which he had left. At one point he wrote a short journal-style account, titled "No Frills Circumnavigation," but he never published this nor did he publish a book of any kind about his voyage. Even among boaty types, his story is barely known.

The elephant in the room of this story of single-handed mariners is that recreational cruising and racing in sailboats has remained mostly a white-male endeavor from the wealthy countries of the global north. Highly skilled small-boat sail-ors, fishermen, and deep-water adventurers, of all races, ethnicities, and nationalities throughout history, have trave-led and worked at sea all over the world. In the modern era, however – due to legacies of colonialism, capitalism, racist elements in publishing, racist economic policies, and the gobbling up of coastal property by primarily white communities – nearly all the early people in the modern era who crossed oceans alone, at least of whom we are aware, were white men, until the likes of Davison, Das, Horie, Adams, and then Teddy Seymour.

I, for example, never sailed in boats while growing up, but came into life on ships after college by getting an off-beat job as an academic teacher aboard for a high-school semester at sea. I had parents who had supported me and allowed me to get a private college education without leaving me in debt. Years later, in preparation for the Atlantic crossing, I bought *Fox* on my own and arrived in Portugal nearly broke, but I still had a part-time job and a graduate-school scholarship to return to, and my parents to lend me some money to pay off the remaining bills. In other words, I had the means, the abil-ity to take the time off, the financial back-up, and the lack of familial responsibilities to be able to even consider an adven-ture like this. Although the boat itself, even after all my additions and improvements, still totaled less than a Toyota hatchback, I lived in a town beside the water and in my girl-friend's apartment while not off at graduate school. I had months off to work on the boat, access to advice, to friends who knew about these things. I could pay to keep the boat in a shipyard and rent a mooring. If my skin were darker, my Judaism more visible, my first language not English, or if I were not a cisgender male, who knows what direct or subtle roadblocks would have been put in front of me—or I might simply have learned growing up that this sort of thing was not for me.

Slocum, Pidgeon, and other well-known single-handers were relatively poor. They did nearly all the work themselves on shoe-string budgets. In the countries they lived in and the ports they visited, though, as white men, even without much money, they had a path to achieve what they wanted if they had the talent and gumption. Any individual and cultural discouragement they felt before departing was but a scratch on the barricades that had been constructed in front of, say, an African American man trying to build a boat and sail around the world in the 1890s, or 1920s, or 1950s—and still today. Maybe Seymour chose to live in St Croix because it was a place at a distance from the racism of America. In one of his rare interviews, with *The Bay State Banner* (Boston's African American-focused newspaper) in 1992, Seymour said that going to sea on his own was hardly the most dangerous thing he had ever done. "The easy part was sailing around the world. I've almost lost my life on many occasions. I've been through Vietnam, I've lived in LA where the cops hassled me just because I was a black man running down the streets in a sweat suit." (Although Seymour said that he never actually said that. This was one of a few early moments that soured him for life on reporters.)

Consider, too, that the nostalgia for the age of sail, of sailing ships, which pervaded much of the Western twentieth-century desire to get away and out to the seemingly unspoiled sea, is not a universal feeling. The ship under sail, the ocean horizon, not even a calm, sandy beach is necessarily soothing and inspiring for everyone. For most Americans the word "yacht" oozes white wealth and exclusion. An ocean voyage in some families might have been the darkest period in their recent or ancestral history. If so, then why would you want to go sailing by yourself to cross an ocean? Nor were the cruising sailors from North America, Britain, and Europe who arrived into ports around the world always, to put it mildly, individuals to be emulated.

Pidgeon and Lewis, for example, saw themselves in the wake of sailing-ship explorers, luffing up into harbors with a colonial privilege to go wherever they wanted. They considered their travels, photographs, and research as benign, even beneficial; Lewis was especially sensitive to treading respectfully, but even he still considered it his right to pursue travel and knowledge and to write and publish his observations of these communities. I am no better.

The idea, however subtle, of the lone white-male colonial sailor as superior and privileged is rooted and germinated in sometimes surprising and even unintentional ways in Western culture. Maurice Sendak's *Where the Wild Things Are*, first published in 1963, won the Caldecott Medal and has remained one of the most popular children's books in English ever crafted. In this picture book a young white boy with dark hair, named Max, wearing a white wolf suit, is misbehaving in his house. He is sent up to his room without dinner by his mother who is not pictured, out of the frame. He is told he's being a "wild thing." Max imagines his room transforming into a forest, the walls disappear, and he tromps off as a wolf toward the moon until:

> . . . an ocean tumbled by with a private boat for Max
> and he sailed off through night and day
> and in and out of weeks
> and almost over a year
> to where the wild things are.

After trying to be brave before an ocean monster, he sails his little wooden sailboat onto a beach. Here Max finds long-haired monsters with yellow eyes and sharp teeth. He tames and impresses the monsters with his ferocity. They crown him "king of all wild things," have a party, howl at the moon together, and the monsters parade him around on their shoulders as the conquering hero. When Max gets lonely and tired of it all, they plead with him to stay. Max casts off anyway, leaving them sad and disappointed. He sails home alone in his boat until he returns to his room and his warm supper waiting for him. What more could a solo explorer want?

Maurice Sendak, personally and symbolically touched by the Holocaust, a theme in much of his works, surely never intended a colonial message. Yet Max's single-handed voyage here is nevertheless a privileged solo sailor's path to exotic pleasures, royal treatment, and then a triumphant, cozy return home with a new appreciation for what he has—not exactly the narrative path of Joseph Campbell's hero's journey, but pretty close.

When read today, many of the early single-handed sailing narratives are injected with racist, colonial observations and combative experiences. With his superior sailing skills off Morocco, as he told it, Joshua Slocum outwitted "Moorish pirates," villains of Mohammed. In the Strait of Magellan, Slocum wrote of the aggression of small groups of Indigenous people, "canoes manned by savages," some of whom had formed into a criminal band led by a multiracial outlaw named Black Pedro. Slocum reveled in these stories, how he brandished his gun regularly and fired often. Most famously, Slocum described how a group raided his boat one night while he slept. Another captain had given him carpet tacks to spread on the deck, so that when these Native pirates snuck aboard with their bare feet, they shouted in pain and retreated, jumping into the frigid water, making animal-like howls. Slocum, the clever hero, bolted up on deck and fired after them with his rifle. He explained that when going ashore for wood for his stove, he always brought his gun: "I reasoned that I had all about me the greatest danger of the whole voyage—the treachery of cunning savages, for which I must be particularly on the alert." Once he wrote that he heard the breeze of an arrow whiz past his head and stick into the mast of *Spray*. Slocum was in real danger in these cases, but as a creature of his time he tangled this up with colonial and technological racism, that all of the world was his domain.

A generation later, Pidgeon was not without racism or judgment, but he defended and was envious of what he believed to be the Pacific Islanders' unmaterialistic, unhurried way of life. He was far more interested in local people than Slocum, but Pidgeon still maintained a tourist's distance. He kept on his white shirts and trousers, his camera in hand. He did not begin wearing lava-lavas or tucking flowers behind his ear, as would single-handers like Gerbault or Wray and then Moitessier.

Even as late as the 1960s, Chichester, in *Gipsy Moth Circles the World*, did not recognize the full story of people in the Pacific: "It took mankind almost the whole of human history to discover how vast the Pacific is—almost to the end of the eighteenth century geographers just couldn't believe there was so much sea." Chichester had lived years beside Māori people in New Zealand and must have known of the work of, among others, his fellow single-hander David Lewis, yet for Chichester the mapping of the Pacific began only with Captain Cook.

In "No Frills Circumnavigation," his brief unpublished account of the voyage transcribed from a few of his at-sea journals, Teddy Seymour reported only good greetings and assistance from the people he met during his twelve port stops. If he encountered racism anywhere he did not write anything about it here. In the months before he died, he sketched out an outline that added more details to his early account. This described gunboats approaching him on both ends of the Suez Canal and officials treating him like a spy in ports in the Middle East. He attributed this more to his U.S. Marines connections than to his skin color. Seymour described enjoying his visits to places such as Darwin and Papua New Guinea and Yemen, where in the 1980s a person of color visiting alone on their cruising yacht, flying the American flag, must have been a novel sight. In his concluding paragraphs to "No Frills Circumnavigation," Seymour wrote of the kindness of the people that he visited, locals who often treated him "like a long-lost cousin":

> [In the Seychelles] there were invitations to visit homes, eat meals, and be an overnight guest.
>
> One new friend encouraged me to take up residency because all that I could ever want is there, and I agree. Now, that was a place that caused me to sit in the cockpit and sadly observe disappear beyond the horizon . . . I [also later sat] savoring thoughts of the people of Yemen and Egypt, the inhabitants overwhelmed me with goodwill and

displayed a keen interest in my journey. It's usually the man making a living with a fishing boat built on the beach or the guy selling tea on the corner with the homemade cart that is willing to offer the shirt off his back as a gesture of friendship.

I like to imagine Teddy Seymour arriving skillfully in *Love Song* alone, greeting people with the voice and patience of a schoolteacher and a long-distance runner – how unique and disarming this traveler must have been.

In terms of his *what-they-saw*, Teddy Seymour's depiction of his relationship with the ocean has a similar feel to that of Harry Pidgeon. His short account is matter-of-fact, with little drama, and the three-chapter story is written in part to provide information to fellow mariners, outlining, for example, costs and procedures for transiting the two major canals, the Panama and the Suez. In the supplemental outline he wrote late in life, it's clear that his time in the Marines pervaded his outlook and sense of self-discipline, the value he placed on thorough preparation and logical decision-making. When relating a story about when he had to go aloft in heavy weather to fix his running lights in the shipping lanes, despite his fear of heights, he wrote: "Semper Fi-Do-or-Die sounds great on the parade field. Way out here in the Indian Ocean it means Do & Die." In the Torres Strait and in his approach to the Red Sea, he was often in waters known for pirates, so he kept a rifle on board and sailed with no lights at night, chewing on coffee beans to stay awake. The problems he described on the voyage were nearly all shore-derived— people, ships, his propeller shaft damaged by a fishing net, how one day off Italy for a few hours he pounded absurdly through seas littered with a patch of floating diapers. Rarely did Seymour write of any significant challenges derived from the ocean itself.

Seymour loved animals his whole life. He wrote that dolphins arrived to keep him calm and safe that day when he had to go aloft. Seymour loved to fish, using seabirds to find them. He was so successful that he often had too much tuna and dolphinfish on board and felt it wasteful, even after he ate fish for every meal for days at a time. When not eating fresh fish, he lived frugally, eating mostly rice and beans, which he reminded the reader is the base food of a majority of the global population.

Seymour's *Love Song* was a thirty-five-foot fiberglass design with proven deep-water capabilities, which he had toughened still further with extra layers of fiberglass on the bow. His boat in 1986 did not bristle with the latest and greatest technological developments, but it was still well equipped. He had a production wind-vane self-steering device, which served him well for the entire voyage, requiring only, he said, a little oil each day. He wrote: "no human can outperform the Aries," which was his wind-vane brand of choice. Seymour had a small electric refrigerator to preserve fresh food on board, and his relationship with his "trusty" engine, a small inboard diesel, was far more favorable than most of his predecessors. His engine got him out of a few potential scrapes, but, at the same time, he was self-deprecating as to its maintenance, joking that he was very good at taking things apart but not as good at putting them back together. In Australia, he needed to bring the engine to a mechanic for repair; it had failed mostly because he wasn't using it enough. Seymour had wired *Love Song* with solar panels, a long-distance two-way radio, and he had, with some guilt—because he knew his celestial navigation and practiced it regularly on the voyage—invested in a new satellite navigation set, a Magnavox MX4102, a predecessor to GPS. This device required some repair along the way, and failed at a couple of key moments, but he found the electronic navigation to be enormously helpful, quipping that he would now never leave port without two things: this satellite navigation machine and a solid supply of peanut M & M candy. Seymour also reveled in the technology of the global credit card, allowing him to fix things in port, to "sail now, pay later."

In the end, Seymour told of a solo circumnavigation that was mostly uneventful—no groundings, no knockdowns, no shark attacks, no rogue waves or typhoons or collisions with ships. Most of the success he attributed to his gear, his boat *Love Song*, and his careful consideration of the safest route and season for sailing. No spiritual guru like Moitessier or a pioneering salt like Slocum, Seymour wrote like Pidgeon with a military mindset: a sailor with long, earned experience giving the reader the feeling that this was an adventure available to nearly anyone if you respected the preparation necessary and remained vigilant. "If you want guarantees," he wrote, "buy a toaster." His ocean was unpredictable but benevolent, a place of beauty and thrill, but never terror. Each day of his voyage the sun rises off the stern and sets off the bow as *Love Song* circles peacefully westward around the world.

Despite the brevity and practical account of the voyage, Seymour did include in "No Frills Circumnavigation" at least one ecstasy-so-pure moment. During his passage in the Indian Ocean, after transiting the Torres Strait, he was surfing downwind on high seas under full cloud cover, mostly locked up in his cabin with a book while the self-steering did the work. He and his boat were gobbling up the miles in the right direction, in "full stride," as if running another marathon. He approached Christmas Island where he had planned to stop:

> *Love Song* experienced unbound freedom, surging with the gusts, lifting her transom while sprinting with the swells, as foam rushed alongside the hull and occasionally along the deck, and the song of the bow wave played over and over. We were not alone during those enjoyable days: dolphins were attracted to the sleek hull and playful movement. Those darting, leaping, squealing creatures adopted *Love Song* as a playmate and devoted many hours, day and night, plowing through the water in concert with the fleeting object, using only a small working jib to answer the call of the strong southeast trade wind. The sensation became captivating, and the experience incomparable. It seemed a pity to curtail all the activity.

So he didn't. Seymour just kept on playing his *Love Song* in a "euphoria" right on past Christmas Island, evoking when Slocum sailed right on past the Marquesas. Seymour continued on his runner's high for another 3,200 miles and three more weeks until finally anchoring at the Seychelles, where he received that warm welcome from the people there, the reminder about what he felt to be most important in life.

Teddy Seymour returned to local fanfare in St Croix. He was featured in a couple of national sailing magazines, received memberships and awards from the likes of the Joshua Slocum Society and the Cruising Club of America, but mostly he returned to his life as it had been in St Croix. He resumed his job as a teacher, still living on his boat. He had three children. He only moved from St Croix in his late seventies for medical care near his daughter in Oregon, intending to go home to St Croix, but he died there at age eighty-one in April of 2023.

While Seymour was on his world voyage in 1986, a librarian and fellow marathon runner named Wallace Williams organized a long-distance running race on St Croix in his friend's honor. The "Toast to the Captain" race has been held annually ever since, in February, to mark when Seymour embarked on his solo circumnavigation, but also to highlight Black History Month. Seymour was a runner all the way up to his final days. He jogged in his Oregon apartment if it was too cold to go outside. Before he died he wrote that he had had more lives than a cat, because he had escaped thirteen near-death moments—six in Vietnam and seven on boats. The last one was in his early seventies, when he was diving underwater with a snorkel, trying to untangle mooring lines after a hurricane, when he was knocked unconscious and lost four of his front teeth.

Teddy Seymour also totaled that he had lived on a sailboat for fifty-one years of his life.

"He always lived on his boat," his daughter Maya told me. Her dad kept his final apartment in the same fashion, clean and minimalist.

# 20. Dolphins, Whales

It's so stereotypical, but for me, too, the most memorable marine animals from my trans-Atlantic crossing were the dolphins. Although I saw a few different species, I regularly encountered what I believed to have been the short-beaked common dolphin (*Delphinus delphis*). I worked this one out because the guide that I had aboard *Fox* had lots of easy color pictures. Dolphins appeared throughout my passage and often at my worst times. In big seas and winds, if Neptune was mischievous, he timed a wave just as I was coming out of the hatch. I did not have a canvas or rigid shelter over the cockpit, called a dodger in America, which many boats have to shield some of the weather. So not only might a tall wave slosh a saltwater smack across my face, but if I didn't have everything shut in time, I'd get water in the cabin, adding to the general mank below that I tried to control by wiping and cleaning daily.

At one low point in the voyage, after a long night of winds over thirty knots, the sea and sky different shades of slate, I was stepping out of the companionway when *Fox* slid off a wave and I heard a bang on the hull by another wave coming from a different angle. Before I got out of the way, seawater splashed down my collar and sprayed a barrel's worth of ocean into the cabin across the electronics. I turned out to the gale and swore, blasphemed at my greatest volume, right out of my belly. At that instant a pod of dolphins approached from windward, as if my shouting had summoned them.

One of the dolphins was escorting a baby about the size of a raccoon. I found myself apologizing for the profanity. The family leaped in unison, swam under the boat, appeared to be smiling, not mocking, as if reminding me to try to relax and enjoy the ride.

Dolphins were there for my high points of the voyage, too. When the stars were out and conditions were reasonable, sailing alone at night by myself was glorious. Over the course of my passage in July and August, I observed an entire cycle of the moon and progressed along a celestial march of time. The days were getting shorter toward the autumnal equinox, while I sailed eastward toward the rising sun and across time zones. In the middle of the North Atlantic, ship traffic was practically nonexistent for me that summer, and since I kept my radar and running lights off to conserve power there was not a light from my boat or from anywhere as far as I could see. As I worked on my star identification with my books on board, I traced the movements of constellations and planets and embraced that gorgeous verse written by the seventeenth-century English poet and priest Thomas Traherne: "You never enjoy the world aright, till the Sea itself floweth in your veins, till you are clothed with the heavens, and crowned with the stars: and perceive yourself to be the sole heir of the whole world."

One evening I had spent more than an hour altering the boat's course, then adjusting the sails and various lines. I did not have roller furling on my boat, which meant I had to crawl up forward on the bow to put up and take down sails. The wind was light that evening, but the boat was still moving in a favorable direction. I was disappointed in myself, though, in how long it took me to try to get *Fox* performing the way I wanted. Exhausted, I decided to go below for a short nap.

Just as I was about to climb down below, I heard a short *ffuh* off the bow: the exhale of a dolphin. I clipped my tether back into the jackline and walked up to the bow. I laid myself on the white deck like a child leaning over the edge of the bed. I could have reached out and touched them: five dolphins swimming and swerving in front of *Fox*, their bodies weaving wide, pale, green-blue wakes of bioluminescence. Through the dark it was too fuzzy to see underwater their fins, tails, or the full shapes of their heads. I could only see their surging outlines, perfectly in sync, somehow never bumping into each other or the bow, always knowing exactly how the other was going to angle, effortlessly swimming at the same speed, then circling back to match my slower progress. Occasionally a black back eased up through the sea's surface for another exhale, dripping water that glowed with green gems of bioluminescence while the wet skin wore the stars of the universe.

It was about 3:30 a.m. local time. In between watching the dolphins I rolled over and looked back at *Fox*, Sandy sailing the boat so quietly on his own, with me as passenger. Gazing upwards I saw the mast and mainsail rocking between the stars Deneb and Vega. I imagined the Earth and its rotation, a mile of black sea beneath me, and I thought about various people all over the world doing different things at that moment: many suffering, longing for something, some sleeping, a rare few blessed and blissful and as free as me at that instant. I tried without success to envision someone living something even nearly as beautiful. How could anyone be as privileged as me in that instant? The entire adventure was worth it for that one night, that one half-hour on the bow with the dolphins.

Just as most Western sailors throughout history seem to have always feared and hated sharks, these same sailors have seemed to have found joy in watching dolphins, perhaps because of their smile-like mouth, their dynamic swimming around boats, and because, well, their teeth are a lot smaller. Sailors in Slocum's day were quite content to enjoy dolphins leaping, celebrating them as good omens, and then kill the same animals for dinner. Yet by the mid-twentieth century, harpooning dolphins for food or souvenirs largely faded from the broader culture of both working mariners and recreational sailors in the West due to increased understanding of our mammalian connections, further studies into their intelligence, as well as popular depictions in stories and film, such as the television series *Flipper* (1964–7). Dolphins and whales in the 1970s and 1980s became the poster animals for ocean conservation and endangered species, just as polar bears are often the icon for climate-change organizations today.

Slocum not only wrote of how ocean dolphins favored sailing vessels over steamships, but he said they leaped out of the water when he sang sea chanteys in the North Atlantic, "vastly far more appreciative than the turtles." Slocum thought of dolphins as fish, but if he ever tried to harpoon them, as he did sea turtles and sharks, he never mentioned this in *Sailing Alone Around the World*. Slocum instead described dolphins as "gamboling" companions to *Spray*. (Dolphins seem always to be gamboling in written works since at least the early 1800s.) Off the Azores, Slocum explained that dolphins were "gamboling all about" his boat, but the animals avoided the steamship *Olympia* which had powered near the *Spray* with a young captain far too confident in his navigation. "Porpoises always prefer sailing-ships," Slocum explained.

In the 1920s, Pidgeon's dolphins were "gamboling," too, seemingly "for the joy of it." He regularly observed schools during one of his long runs in the South Pacific. He began to distinguish individuals by their "peculiar markings or scars." In 1950, Edward Allcard's dolphins were still "gamboling," rushing toward his boat and leaping out of the water, "bent on getting the maximum enjoyment out of life."

In the late 1960s, dolphins kept up the mood of teenager Robin Lee Graham, the same sailor who shot sharks on sight. The first pod of dolphins that Graham saw was near Hawai'i. He could hear their squeaking on the surface and through his fiberglass hull underwater, especially after one thumped into the keel. The next day they were again swimming alongside. Speaking into his tape recorder, he said: "It has been so long since I heard any voice, and it's almost as though someone was trying to answer me." Leaving his anchorage in American Samoa, and then later out of Darwin, Australia, Graham wrote that dolphins seemed to be welcoming him back to the sea. When he met and fell in love with his future wife, Patti, she reminded him of a dolphin when she swam. When the two walked naked on the beach in the Galápagos, Patti now five months pregnant, Graham wrote that the dolphins came up to the shore "and sort of tilted their heads sideways to take a look." He expands from here to talk about their

Garden of Eden, the prolific wildlife, and the dolphins' lack of fear of humans: "they sort of accept us."

Dolphins have kept on playing happy protective roles in single-handed sailor stories. It happens so often, dolphins arriving at the right time to welcome or encourage, that it cannot always be a coincidence. On Neal Petersen's first ocean passage up to Ireland, dolphins appeared just at the moment when he was beginning to believe his naysayers, the "critics at the yacht club." He had lost his rudder, had no wind, was low on drinking water, and he knew he would have no money to repair anything when he got ashore. This was when the dolphins came leaping, flipping, "dancing on their tails" along both sides of his boat: "As if to lift my spirits, Nature answered on cue."

The most extraordinary sea story about ocean dolphins that I've heard or read was told by Moitessier. It's noteworthy that among the books he said he was reading on board was Robert Merle's *The Day of the Dolphin* (1967), a science-fiction novel about dolphin intelligence and a biologist based on John Lilly, the researcher who explored single-handed sailor narratives and, more famously, studied LSD, water immersion, and dolphin-human communication. Moitessier and *Joshua* were nearing Rakiura Stewart Island, at the southern tip of Aotearoa New Zealand. He knew that submerged rocky shoals extended far out beyond the island. Although it was mostly overcast, he managed a sun sight. Confident as to where he was, he continued sailing swiftly at over seven knots with a steady favorable breeze, making sure to give the shoals a wide berth. Once past this point he would be truly eastbound in the South Pacific, able to pop some champagne and free from worrying about any more land for thousands of miles.

The sky filled with clouds, but the waves remained small.

The wind held as he sped along, eager to pass this last hazard. When he was down below drinking coffee and looking at
the chart, he heard the "familiar whistlings," so he poked his
head out of the hatch and saw a rush of over one hundred
dolphins schooling around his boat. By his description, geography, and their behavior, these were likely dusky dolphins
(*Lagenorhynchus obscurus*), which have very small beaks, black
backs, and white bellies. They acted in a way he had never
seen any dolphins behave before.

Moitessier wrote: "A tight line of 25 dolphins swimming
abreast goes from stern to stem [bow] on the starboard side,
in three breaths, then the whole group veers right and rushes
off at right angles, all the fins cutting the water together and
in the same breath taken on the fly."

Moitessier watched them repeat this behavior over and
over. He sensed that they were agitated, "nervous." Normal
dolphin behavior would be to swim on both sides of his boat
or play in his bow wake, especially since he was sailing so well
and quickly. But this time, among the huge school a smaller
group swam alongside his boat then sharply turned right, to
starboard. The dolphins repeated this group turn about ten
times. Moitessier decided to look at his compass. The wind
had shifted roughly ninety degrees. With the calm waters and
the disorienting overcast skies, he hadn't noticed that *Joshua*
had turned itself northerly and was heading toward the submerged reef, the jagged edges that would have ended his trip,
if not his life in these cold seas.

Moitessier turned right to follow the dolphins, adjusting
his sails and the self-steering gear to a new safer course. The
dolphins stopped their veering behavior. The entire school
stuck around, though mostly on the starboard side of his
boat. One of them leaped out of the water three times,

Teenaged single-hander Laura Dekker watches dolphins from the bow of her boat *Guppy* en route to the Galápagos Islands (2011).

spinning in the air. Moitessier could not help interpret this to mean that the dolphin was celebrating their communication and cheering him on. Although he was tempted to steer back to the left again toward the rocks, just to see what would happen, he wrote that he was afraid to ask for too much, to probe his fairy tale too hard.

"I can't risk spoiling what they have already given me."

The dolphins continued beside him, seemed to look up at him, and they kept playing around *Joshua* for about two more hours—longer than he had ever been surrounded by dolphins in all his years at sea. Even when the group left, two stayed with him, one dolphin on each side of the bow, "two fairies in the waning light," for another three or so hours, through twilight, until after he and *Joshua* had cleared the shoals.

When it comes to whales—by which I mean the larger toothed whales like orcas (killer whales), pilot whales, and sperm whales, and the large baleen whales like humpbacks and blue whales—solo sailors tend to have more conflicted perceptions. The sheer size of whales is magnificent and awe-inspiring, but for vulnerable sailors by themselves whales also represent a genuine threat to their safety.

Teddy Seymour, for example, had an encounter with an orca that could have sunk his boat. Sailing alone in *Love Song* in 1986, he was cruising across the Gulf of Aden, bound for the Suez Canal. Seymour was using his Aries self-steering system with its separate rudder suspended off the stern, about two feet under the water. He had passed through a region of light winds and was making good time, sailing safely and calmly. All was going well. Earlier that day he had seen an orca, which is easy to identify at sea because of its black skin, distinctive white patches, and tall thin dorsal fin, which for males can jut out of the water as tall as a person, like a giant witch's hat slicing through the waves.

After dark, the same orca, or maybe another one, approached his boat.

"A mischief maker pushed *Love Song* sideways," Seymour wrote, "and made teeth marks in the Aries rudder. By the time I leaped to the cockpit, the rudder was being molested as the boat continued to be pushed and slightly tilted."

Seymour did not give an estimate of the killer whale's length, but orcas can grow as long as thirty feet. His boat *Love Song* was thirty-five feet long.

"As the hull slid off the emerging monster," Seymour explained, "a part of the mass appeared; then it quietly submerged. Operating the engine and striking the engine with a hammer were two techniques used for the next half hour to deter foul play."

Orcas, like all toothed whales, are highly tuned to hearing underwater: sound and echolocation are their primary methods for hunting and social communication. Seymour must have read or heard somewhere that engine noises deter killer whales and reduce their ability to talk to each other and to find food. In the 1980s, the branch of marine biology that studied whale echolocation and their sensitivity to underwater sound had only just begun to emerge.

Seymour concluded his account with some humor.

Explanations submitted to account for this obnoxious behavior suggest both innocence and violence. Was the nudging an act of passion? Could it have been love at first sight? Were the teeth marks a display of affection to be viewed as a memoir? Perhaps the light-grey colored Aries rudder flashing side-to-side in the phosphorescent matter of the sea lured the animal into regarding the device as an evening snack. For the same reason that a patent log rotor is painted black; namely, shark avoidance, I accepted this incident as a suggestion to paint the Aries rudder a darker color.

Perhaps the pale rudder moving through the bioluminescence might indeed have looked to a hungry killer whale like a fish or a whale's fin? The rudders of these devices are hardy, made of thick fiberglass, but I suspect if that orca had really wanted to take a full confident chomp, with each tooth longer than your finger, it would have done far more damage.

Nor was Seymour the first or the last sailor to come hull to head with a killer whale. There was a theory that Bill King's boat, holed off Australia, was not bashed by a great white shark but instead by a killer whale. In 1972 at least three killer whales sank a cruising boat off the Galápagos, setting the Robertson family into their life raft and sailing dinghy for over a month before they were picked up by a fishing vessel.

Single-handed sailors have also had close encounters with a range of other whale species. One September day in 1892, when William Andrews was sailing alone across the North Atlantic and only about a week from landing in Portugal in his 14.5-foot boat, he maneuvered through a pod of what he identified as finbacks. Andrews wrote, perhaps referring to a boat hook of some kind: "I seized my shark tickler, rattled it on the boat, made a noise and yelled at them. All to no avail. On they came, with their mouths wide open and with blow holes big enough to crawl into. I commenced to tremble and feel shaky in the knees. When within fifty feet, oh, how they made the water boil!" The whales made a commotion around his boat—presumably he was in an area where they were feeding. He reported that it lasted a terrifying fifteen minutes, turning his little boat every which way, "they blowing their misty breaths in my face."

A few years later, in *Sailing Alone Around the World*, Slocum was in awe of the feeding behavior of whales, likely humpbacks, doing what biologists now refer to as "bubble feeding" in which they corral a school of fish using air bubbles. Slocum experienced the danger of whales, too, when after leaving Juan Fernández off the coast of Chile he and *Spray* had a near collision with a large whale.

In Slocum's 1890s, as you might expect, there was little talk about ocean conservation or even much human impact on deep-ocean animal populations, other than the recognition that the whalemen and sealers had impacted and even sometimes decimated local "stocks." Extinction at the hand of human hunting and loss of habitat was well known *on land* by then, but although fishermen recognized the reductions of many populations and worried about the impacts of higher-capacity technologies, very few ocean species beyond fur seals and a couple of seabird species, such as the great auk, had actually been identified as extinct or even severely threatened by Western communities. Few if any early single-handed sailors mention loss or reduction of marine populations of any kind during their travels. For example, in Durban, South Africa, Pidgeon anchored his *Islander* beside three steam whaleships—steel vessels with explosive harpoons that hunted the fast rorqual whales—even as that very year the absolute last of the American wooden whaling ships under sail were limping out of New Bedford, Massachusetts, to try to find any remaining slower-swimming sperm and right whales. Pidgeon ate and socialized with the whalemen in Durban, but he had nothing to say about whale populations or hunting. In fact, over his entire circumnavigation, Pidgeon reported very little interaction with whales themselves, although he once mentioned how surprised he was by the duration of one whale's breath. Seeing the world as he did, Pidgeon concluded that whales were of little danger to small boats, because they were well aware of their surroundings— as long as you didn't surprise them.

In the 1940s, sailing much farther south, Vito Dumas often wrote of seeing whales yet almost entirely in terms of danger to his vessel. He reported at least ten close encounters with whales—large baleen whales, sperm whales, and mid-size toothed whales, perhaps pilot whales. His solo transect might be a record of healthier whale populations in the Southern Ocean before the industrial-scale increase of hunting whales there after the war. Sailing as he was during wartime, his language to describe *what-he-saw* follows in kind. During one calm on the approach to South Australia, with the horizon and sea blending together, Dumas wrote that "the stertorous breathing of the whales sounded like a far-off naval bombardment, punctuated by the splash of projectiles." At another point a fifty-foot sperm whale, twice the size of his boat, made multiple passes around his *Lehg II*, as if the whale were examining the vessel and its human inhabitant. On another occasion his boat ended up "elbowing her way between two whales," and when the wind puffed, his boat rolled on the back of one of the whales before he could sail free. In that case the animal did not react at all, as if soundly asleep. Dumas recorded two other instances of whales directly ahead, including "an enormous cachalot [sperm whale]" that dived just before what would have been a "catastrophe," and another event when other whales of an unspecified species passed him too close. Dumas tried to scare the whales off by flashing a light or shooting off his gun.

By Davison's 1950s, the whale at sea was becoming more established as a majestic creature to most Western cultures, although it remained a threat to mariners in small boats. Sailing north in the Caribbean chain up toward the Bahamas, Davison watched a large whale from her cockpit, within a boat length, and she was nervous it might damage *Felicity Ann*: "At close quarters it was not so much a sea creature as a panorama. My eyes did not take it all in at once, but traveled along it as it ploughed, majestically spouting, across our wake, no more than twenty feet astern." In 1962 aboard his nineteen-foot *Mermaid* on the North Pacific, Horie ate canned whale meat brought from home, and he had his own close encounter with what seems by his description to have been a pod of sperm whales, of which he sought to dispel myths about the power of their spout and referred to them as companions, indifferent to his boat.

Perhaps the evolution among single-handers in their thinking about whales is best exemplified by Clare Francis, who sailed alone from England to Newport, Rhode Island, in the 1976 OSTAR and came home to write and publish *Woman Alone* (1977). Francis wrote often about marine mammals, including a loving portrait at one point of a seal. The trans-Atlantic racers had been asked that year to record their sightings of dolphins and whales, to keep track if possible of any markings and to take photographs. Francis wrote about one day, roughly midway between Ireland and Nova Scotia, when she saw dolphins off the bow, then larger animals astern: "After the number of yachts sunk by killer whales in recent years," Francis wrote, "I hurried below to get the reference book and flicked through the soggy pages with fumbling haste. But with relief I was able to rule out killer whales or, the worst of all, baby killer whales with angry mothers in hot pursuit. No, these appeared to be pilot whales, which were harmless and, apparently, not too bright because they followed their leader anywhere, even up beaches. I was very flattered that they had chosen to follow me but hoped they would find their leader soon."

Later that same day, Francis sailed directly toward a larger whale floating still in the water. She wasn't certain if she should try to steer off. She was paralyzed with indecision. Fortunately the whale at the last moment ducked below, slowly, just as her boat sailed across. Francis expected it to graze her boat's keel, but felt nothing. The whale had "his radar" on, she wrote.

As Francis neared the Canadian Maritimes, she found herself in a calm with a large whale that she estimated to be about fifty feet swimming alongside. In the moment, she did not think to get her camera but tried to identify it with her book. She could not get enough clues before it sounded. Along the same lines as her fellow English solo sailor a few years earlier, Nicolette Milnes Walker, Francis concluded her thoughts on whales by revealing the emerging environmentalism and nationalistic finger-pointing of the early 1970s: "Whatever the species, it was cheering to have seen a large whale, when the Japanese and the Russians were almost fishing them to extinction." Clare Francis was reflective of her era here, at the height of Western pressure on whaling nations, which resulted in the international moratorium on commercial whaling that went into effect in 1985.

Many sailors know the story of single-hander Steven Callahan who in 1982 was westbound across the Atlantic when his boat was holed and half-sunk during rough weather by what he believes was a whale, however accidentally. Callahan survived seventy-six grueling days in his life raft, drifting to the Caribbean. During the 1984 OSTAR five different boats collided with whales in the North Atlantic, including one before the starting line. One of the boats had to head back to port and drop out, while another, the *Tjisje*, took on so much water that it sank. The solo captain, Henk Van De Weg, was airlifted out of the water by a Coast Guard helicopter. In 2021 more than fifty boats reported close encounters initiated by killer whales off the coast of Portugal and Spain in the Canary Current, half of which resulted in damage that required heading into port for repairs.

In short, however, whales have emerged as conservation icons ashore, whales for the solo sailor remain a mixed experience out at sea, not nearly universally feared like sharks, but not universally adored like dolphins.

For Bill Pinkney, sailing alone out of Boston in the summer of 1990, bound for his circumnavigation and skimming across the recently established National Marine Sanctuary of Stellwagen Bank, a medium-sized whale was the symbol of the deep ocean, finally away from humankind. He observed this pilot whale swimming beside his boat, close enough for him to smell its breath. Pinkney did not see this whale as any kind of threat, but as welcoming him to the ocean, an escort: "I had never been so close to a real wild animal," he wrote, "and this was such a large and powerful one that I sat in absolute amazement for about fifteen minutes until it disappeared into the sea." It was a moment that stuck with him for the rest of his life.

# 21. Bill Pinkney and Neal Petersen: For the Children

Less than three years after Teddy Seymour tied up *Love Song* at the dock in St Croix after altering his entire cruise track to avoid South African racists, another African American man named Bill Pinkney sailed into Cape Town. It was on the morning of 13 December 1990. This was Pinkney's first sighting of "Mother Africa" after a thirty-four-day passage from Brazil. It was shaping up to be a bright, clear day in Table Bay. As the day opened, the wind blew favorably, allowing him to set a huge, light air spinnaker that had bold red, green, and black stripes to symbolize the African American struggle for freedom from discrimination in the United States. He had commissioned this sail particularly for this moment.

"I wanted all to see who I was and where I came from," Pinkney wrote in the story of his voyage, titled *As Long As It Takes: Meeting the Challenge* (2006).

Once beside Robben Island, the prison island from which Nelson Mandela had been released only months before, Pinkney steered his boat *Commitment* beside another sailing yacht that had emerged out from behind the harbor's breakwater, the only other boat out that morning. This was skippered by Neal Petersen, a lighter-skinned South African who also identified as Black. Petersen was sailing with his parents on board. This meeting on the water in Table Bay would hold profound significance, connecting national histories, generations, geographies, and the sail-racing communities.

Bill Pinkney, fifty-five years old, was balding, with a salt and pepper beard. This was his first solo ocean-crossing, and he was attempting to become the first African American to sail around the world by way of the Southern Ocean. Several years older than Teddy Seymour, Pinkney had grown up in poverty on the south side of Chicago where he endured several events as he grew up that painfully proved to him the racism inherent in American society. Raised by a single mother who cleaned people's houses, Pinkney did not find a passion for school until the seventh grade when he discovered a love of reading, enjoying books given to him by an energetic, committed teacher named Gladis Berry. Here he came upon *Call It Courage*, a story with which he immediately identified and would carry with him his whole life. He fantasized about sailing off and returning as a new man. "It was a dream of a great adventure like the young boy's—sailing off to become my own person and to return home a hero," Pinkney wrote. "That was the beginning of what was to become my dream to sail around the world."

To make his mother proud and secure a better job, he traveled across town to a pre-engineering high school. One day he arrived to find that someone had spray-painted in enormous letters "N****R TECH" on an outside wall.

After graduating from high school in 1954, Pinkney chose not to go to college. Like Seymour, he saw the US military as a path of opportunity, so he joined the Naval Reserve, still thinking about *Call It Courage*. He tested well and became an officer in the medical corps—despite the white recruiter urging him to be a ship's steward, to be with his "own guys." During his time serving his country, Pinkney experienced first-hand the harsh realities of the Jim Crow south, where he was forced to ride buses separated by race, watched new friends step off the sidewalk when white people came in the opposite direction, and found he would not be served in certain stores.

After his service in the Navy, Pinkney, feeling suffocated in the south, divorced his first wife, whom he had met in Florida. He left behind a young daughter and ran away to Puerto Rico. Here he found work with an elevator installation company and as a hired limbo dancer in clubs where he faked a Caribbean accent for tourists. In Puerto Rico he learned how to sail, volunteering on an inter-island ferry. It was now the early 1960s. He moved to New York, converted to Judaism, continued to read sailing stories, got a bit of ocean-sailing experience as a crew member, and remarried. He worked as an X-ray technician and then trained as a make-up artist for low-budget films before moving to mainstream celebrities, specializing in Black skin and hair, which all led him to move up the ladder until he was an executive at Revlon. This profession brought him back to Chicago, working for a highly successful Black-owned beauty products company. Now Pinkney and his wife had a bit of money, so he began to sail regularly on Lake Michigan. He bought his first boat (a Pearson Triton, coincidentally, the same design as my boat). Pinkney became the only Black member and then the commodore of his yacht club in Chicago. At the age of forty-eight, he lost his latest job in public relations for the city of Chicago because of a change in administration. So now with his fiftieth birthday looming, he decided he wanted to make a solo world voyage happen while he was still physically able. He had reconciled with his daughter, who had two kids of her own. He thought often about how his life had gone, the choices he made to leave his young family. He wanted now, he said, to leave a legacy, a "benchmark" of which they would be proud. He decided that along the way he would write letters to his grandkids.

Pinkney began the grind of finding a boat and raising the money. Single-handed sailing narratives, beginning in the 1980s, especially those with an interest in racing, now nearly all included the trials not of building a boat but of raising money and finding sponsors to fund and fit it out. Pinkney spoke about education and inspiring schoolchildren. When word got around that he was going to write letters home, not only to his grandkids but to his former elementary school, the entire Chicago public-school system wanted this correspondence. So he planned to film himself on board with a hand-held camera and then mail the videotapes home when he got to port. Kids in schools, he said, could follow the vessel's progress and occasionally even connect to him over the long-distance ship-to-shore radio. Pinkney found a major sponsor in Boston, who arranged a similar program for public-school kids there. It became essential to Pinkney's *why-go* for him to prove to children the value of following a dream and to model for them his commitment to keep going, to endure and make it around the world. "Now I had thirty thousand grandkids," he told me.

Pinkney explained that as he planned his voyage he did not know about Teddy Seymour, or about Neal Petersen, a teenager in South Africa, who was growing up desperate to sail around the world. Pinkney did know, however, reading his *Cruising World* magazine, about Tania Aebi sailing alone into the Pacific that year and about Dodge Morgan, who became the first American to circumnavigate the world non-stop. He would watch Morgan's documentary *Around Alone* (1987), made from footage he took while on board, and he read Morgan's narrative, *The Voyage of American Promise* (1989), over and over again as his primary logistical reference. Pinkey had read his Slocum, too, and had read *Dove*. Meanwhile Pinkney continued to plan, raise funds, and organize. He networked with various businesses and contacts with connections to sponsors. Through a contact of a contact, he was flown to London, where his host arranged a visit to a house with a large bronze dolphin door knocker, the home of none other than Robin Knox-Johnston. Pinkney was in "hog heaven," sitting around petting the family dog, eating tea and toast, and gawking at the Golden Globe trophy and other sailing ephemera. Knox-Johnston told Pinkney that a circumnavigation using the canals would be quickly forgotten, because whatever record he set as the first Black person to do so would be quickly surpassed. "They'll never know your name," Knox-Johnston told him. "If you're going to do it, do it like a man." He told Pinkney that he must go around the big capes by way of the Southern Ocean. Pinkney walked out of Knox-Johnston's house convinced that he should indeed circumnavigate via Cape Horn.

Although Pinkney was not exactly racing, he had no plans to sail the Southern Ocean in the likes of Slocum's *Spray* or even a stout pocket cruiser like Seymour's *Love Song*. Even if he could get a suitable boat on loan, which he eventually did, he needed to raise several thousand dollars for the voyage. Through a major sponsor, Pinkney managed to borrow a large, stout forty-seven-foot ketch, a proven vessel that another sailor named Mark Schrader had already sailed to complete a circumnavigation race. Pinkney renamed the boat *Commitment*.

During his preparations for the voyage he read a book by D. H. Clarke, who kept track of small-boat milestones for the *Guinness Book of World Records*, titled *The Blue Water Dream: The*

*Escape to Sea Syndrome* (1981). Pinkney sent Clarke a letter requesting advice. He received a kind but sobering reply. Clarke said that of all the people who wrote to him about solo circumnavigations, only five percent even got a boat, and of them only five percent ever left the dock, and of them only five percent ever sailed beyond their closest ocean. At the top of his computer, Bill Pinkney posted a sign to remind him of this attrition rate.

After that morning in Table Bay and his visit to Cape Town, during which he toured around and reflected on the apartheid of South Africa—finding the people there far kinder than the system—Pinkney continued on to complete his world voyage, including the rounding of Cape Horn. He stopped in Tasmania, Brazil, and Bermuda. Beyond his moments with pilot whales, discussions of threatening waves, and a seemingly encouraging albatross he imagined to be a reincarnation of someone at home helping him persevere, for Bill Pinkney the organisms at sea, or even the ocean itself, although "all-powerful" and "relentless," were barely present in his story of his life and this voyage, *As Long As It Takes*. Pinkney, who sailed with the new GPS technology, more often described the logistics of planning and running the voyage. He wrote of gear failure, inspirational communities in ports, cultural observations, and his bouts with fear, fatigue, and loneliness. On Thursdays while at sea, he rewarded himself with watching videos of television shows recorded for him at home. Once in a lightning storm off the coast of Uruguay, his boat stable, he stopped fretting about what he could not control, went below, had a shot of whiskey, and put on headphones to listen to the operatic soprano Kathleen Battle. He ignored the threats outside as his wind-vane self-steering took care of the sailing. Another time he was so ill at sea, perhaps with the flu, that his voyage track for a few days looked to those ashore as if he must have fallen overboard. With something like this in mind before he left Boston, Pinkney had filmed a video of himself addressing the children in case he were to die out at sea. He remembered the community trauma when the teacher Christa McAuliffe and six other astronauts died in the explosion of the NASA space shuttle *Challenger* in January 1986. As soon as he was well enough, he made his contacts to shore to make sure they knew he was okay: no need to play that video.

Despite his emphasis on his connections to schools and the logistics of the voyage, Pinkney did write about "one of the most spiritual experiences of my life." One night he sailed *Commitment* on a flat sea with "billions of chips of light" in the sky reflecting perfectly in the calm dark water. The vision led him to feel, just for one second, that he was part of the universe and the span of deep time: he had a humble destiny, and he felt at peace with his small role, no lesser or greater than any other person's for their blip of time on Earth.

As a storyteller, Pinkney perfectly placed this lovely moment at sea directly before his arrival in Cape Town, contrasting it with his fear of the racism he would see and experience. This evening of starry peace also happened the day after a near-death experience with a large fishing vessel from Taiwan. The ship crossed his bow while he was napping during the day. Pinkney woke up for his visual check on

Holding up his hat from Madison Park School in Boston, Bill Pinkney hosts local schoolchildren on his boat *Commitment* during his stop in Tasmania (1991).

deck and saw the stern of the vessel, reading "Taipei" as the home port, only "spitting distance" away. He had forgotten to set his radar alarm. As his heart was pounding and the ship's wake slapped against *Commitment*, he thought, "Had the ship seen me and changed course? Or had this near miss been an incredible piece of good luck?" In his narrative he does not return to this moment again, but it was an event that stuck with him, a story he still selects when telling of his voyage now in his eighties, and it has become exceptionally poignant for me. Pinkney told me he does not remember the smell or the sound of the engines. "It was one of those things that the visual stopped everything. And boats that size when they're really moving don't make a lot of wake or engine noise."

"Six feet off the water, your horizon in any direction is two and a half miles," he said when remembering this near miss. "A big ship like that can be down below the horizon, over you, run you down, and be back over the horizon again in something like twenty minutes—or less depending on how fast he's going. No one would know." Pinkney told the story of a photograph he once saw of a big freighter with its anchor sticking out of the hawsepipe on the bow. "And on the anchor is the upper portion of the mast of a sailboat." He reasoned in retrospect that the vessel had been illegally fishing in Brazil's exclusive economic zone, so the crew was not only unwilling to reply on the radio, but would never have reported any collision.

On Bill Pinkney's return home to Boston, the docks crammed with kids, he primarily saw his solo circumnavigation as an act of personal and patriotic pride, for his family legacy, and, again, to inspire children. Consciously representing Black America, he wrote in *As Long As It Takes* that the ocean, if you could get out there, offers a chance to prove oneself on "a level playing field," regardless of skin color. Officials in Chicago named a street after him. His feat was read into the Congressional Record. A film documentary came out soon after and his memoir and narrative of the voyage followed several years later. "In hindsight," he wrote, "I see that sailing has also served as a visible metaphor for the voyage of life itself."

Pinkney went on to skipper a large sailboat from the Caribbean to Brazil and across the Atlantic to historical slavery ports in Africa, with high-school teachers aboard in order to teach children back home about the Middle Passage. Then in 2000 he became the first captain of the schooner *Amistad*, a replica of the coastal ship aboard which African captives rebelled off Cuba in 1839 and eventually, by way of the US Supreme Court, claimed their freedom to go back to Africa. He commanded *Amistad* across the Atlantic and to ports in Africa. At the time of writing, Pinkney, at age eighty-six, is back living in Puerto Rico again and running sailing charters out of Old San Juan with his third wife. His most recent work is a children's book, *Sailing Commitment Around the World* (2022).

Bill Pinkney's boat *Commitment* had originally been built to participate in a solo sailing race called the "BOC Challenge," one of the many single-hander events that began emerging from the 1970s into the 1990s, after the Golden Globe race of 1968 and the ever-growing popularity of the OSTAR, that trans-Atlantic race that began in 1960 with five people.

In 1978 another trans-Atlantic race began; this one going more southerly and downwind, named the Route du Rhum, which left from Saint-Malo in Brittany. British Oxygen Corporation founded their BOC Challenge round-the-world race in 1982, which went around the southern capes with four stops along the way. This was held every four years, scheduled not to conflict with the OSTAR. Then in 1989 another solo round-the-world race began, the Vendée Globe, starting in Les Sables d'Olonne in the Vendée region of France. This was in the spirit of the first Golden Globe, totally non-stop. The OSTAR, and a similar race in the North Pacific, a "Trans-Pac," had now become a sort of training run, an appetizer, for the single-handed round-the-world races.

Although several amateur cruisers entered the OSTAR or the larger races just to try to finish, the *why-go* of these solo races became more aligned with technological development, financial backing, and nationalistic pride. In contrast to cruisers, the new racing single-handed sailors, aiming foremost for speed, now required large high-tech boats, significant capital, and a shore-based team to support them before and during the voyages. The smaller races, including the OSTAR and its spinoffs, still allowed for a few shoestring sailors who wanted to challenge themselves just to cross the finish line. But even this became harder and harder for sailors on a small budget as the years progressed.

On the morning in Table Bay in 1990 when Bill Pinkney sailed in aboard *Commitment*, Neal Petersen was the person at the wheel of the much smaller racing yacht, a boat painted bright red and named *Stella-r.* Petersen had directed the design and the building of this himself. Born in 1967, he was still in his early twenties and more than a generation younger than Pinkney and Seymour. Petersen wanted to be a single-handed racer, to compete, and, like Bill Pinkney he felt that his *why-go* must be at least in part to inspire children and instill the potential for the realization of dreams: transcending any person's disadvantaged upbringing and pursuing a given passion and goal.

Petersen had scraped together the money for his boat by working as a scuba diver for a diamond-mining company. Tall, even gangly, he had been born with a hip defect. As a child he suffered through several surgeries on the "blacks-only" side of the hospital and then spent nearly a year in a cast, requiring him to walk with a cane into his teenage years. Yet as early as the age of twelve he began dreaming about sailing and the ocean.

"The solo sailors Joshua Slocum, Bernard Moitessier, and Francis Chichester and the diver Jacques Cousteau were my idols," Petersen wrote. "The libraries were segregated. I was supposed to use 'our' one-room branch, but I'd make the painful hobble to the white library. The librarian there recognized my hunger, my ambition, and, being a brave woman, she turned a blind eye to my color and went out of her way to gather sailing books for me."

Petersen never got out of his head the dream of sailing around the world alone. His father dived for abalone, so he learned to dive, too. Then he talked his way onto sailboats, all owned and sailed by white people in Cape Town. As the years went on, he scrimped and saved and studied to design and help build his boat. While training for a professional dive license in the US, he traveled to Chicago to meet Bill Pinkney to learn about how he was making his voyage happen.

Now in Table Bay in 1990, after waving goodbye to Pinkney from the decks of their boats and then connecting later ashore, Petersen soaked up the inspiration. As Pinkney was sailing southeasterly into the Indian Ocean, Petersen began his sea trials on *Stella-r.*, named for an unrequited love, then sailed north, his first solo passage, having never navigated in the open ocean before or used a sextant in real conditions. He made it successfully up to the Cape Verdes and then to the Azores, with the plan to compete in the OSTAR in 1992. About ten days away from his arrival in England, Petersen was sailing at top speed, surfing at over fifteen knots, when he hit something: what he believed to be a submerged container that had fallen off a ship. This snapped his rudder, broke supporting timbers inside his boat, and loosened the keel's connection to the hull. He rigged a clever makeshift steering system with a bucket towed astern and sailed slowly ahead. He limped toward shore and then was towed by a fishing boat into Galway, Ireland, nearly dying of thirst because in bad weather half his water supply had broken its lashings and leaked out.

Petersen's sailing career from here is a continual story of extreme single-minded determination, decades-long response to misfortune and trial, toward which each time he responded by dusting off and then getting back out to sea. Petersen found a home base in Ireland, competed and placed well in the OSTAR (having to turn back at the start after running into a floating plank), and then on the return to Ireland he met a woman named Gwen Wilkinson who would be his romantic partner for several years. Wilkinson cared deeply

about the natural environment, inspiring Petersen and helping him tap into new sponsorship. He renamed his boat
*Protect Our Sealife*. Petersen's *why-go*, however, was really more
focused on personal challenge than marine conservation.
Like Pinkney he was passionate about inspiring kids to persevere and dream, writing in his narrative *Journey of a Hope
Merchant* (2007): "From Bill I would learn to tie racing sponsorship to the education of children and inspirational
speaking." Petersen has a gift for holding an audience, and
even today he still loves to visit schools.

Petersen next competed in a westbound trans-Atlantic
race, which, despite some damage along the way, he finished.
He entered the BOC Challenge around the world, but after
a triumphant return to Cape Town for the first stop, he capsized soon after leaving on the next leg, barely off the Cape
of Good Hope. His mast snapped, and he had to return
home. Dauntless, he fixed up the boat and completed the
final leg of the race from Uruguay back to Charleston, South
Carolina. Before this final leg, though, his sailing mentor, his
"seagoing father" Harry Mitchell, aged seventy, died without
a trace in this same race. It is presumed that he capsized and
sank in exceptionally heavy winds and seas off the coast of
South America after rounding Cape Horn. This was the same
weather system that capsized the boat of single-hander
Minoru Saito, who was also presumed lost until he re-
emerged weeks later, having lost all his electronics, radio, and
steering. Mitchell had activated his distress beacon, but at
that point he was beyond the reach of search planes. A vessel
from the Chilean Navy had to turn back because the weather
was so bad.

Still undeterred, Neal Petersen kept racing. He sailed in
the 1996 OSTAR. Despite *Protect Our Sealife* being holed

Neal Petersen sailing his boat *No Barriers* out of Cape Town, bound for Auckland on the second leg of the 1998–9 Around Alone circumnavigation race (1999). Note the servo-pendulum wind-vane self-steering gear, with the little rudder tilted up and not in use.

after a glancing blow from a Russian merchant ship, leaking once again mid-ocean, Petersen pumped his way along, as before, and finished in third place in his class.

He continued to court sponsors and repair his boat, now named *No Barriers*. He entered in the next four-stop circumnavigation race in 1998. His partner by this point, Gwen Wilkinson, who had been traveling from port to port and living with him whenever possible, had endured enough and returned to Ireland for a different kind of life. Petersen chose his sailing goal over the relationship.

Petersen at last successfully sailed solo around the world, making it around Cape Horn and below the other scary capes. Along the way, like Pinkney before him, he sent home videos—technology now enabling this over email—and from his cabin at sea he wrote a newspaper column and connected live to children in their schools through his No Barriers Education Foundation. He finished safely this time, in the middle of a pack of nine people (out of fifteen entrants) who managed to finish. He was the only South African and aboard the only home-made boat in the race, which was the smallest of the fleet.

Neal Petersen has done little sail racing since then, but he has remained heavily involved in the education of kids around the world. He has been traveling with his new partner, sailing on a boat in the Caribbean, and giving motivational speeches whenever he can. He and Bill Pinkney remain in touch and are friends.

# 22. Ships Again, Rescue

For the purposes of shameless foreshadowing, after Pinkney's harrowing near miss and Petersen's collisions, an additional aside on ship encounters is worthwhile here—as are a few further thoughts on the solo sailor's risks and methods for rescue.

By the letter of the law, unless a merchant ship is restricted because of a narrow channel, the nature of its work, or it is in a shipping lane or some other navigational limitation, a sailboat, no matter how small, has the right of way—even if meeting a tanker twenty times its size. However, it is understood among reasonable mariners that small boats should not bother a merchant ship, but alter course themselves and stay out of a big ship's way. In a few situations, though, it's hard for a little boat to turn, and it just takes a touch with a joystick for the on-duty officer on a merchant ship to steer away for a few minutes with no impact on their schedule.

Seymour perhaps put the matter best in the 1980s: "I'm convinced that watch personnel aboard ships cannot see the tiny, low-range lights displayed by yachts until dangerously close. In addition, it is foolish to rely upon the detection of a little boat on shipboard radar. Therefore, it is mandatory for the solo sailor to accept responsibility for being seen and staying out of the way of everything that moves." When he was sailing in areas with heavy ship traffic, Seymour used a high-powered strobe light, even though that's

The containership *Berlin Express*, the only ship Bill Pinkney saw during his 56-day passage from Cape Town to Tasmania (1991). The *Berlin Express* came up astern of *Commitment* and the two vessels snapped photographs of each other.

not any kind of official navigation light and is technically illegal internationally.

In the summer of 2022, Kenichi Horie, just before crossing the Pacific alone for the seventh time, told me that he rests easily with modern electronics. His boat has an Automatic Identification System (AIS), a technology required on merchant ships since 2004, but not available to small boats until a couple of years later. AIS pings on to an electronic chart plotter the exact name, course, speed of vessel, and the projected closest point of approach. Ship officers will presumably see the little boat on their computer screen and avoid it or make contact by radio if they cannot. Horie explained that he simply goes to bed when it's dark and wakes up when it's dawn, only getting up at night if there's a shift in weather or something else that needs tending. With AIS he can also set an alarm, just like radar, if a vessel crosses a certain distance that you key in.

The statistics, the risks of encountering a ship out at sea, are difficult to calculate, because the danger increases significantly if traveling in known shipping lanes, approaches to ports, or closer to the coast. Fishing vessels normally congregate around known fishing grounds, but could transit from anywhere to get to them. With steadily increasing global trade, ships over time have been gradually growing larger and faster and with smaller and smaller crews. For example, the *San Quirino*, the British oil tanker that stopped to try to help Harry Pidgeon, only to crash into his boat, was a new vessel in the 1920s and was 415 feet long. Most of today's ocean-crossing oil tankers are close to 1,000 feet long and are usually run by only twenty or so people on board.

It is also difficult to know how many solo sailors have died at the bow of a merchant ship or fishing boat, beginning in the modern era perhaps with Si Lawlor or likely Joshua Slocum. In 1968 the American boatbuilder and single-hander Arthur Piver sailed across the North Atlantic to participate in the OSTAR, but he was never seen again. In 1976 the English sailor Mike McMullen left the dock to sail solo across the Atlantic in the OSTAR race only days after his wife Lizzie was fatally electrocuted at the dock in an accident with a power tool that fell in the water. He was never seen again, and only a few pieces of his boat and a piece of sailcloth have been found washed up in Icelandic waters. In 1978, in another trans-Atlantic race, the French solo circumnavigator Alain Colas and his boat disappeared without a trace after a report of all's well to the north of the Azores. In 2009 another experienced single-hander, Hubert Marcoux, disappeared off the eastern seaboard of the United States, heading southbound. Winds in excess of sixty knots might have been in his area. Were any or all of these sailors run down by a ship?

We only get accounts from the near misses, like Davison's and Pinkney's. For example, in 1964, after John Letcher sailed his little wooden boat alone from Hawai'i to Alaska, he sailed along the coast of California where he found himself in light winds at night, directly in the shipping lanes. A ship bore directly down on him and didn't respond to his searchlight. He had no engine. Letcher dived into the cabin at the last minute and the bow wave seemed to push off the boat enough so that he was not sunk, but the mast, rigging, and bowsprit were all torn to shreds as his boat rolled and scraped against the side of the large ship, similar to what had happened to Pidgeon and Moitessier when big ships got too close.

Before my trip I did a lot of reading and thinking about what I would do if *Fox* began to sink or catch on fire or if I had to abandon the boat for some other reason and needed rescue. As mentioned earlier, I purchased an EPIRB which would send out a signal that my boat was in danger if I clicked it on manually or if it was submerged under a given amount of water. I had a red neoprene survival suit. I had flares, a ditch bag, and a satellite phone in a waterproof case. Mostly because of space and expense, I chose not to purchase and try to mount an inflatable life raft on deck, using the rationalization that I was already in a small boat, so my job was to keep this one floating. I had a tiny inflatable row boat for getting to shore when I was anchored, but this was folded up on deck and would easily take twenty minutes, even when highly motivated, to get pumped up and ready to put over the side. In order to keep their sailboats afloat, some mariners have added extra flotation in all sorts of ways inside their cabins, while others have added watertight bulkheads so any flooding could be contained in one section of the hull.

The single-handed sailor "should have the decency to drown like a gentleman and not bother rescue people," said Blondie Hasler, the veteran officer of the Royal Marines who founded the modern trans-Atlantic race in 1960. Written into the rules for this first race was that the sailors had to be ready to make their own repairs, and that they "have no right to expect or demand rescue operations to be launched on their behalf."

This bravado is easier to support from the safety of shore, of course, and nobody knows how you will react in a moment of stress when your life is on the line. It is true, however, that rescue efforts can put other people in danger. In 1972, for example, seventy-year-old Sir Francis Chichester set out across the Atlantic for another go at the OSTAR. When he dropped radio contact for over a week, most presumed he was lost. It turned out he was indeed ill and his self-steering had broken, but he was heading for the Azores or maybe back home to England. Several misinterpreted communications followed while it seemed all of Europe tumbled out to rescue Sir Francis. The French weather ship *France II* got too close to Chichester's boat and snapped some of his rigging and part of his mizzen mast. Then he really did need a rescue, which was conducted by a Royal Navy warship. On the way home, the *France II* then collided with an American private yacht in the Bay of Biscay, which the press reported (incorrectly) had also been outbound to rescue Chichester. "I had not asked for help," Chichester wrote in *The Sunday Times*, devastated, before he knew the truth, "but that cannot alter the fact that those who lost their lives were trying to help me. They acted in the highest tradition of the sea, and I am deeply distressed that their generous action ended so disastrously." The yacht had sunk, drowning seven of the eleven souls on board.

High-profile rescues of single-handers have continued to increase as the boats, designed for speed, have gotten lighter and faster, venturing farther, and solo sailors are pushing their boats harder and harder to win races. Although race officials have put in place more safety measures, including mandatory boat inspections and proof of at least one previous single-handed passage of a given number of offshore miles, there have been more than a few tragedies. In 2017, for example, even with all the weather routing and modern technologies, only seven of twenty-one entrants finished the OSTAR and four needed rescue due to an enormous and unusual storm in June. Among those rescued were experienced single-handers, veterans of other races and of severe conditions.

In the first BOC Challenge Race in 1982, seventeen sailors entered, ten finished all the way around the world with the four stops, and one person had to be rescued at sea. In the 1986 BOC Challenge, twenty-one sailors entered, sixteen made it all the way, one person had to be rescued at sea, and this time one person died. His name was Jacques de Roux, a former officer aboard French nuclear submarines. He was off the southeast of Australia. They recovered his boat, undamaged, but he was never found. In the previous BOC race, de Roux had capsized and lost his mast, but he had been miraculously saved by another single-handed sailor. This time, although in the lead, Jacques de Roux was exhausted, his self-steering hadn't been working, and then something happened that we'll never know. In the 1994 BOC round-the-world race, Frenchwoman Isabelle Autissier, who had successfully finished a previous circumnavigation race, this time lost her mast and after clinging to a damaged hull was airlifted by a helicopter launched from a frigate of the Australian navy. During the race that Neal Petersen completed in 1998–9, Autissier was leading the race but capsized in the distant Southern Ocean. She was rescued this second time by a fellow sailor (who went on to win the race).

As with Donald Crowhurst, Bas Jan Ader, and Jacques de Roux, occasionally a single-hander's boat is found with no one on board. The cause of death here is presumably not a ship collision. In 1966 an experienced single-hander named John Pflieger, for example, still sailing well at sixty-eight years old, cleared out of Bermuda, but then his boat, without a soul on board and the jib set, tiller lashed, and a pipe still filled with tobacco, grounded on a sand bar off Antigua. Pflieger was never found. In 1968 one of the more famous of the single-handed ascetics, William Willis, who had traveled alone with practically nothing, on slow-moving sailing rafts across the South Pacific, died at age seventy-four while sailing by himself on a trans-Atlantic crossing out of Long Island, New York. A few days from Ireland, a Latvian fishing vessel found his boat with his logbook inside, but Willis had been long gone. In 1992, Mike Plant, a veteran of three solo circumnavigations, was crossing the Atlantic on the way to participate in the Vendée Globe, when he disappeared—a ship found his boat floating a month later, capsized, the keel broken off, about halfway between the Azores and Ireland. In 1997 a ship off the coast of Chile found the floating wreck of Vendée Globe racer Gerry Rouffs—he had been in second place. I could go on.

Just as Pidgeon and Moitessier bent steel or sawed off spars after collisions with merchant ships, and Bill King strung an old sail over the hole smashed in by a great white shark, a staple of single-handed sailor stories is the makeshift repair, in which our hero after a dangerous mishap must cobble together some fix in order to limp to port. For example, after heavy weather knocked over his mast, Robin Lee Graham had to use his boom as a mast and cut up existing sails to fit the makeshift rig as he managed to blow slowly over to the South African coast. Although Neal Petersen must also be in contention, I don't think anyone suffered more often than David Lewis, who seemed to be constantly losing his masts. Lewis' first book includes diagrams for a jury-rig he was forced to perform during his first trans-Atlantic crossing. Years later, after losing his mast in Antarctic waters during knockdowns aboard *Ice Bird*, Lewis required two different strategies to keep steerage and drift slowly along with extra-ordinary concoctions of bits of sail and pieces of spars and wire and an ice axe.

Today, to help those who are beyond a jury-rig, Coast Guard teams around the world have helicopters and aircraft on stand-by, with international agreements and protocols about range and jurisdiction for clear communication plans to rescue recreational sailors, as well as anyone else at sea who is in danger, such as ferry and cruise ship passengers and mariners on fishing vessels and merchant ships. These Coast Guard rescue teams will coordinate with any private,

David Lewis sailing alone to Antarctica aboard *Ice Bird* (c. 1972).

commercial, or naval vessel who might be traveling through the area, all of whom are duty bound by international custom to assist any seafarer in trouble.

The thought of death for the single-hander—drowning, sinking, dying from fire or thirst or an infection or blood loss—all comes not only with one's instinct for self-preservation, but the consideration of one's potential death also comes with a significant element of guilt for those left on shore: family, friends, or a professional team supporting one's voyage. In her narrative, circumnavigator Naomi James wrote about the contradiction of wanting to push herself beyond what she thought possible, for herself, but then also pangs of guilt over how her failure would hurt those who had encouraged, even enabled her trip. This included her new husband, Rob James, himself a highly experienced ocean sailor who knew well how little experience she really had: "*They* believe I can do it because *I* believe I can, and such a belief in a person's determination is an incredible expression of faith. But if I *fail*, then, in the eyes of the world, they will be the ones to blame. And they won't be able to exonerate themselves by saying she died because she made a mistake, even if it were the truth. Poor Rob. I'll have to make it. It would be just too terrible if I didn't."

Dame Naomi James did make it back and all the way around the world. A few years later, Rob James drowned off the coast of England. He was not sailing alone, but he fell off the boat that he was racing. This was ten days before their daughter was born.

# 23. The Case of Youth: Laura Dekker, Jessica Watson, and Abby Sunderland

To drive ships commercially with passengers or cargo in nearly all countries you must obtain and earn a license, which is earned from years of experience, a suite of professional training courses, and classroom and practical examinations. But beyond a shortage of cash, there is little stopping a private citizen from buying a recreational boat—the paperwork and licensing in most countries is easier than buying or driving a car. For less than the cost of a camper van, you could today buy a small seaworthy old fiberglass boat, fit the craft out for offshore sailing, and then pull up the anchor and aim across an ocean, regardless of experience, physical or mental fitness—or age.

In 1965 the youngest known sailor to take off to cross an ocean alone was Robin Lee Graham at sixteen years old. Graham had grown up sailing small boats, cruised with his family in their boat in the South Pacific, and had read his Slocum. Although he seemed to care little about this, he held the mark for the youngest solo circumnavigator—he explored the world for five years—until Tania Aebi finished her trip in 1987, also aged twenty-one but about three weeks younger than Graham at her finish line. Several years later, in 1996, another American named Brian Caldwell, who had also spent years cruising with his family, finished a solo non-stop circumnavigation at the age of twenty, sailing in and out of Hawai'i. (That same year a fourteen-year-old boy named Subaru Takahashi sailed from Japan to California.) In 1999 the Australian Jesse Martin at eighteen became the new youngest person to sail around the world non-stop, which he did via the Southern Ocean. Martin set off after only three hours of solo sailing his boat beforehand. Shortly after Jesse Martin's voyage, the World Sailing Speed Record Council stopped certifying age and other "human condition" records, such as oldest or youngest, and really any other category beyond speed—not marital status or disability or race, stating that these categories can be expanded endlessly and the verification is "a less exact science." There had been special concern about encouraging young people, because in order to secure sponsorship and raise money for a boat, it was usually necessary to say they were doing something new or breaking some kind of record.

In 2007 (the same year I sailed in the other direction) an English boy named Michael Perham sailed across the Atlantic to the Caribbean at the age of fourteen; his father sailed behind him in another boat. Perham then set out to sail solo around the world, this time with a major sponsor funding his high-end offshore racing boat. An American teenager named Zac Sunderland was already doing the same, but on a fitted-out pocket cruiser. Sunderland, who had been inspired by growing up reading Robin Lee Graham's *Dove*, definitively decided to do the trip after watching *Deep Water* (2006), a documentary about Donald Crowhurst. Sunderland finished his voyage and held the record for the youngest solo circumnavigator for about a month—until Perham finished, since the teenager from England was sixty-five days younger.

Then during the years 2009 to 2012 three teenaged women from three different countries—Laura Dekker, Jessica Watson, and Abby Sunderland (Zac's younger sister)—set out to sail around the world alone. All three, at least in part, sought to claim the new record for the youngest person to circumnavigate single-handed. The story of these three teenagers—Dekker, Watson, and Sunderland—is extraordinary in part because the three young women had the further hurdle of social judgment in front of them, even though a handful of young men had already done the same types of voyages. "For women, and young women in particular, risk-taking is something to be avoided," wrote social science researchers Mike Brown and Dawn Penney, who had found that the general public believes that risk-taking is primarily the "preserve of males." In each of their books, published shortly after their voyages, Dekker, Watson, and Sunderland's *why-go* and *what-they-saw* reveal a new technological viewpoint and a method of communication that Slocum or even Davison could never have imagined.

Her father bought her a little sailboat at age six, and by age eight, Laura Dekker so regularly won all the youth events that she was no longer allowed to compete against the other kids and had to sail against adults. In her narrative, *One Girl One Dream* (2013), Dekker explained that at ten years old her father allowed her to go camping alone with just her dog for six weeks. At thirteen, she sailed in a small boat alone from her home in the Netherlands across the North Sea over to England. After she had been there a couple of days at the dock, the police showed up to inquire. Her father was required to fly over, after which he then (legally) allowed her to sail back home by herself.

This was the summer of 2009. The American and British sixteen-year-old boys, Zac Sunderland and Michael Perham, were finishing up their world voyages, and Jessica Watson in Australia, also sixteen, was preparing to leave. Dekker likely saw all this in the news and thought *I could do this, too.* But she declared later: "I wasn't looking for fame. I just wanted to sail and be left alone." Her father helped her get a boat ready, for which Dekker came up with half of the money by working odd jobs. After they went to the Department of Education to register her for the distance school program set up for Dutch kids living abroad, the official leaked their plans to the press. Soon she and her father were overrun by phone calls from journalists and television reporters.

In the footage from the news cameras at the time Laura Dekker looks calm, partly confused, very young, but also maturely, mildly amused by the absurdity of the attention. She wrote in her personal notes at the time that she felt terribly depressed and exhausted by the trials, writing "It's a good thing I'm a fine actress." The Dutch Council for Child Protection saw Dekker's idea primarily in terms of child neglect and seemingly a fear that this might break the compulsory education system in the country. The case about the girl who wanted to sail the world alone received enormous media attention. The Dutch Prime Minister weighed in on television that Dekker had to stay in the country to attend school. The court assigned a guardian (who was male) to keep a close eye on Dekker and make sure she did not try to sail away. The courts sought to evaluate Dekker's technical competence as a sailor and her emotional, social, and cognitive development. The appointed psychologist found that Laura had an emotional "flatness" and that she "is inclined to operate independently . . . so that friendships take on a somewhat functional character." She had very little interest in peer approval, the report said, and she "is self-centered and very self-satisfied." The courts tried to decide whether her father, Dick Dekker, had shown gross negligence by supporting this voyage.

As Laura Dekker lived under surveillance and her case made it through the courts, on the other side of the world, in the early hours of 8 September 2009, Jessica Watson was outbound for a final shakedown cruise aboard *Ella's Pink Lady*. Watson was sailing the boat alone from her home port in southern Queensland down to Sydney, which would be her official start. Watson's parents had taken their four kids to live on a motorboat for a while, but both of them really hoped Jessica would abandon this circumnavigation idea— or at least put it off for a very long while. Yet Jessica had been persistent over the last few years in getting offshore passage experience, seeking expertise, taking training courses, and researching sponsorship. Her parents kept asking experts and people with whom she sailed if they thought Jessica had the stuff to do this. They kept receiving green lights. Against their instinct, they began to help with the business side of things, and Watson's parents had a trusted friend, a true ocean-sailor and single-hander, who advised her (and them).

*Ella's Pink Lady* was a proven rock-solid offshore fiberglass boat design, a thirty-four-foot Sparkman and Stephens, built to cruise anywhere—similar to Teddy Seymour's boat. It was no coincidence that Watson's was the exact same design that previous teenagers Brian Caldwell and Jesse Martin had single-handed around the world non-stop. Sailing out of the harbor, the hull painted a glossy pink, *Ella's Pink Lady* displayed a mosaic of sponsorship advertisements on the hull and the sails shouted in enormous pink letters the name of the cosmetics sponsor that enabled the final push to get ready.

On this first night out, a little seasick and mentally and physically exhausted from the emotional departure, Watson was thankful that the winds were favorable, the night calm, and the visibility good with some moonlight. At 1:46 in the morning, she looked out at the horizon, set her radar alarms, and went below to catch a short nap. In her book *True Spirit*, Watson wrote: "A horrible bone-shuddering explosion of noise woke me as *Ella's Pink Lady* was suddenly stopped in her tracks and violently spun around. I jumped up as the awful grinding noise continued, and a quick glance up through the companionway told me that we'd collided with something huge: a ship." The black ship towered over and blocked out the stars. "The roar of the engines filled my head and my whole world."

Watson hurried out to the tiller and turned off the electronic autopilot, but steering was useless as the boat had already been knocked to port and was now pointing forward as it was "shuddering and screeching" along what she would learn later was the port side of the northbound *Silver Yang*, a

740-foot-long bulk carrier delivering coal from Australia to China. The ship had not been traveling all that much faster than *Ella's Pink Lady*. The officer and the deckhand on watch up in the bridge had, far too late, tried to steer to starboard to avoid the collision. When Watson saw that the hull of *Silver Yang* was going to clip her spreaders, she rushed below and listened with her hands over her head to the gunshot explosion of her rigging bursting out of its steel chain plates.

Once clear of the ship, Watson searched and saw that she was not sinking. Although most of the rigging was down, the mast had snapped at only about halfway up. Watson called her father on the satellite phone. As they talked, her mother immediately called the Rescue Coordination Center, who then called Watson directly. She confirmed that she was not hurt and did not need assistance. Watson then called the ship, reading its name on the AIS, and finally made contact, confirming she was fine and not sinking. The watch officer did not speak English well. The *Silver Yang* carried on without stopping.

As revealed by a later official report, both parties were in the wrong here. It was a clear, moonlit night, but Watson missed seeing the dark hull or the ship's two white masthead lights and single red side light. She also did not see the ship on her radar, nor did she read its name on her AIS, which said how close the ship was. Before going below to nap, Watson checked that her boat's running lights were on and she set her radar alarms, but these were adjusted to warn of ships crossing circles of four and two miles away; the *Silver Yang* was already too close at one mile. On her AIS, Watson broadcast only her identification number, not more specifically her boat's name and the type of vessel she was. She did not have any passive radar reflectors, and she'd forgotten to turn on her electronic radar transponder, a device aloft that increased her visibility on another ship's radar. None of this is intended to diminish Watson's seamanship. She was still getting used to her suite of electronics, and lookout in the middle of the night is riddled with challenges and mistakes. It's very easy in the dark, for example, regardless of how much sleep you've had or however preoccupied, to mistake the masthead lights of a ship for a much smaller vessel or even as two stars.

Aboard the *Silver Yang* meanwhile two presumably well-rested, professional-licensed mariners failed in their duties. The second mate and deckhand, it seems, were chatting to the point of distraction. The officer did not properly observe his radar or his AIS. The two men only saw the single green light of the sailboat visually a few minutes before the collision—assuming at first it was just a fishing boat or an anchored buoy.

In other words, all of the electronic devices on both vessels, through user error by both parties, had failed to avoid the crash. Regardless of any official right of way, international law and custom demands that the watch officer on both vessels identify imminent collisions miles beforehand and try to make contact and take steps to avoid it. The mate of the *Silver Yang*, aware of the scrape, should have immediately cut his engines and made certain that the small boat was okay before continuing on. Watson had hoped that night to get farther out to sea and out of the shipping lanes, but the wind had been light earlier in the evening. Now she was lucky to be alive. In the previous twenty years, there had been at least thirty-eight collisions or near misses in Australian waters and more than half the time the merchant ship had not stopped to offer help.

After cutting away the torn sail and stabilizing the rigging, Watson began motoring back to port. She somehow suppressed the terror, then the shame, to stay resolved. She later wrote that as she returned to port after this experience she knew then that she was going to be able to accomplish her goal of sailing alone around the world. She had proven to herself that she could respond methodically and sensibly to a crisis. "I am not playing down what happened at all," she wrote later. "It was terrifying. But after living through it, I had no doubt that I was going to set off on the trip. I was more determined and more focused than ever."

Watson's collision made international news and fueled criticism in the Netherlands of Laura Dekker's plans. Yet once her boat was repaired, Watson set off again to sail single-handed down to Sydney, but this time with family and friends on another boat in company. She then sailed alone out of Sydney harbor, bound north to cross the equator to get more experience in more forgiving waters and to put in enough miles so that this 'counted' as a true circumnavigation. By mid-December 2009, after two uneventful months alone at sea, Jessica Watson was barreling southeast, blogging away cheerfully as she prepared for heavy weather and the passing of Cape Horn.

Desperate and frustrated in the Netherlands, on 17 December 2009, Laura Dekker, now fourteen, gathered all her remaining money, then wrote a goodbye note to her dad. Dekker boarded a plane to Saint Martin, the French-Dutch island in the Caribbean, where she had found a suitable boat for sale on the internet. She wrote that she had to use another laptop because the government was spying on hers. Once in Saint Martin, she posed as a seventeen-year-old with a fake name. After reviewing the boat and finding it suitable, she was about to sign the agreement with the broker when the man got a phone call. The Dutch authorities had tracked her down. She was arrested and sent home. Before it was all over, Dekker and her father would be forced to sit in total for six different verdicts from three different courts.

A couple of weeks later in January of 2010 a third teenager, Abby Sunderland, aged sixteen, set out to go around the world alone. From southern California, she, like Watson, wanted to sail around non-stop.

Jessica Watson had rounded Cape Horn by now and was recovering from her worst weather so far, which she encountered in the South Atlantic with gusts of sixty-five knots. Her boat was knocked on its side a few times, including when one massive wave rolled her so far that it buried her mast underwater, bending the steel frames above the cockpit that held her solar panels, twisting part of the railing, and forcing a few splits in the mainsail. She and the boat were bruised, but okay, and now she was charging along again, ever eastbound. In her blog a few days later on Australia Day, after writing how she received a call on her satellite phone from the Australian prime minister, Watson wrote: "P. S. Congratulations times a million to Abby Sunderland for departing on her voyage last Saturday, I know what a challenge it is just to get to the start line. Despite the fact that there seem to be a lot of adults determined to see Abby and me pitted against each other as rivals, I only wish her the best of luck and am totally thrilled that there's another girl going for the record!"

As it turned out, the starting line had to wait for Abby, because she had steering-gear and electrical problems and had to pull into a port in Mexico. She sailed with two electrical autopilot steering systems only, because a wind-vane self-steering system would not work with her boat's racing hull. Her father and her support team flew down and fixed the problem. Off she went to start again, southbound for Cape Horn.

Although Sunderland appeared taller and physically stronger than Dekker and Watson, Abby projected on camera a quieter, more passive persona—an ever so slight deer-in-headlights vibe. When she was little, the whole family had cruised in a sailboat for three years along the coast of Mexico. One of their favorite books to read as a family was the story of Robin Lee Graham and *Dove*. Back home, her father self-published a book of their family adventure as cruisers. As her brother Zac was planning, then sailing on his circumnavigation, Abby was fourteen, helping out—and telling her mother that she wanted to do it, too.

For her "campaign," as the Sunderlands, Neal Petersen, and other modern racers call a major voyage, Abby was able to secure sponsors. They purchased a high-tech deep-water racing boat named *Wild Eyes*, with the thinking that if she could sail faster, she might avoid the worst weather, and spend less time in the Southern Ocean. This boat had already been sailed solo around the world by another person, and it was a design that was lightweight but theoretically unsinkable because of its several separate watertight compartments and extra flotation. Part of the reason that Abby aimed to sail solo around the world non-stop, instead of pulling in to ports, was that, as her mother put it in one interview, there was the worry about her as a teenaged girl, "this young blonde thing," in ports "filled with political unrest, violence." And there was, too, the matter of moving quickly to be able to set the record as the youngest person to circumnavigate the world alone.

As with Watson and Dekker, people from all over questioned the parents and Abby's experience and maturity—even though the family had just supported their teenaged son in a safe circumnavigation. The parents opened themselves up to further criticism, because they welcomed a film crew in to observe their family and their seven kids as Abby prepared for her voyage. The idea was that this would be a family reality show about home-schooling, Christian life, and a way to raise children away from, as Abby's co-author put it, "the electronic cages of Facebook, texting, and video games, and to aspire to achieve great things." The show never happened, but it was to be titled *Adventures in Sunderland.*

Abby embraced this idea that to sail around the world alone *is* an important, laudable feat. Her explanation of her *why-go* feels like a young Western anthem, a striving for individual prowess in service of a trophy, a dream—which somehow rings slightly different, perhaps unfairly so, from what, say, Davison expressed. In her book *Unsinkable: A Young Woman's Courageous Battle on the High Seas* (2011), Sunderland was sailing southbound toward the equator, getting her sea legs, having success taking care of her engine, when she mused, "It seems like people my age are over-protected today." She wrote that the "Student of the Week" stickers on the back of minivans are meaningless and that when America was founded, boys her age were running farms, apprenticing in a trade, and going to war, while girls her age were starting families. She questioned the very idea of "teenage years":

> If you belong to a church, you might go on mission trips to foreign countries, which is cool. Other than that, it's hang out at the mall, surf the Internet, and wait until you're eighteen to start your life.
>
> As I passed weeks alone at sea, especially when watching amazing sunsets or night skies filled with shooting stars, I was so thankful that my parents trusted me enough, and had enough faith in my abilities, to let me follow my passion and try to do something great, even if I might fail. And it was little successes along the way that changed me, built my confidence, and helped me grow.

Dekker, Watson, and Sunderland all espoused pretty much the same idea, just as did their contemporary male teenaged solo sailors. To sail alone around the world was something awesome, with a somewhat pompous suggestion that every person wanted to do something like this but did not have the courage to pursue their ultimate goals.

"Why are some people strong and others weak?" Laura Dekker wrote later in her account, *One Girl One Dream*. "Why was I able to fight so hard against the Dutch state to be able to sail, while others don't pursue their dreams and most just carry on dreaming endlessly?"

On 14 May 2010, Watson returned home to an adoring crowd of thousands of people after her non-stop around the world of 210 days alone. A flotilla of hundreds of boats surrounded *Ella's Pink Lady*, with passengers waving and honking and shouting as they all escorted her in. Helicopters whirred overhead. Jessica yelled happily over to her family and from a grocery bag handed over the rail she slurped cold whipped cream right out of the dispenser. When her boat tied up to a pink-carpeted quay at the base of the Sydney Opera House, she stepped off and hugged her parents and sat immediately for speeches, delivered her own, and cried and waved and smiled.

Watson wrote in her book *True Spirit* that she was timid as a child, the last of her siblings to hop into the sailboat. She also had significant dyslexia growing up, so that it took her a while to read and her spelling remained a challenge. Part of her stated *why-go* was to prove to herself she could do this and to inspire young people to follow their dreams. She felt stung by being continually underestimated at the docks or elsewhere because she was a young woman. Her mother had once read to her Jesse Martin's *Lionheart*, in which the Australian teenager ended his book saying he was just a regular person. "He was someone I could relate to," Watson wrote, "and it made me wonder . . . Could I do it?"

Watson read more as she grew up. She read her Slocum, her Chichester, her Graham. (Neither Watson, Dekker, or Sunderland mention or seem aware of Ann Davison or Sharon Sites Adams.) Watson reread *Lionheart*, and she read over and over *First Lady* (1989) by Kay Cottee, the Australian single-hander and the first woman to sail non-stop around the world. Watson read about the recent racing champion Dame Ellen MacArthur, who a few years before had not only nearly won the Vendée Globe around-the-world race as the youngest ever entrant but later set the record at the time for the fastest solo non-stop trip around the world by anyone.

While out at sea during her circumnavigation, Watson sent a regular blog home. From the start of her voyage she had a gift for storytelling, for delivering a voice that was humble, fun, self-deprecating, and inspiring. Watson wrote about chocolate, her hair, how she liked to talk on the phone. She did not challenge broad stereotypes, seemed even to play with them. For most of Watson's voyage hers was the most read blog in Australia. She used her satellite phone for twice-daily phone check-ins with her parents, advisors, and weather forecasters. She also called her friends just to chat. She called other single-handers on their boats or ashore, to get their advice or just to connect.

In her blogs Watson embraced the sort of animism so frequently found among solo sailors. She personified her much-loved boat, extolling its sea-kindliness, how they were in this adventure together. She named her wind-vane self-steering gear "Parker," after the character in the British science-fiction puppet show *Thunderbirds* who is the butler and chauffeur for the impeccable Lady Penelope. In the show Parker drives a futuristic pink bullet-proof Rolls-Royce convertible. Likening her Parker to "Wilson" the volleyball in Tom Hanks' movie *Cast Away* (2000), Watson explained, "I did have some pretty complete conversations with my stuffed-animal crew members and my trusty friend Parker."

When Jessica Watson stood onstage at the Sydney Opera House that day, she declared: "I'm actually going to disagree with what our Prime Minister has just said, I don't consider myself a hero. I'm an ordinary girl who believed in her dream.

You don't have to be anything special, anyone special to achieve something amazing. You just have to have a dream and believe in it, and work hard."

Jessica Watson's triumphant return to Sydney was in May 2010. Laura Dekker was still sitting in a courtroom. Abby Sunderland had by then successfully, uneventfully sailed south from Mexico and rounded Cape Horn. Sunderland and her team decided to abandon the non-stop endeavor, however, because her electronics and automatic self-steering gear continued to be unreliable. She stopped in Cape Town, where her team flew out to meet her for an electrical overhaul. It was in Cape Town where Sunderland watched Watson's return on television. She blogged out her congratulations.

*Wild Eyes* rejuvenated, Sunderland sailed back out eastbound. It was now the start of winter in the Southern Hemisphere. She rounded Good Hope and sailed into the Indian Ocean, making excellent speed. Within a week conditions deteriorated and then a line got stuck up aloft which stopped her from pulling the mainsail down. If she were to try to free it, she would need to climb aloft in near-storm conditions. She conferenced with her team ashore about what to do. Her mother sent out a group "Urgent Prayer Request" email to help Abby for her climb the following day. But in the morning Sunderland didn't have to go up after all. As if in answer to their prayers, the line managed to free itself.

A few days later the weather again piped up, with gusts of wind forecast to sixty knots. On 10 June her boat was rolled over on its side. Four times. The mast slammed down into the water, but the boat levered back up again. When the weather seemed to ease off a bit, she set some more sail. Soon after a phone call to her dad about a problem with the engine—she was running out of power to run the autopilots—Sunderland was below when she heard a roar "like a jet engine." The boat was lifted up. Abby was thrown. The back of her head banged against a set of metal gauges. *Wild Eyes* rolled over through a complete 360 degrees. Sunderland blacked out for a short period. She remembered later a few seconds when she was lying flat on the roof of her cabin, with tools, the tea kettle, the engine cover falling, attacking, crashing on top of her.

Back upright, regaining her senses, Sunderland saw the cabin was flooded, but the boat was not sinking. She looked on deck and saw the mast snapped and the rigging hanging over the side, like a trampled marionette. Her dodger, the solar panel frames, the wind generators, everything was twisted and broken. Ropes, sails, and rigging were so tangled that she had to use a knife to cut herself out of the cabin to open the companionway hatch.

Sunderland tried to gather herself. Her electronics and her two satellite phones were swamped and useless. She knew her position exactly, however: this was several hundred miles from the nearest land in quite literally one of the roughest, most desolate locations on Earth.

She found the EPIRB. She removed it from its bracket. She prayed to God. The wind and seas were still pounding on deck. She sat there down below, listening to the slosh of water around her feet, wedging herself as the swells bucked and heaved the boat, holding the object that would end her trip and set so much else in motion. She weighed her options.

She concluded there was simply no possibility for any kind of jury-rig. She lifted up the plastic flap and activated the signal for rescue. The white box began to flash a little red light in the dark cabin.

"Flipping that switch," she wrote, "was the hardest thing I ever had to do."

Less than two months later, despite the disastrous news about Sunderland and *Wild Eyes*, Laura Dekker and her father received a release from the courts in the Netherlands. They wasted little time, leaving the country and sailing south together along the coast of Spain and Portugal in the Canary Current, silent about their intended ports because they weren't sure if the Dutch authorities might change their minds. A few weeks later, Dekker left alone to cross the Atlantic from Gibraltar aboard *Guppy*, a forty-foot ketch. Seeing family at each port for assistance and sightseeing, she stopped at the Canary Islands, then the Cape Verdes, from where she sailed uneventfully and quite quickly alone across the Atlantic in seventeen days to Saint Martin, the same Dutch island where she had been arrested. Now she received a warm if cautious welcome.

Dekker argues in her narrative that she chose the *harder* route of stopping in ports, because she wanted to see the world as she went. It is almost always a safer route to stay in mid-latitudes and travel via the Panama and Suez Canals, thus avoiding the Southern Ocean and the scary capes and their enormous waves, isolation, and the march of weather

Under the eye of reporters in the harbor of Den Osse, Netherlands, Laura Dekker walks the gangway to her boat *Guppy* to begin her sail around the world (2010).

systems with an endless fetch. But the equatorial route is not necessarily easier. Most sailors feel safer far away from the coasts, away from rocks, coral reefs, shoals, currents, and shipping and fishing traffic near shore. Navigation is easier far out at sea, while approaches to harbors are often the most difficult parts of a voyage, especially if you have to manage this on your own. So there's a trade-off. Stops in port allow regular maintenance, replenishment of supplies, and the opportunity to rest and recover, but port stops and coastal sailing require a wider range of seamanship skills.

Dekker traveled through the Panama Canal, stopped in the Galápagos Islands, then made her way west across the South Pacific. She stopped at ports for a few days at a time, watching the seasons ahead for favorable weather, while mindful of the days ticking by to make sure she could still set the record for the youngest solo circumnavigator, taking longer and longer jumps. She wrote that in Cape Town she needed a security detail and her father to fly in because the Dutch government still did not want her to complete the voyage and claimed she had not kept up with her schoolwork. On 21 January 2012, shunning a return to the Netherlands, Dekker finished her circumnavigation in Saint Martin. She was sixteen years and 123 days old, the youngest solo circumnavigator ever. She still is at the time of this writing.

Tania Aebi wrote the foreword to Dekker's *One Girl One Dream*, in which she eloquently expressed the matter of technology and the modern, young single-handed sailor—both the *why-go* and the *what-they-saw*:

> But, we live in different times, and only seagulls have the luxury of disappearing at sea. Modern sailors are not Bernard Moitessier, sending messages to loved ones with slingshots aimed at passing tankers. They keep daily blogs and use satellite phones to call home. GPS and chart plotters provide up-to-the-minute positions and EPIRBs pinpoint them immediately in the event of a disaster. All this can be a double-edged sword. At the same time that technology has made the high seas feel safer and more accessible to everyone, it also keeps the sailor tethered to land. In the middle of the ocean, Laura was still on stage, and I got the impression that she saw this as a necessary evil, the price she had to pay to fulfill her quest.

It would be a mistake to underestimate the number of hours, days, and weeks of quiet, solitary time that Watson, Sunderland, and Dekker spent sitting in their cockpits looking out at the surface of the sea alone and pondering their smallness on the ocean as they recalibrated the meaning of their lives. Yet as is true for most of us in the twenty-first century, their relationship with the ocean, their sense of patience and knowledge, was quite a different one, from, say, Harry Pidgeon or Ann Davison.

In her writing, for example, Sunderland communicated her ocean world with technological metaphors, "being at sea is like watching the whole world in high-definition," and watching bright white cumulus clouds was "almost like you're watching a 3-D movie." Sunderland flicked the icky squid off her deck, "making as little skin contact as possible." At the beginning of the trip she enjoyed the dolphins, who seemed to welcome her to the sea and always looked happy. One dolphin swam in front of her boat on the way to Cape Town, when she was feeling down about having to stop, "kind of like he was guiding me, and that cheered me up a little." At one point she saw a seabird as an agent of God. This was in the Southern Ocean when a bird flew above her mast, after her mom had emailed out the prayer request and just before she saw the stuck rope had freed itself somehow: "It might sound corny or overly religious, or whatever, but maybe God really did send an angel to untangle the line."

For her part, Laura Dekker's flying fish were "smelly beasts" and the squid "caused even more mess." Dekker hated seabirds, which merely represented something to clean up after. As she was reading Moitessier's *The Long Way*, she nicknamed a white bird that landed in her cockpit "Messy." (By the photo and video, this was a red-tailed tropicbird,

*Phaethon rubricauda*.) Dekker tried to feed the bird, but it was not interested in her canned fish, and its droppings splattered on her gear and into the cabin. The seabird stayed on board through the day and even as she came to anchor in Vanuatu. When she returned to the boat after clearing customs, Messy had left. "I can now start cleaning up all the bird shit," she wrote. Dolphins fare a bit better through Dekker's eyes (see p. 288). She was cheered by pods of them, especially once toward the end of her voyage when dolphins appeared for several hours in the middle of rain and squalls.

Jessica Watson's narrative *True Spirit* is also mostly focused on the survival and technical aspects of the voyage, but through her blog entries and the backstory and perspective she wrote alongside them (as well as the QR codes linked to onboard video clips), she had among the three teenagers the most interest in the natural world. Watson occasionally offered a blue environmentalist message. She was more sympathetic to the seabirds, for example, berating herself for not bringing a bird identification guide, and she looked forward in particular to the albatrosses during her voyage, their signaling of a change in latitude and their dynamic beauty as part of the character of the Southern Ocean. About a month into the voyage, heading toward the equator in the South Pacific, Watson wrote in her blog:

> Tonight I've got company out here. Let me introduce you to Silly. He's a little brown seabird who's landed on the Sailor 250 satellite dome on the stern of *Ella's Pink Lady*. Silly earned his nickname because of his dangerous fascination with the wind generator and his amusing attempts to land on the bendy windvane blade. Even though the wind generator isn't spinning too fast at the moment, watching him fly

so close to it again and again was a little nerve-racking! Anyway, he's been sitting there for well over three hours now and seems to have made himself quite comfortable perched on the dome.

In addition to Silly, I've been seeing a lot of birds out here today, mostly little Jesus petrels and brown gannets (at least that's what I think they are!), which is kind of surprising as the nearest island is about 200 nautical miles away.

Trying to fish she nearly killed a bird that hooked itself on her line, about which she felt terrible and it put her off fishing for several weeks. Later, Watson was able to catch a tuna, and she had a go, too, at cooking calamari with the squid that ended up on deck. And dolphins perked her up as well when she was feeling down.

Most significantly in terms of environmentalism, in *True Spirit* Watson comments on ocean plastics. She explains that on her voyage all non-biodegradable garbage was compressed and packed up for the end of the trip. While sailing in the South Atlantic she saw a lot of plastic garbage floating by. "It looks so out of place and ugly drifting by on the swell," she blogged. "So I've resolved to put a lot more effort into refusing plastic bags and using less plastic when I get home." Later, as she was approaching Western Australia, Watson wrote in her commentary about how having to collect all her garbage for the voyage in one place made her think carefully about consumer waste when ashore. She explained how her fellow Australian single-hander Ian Kiernan, who completed the BOC around the world race in 1986–7, returned home to report how much garbage he saw en route, inspiring him to co-found the nonprofit *Clean Up Australia*, which organized a Clean Up Sydney Harbour Day. This grew into a worldwide campaign, *Clean Up the World*, now organizing cleanups in 120 different countries. Watson cheered: "From little things big things grow!"

At first Abby Sunderland's parents assumed that the EPIRB had gone off by mistake. They had just spoken to their daughter on the phone thirty minutes before and conditions sounded as if they were improving. But the US Coast Guard rescue response operator explained that the boat's EPIRB had been manually activated, as had her smaller personal EPIRB.

Abby, with no communication at all, as *Wild Eyes* lay ahull in large seas, could only at first try to nap and stay warm. Although she saw the EPIRB bulb flashing, she could not be sure if this message was received anywhere. And if it were, how long would it be until rescue came? She tended to a gash on her foot, stabilized the boat and tidied the mess on deck as best as she could, and then tried to bail out the water. She tried unsuccessfully to get the engine going.

Yet everything would work out perfectly from a communication and operations standpoint. It was, in fact, a model rescue, something astounding even in the twenty-first century. A large industrial fishing vessel happened to be on the way to Kerguelen Island. It diverted its course toward Abby's location. Meanwhile, the Australian authorities chartered a large aircraft and sent their own search-and-rescue staff and a dozen volunteer "spotters." From Perth they flew for six hours and due to a fortunate break in the clouds saw *Wild*

After her boat *Wild Eyes* was dismasted by a rogue wave, Abby Sunderland stands by for rescue in the middle of the Indian Ocean (2010).

*Eyes* exactly where the boat was reported to be. Sunderland was able to speak to them on her VHF radio. They explained that a fishing vessel would be there in about twenty-four hours. The plane then returned to Perth to refuel. She assembled a bag and waited.

A little over a day later, Sunderland was rescued from the middle of the Indian Ocean. They abandoned *Wild Eyes*. (Eight years later fishermen would find the hull, still floating, off the coast of southwestern Australia.)

Once home in California, the Sunderland family repelled the photographers and news trucks outside their house, deciding to hold a news conference the very next morning. That same day, going into labor during the press conference, her mother gave birth to a baby boy, whom they named

Jean-Paul after the captain of the fishing vessel. Soon Abby, her brother Zac, and her father appeared on the television news shows. Her father deflected criticism for the cost of the rescue operation to the Australian taxpayers. As Abby sat there, her father answered questions: had the whole operation been too dangerous from the beginning? Should his family help offset the rescue fees? And even, had he and his wife pushed Abby for the purpose of selling the reality TV show? Abby kept a brave, composed face during these interviews. She spoke of still loving sailing, the unfortunate nature of the rogue wave, and that she was proud of what she had accomplished. She had after all, at sixteen years old, sailed from Mexico to South Africa via Cape Horn, alone.

# 24. Storms, Waves

I had a few methods to predict the weather during my trans-Atlantic crossing aboard *Fox* in 2007. I had a barometer and I had eyes, so about every four hours I recorded the atmospheric pressure and observed the clouds and the state of the sea in the hopes of making predictions. I often consulted the books I had aboard about ocean weather, but rarely with the proper patience or acuity.

For longer-term predictions, I relied on my connections to land. Due to limited funds, I did not have the level of internet contact and weather routing that, say, Jessica Watson would have a few years later, but I wasn't that far off. Within a couple of hours' range from the coast I could hear weather stations with the VHF radio. When too far for the VHF, I had my portable multi-band radio receiver, so all the way across the Atlantic, when I could tune them in, I listened to all sorts of transmissions, both private and public, including weather predictions. An amateur weatherman named Herb Hilgenberg helped numerous sailors plan their offshore passages. Herb was a retired, opinionated gentleman working out of his home in Ontario. Again, my radio could not transmit out, but I could listen in on his advice and conversations with other sailors, a couple of whom were within a few hundred miles of *Fox*. Some days I could not hear Herb's transmission at all, or I could only get his pearls of wisdom with the antenna fully extended and its metal tip touching the stove while I delicately turned the tuning knob. During the last week of my trans-Atlantic crossing, when the weather advice was most crucial, Herb went on vacation.

I had other means. Via the Iridium satellite phone I made my almost daily two-minute calls to Lisa, an oceanographer, who gave me weather that she interpreted from the National Oceanographic and Atmospheric Association website.

As a final piece of insurance, I hired a weather-routing service. For an extraordinarily high fee per call, a guy sitting in an office in upstate New York, monitoring all of the latest satellite data, told me what weather to expect in the next few days and helped me decide which way to go. Although most of these weather-routing people with whom I spoke seemed to have never been on a small boat before, unaware of how much mileage I could actually cover in a day, for the most part their predictions were accurate and helpful. They sent me daily texts.

I turned to this weather service at the last minute before my departure, because when speaking in a phone booth in Portland, Maine, with the rain pounding the roof, to a fatherly friend named Don Treworgy, he explained to me why he could not monitor the weather for me as had been our original plan. Don was a saintly and inspiring figure at Mystic Seaport Museum, the planetarium director there for over forty years. I had taken his celestial navigation class, and we had worked together often. He had done weather communications for the schooner on which I had sailed as a watch officer several years before. Don's last-minute decision was a dark omen for my trip. He had been feeling ill, he said, was tired and overworked, and he said, as gracefully as he could, that he just could not bear the responsibility. He wrote a long apologetic email that Sunday morning before our phone call. He did not try to discourage me, although he had gone to speak with Lisa while I was out on the shake-down cruise with friends. "Learning in more detail of the thoroughness of your preparations and the design of FOX," he wrote, "I feel somewhat more at ease about your voyage of exploration. Adventures like sailing across an ocean alone or climbing a mountain are as much to learn about the inner self as to complete the challenge and that seems good to me."

As we talked further on the phone, I watched the rain out-side the booth pelting the boats in the marina, and I remembered the black and white photograph that Don had of a lovely young woman named Sue Howell taking a sextant sight. This was up on the wall of his teaching classroom at the museum. Among a total crew of twenty-eight, Howell and eighteen other people drowned in 1984 during one of the Tall Ships Races when the *Marques* sank in less than a minute, foundering in a squall under big seas a day out of Bermuda. Don had been doing weather communications for them. He wrote me in that email about how "in the back of my mind, I know I failed 19 people."

After I got off the phone with Don, I tried not to think too hard and just called to set up that weather service instead.

In the end, I had all the information I needed thanks to the weather service and Lisa's forecasts. This new world is not without its negative aspects. Certainly knowing that a gale was on the way was helpful so I could be prepared. My logbook was filled with little sketches as I tried to align myself with favorable winds around the circular lows that march eastward across the North Atlantic. Yet the reality of life in the open ocean on a simple small boat is that it doesn't take long to get the vessel ready for heavy conditions. In most cases, *Fox* was too slow to avoid anything in the short term.

My boat's top speed was roughly six knots. That's equivalent to a slow jog. I would, however, stress and fuss for days when I knew stronger winds were coming. I grew dependent on these outside forecasts and did not force myself to work enough with my own observations. I listened to their predictions too closely and did not trust my own judgment enough. *Fox* did not have a gauge for wind speed and judging wave height is tricky. Book diagrams, photographs, and the Beaufort Force wind chart help get you into a range. But if Lisa or the weather service told me to expect ten-foot seas, that's usually what I saw, if you get what I mean. If they said a wind speed of twenty-five knots, unless it was way off, that's usually what I felt and wrote down in my logbook.

Forecasts were often the most helpful when they told me when rough weather or calms were going to end. They were often wrong by several hours or even a day or two, but knowing that a change was ahead was helpful. When I was holed up in the cabin during beastly winds from the completely wrong direction, I took solace from wisdom more useful than the texts of the weather service: the words of the lobster captain that I had worked for part-time just before I left on the trip. While we were out hauling pots one morning, I asked him if it was going to stop raining. He said, "Always does."

Perhaps the most challenging weather experience I had on my trans-Atlantic passage was about midway across. A cold front blasted in, followed by a high-pressure system. This had not been predicted, and then it lasted much longer than either the weather service or Lisa thought it would. I felt helpless, even a little betrayed. It happened after some odd shifts in wind direction. Then a chilling rain swept in. More experienced mariners would have recognized the signs, but I was unprepared when the wind came in on a squall, blowing so hard that the waves were blasted round and soft. White foam laced and streaked over a sea that had turned an oddly green hue. The sky was white behind a dense gauze of gray, lower clouds moving quickly. I had too much sail set. I was not dressed for the cold and wet, either, and Sandy, who had his light-air wind vane up, could not handle this. Flicking the chain off the collar at the end of the tiller, the handy system that Sandy Van Zandt had fashioned for me, I disengaged the self-steering. I thought this would be something quick so I'd just take the tiller and steer myself to ride it out. But the winds did not subside. *Fox* heeled hard and scudded across the surface. While soaked to the skin, shivering, struggling to lash the tiller so I could go forward to reduce sail, I saw a half-dozen shearwaters astern, ambivalent to the burst of wind, flying down to grab at a fishing lure that I had stupidly streamed at daybreak that morning. Because of the boat's speed, the plastic squid skipped above the waves.

"Yah—yah!" I yelled. "Get away from that! Shearwater, yah!"

After some gymnastics and the boat nearly broaching, the leeward rail scooping into the frothing ocean, I got the fishing line in before a shearwater bit into it. With a bungee cord on the tiller (my electric tiller pilot was safely in a bag below that I could not reach), I managed to reset Sandy, bearing downwind for enough time to reduce the amount of sail I had set. Holding on with one hand to the mast, I lowered the mainsail then held on and tied a double-reef into the canvas, raised the sail back up, cranked it up with the winch, and then changed out to a smaller jib, sitting and sliding and bucking up and down on the bow, holding on at times as if I were working on the wet hood of a car that was barreling around a bumpy hairpin turn—barely half-on, splashed and shivering, as I tried to clip and unclip a series of hanks from the slippery edge of one sail while keeping the other sail from blowing away. Before the full weather system passed hours later, the wind increased further so that I had to tuck in a third reef and drop even the storm jib.

I remember incidents like that one, moments in what seem to me like coves or harbors. I see in my memory various specific events from this passage in patches of water that seem enclosed, even though at times I was over five hundred miles from the nearest land. I do not mean I envision them within the half-dome of the horizon, but in far smaller and more specific spaces, as if inside a sports stadium. It is almost as if my mind sculpted a bank of clouds into resembling a hillside or made a set of low stars into a line of distant house lights. This creation of enclosed spaces, of locations in the middle of the Atlantic, is for whatever reason a way my little brain strategized to cope, or at least recall the stages of the crossing. As another example, I remember quite clearly one bright morning in a flat calm when I was on deck and a large merchant ship seemed to slow down several miles away. My mainsail was up with the orange triangle, and I wondered if the ship thought I might be in distress. After slowing down, they did not respond to my radio call and then seemed to decide I was okay and moved on—similar to the moment that Kenichi Horie described. But I remember this event as if it took place in a small, sunny, hot pond. I haven't done this to memories of when I have been on ships with other people on board. I am not sure what to make of it. In other words, I remember that sunrise with the ship that I chose not to call on the radio and the spangly night with the bioluminescent dolphins off the bow as small static shrines on the ocean surface, places that I might go back and visit, illustrations in a book. In my memory these events have physical borders, mental addresses.

For all my talk of stress and worry, one benefit that I had when I went to sea aboard *Fox* is that I had already spent a lot of time on ships and had a certain comfort, some understanding visually of sea states. But then again, I also knew from experience and too much reading all that can go wrong with the weather. And I'd never experienced these things in so small a craft. Nor did I fully know wet and mold until this small-boat passage on open water. Fortunately I never saw a full storm on my crossing. I had enough experience at sea to know I had no interest whatsoever in storms either on *Fox* or any vessel ever again. Over the path of my crossing I sailed through four gales, all with winds likely exceeding thirty knots. These were bathtub splashes, though, compared to the winds and waves that the likes of Dumas and Moitessier and Pinkney and MacArthur and so many others have encountered in the Southern Ocean. I was, however, approaching the same waters at the same time of year as the 1979 Fastnet race, when an unexpected storm blew up and capsized seventy-five boats, sank five others, and drowned nineteen people.

I had in fact prepared for the North Atlantic as if I were to be in a constant hurricane. Before the trip I had a new storm jib made and had the sailmaker put a third reef in the mainsail. I read up endlessly on storm techniques and gear. I had spare bolt-on rigging, a storm drogue, and wore my knife on a belt always at the ready. Once underway I checked all the rigging constantly, looking for wear, lines chafing, or shackles, screws, or bolts pulling out. Out of sight of land, I inserted and sealed in the bottom of three washboards in the companionway opening that leads down to the cabin, to reduce flooding if the boat were knocked over or swamped by a heavy wave. During the gales, I inserted the other two washboards and closed the hatch. Under the beam that supported the mast, I twisted a jack stand, the kind that construction workers secure under beams in a basement.

During the worst of the gales, I usually rode it out with my best version of hove-to. I learned that *Fox* was a little tank. And Sandy was tough and reliable, steering the boat unfazed in the worst of the gales. Although I rarely felt so, I was actually quite safe.

Storms are typically the main course for the sea story, but since sailors are readers, as sailor-writer Jonathan Raban has explained, they can struggle to describe their experiences without slipping into long worn tropes, especially anyone writing after Joseph Conrad. This anxiety of influence has in turn impacted the single-handers' *what-they-saw*, their face staring into the wind and perceiving the rough weather live and in color. In his fiction, especially *Typhoon*, Conrad wrote vivid, accurate, and extravagant descriptions of waves and storms—perhaps more passionately than any other writer before or since writing in English (his third language after Polish and French). Here are a few sentences from *Typhoon*:

> It was something formidable and swift, like the sudden smashing of a vial of wrath. It seemed to explode all round the ship with an overpowering concussion and rush of great

waters, as if an immense dam had been blown up to windward. In an instant the men lost touch of each other. This is
the disintegrating power of a great wind: it isolates one from
one's kind. An earthquake, a landslip, an avalanche, overtake a
man incidentally, as it were—without passion. A furious gale
attacks him like a personal enemy, tries to grasp his limbs, fas-
tens upon his mind, seeks to rout his very spirit out of him.

David Lewis, for example, wrote eloquently of storms in the
far Southern Ocean while alone aboard his *Ice Bird*, trying to
circumnavigate Antarctica, yet even here there is a certain,
almost unavoidable predictability to the language:

> The waves increased in height with unbelievable rapidity.
> Nothing in my previous experience had prepared me for
> this. Yet I had known the full fury of North Atlantic autumn
> gales . . . Barry [his son] and I had weathered Coral Sea cy-
> clone "Becky" . . . but this storm was something altogether
> new . . .
>
> And still the wind kept on increasing. It rose until, for the
> first time in all my years of seagoing, I heard the awful high
> scream of force thirteen hurricane winds rising beyond
> 70 knots.
>
> The remains of the already-shredded canvas dodger
> streamed out horizontally, flogging with so intense a vibra-
> tion that the outlines blurred. Then the two stainless steel
> wires supporting the dodger parted and in a flash it was
> gone. The whole sea was white now. Sheets of foam, acres
> in extent, were continually being churned anew by fresh
> cataracts. These are not seas, I thought: they are Snowy
> Mountains of Australia—and they are rolling right over me.
> I was very much afraid.

Words, like people, just seem to fail before the most significant tempests. In the storms of the Antarctic, Lewis
seemed to be holding on with the only solace or purpose
being that this would make a good story if he survived. He
was like the painter J. M. W. Turner, who famously claimed for
the purpose of art to have strapped himself to the mast of a
small boat as he sketched a distant ship foundering in rough
weather. Lewis wrote: "All of my perceptions were increasingly heightened; while art is a distillation and refinement of
life at secondhand, here was I living the actual raw material
of poetry."

Kay Cottee, sailing alone in the Southern Ocean in the late
1980s, also wrote with a vision of the Romantic sublime, that
mixture of sheer beauty and terror, as she and her boat
surfed in storm-force conditions. She wrote in *First Lady*
how she tore down sixty-foot seas under bare poles, meaning
no sails were set at all, even as she dragged over 260 feet of
chain and rope astern to try to slow her boat down. The
waves rose up behind her, occasionally breaking ferociously
into white water, yet "When we were in the troughs I looked
up, and despite my fears of being pitchpoled I was captured
by the beauty of the aquamarine colours of the sun shining
through the peak of the next approaching wave."

Sometimes, conveniently from a narrative perspective,
sailor-authors such as Abby Sunderland are not required for
their climactic storm moment to try to describe particular
conditions, like the rogue wave that rolled over her *Wild Eyes*.
Sunderland wrote that she only heard the wave—a roar "like
a jet engine"—then the wave simply, invisibly overwhelms
*Wild Eyes*. She shows readers the terrifying results, the objects
of the cabin flung below.

The film documentary about Sunderland's voyage puts

the wave at sixty feet high, but her rogue wave's size is impossible to know at this point, other than to recognize that large outlier waves, rogue waves, do very much build and live and die out at sea all the time. Slocum fell victim to one on the way to the Strait of Magellan. Rogue waves often come out of big storms—a single random wave can be twice the size of all the others—or they can be completely unpredictable, in all oceans, reaching heights over ninety feet high. Rogue waves sink even large ships, can break oil tankers in half. In the winter of 1978, for example, a large container ship on the way from Germany to the southern United States sank with all hands after a distress call. Some scattered debris and the finding of a lifeboat that had not been manually launched— but instead torn from its attachment pins by force—suggest the containership was pummeled by a wave that was some sixty-five feet high, then sank. Considering events like these and the results of some recent satellite research, oceanographer Gary Griggs reported research that suggests "large rogue waves are far more common than previously believed and not just the result of sailors' imaginations".

It's reasonable to conclude that rogue waves have taken the lives of at least some of the single-handers who have disappeared.

If you have ever been in a larger ship in a gale looking down on a small boat in the same sea state, or even seen people on a little boat off the coast while standing on a cliff in heavy weather, you cannot help but be struck by the extreme

Jessica Watson sailing in heavy weather in *Ella's First Lady* under just the storm jib on the final approach to Sydney to finish her non-stop circumnavigation (2010).

motion, the extravagant dipping and heeling, pitching and rolling of the tiny craft within the waves. The boat will sometimes be bashed by the wall of a wave with a thud and splash of ocean that engulfs the entire deck. You think there is just no way that a little boat can rise up for another moment.

What more common metaphor is there than a small boat in a storm?

Few solo sailor-writers can manage to write today as did Conrad about a storm's personal and wrathful intentionality, but I suspect the feeling is nearly universal, whether they ascribe the hand of that storm to be sent by the gods of Olympus, as did Odysseus, or the Christian God, as did Florentino Das, or under the control of some other force that has conspired to intentionally test one's individual faith or mettle. Sailors seem to have always seen the storm in these terms, even while somehow simultaneously seeing the ocean as indifferent to human struggles. It is foremost the storm that is the proving ground for the individual, not the doldrums or the sharks or the logistics or the ship avoidance or even the loneliness. The solo sailor might interpret their safe emergence out of a storm as a success born of experience, toughness, personal philosophy, technological expertise, the good boat, the aid of one's ancestors, the mercy of their god, or just merely dumb luck. Or a mixture of all these things.

Like Kay Cottee, single-handed mariners have also throughout history seen the storm both as sublimely beautiful and as a reminder of their smallness before the ocean's power, no matter how tough or experienced they might be. As early as 1870, E. E. Middleton, while sailing alone around Britain and depicting himself as a model of fortitude and morality, seemed to sail from one gale to another, scudding into tight harbors between rocky skerries and rip currents (see p. 44). Middleton wrote that he never turned back after leaving a port, regardless of the weather. At one point toward the end of his voyage, as he barely nipped into an anchorage before a dreadful thunderstorm, he cited a passage from Virgil's *Aeneid* (c. 20 BCE), first in Latin, then in English. He was presenting his voyage, seeing himself on the stage of epic heroes, even as he deferred to the sea's immortal power:

> Men shout; the cordage creaks; and darkness reigns;
> The thunders crash; reflash the lightning's chains—
> All nature threats with death, as if, indeed,
> The heavens bowed to crush the earthly seed.

The image of the solitary figure, stout and brave alone out at sea in a storm, has continued to be recycled in popular culture and artistic works, from that description of the resolute spirit of Josiah Shackford written in the 1860s, to the painting of *Gipsy Moth*, so tiny and battered in the black waves of Cape Horn, an image that blasts across the cover of Sir Francis' bestseller a century later. For those sailors who see and live their voyages alone on the ocean as stories, seeking meaning, nothing has more potential to define than the storm. John Rousmaniere put it this way: "Few events can thrash a life—or glorify it—as effectively as a storm at sea."

Then again, what we expect to be the climax, the final trial of our journey alone, the defining moment in our voyage of no return, is in practice rarely so.

The times I did the most reading that was not directly related to the passage was actually during those more extreme conditions, in one of my four gales, when there was nothing to do but sit below and wait it out while Sandy bravely steered *Fox* and the hull thumped along at whatever course felt safest to me at the time. For hours, even days—though the cabin often steamed up down below—I wore my full foul-weather gear, including my thick red jacket with its neon yellow hood. This jacket had a thick wide collar that I velcroed tight on my face whenever I went out on deck. The collar cinched just beneath my eyes, sealing in that smell of sweaty, damp fleece right against my nose. Although they kept my feet wet and clammy, I preferred to wear scuba booties rather than sea boots, because I had more traction and felt a tad more dexterous and safe when crawling around the little deck in heavy weather.

In gales with nothing to do, I still rarely had any motivation or mental power to write anything thoughtful. I had a few novels on board, but I never got beyond a paragraph or two with these. Instead I flipped through the Sunday *New York Times* that I had bought in Portland. I read absolutely every sentence in this newspaper, multiple times. Trying not to mind the jaw-jarring bashing of *Fox*'s bow into heavy seas, I read about Steve Jobs' rationale for lowering the price of the iPhone, what I should do if I had only thirty-six hours in Vancouver, and that Lindsey Rosenbaum's new husband went to Princeton and is the son of a life-insurance salesman from Katonah, NY. Instead of a trail of popcorn, I dotted my wake with the balls of a Sunday newspaper, crumpling up a page that I simply could not read again. I quickly opened up the hatch, reached over the wood weatherboards, and flung each paper ball into the gray sky to watch the wind snatch it away and astern. I fancied it made Sandy laugh in a graveyard-humor sort of way, like how you hear stories of soldiers in foxholes throwing up an empty can and listening to it getting shot in the air by the ever-watchful enemy.

Sailors spend a lot of time waiting out storms, watching the clock, the GPS, the wind gauges, the speedometer, the seas, trying to decide if the gale is beginning to abate or if it is getting worse as their bodies are thrown around down below, their minds mentally on edge for hours, sometimes for days. Once during the third gale I finished reading a newspaper page for the umpteenth time and could no longer stand watching the leeward porthole dip into the gray-green ocean, that washing-machine window, and that sound of wind-shriek getting into my bones and burrowing into my memory. I balled up the page and zipped and strapped up my foul-weather jacket. It was about 7:45 p.m. I pulled on my hood, velcroed the collar across my face, and opened the hatch, ready to get a wave of water on my head. I looked back at faithful Sandy steering away, the wind vane hard over against the gale. The gale tore the tips of the waves into white-foamed spray. *Fox* lurched. I banged my shoulder against the hatch. The sky was charcoal gray, the blacker night impending, and I could see a higher layer of clouds blown by that relentless wind, while the foreground clouds with dark, heavy bottoms and scary purple and olive fringes, rolled along at a different rate than the background stratus.

It was then that I saw one storm-petrel, distant cousin to my old friend from the Caribbean. I observed its face, its little glistening black eye. The bird, a ball of ash, was not flapping. Its wings seemed locked at an odd angle, as if they had been pinned open and its body flung across my stern at great speed. It seemed as if paused mid-flight, considering me.

Was this still its element? Was this storm-petrel still thinking, "Thank God, I am safe"?

Or was it thinking: "My God, how are we going to get out of this?"

*Fox*, Sandy, and I had now sailed easterly past 40° W longitude, then 30° W, then 20° W. I continually attempted to nudge farther north, which would shorten the distance to England, but this always resulted in heavier winds and waves. After nearly a month at sea, I learned in early August that an especially large low-pressure system—with predicted sustained winds of over forty knots and seas of more than fifteen feet, almost storm conditions—was barreling up behind me. Here was information from shore that I could act upon with enough notice for my safety. I rushed southeast to get out of its way and was in large part successful, able to deal with winds of about thirty knots and from behind me, a more comfortable direction. This last bend, however, put *Fox* and me much closer to the Iberian peninsula than to England. I would be facing both unfavorable winds and the strong southbound Canary Current if I wanted to claw back northeast to a landfall at Falmouth.

By this point, I was starting to really wear down. The march of gales and calms had left me tattered emotionally and physically. I did not want to approach the English Channel and the crowded shipping lanes without an engine or the possibility of a dead battery and no running lights or radar. In rereading through my notes in my engineering logbook, I tried a bunch of things, checked the impeller, but was never able to get the engine running properly. Maybe water had got into the gasoline from waves and rain washing over the fuel cap or by way of the fuel jugs that I kept in the cockpit. Whatever it was, the engine kept getting worse. I figured I'd only try to turn it over one more time if I needed it on an approach to a harbor. (I did have a spare third battery that had been fully charged when I left Maine, but until the other two died completely I did not want to hook this one up for reasons that are too boring and too embarrassingly illogical in hindsight to detail here.)

So at the knees of this last and strongest gale, I adjusted my course and my waypoint to aim downwind and down current to Cascais, Portugal. Cascais is at the mouth of the river that leads up to Lisbon and was a port where I had docked several years before on that previous trans-Atlantic crossing. Since I did not have proper harbor charts for Spain or Portugal—I had never planned to go there—familiarity with this marina was significant, and I knew it did not require a long approach under power.

For the previous week or so I'd hung the Union Jack in the cabin to provide me with strength. Ceremonially, I took this down and pinned up the flag of Portugal.

# 25. The Environmental Epiphany of Ellen MacArthur

You can be nearly certain as you read this right now that a person is on a boat out there trying to cross an ocean alone. Beginning perhaps in the 1980s, for the first time in human history, as far as we know, at any given point on any day of the year there is assuredly at least someone, if not several someones, out on the global ocean voluntarily by themselves in a small boat, cruising on their own or racing against others. In 1988 the late historian and single-handed sailor Richard Henderson compiled a blue-water "honor roll" of solo sailors. He totaled 421 people, presumably all of whom had crossed at least one ocean alone. Of these 421, 94 had sailed alone around the world. In 2021 the International Association of Cape Horners created a revised list that totaled 330 people who had sailed alone around the world, including 180, beginning with Robin Knox-Johnston and Bernard Moitessier, who had done so without stopping. Many of the sailors on this list have circumnavigated alone more than once. There are certainly more people who have not been recorded in any published list, and then there are several hundred people by now, maybe even thousands, who crossed at least one ocean alone or did significant solo passages, but never went around the world by themselves.

Among the circumnavigating cruisers who did so more than once is an Australian by the name of Jon Sanders. He has sailed around the world eleven times. That is not a typo. He grew up in Perth, interested in boats since he was a boy.

He read his Slocum and his Knox-Johnston and got involved in ocean sailing, funding his voyages mostly by his sheep-shearing business. Quiet and self-deprecating, Sanders bettered David Lewis by completing a single-handed circumnavigation of Antarctica. Between 1981 and 1982 he did this twice without stopping. A few years later he sailed around the world three times without stopping, a total of 70,000 miles. He has written just one book, *Lone Sailor* (1984), which is long out of print. This sort of art or messaging seems never to have been of much interest to him. Sanders finished his most recent circumnavigation in January of 2021 at the age of eighty-one. As the Covid-19 pandemic ripped around the globe, he was out at sea. He had been sponsored to raise awareness about microplastics. His mainsail carried an enormous logo that read "NoPlastic-Waste.Org," and he had a specially drilled intake to filter ocean water for one hour every day. When he returned home to Australia, scientists found tiny bits of plastic in nearly every single sample.

The single-hander racers have continued to push almost inconceivable boundaries. The French sailor François Gabart, for example, won the Vendée Globe in 2013. Then in 2017 he set the record, which is still held at the time of writing, for the fastest full solo circumnavigation of the world. In charge of a stunningly high-tech foiling trimaran, he *averaged* a speed of twenty-seven knots over his 27,000-mile voyage. Gabart surfed and pounded and hydro-foiled across the oceans of the Earth in forty-two days, sixteen hours, forty minutes, and thirty-five seconds. To put that into perspective, in 1969 Knox-Johnston did so in 312 days.

The difference between modern single-handed racing and small-boat solo cruising, comparing the passages of, say,

François Gabart to that of Jon Sanders, is like juxtaposing a Formula 1 Grand Prix car race to a camping trip in a 1960s Volkswagen bus. The cost of Gabart's mainsail could fund five of Jon Sanders' boats and all of the equipment and stores for each of them to last around the world.

The Vendée Globe, the Velux 5 Ocean Race, the Route de Rhum, the Mini-Transat and Mini-Transpac (ocean-crossings in small racing boats), even the modern evolution of the OSTAR, which has now been split into a more professional race and one that is more for amateurs, are all big businesses and high-tech endeavors. In the wake of Alain Gerbault, Bernard Moitessier, Eric Tabarly, and Alain Colas, France has entirely dominated the sport. French solo sailors comprise the majority of winners, record-holders, and entrants of all the major solo races. In 2018, for example, organizers staged a fiftieth-anniversary re-enactment of the 1968–9 race—the one with Moitessier, Knox-Johnston, and Crowhurst. The 2018–19 sailors aimed to circle the world non-stop in boats that were similar to the 1960s-era size and designs, and they navigated without computers or GPS and other modern equipment. No one died, but only five of the eighteen entrants finished the race. Jean-Luc Van Den Heede, an experienced champion single-hander from France, won this retro-Golden Globe. Van Den Heede has now sailed alone around Cape Horn a full twelve times.

Although still dominated by the French sailors in the high-speed races, solo sailing has continued to expand around the world. For example, in the 2022–23 version of the Golden Globe circumnavigation race, sixteen entrants flew flags from countries such as Ireland and Canada. The winner was Kristen Neuschäfer of South Africa, the only woman entrant, finishing in 233 days. She finished ahead of the only two others who managed to complete the voyage nonstop, Abhilash Tomy from India and Michael Guggenberger from Austria. Ian Herbert-Jones from England was rescued after being rolled and dismasted after rounding Cape Horn. Neuschäfer herself rescued fellow competitor Tapio Lehtinen, from Finland, who was floating in a life raft in the southern Indian Ocean after his boat sank under his feet in about five minutes.

Meanwhile, among the solo cruisers and even among some of the racers, a sense of environmentalism has grown, influencing their *why-go* and their *what-they-saw*. The French solo circumnavigator and racer Isabelle Autissier in 2009 became the head of the French branch of the World Wildlife Fund. She writes and advocates for climate-change action and has proposed that racing boats post their carbon footprint on their hulls before departing on an ocean crossing. For the 2024 Vendée Globe, the Swiss single-hander Oliver Heer (#RaceforChange) aims to run a climate-neutral race and will be sampling seawater for levels of carbon dioxide, temperature, and salinity, sending out the data in real time to the Swiss Polar Institute. Gabart himself told the press after setting the world record that the most likely restraint to the next person breaking his time will not be anything related to boat design, but the fact that the melting of Antarctica's edges due to global warming has made sailing in the furious winds of the Southern Ocean increasingly more hazardous.

Solo sailors have rarely led the way of blue environmentalist movements, however. Of any sailor, Moitessier lived and wrote the most earnestly about his spiritual relationship with ocean life and the sea itself, but even he never really waved a flag to preserve, protect, or diminish our impact on the ocean specifically. Even in his later writings, Moitessier was more focused on people on land, both in cities and on South Pacific islands. The next generation of published solo mariners, often going when quite young and having grown up with public concern about ocean plastics, oil spills, and overfishing, such as Robin Lee Graham, Nicolette Milnes Walker, and Tania Aebi, began to lean in a little to marine conservation. These sailor-authors wrote of pollution, beautifully diverse marine settings, and anthropomorphized sea turtles. None of them afterwards, however, did anything professionally in terms of ocean advocacy. Nor have Watson, Sunderland, or Dekker in the 2010s been active in marine conservation after their voyages. As eighty-three-year-old Kenichi Horie explained to me beside San Francisco Bay in 2022, the *why-go* for him, which I think goes for most single-handers, especially at first, is more often about the personal mission.

For example, in May of 2022 the Australian sailor Lisa Blair became the first woman to circumnavigate Antarctica non-stop aboard her vessel *Climate Action Now*. She completed this goal on a second attempt, setting a new speed record. Her boat was covered with a design that depicts hundreds of sticky notes about how individual people can make changes. "I run a paperless office. Donna, Gold Coast," says one. "I embrace plastic free July, Cleo W., NSW," says another. Blair's first book was called *Facing Fear* (2021). Addressing climate change was an opportunity for sponsorship and almost certainly a far distant second to Blair's mission to solo sail around Antarctica. This does not diminish her genuine care and desire to make a broader impact. It's like people running a marathon for a cause.

All of this in mind, then, renders the story of Ellen MacArthur, our final character to sail onto this watery stage, all the more exceptional.

"I loved the sea, I was drawn by the sea, and my job and motivation were to race on the sea," declared Ellen Mac-Arthur in her first book, *Taking on the World* (2003). In this she tells the story of her life up to her second-place finish in the 2000–1 Vendée Globe, a feat that she accomplished as the youngest (aged twenty-four) and only female entrant. The Vendée Globe is an event that transcends analogy or parallel: roughly three months of relentless high-speed sailing alone in the harshest conditions in the world as sole navigator, engineer, software technician, tactician, rigger, meteorologist, cook, and sailmaker on racing boats sixty feet long—propelling oneself by the powers of the wind while thousands of miles away from any physical assistance and constantly trying to balance simple survival with the desire to go ever faster. When Ellen MacArthur sailed in the Vendée Globe in 2000–1, one person had died in each of the previous two races.

As with nearly all of the world's single-handers, the path to this sort of life and her motivation to go could hardly have been predicted—but MacArthur's passion and talent for this seemed like a rare, recessive gene emerged in this special individual. She was born in 1976, the oldest daughter of three children, in the farming village of Whatstandwell, Derbyshire. At age four she went on her first sailboat with her aunt, who owned a little pocket cruiser by the coast. Like a young Mozart finding a keyboard for the first time, a prodigy discovering her talent and passion, Ellen was immediately enthralled and devoted.

"The most amazing feeling was the feeling of freedom, the feeling that I felt when we hoisted her sails," she said later about that first day. "It was the greatest sense of freedom that I could ever imagine. I made my mind up there and then after that first sail, somehow, I was going to sail around the world."

As MacArthur saved her lunch money to buy her own boat she read every book on sailing she could borrow. She remembers in particular reading *Gipsy Moth Circles the World*. Her school library still has the lending card showing that she checked it out multiple times. Meanwhile, she passionately looked forward to the small annual trips with her aunt. When she at last bought her little dinghy, she sat in the boat on the grass in her backyard. Soon she was taking lessons. By the age of seventeen, after learning she had not passed her examinations to become a veterinarian, mostly due to a poorly timed illness, MacArthur decided she would skip university, earn her boat captain's license, and begin teaching sailing. She bought herself her own pocket cruiser. In 1995, because of her devoted teaching and excellence and speed in achieving her certifications, MacArthur was awarded the BT/YJA Young Sailor of the Year Award in Britain, sharing the stage with none other than Sir Robin Knox-Johnston, who was receiving his second Yachtsman of the Year Award. No one at the time, not even MacArthur, had any idea what she would go on to achieve—and that these two would be sharing the stage again ten years later.

MacArthur decided that she wanted to sail her boat alone around Britain. The round-Britain solo voyage had been first popularized a century and a half earlier by previous M-surnamed British yachtsmen—Middleton, McMullen, and MacGregor—and was later spun into literature by Jonathan Raban, who after his own solo trip around his home island wrote *Coasting* (1986). At eighteen, MacArthur found a sponsor and accomplished the trip without incident, navigating all the tides and currents and coastal rocks and rips that make a solo trip like this so difficult.

MacArthur next earned a position helping to prepare boats for ocean races, which led to her assisting in the delivery of a racing boat back across the Atlantic from the Canadian Maritimes. As she approached the coast of France and saw the chimneys of Les Sables-d'Olonne, sitting at the helm alone with her shipmate down below, MacArthur found herself wanting to put the tiller over to go back out to sea. Her *why-go* was now forged in carbon, kevlar, and stainless steel: "Although we had been out there for two weeks and sailed through testing conditions, I had absolutely loved it. We really had sailed across the Atlantic, and I knew I was doing what I'd been born to do."

MacArthur worked relentlessly on ocean racing with her eyes set on competing in the Vendée Globe, teaming up with the single-handed sailor and marketing manager Mark Turner. She worked to prepare others' racing boats and hustled for sponsorship to race herself. She began to work on her French so she could communicate with the major players. In 1996, as the only female competitor among the fifty-two entrants, she sailed in her first ocean-crossing race, the Mini-Transat, which is a single-handed event in boats that are by rule only twenty-one feet long. The Mini-Transat had proved nearly as dangerous as the Vendée Globe; before MacArthur's year, one person had died on average every time the event was held. MacArthur finished first in her class and seventeenth overall.

From here she, Mark Turner, and a growing support team found a major sponsor to finance Ellen's entrance in the

Route de Rhum, another trans-Atlantic race. When Mac-Arthur won first-in-class and fifth monohull overall in this high-profile event, the racing world really began to sit up and take notice. Her sponsor committed to fully financing a new custom racing boat, *Kingfisher*, built to compete in the Vendée Globe. As she continued to train and prepare, she raced with other sailors, including with a Vendée Globe veteran from France. She raced on high-performance dinghies and enormous trimarans to practice technique and to understand how to harness the power of these ocean rockets. With her new boat completed in Auckland, MacArthur sailed with part of her team to Cape Horn, then by herself with *Kingfisher* up to France. As a further test, she raced her new boat across the North Atlantic in the 2000 OSTAR (now called the Europe 1 New Star). She won this race, too, earning first among the monohulls and setting a new OSTAR monohull record, crossing in fourteen days—the youngest ever to win. To exemplify how boat design and other factors have evolved, consider that Sir Francis Chichester first won that race in 1960 by finishing in forty days.

Later that year, in the northern hemisphere winter of 2000, MacArthur lined up to compete in the Vendée Globe. Modern racing boats, whether mono- or multi-hulls, as with Abby Sutherland's *Wild Eyes*, cannot be steered by wind vanes. All of MacArthur's self-steering aboard *Kingfisher* was electronic, dependent on a diesel generator and auxiliary solar power. On her boat there was no shower, no toilet, no laundry, no insulation, no comforts whatsoever. Her food was freeze-dried and heated with a little stove. Her water was desalinated from seawater. All of her systems had backups and backups of backups, and via a large satellite dome at the stern of *Kingfisher*, MacArthur could call or email her team for technical advice and regular check-ins. She could hear her position in relation to the other racers, and she could look at Internet-posted weather, but she was not allowed weather-routing advice from anyone ashore nor could she receive suggestions on when and where to tack. In other words, in addition to the brutally exhausting physical conditions, Mac-Arthur and her Vendée Globe competitors at the time had to constantly make all their own decisions.

After coming from behind, MacArthur held the lead for a couple of days in the final stretch in the Atlantic, but she eventually finished in second place, only a day behind the winner, Michel Desjoyeaux of France, who set a new Vendée Globe speed record. Of the twenty-four entrants that year only fifteen finished. Over the course of the race, MacArthur had to replace fiberglass shelving, repair large patches of sail, flip and reset a battered daggerboard that was nearly twice her body weight (only a couple days from the finish this board had been struck underwater, perhaps by a floating shipping container), and on several occasions MacArthur had to climb to the top of her ninety-foot mast in the most extreme conditions to do electrical work, drill holes, and repair battens. Coming down from one of these trials she told her camera that this had been the closest to death she had ever felt: she had been pinned at the top of the mast on the leeward side as the boat gybed itself, since she had no way to alter the self-steering while up aloft. If the boat had heeled all the way over, she would have drowned—if not been killed immediately by the impact. In the final days of the Vendée Globe, she sailed with only one of her two forestays, a crucial part of the rigging that keeps the mast upright.

MacArthur had already been popular in France before the race, but with this second-place finish in the Vendée Globe her celebrity went to the moon. Hundreds of thousands of people lined the docks to welcome her home. "*À donf! Ellen! À donf!*" they shouted, which translates as "Go for it," or "Full-on"—which started after a French interviewer asked MacArthur what her favorite French phrase was.

After the Vendée Globe, MacArthur wrote her first book, *Taking on the World.* Despite the pressure from her publisher, she took a full extra year to do so, because she felt she was too rushed and pulled in too many different directions. She wanted to carefully write the best book she could. *Taking on the World* even includes her own line-drawing illustrations. Meanwhile, MacArthur continued to sail and plan intensely, racing on her own, with others, and as captain of a fully crewed trimaran attempting to set a new world speed record. They lost their mast in the Southern Ocean, but they were all fine, and the endeavor gave MacArthur confidence that she could take a powerful trimaran by herself around the world to try to set the single-handed record. By December 2004 she was taking a new custom-built trimaran, an enormous seventy-foot-long boat named *B&Q Castorama*, which she nicknamed "Mobi" after the white whale, on a trial race across the Atlantic. She took this boat, built just for her in Australia, from New York City to Cornwall in just over seven days, arriving seventy-five minutes shy of the world record.

Later that year, MacArthur sailed her new trimaran solo around the world in an attempt to beat the fastest time for a circumnavigator. Among the most high-tech sailing vessels ever built, with the most advanced materials and technology, this vessel was also stunningly dangerous. A trimaran, like a raft with a pole in the middle, is more stable upside down, so if the boat pitchpoles or is flipped over sideways, which is more likely at great speed, it's nearly impossible to right the

Ellen MacArthur aboard *B&Q Castorama*, approaching the finish line, about to set the world record for the fastest non-stop circumnavigation at the time (2005).

vessel, even for a team of sailors. The mast of her *B&Q Castorama*, "Mobi," reached one hundred feet high.

Arriving back in February 2005, standing once again on a stage with Sir Robin Knox-Johnston, Ellen MacArthur had achieved what she set out to do, rocking the sporting world by setting a new circumnavigation record, making it around the Earth—from a pre-set line off France and back—in seventy-one days, fourteen hours, eighteen minutes, and thirty-three seconds. Since this wasn't within any racing rules, she received regular weather-routing advice and constant assistance from her shore-based team, but the weather routers were occasionally off or even incorrect—the reality of weather forecasting. As she neared the finish, over 30,000 emails from around the world came in each day, encouraging her on, dozens of which Ellen would scroll through and read on board for inspiration as she was sailing. Over the course of the ten weeks, the most she ever slept at a single stretch was three hours—which she did only once—and she averaged over the whole circumnavigation no more than four and a half hours of total sleep during each twenty-four-hour period. MacArthur said she found this trip twice as hard as the Vendée Globe race, admitting that her mind visited some very dark places due to physical and mental exhaustion. Although she was sailing alone, she wrote that this truly felt like a team effort, even more than any other previous race, a culmination of years of collective work from dozens of people. This feeling of doing it for others helped pull her through. Her devotion and partnership with her "Mobi," too, was as cherished and emotional as her relationship with *Kingfisher*.

Ellen MacArthur and "Mobi" were accompanied back to England by a Royal Navy escort and a private fleet of hundreds of vessels. Queen Elizabeth II named her, at twenty-eight, the youngest woman in modern times to be Dame Commander of the British Empire. The President of France awarded her the Légion d'Honneur. Although her world record would only stand for a couple of years and then would be slashed by François Gabart a few years after that, the other awards and opportunities continued to flow in, and she continued to race at the highest level, alone, as skipper, and as part of a crew.

Yet five years after her solo circumnavigation record, she quit competitive sailing entirely.

To explain why MacArthur left the racing life at the top of her game, it is important to delve into her *what-they-saw*, the evolution of her perception of the ocean and marine life. As presented in her writing, her blue-water world was at first more Chichester than Moitessier. She sailed with her eyes constantly on boat speed and weather, often sailing her boat white-knuckled at more than twenty knots across the surface. Periods of calm seas and low winds were moments of anguish and times to repair the boat frantically before the next blow. As MacArthur spent more and more time at sea, however, in her storytelling she began to increase her observations and extend her sympathies to the nonhuman world at sea.

MacArthur, for example, never had the time to fish at sea, but she wrote that she preferred not to eat flying fish that landed on deck, to throw them back, because she felt sorry for them. She loved her dolphins, felt welcomed and accompanied by them, and she had been particularly struck early on in her career at the prolific marine life in the Gulf of St Lawrence as she began her first trans-Atlantic crossing. Here they sailed past belugas and pilot whales, over fifty dolphins approaching from all directions, and sharks "silently slipping along." She was, as she wrote in *Taking on the World*, "hypnotized by the wildlife . . . amazed at how many species were around us."

Early in her career and in *Taking on the World*, MacArthur wrote little of seabirds. But as she spent more time in the Southern Ocean, she became mesmerized by the albatrosses and other birds of this desolate region, recognizing that their sightings often signal land and icebergs nearby. Describing the albatrosses during her first Southern Ocean crossing alone, this bird is a "friend," but she admitted to not having time or energy to think more about them. By her later trips she was able to spend time differentiating their species, and they came to symbolize these stormy seas and were her regular companions. In her second book, *Race Against Time* (2005), about her record-breaking solo circumnavigation on *B&Q Castorama*, MacArthur wrote the following one day after clearing the Cape of Good Hope:

> Sunrise, though, was amazing—the light fantastic, and the seabirds, as ever, around us all the time. Wandering albatrosses, sooty albatrosses, black-bellied storm-petrels, and little shearwaters—dancing not just in the wind but with the immense waves. I guess for them it's just another day in the Southern Ocean. As for me, sometimes I find it hard to come to terms with the idea that this is in fact my job.

*Race Against Time* includes several photographs of albatrosses, including ones taken from stills or video by MacArthur herself from her cockpit. On the bulkhead of "Mobi," amidst small motivational sayings for herself, she drew cartoons of albatrosses, both comic and dramatic. After rounding Cape Horn, wrung-out tired and having to work aloft, she watched a single albatross seem to say goodbye to her as she left the Southern Ocean, bound north, still pushing to break the record.

In *Race Against Time*, MacArthur's interest in seabirds continued up into the Atlantic on the way home. She wrote specifically about what she believed to be a masked booby (*Sula dactylatra*) near the equator, mentioning how she looked it up in her bird book. By *Full Circle: My Life and Journey* (2010), her third book, which was a memoir of her years after the Vendée Globe and beyond the world-record circumnavigation, MacArthur now began writing of the cape petrels in the Southern Ocean, and she described her stop in the Falkland Islands on her trial sail with *B&Q Castorama*, during which she had her brief meeting with the albatross conservationist Sally Poncet. "Little did I realize then," MacArthur wrote, "the significance of the conversation."

Beyond the seabirds, she described her experiences in the Southern Ocean as that sublime mixture of terrifically threatening yet mesmerizingly beautiful. At one point during the Vendée Globe race in 2000, MacArthur was napping far southeast of the Cape of Good Hope when she looked out of a portal and saw her boat sailing closely past an iceberg, within twenty feet. She ran into the cockpit in her socks. MacArthur told her camera immediately afterwards that she did not even want to think about what could have happened, wondered out loud how in all this vast ocean she could get so close to something like this. Sailing at over twenty knots and surfing down massive waves, she said: "It is a very subtle mixture of exhilaration and terror. And yes it's amazing to be going so quickly, but you're on your own and if something goes wrong there is no one there." In all her trips to the Southern Ocean alone she had to be afraid of icebergs, however beautiful they were, because the radar alarms were unreliable, and she occasionally had to slalom past the smaller growlers at high speed in rough weather, even when it was dark and moonless.

MacArthur's description of the enormous Southern Ocean sea states are harrowing, evocative of Kay Cottee's descriptions of aquamarine wave faces backlit by the sun as the seas towered threateningly overhead. MacArthur wrote in *Race Against Time*, for example: "It's about to go dark down here, and the waves are no smaller . . . I'm completely in awe of this place. The beauty of those immense rolling waves is endless, and there is a kind of eternal feeling about their majestic rolling that will live on for ever. Watching them roll along—with nothing to stop them—makes me and *B&Q* feel completely insignificant." MacArthur, as if in a nod to Moitessier, continued on to explain how sensory it all was, how tiny she felt before the indifference of these seas, and how she was both afraid and feeling gorgeously alive—even in winds gusting to over fifty knots. MacArthur was isolated but felt free as she coped with the boat's high speed in a storm, in the dark, when she couldn't even see the waves coming. In *Race Against Time* she ended this onboard entry with a surprising shift in tone, as she tilted her hand toward what she was thinking about as her future calling after her sailing career: "I'm glad we've come down here and seen this storm. It's a reminder of how small and insignificant we are on this planet—but at the same time what a responsibility we have towards its protection."

After setting the world record, even as she continued to race for a couple of years, MacArthur had really moved on to her next mission: human sustainability on Earth. As she explains in *Full Circle*, she began to learn about the crash of the cod fishery in the North Atlantic by a chance tour of a mothballed French factory trawler and then a friend giving her a copy of Mark Kurlansky's *Cod* (1997). She reconnected with Sally Poncet and visited the island of South Georgia and a couple of the other sub-Antarctic islands, where she learned about the impact of nineteenth-century sealing, twentieth-century industrial whaling, and the decreasing populations today of wandering albatrosses. Here she learned that seabirds are the most threatened of all groups of birds on Earth. Of monitored global populations, seabird colonies have declined by nearly seventy percent over the last seventy years. Their plummeting numbers are due in part to human development on their island habitats, introduced species like rats and pigs that eat their eggs, and because of plastic and chemical pollution at sea. Although this problem is lessening due to new regulations on the type of gear, in part due to the work of Poncet and her colleagues, tens of thousands of seabirds are also still killed each year due to industrial fishing practices, such as long-lining, which streams miles of lines with baited hooks near the surface, attracting and killing birds that mistake the bait for prey. As MacArthur helped to collect samples, count nests, and record advocacy videos, she found herself mesmerized by the albatrosses, their peaceful nature away from any people. She could now slow down, sleep through the night, watch the enormous animals up close and waddling around on the cliffs; before, she had only seen them out at sea on the wing in heavy winds, thousands of miles from land. With time to think, sitting on the islands that she had previously only screeched past, Mac-Arthur began to reconsider her life, re-evaluating it thus far as even a bit selfish and self-centered.

"It was a bit like seeing something you weren't expecting under a stone, and having two choices," she said at one public talk. "I either put that stone to one side and learn more about it, or I put that stone back, and I carry on with my dream job of sailing around the world. I chose the first. I put it to one side and I began a new journey of learning."

As MacArthur told it, what she saw under the stone, what she began to realize from her time alone in the Southern Ocean, was how her carefully measured supplies and materials on her boat so closely parallel the finite materials on Earth, materials such as coal and liquid petroleum, but also copper, tin, zinc, and silver—all projected by some research to be exhausted within this century. Sustainability of resources was a bigger issue than saving the whales or stopping coastal pollution. This was everything. MacArthur committed to leaving ocean racing altogether for this greater challenge: "the future of our global economy." MacArthur's growing sense of existential crisis about the human impact on the Earth crystallized during her "journey of learning," over the four or so years after her 2005 record-setting circumnavigation. The emergency around climate change and the rapidly rising alarms about carbon emissions were getting louder.

"If we want a world that works," wrote the conservationist writer and activist Bill McKibben in 2010, responding to a lack of action in the US Congress, "we're going to have to raise our voices."

So today one of the greatest single-handed sailors ever to have lived now uses her star power and logistical talents and experience to propel two initiatives. The first is the Ellen MacArthur Cancer Trust, which she started after the Vendée Globe. This program gets together on a sailboat young people who have had or are still fighting cancer, bringing them aboard as a crew to haul lines and steer the boat and just be with other kids in the same situation, including survivors, who really understand each other. The second, started in 2010, is the Ellen MacArthur Foundation, which raises money, funds research, and conducts outreach to achieve a more circular global economy, not only recycling materials and products, but designing them, building them to be reused and repurposed from the start, to get closer to zero waste. MacArthur explains that she has found it is not enough simply to lower our impact and use less, travel less, buy less—the mission at hand is to realign the entire operating system of capitalism, shifting from a linear economy to a truly circular system. She explains that being on a boat alone, with all her supplies while several thousands of miles away from human contact, had inspired this perspective. When she stepped off "Mobi," after setting the world record by traversing the Southern Ocean alone in 2005, running for her life before hurricane conditions off Cape Horn, MacArthur had her epiphany, connecting her sailing life to the world as a whole.

"No experience in my life could have given me a better understanding of the definition of the word finite," she says in her public speeches, which have reached millions. "What we have out there is all we have. There is no more."

Toward the end of *Full Circle*, MacArthur explained that she bristles at any perception of her as an "eco-warrior." She is focused on inspiring innovation and positive change. Her beloved sailboat had become a symbol of Earth and her experience alone at sea had stood for all human life. Like the first solo circumnavigator Joshua Slocum who had returned home a century earlier, Ellen MacArthur also tied up at the dock and burned to be of greater use.

As the solo sailors have changed over a century, so have the stories created about them. In 2016, for example, a half dozen years after the establishment of the Ellen MacArthur Trust and the voyages of the three teenaged-girl single-handers, Disney released the animated film *Moana*. This was nearly 150 years after that heroic description of Josiah Shackford, seventy-five years after *Call It Courage*, and over fifty years after *Where the Wild Things Are*.

*Moana* slots neatly into the hero's journey structure, with more than a brief nod to *Call It Courage*. In the animated film, the hero, Moana, the daughter of the chief, has been chosen as the special person favored by a personified ocean. However, unlike Mafatu in *Call It Courage*, Moana is not afraid of the ocean. She is instead blessed, chosen by the sea. Moana's home island is in trouble, so she sets out alone, beyond the reef with her pet chicken, teaching herself to sail as she goes. After a storm leaves Moana and her small *waka* shipwrecked on an island, she solicits the help of the demigod Maui, allowing her to voyage back out to sea, where she scrapes through several trials until she passes her final test by using her recently learned dynamic sailing skills to restore the ecological balance of the region. She saves her home island and the health of the food and her people, to whom she returns to be the next-generation chief. A major thread throughout the movie is that the main character learns of her people's history, that they were once great voyagers across the oceans. The final scene of the film is Moana as a young captain-chief, a figure evoking master navigators like Mau Piailug who rejuvenated their Pacific Island communities in the 1970s. Moana's fellow islanders sail gloriously over tropical swells in a fleet of traditional vessels while a stingray, the spirit of her grandmother, swims alongside the boat and a sea eagle, the spirit of Maui, soars by the masthead.

In other words, in Disney's *Moana*, the new version of the solo-sailor story, the young mariner hero returns as an environmental and community savior, a reviver of traditional seafaring culture, and with the crown as new chief of her island, swarmed by hugs and cheering, beloved by her family and her community, whom she now serves.

Ellen MacArthur's radical life-shift to focus on the betterment of humanity is mostly terrestrial, focused on humans on land, on the things we make and the preservation of materials, but it arose out of her study of seabirds and other twenty-first-century marine issues. She followed in the wake of solo-sailor environmentalists such as the Australian Ian Kiernan, one of Jessica Watson's heroes, and other sailors turned activists, such as Sir Peter Blake of Aotearoa New Zealand and Isabelle Autessier of France.

Looking ahead toward the future of solo sailing, cruising or racing, regardless of what type of boat people choose to go on and at whatever speed and however connected to shore, the single-hander will always return home with a deeper appreciation for a single human's smallness in time and on Earth. Sailing a small boat at sea is, especially for the cruisers, a commitment to a low-impact lifestyle that teaches one to adapt and pay careful attention to the natural world.

Robin Lee Graham put it well after his five years on *Dove* in the late 1960s: "One learns from the sea how little one needs, not how much."

Solo sailors will continue to try to bring back to us how truly large our ocean is, how for weeks across the surface you can see no one else, nothing created by human hands. Although today they know intellectually that this is no longer the case, on the surface of the ocean the mariner still feels and looks on what appears to be an untouched, unspoiled, elemental and wild and immortal sea. Small-boat sailors in particular will continue to perceive the ocean this way and will write about it in kind. Yet sitting on the quiet deck alone with only the sound of the hull gurgling along over the royal blue surface, the solo sailor, regardless of their artistic aspirations, will always feel limited, by pen or now film, in what they can genuinely retrieve for those of us on shore as to the true experience of what they saw.

During one of Ellen MacArthur's first ocean passages across the North Sea as a teenager, she tried to bottle up some bioluminescence to bring home. "I began to realize that the beauty of the water can't be taken away or captured," she wrote, "It can only properly be appreciated first hand . . . I was desperate to understand much more."

# 26. The Solo Sailor Survives and Tries to Find Meaning

To deliver and retrieve all manner of solid and liquid things in gargantuan quantities, a dense highway of merchant-ship traffic parades along the coast of the Iberian Peninsula all year long. Containerships, oil tankers, bulk carriers, roll-on-roll-off automobile carriers, naval vessels, and cruise ships combust millions of barrels of oil to power southbound through the Bay of Biscay and ride the Canary Current conveyer belt down eastward toward the Mediterranean and the Suez Canal, or curl westward across the Atlantic toward the Panama Canal. Northbound ships stay closer to the coast, riding a counter-current as they charge up toward the English Channel on the way to the UK and the large ports of Antwerp, Rotterdam, and Scandinavia.

When Slocum approached this coast to "discover Spain" in 1895 he would have found these waters busy with fishing vessels, some merchant vessels under sail, and an occasional steamship passing through. When Ann Davison sailed through this Canary Current region in 1952, she was nearly run down by a merchant ship on her way to Gibraltar—saved at the last moment by her quick action and her engine. During August of 2007, when I was traveling there, about 120 ships each day plowed up and down past Cabo da Roca, the tall peninsula that forms the western mouth of the Tagus River and the route to Lisbon. This shipping lane is one of the more monstrous multi-tentacled leviathans for small boats who wish to pass.

On the afternoon of 18 August 2007, a Saturday, I was sailing along with only the storm jib. This was my boat's smallest sail, hoisted at the bow. Having abandoned my land-fall of England to head along this path of least resistance, I was aiming southeast of the heaviest of the forecast weather and steered downwind and with the current toward Cabo da Roca and Cascais, Portugal. I had been at sea alone for nearly five weeks. I just wanted to get to port safely and figure out the rest later.

I set Sandy to steer on a broad reach on the port tack, meaning with the wind coming across the back left corner of the boat. This had *Fox* headed 125 degrees magnetic, south-easterly. There was approximately twenty-five knots of wind out of the north-northeast. The waves were about eight to ten feet high, some white caps, occasional streaks, some breaking foam. *Fox* was making 3.2 knots over the water, which is really slow but felt safe in those conditions at that point of my passage. I had taken down the reefed mainsail earlier in the afternoon, at 12:45 p.m. local time, for a motion that felt more controlled. I was in no rush to sail faster, since this course was exactly the direction I wanted to go, and I did not want to reach the coast in the dark, especially since local weather forecast a gale near to shore. The barometer had been slowly dropping and was at 30.41 inches. The sky was overcast, thick with cumulus and stratus clouds. I was about 180 miles away from Cascais. I spent the afternoon studying the tides along the Tagus River, finding the boat fenders, checking my anchor and chain in case they were necessary, and making other small preparations for coming in to port. All of this I recorded in my logbook.

At about 3:40 p.m. I went down for a nap. I was lying on the starboard settee where I normally slept, especially when on a port tack. In rougher seas I would stuff a blanket and extra pillows underneath the inboard edge of the mattress to give me more of a bowl so I wouldn't spin out of bed if the ship heeled steeply to windward. I don't remember how bad the motion was that day, but I wrote in my logbook in the noon entry "roll-roll-roll," which probably meant the boat was lolling side to side, although it might have been some sort of words of motivation about being almost there, sort of like "keep on truckin'." I occasionally wrote little things in the logbook to keep my spirits up.

At approximately 4:00 p.m., after I had been asleep for about twenty minutes, I woke up to the jib luffing and the boom rattling around.

I thought, *Why is Sandy doing this?*

I had felt no appreciable wind shift or a change in sea state, no change in the angle of light coming into the cabin. I was confused. I don't remember hearing or smelling anything out of the ordinary.

Still half asleep, annoyed, I put on my glasses and dragged myself up into the cockpit. I usually wore my harness while I napped, so I grabbed the tether from its hook, clipping it into my waist as I walked up the ladder. I stepped into the cockpit and clipped the other end into the windward jackline. By that point in the passage this was so much my practice, regardless of weather, that I did this without thinking. I relieved Sandy of his duties, thanklessly, gruffly, flipping off the chain connection. I took the tiller to steer and looked up, began to focus, to figure out what was going on, why the boat had gybed itself, why it had turned its stern through the wind, from pointing to about ten o'clock to two o'clock, stalling at this previously consistent point of sail. The boom was now jerking back and forth on the wrong side, although kept from too hard a swing by Philip, the boom preventer, which I'd rigged up after I took down the mainsail. The boat had been doing fine for the last few hours.

*What was going on?*

Somehow, blindly unaware of what loomed, I stared at the compass. I huffed at being over 50 degrees off course.

As I looked forward to the luffing jib, I gazed up and began to focus to the left. I'm not sure how I did not immediately see this when I came on deck. A red containership took up the entire sky in front of the boat and to port. It was like staring at only your shoes as you step onto a sidewalk, then suddenly looking up at a wide windowless warehouse a city-block long and ten stories high. White letters, each larger than a house, passed in front of the bow. Above the deck, as I was looking up, were several rows of stacked corrugated steel containers of many colors. I remember the color green, a few different shades. Some were orange. The ship was moving away, steadily steaming almost parallel but at just enough of an angle to point in front of *Fox*. My boat was pretty much stationary in the water, although bucking in the waves while being blown to leeward as the boat luffed.

*Fox* had inexplicably stopped itself, steered away from impact, stalling the boat just short of getting crushed by the containership.

I recall no noise from the ship, which does not square with the event, the closeness of the encounter. What I remember instead is eerie quiet. The metal blocks on my boom clanked around. The jib fabric shook, flapped, and clinked like a shower curtain. I felt *Fox*'s bow pitch in the wake of the ship. I watched the containership's bulbous bow pass in front of me. From its deck no one looked down shouting or even staring. I saw no person at all on the containership. There were no horns or whistles from the ship. And I did not sound the horn on *Fox*. I just watched the churning faceless city-scape of the red ship pass through the water, its white wake off the bow, off the sides, from the stern. I was certainly close enough to hear engines, generators, to smell exhaust, but I just do not recollect any sounds or smells from the contain-ership at all, even though I'd swear in court that I could have hit that red hull with a tennis ball.

This event occurred at approximately 40° 26.6' North by 12° 30.0' West.

The containership kept going. The letters on the side were the name of the shipping line. All caps, no serifs. I looked up at the bridge. I easily read the words of both the shipping line on the side and the name and home port on the stern as it came across. I had binoculars on board, too, always ready on a devoted hook. I must have read the name of the ship and its hailing port on the stern. But I did not write this down in my logbook. I do not remember any of the words. I only remember, mostly, the looking up, the shock, the enormity, the silence. The ship was so close. It happened so slowly that I was not terrified, because by the time I focused I was no longer in danger. It was a silent open-mouthed sort of stunned realization. I felt outside of it. Disassociated. I had no one with whom to lock eyes. I just stood there, now wide awake, looking around, watching the ship steam away with an imperfect, incomplete memory seared in my mind at that particular circle-rimmed pelagic address in the North Atlan-tic Ocean.

I'm telling all this to you exactly how it happened, as best I can. I do not know how in the world I cannot remember the name of the ship or at least the shipping line or why I would not have written this down. I scrawled only this in my logbook:

> 1600 Very <u>very</u> close call. Woke up to the boat gybing—on its own out of the way of a containership. Wow. I came up, completed the gybe. GPS pos 40° 26.6 12° 30.0 3.2 kts

I resumed steering 125 degrees by the compass, and I did not write another log entry until 9:00 p.m., which was an uncharacteristically long time between entries. I wrote only the same course and an updated GPS position.

In literature, in the crafting of fiction, this is all a pretty cheap *deux ex machina*. "A god from a machine" is a contrived plot device to resolve an ending—as in, *suddenly it was all a dream* or *just as all is lost an asteroid comes in and blows up the villain*. The term comes from how some playwrights in ancient Greece would end their dramas by lowering down an actor who was playing a god by way of some mechanical apparatus, probably with block and tackle as on a ship (in addition to metaphorical ones, there have always been a lot of physical connections between ships and stage performance). This god character would end the play by delivering to the mortals on Earth—on stage and in the audience—some judgment or command from Olympus.

What was the message sent down to me? Sandy, the wind vane, had acted with what appeared to be nothing less than improvisational behavior, something entirely out of his mechanical character. The little god of a machine seemed, on his own, to have granted me another day. I should have been drowned in a crumpling of fiberglass, aluminum, and wood under the steel bow of that ship. No one working on the ship, it seemed, had any idea and perhaps might never have even known if I were run over. If a few scrapes had been left on the bow, they might have been observed in port as a curious afterthought, quickly painted over for fear of litigation.

I have been privately processing that near miss for the last fifteen years, trying to figure out what really happened, what it might mean for me, and if this particular brush with death is a metaphor for something bigger than me. If the solo voyage, Ann Davison, is about the path, the meaning of life, then what am I to make of this?

From a practical perspective, though I kept my radar off for weeks at a time to conserve power, I had thought that I had taken all reasonable precautions to avoid a collision with a ship. I had even, I thought, gone a bit further than many others, such as with the orange triangle stitched into my main sail. In hindsight, though, I did not have all my tools at the ready that afternoon, which is perhaps why Sandy needed to step in. My lack of vigilance is all the more puzzling because I had recorded a northbound ship at 12:45 p.m. More importantly, something had happened with another ship the previous night.

Over the course of my entire Atlantic crossing, before arriving at the Canary Current, I recorded seeing ten merchant vessels in the open ocean. I talked to an officer of a couple of them on the radio, but in this time before AIS on small boats I only got one definitive ship name from early in the passage, the *Ocean Atlas*. I never saw a single sailboat of

any kind during the crossing, although I know that other recreational boats were out there eastbound, such as the sailboats
*Prince William* and *Decision*, since I heard them talking to
Herb, the ocean-weather guy in Toronto. These boats were
at their closest a few hundred miles away.

What happened the night before, which should have
alerted me that I had fully entered the shipping lanes, was
that at 12:30 a.m. I saw a masthead light and sidelights on the
horizon. I still had the mainsail up, double-reefed, and was
making about 4.5 knots over the ground. I saw that the compass bearing of the ship's lights stayed the same, and the
range was closing to within three miles as per my radar, which
I had turned on as soon as I saw the sidelights.

I roughly calculated the ship's position and called it on the
VHF radio.

I got no reply and tried again.

Soon the ship clearly altered course to pass astern of me.
I could see the red port sidelight. I thanked the officer over
the radio. No reply. But then as the minutes progressed, I
realized that the ship was coming very close. I grew nervous
as it bore down still closer. I lit my mainsail with a spotlight.
I saw the outline of the ship's bow in the dark. I could identify this as an oil tanker because of its long, low midsection.
The tanker was close enough that I could see with my binoculars the figure of a watch officer high up in the bridge
toward the stern. It looked like a man in a baseball hat. He lit
a spotlight back at me through the glass, which I took as a
polite gesture to indicate he saw me. He wasn't flashing any
kind of Morse code or anything like that. I think the watch
officer just didn't realize how slow I was moving and how
massive and frightening his ship looked to me.

I wrote in my logbook about this being a very close

encounter with a "BFS," meaning big f---ing ship, yet this seemingly did not startle me into wanting to keep my radar on all day. Two hours later at 2:30 a.m., I tucked a third reef in the mainsail, keeping the same course, but I wrote "even this a bit too fast." With the coastal forecast in mind, wanting to thread the slot between the open-ocean storm and the coastal system, I added: "Would be very pleasant sailing if not heading toward a gale."

I should have started to just keep my radar and VHF radio on all the time, regardless of the drain on the batteries. I did not realize the true density of this behemoth parade or how far it extended out into the Atlantic. I never intended to go here, I had not done my research on this shipping lane. But that's an excuse.

I wish I could claim some extrasensory perception that afternoon or at any other time in my passage. I don't think that I had sailed enough alone to earn that. If the rattling of the boom and the shift in the boat's movement had not woken me up, I would simply have opened my eyes briefly before I died on impact. The EPIRB, clicked off due to water pressure as the boat sank, would have given my last position.

There is certainly the real possibility that the officer of the watch aboard the red containership saw me that afternoon and avoided the collision actively, but ended up cutting it almost too close. Maybe they had a lookout posted forward. Mid-ocean, the ship was probably traveling in the range of thirteen or fourteen knots over the surface. Maybe the watch officer had tried to call me. I'm fairly certain my VHF radio was on, but I can't testify to this confidently. I do know that at the time my radar was not. The ship might have been more likely to see me on their radar if mine were transmitting, assuming they did not see me visually, since it was during the day. I must have been hard to see. I did not have my mainsail up, with the orange triangle that I had ordered precisely for this scenario. On this overcast day with just one light-gray mast and one small white sail and a twenty-eight-foot-long dark-gray hull low in the water—and no helmsperson in the cockpit—I was a little ghost. To the watch officer looking down from over one hundred feet above, my white deck would have blended in with the occasional crests, the white-caps, on the top of the waves.

I did not try to call the ship on the radio. I do not even remember picking up my binoculars. I was in shock. There was nothing more to be done. Looking back on it, I wish I had found out if they saw me.

When I told Kenichi Horie through an interpreter about my experience—I sketched out what happened on a piece of paper—he listened with kindness and interest. He concluded that the ship saw me and altered course. This has always been his experience.

But this does not explain Sandy gybing the boat.

I have discussed this over the years with a few experienced open-water sailors and watch officers that work on these big ships.

Firstly, the gybe did not happen because I was pushed away from that ship by its bow wake. Something that close would have rolled *Fox* so aggressively and her motion would have been so far altered that it would have woken me up earlier.

A second possibility for the gybe was a well-timed wind shift, a sudden puff from a different direction. But Sandy would not have gybed or stalled out. He just would have altered course to maintain the relative angle. A temporary wind shift seems unlikely anyway, because after the ship had gone and I regained my senses, I returned to the same course and sail plan. Sandy held the same course all the way to Cascais for over another full day just as he had done for four hours before the near miss without gybing once.

The most likely explanation then, if there is a rational one, is that as the red merchant ship approached *Fox*, its hull and all its containers stacked four or five high above the deck eclipsed the wind on the surface—even from a mile or two away. The red containership disrupted the path of the wind enough that Sandy, suddenly with the same seas but now not enough wind, could no longer hold the course, allowing *Fox* to gybe with the waves, the jib to flop over, and the boat to point away from the oncoming impact. The course of *Fox* and the red ship, and the wind direction, all render this theory the most plausible.

Maybe it was both. Maybe the watch officer altered course, too closely, and then uninentionally cut off the wind to *Fox*, what sailors refer to as blanketing. Any concrete explanation, however, still requires jackpot sort of odds: a confluence of coincidental, extraordinary alignments of wind angles and courses and the timing of human decisions that started many days before so that the position of our two boats intersected in that exact place on the ocean at that precise moment.

Several single-handed sailors have written of a sort of divine assistance, something different from their own extrasensory intuition, what was perhaps more than a hallucination. Slocum's pilot from the *Pinta* being the most famous, or Horie's second self telling him to get working, or, most appropriate to my situation, Adams' "angel at the helm" or Sunderland's seabird freeing the knot at the masthead. Slocum once wrote to a magazine writer, "No man ever lived to see more of the solemnity of the depths than I have seen, and I resent quickly the hint that a real sea story might be other than religious." Moitessier's fairy tern told him a story to save his soul.

I will tell you honestly what I have come to believe after many years of thought. I have never said this aloud. And I know this might put me on a shelf in the crockpot department. I genuinely, truly believe in the spirit of Sandy Van Zandt, the lovely, kind old man who helped me prepare for the trip, who set up the self-steering gear for me and showed me how to use it. He would have been standing beside the Mystic River at that moment, looking toward Long Island Sound and the Atlantic Ocean. It would have been his lunch-time, a late August afternoon when the ocean water there is the warmest all year. Kids would have been swimming off the dock, daring each other to jump off the tall piling on the corner, just across the street from his house. Sandy would have gazed to the east. Knowing I was in trouble, he placed his warm, thickly veined hand on his wood railing, which was my tiller, to pull this just to windward, to gently turn *Fox* and sleeping me in the cabin over to starboard, flopping over the storm jib. I've never told this to Sandy or written to him about it, though I suspect he would understand.

The very same week that I wrote the above, arriving at this conclusion after so much thinking it all through, I was flipping through a boating magazine in a marine supply store. All this research has had me drawn back into these places, walking the aisles, looking longingly at ropes, paints, even plumbing hoses, then combing through advertisements in periodicals to see if I could possibly afford to keep a small boat again, maybe sail to Hawai'i, since I live in California now. So I'm flipping through this magazine, when I see a photograph of Sandy Van Zandt. I'm not making this up. He's standing next to a tall, curly-haired, sixteen-year-old boy named Cal Currier. Cal and his father had bought Sandy's boat so the boy could sail it solo across the Atlantic. In the photograph Sandy and Cal are standing on the boat in the Mystic River, in the same mooring field, in front of the same town where I launched *Fox* over fifteen years ago, in front of the dock where the kids swim.

I biked home and wrote to Sandy immediately.

He replied:

Great to hear from you. We sure miss having you here . . . We decided that the time had come to sell the Tartan 30. I turned 90 in October . . . As much as I would have liked to sail her to Europe myself we lucked into a great young man who was a real pleasure to work with. Cal caught on to using the wind vane in no time . . . He had a very good weather router who kept him clear of an early season hurricane and very good weather all the way to the Algarve in southern Portugal. He stopped for 24 hours in Horta. The wind vane was the same one as the one you had on your Triton. We made a few modifications to it in the 6–8 years that we used it but it worked awfully well.

I had mentioned nothing to Sandy about the wind vane when I wrote to him, and I have since resisted as we've reconnected. It's been hard not to ask what he thinks about what happened to me that day with the containership. Cal Currier lives less than an hour away from where I do now, but I do not want to freak the young man out. I suppose in my own small way it is like how Moitessier decided not to steer his boat back towards the rocks to see if the dolphins would begin that behavior of swerving to starboard again. He did not want to prod a fairy tale. I do not want to take Sandy's warm hand off the tiller. I did not, nor do I now, deserve that generosity, that moment to be chosen to live longer. Maybe it was really about kindness to my parents.

After Sandy steered me away from the red containership, I stood in the cockpit for a while. The jib was luffing, the boat drifting slightly ahead to leeward. After some time, maybe only five or ten minutes, I brought the jib back over, re-engaged the self-steering, and began sailing on the same southeasterly course again. I reached below and got out my camera. The photograph I have of the ship off in the distance is low quality and taken way too late. But there's just enough to confirm this was a largish containership, something in the range of seven hundred feet long, which fully loaded would have a total of about 2,000 or so containers, each of which would fit on a trailer truck, potentially filled with nearly any product imaginable.

My satellite phone call to Lisa that night was at 9:00 p.m. my time, aligning with my logbook entry just before. In her notes that she kept of our brief check-ins, she wrote that I reported that the barometer was stable with winds up to thirty knots. In our call the following day, Sunday, I was complaining to her about the madness of how many ships were out there. Apparently I never mentioned the event with the red containership. Perhaps this was not to worry her. By the time I got to shore, there were so many other things to talk about that it wasn't really until months later that we discussed the event.

As I closed in on the coast of Portugal aboard *Fox*, I stayed sailing with just the storm jib on the same course. Sandy did not gybe unexpectedly again. I often saw two or three large merchant vessels at a time and three or four targets within twelve miles on radar. It was like living a "Frogger" video game. I did not sleep at all that Sunday night. It was the hardest twenty-four hours of the trip because of the high winds, seas, and the ships being so numerous as I tried to intersect the shipping lanes at as perpendicular an angle as possible. It was at times difficult for me to contact anyone confidently on the VHF with what I estimated as their position. I just did not have enough time.

The ship officers that I did speak to said I was not appearing on their radar. I supposed my profile was mixed in with sea clutter on their screen. During the heavy weather, in addition to a visual lookout, I was now checking the radar all the time. I could see the glow of Lisbon ahead. At 2:30 a.m. I had another very close encounter with a ship: the watch officer said she saw me, was altering course, but then it got so close that it felt like I was being sucked into the Death Star. I frantically gybed myself away, which I probably should have just done from the start. But I was so tired and desperate not to give up miles or my angle bisecting the shipping lanes. I remember thinking that now I really am a fox, crossing a highway at night.

Hours later, and beyond the traffic, the sun rose. What I had taken to be a mass of clouds turned out to be the tall cliffs of Cabo da Roca. At 07:50 on 20 August 2007, my thirty-sixth day at sea, I discovered Portugal. I identified the shore on radar to align with my paper chart and the map that I'd torn out of the cruising guide, over which I'd drawn longitude and latitude lines with a ruler. I set up the anchor on the bow. I hoisted the American flag astern, then raised up to the spreaders the Portuguese flag and the yellow quarantine flag that says you have yet to clear customs.

The seas rolled high and long. Dolphins zoomed in to welcome *Fox* by surfing down the crests of the waves in parallel with my course, gamboling as dolphins have never before gamboled. They carved across the swells in twos and threes then curled underneath my keel. As Sandy steered and *Fox* drove forward, aware of imminent rest, I took photographs of the dolphins and everything rapid-fire, snapped selfies in front of the flags. I was wearing sunglasses, unshaven, the sun was bright, the sky clear. I remained bundled up to my nose in my foul-weather jacket as the wind was still whipping up a near gale. I took selfies in front of the cliffs, in front of the dolphins. Then I was greeted personally by a flock of seabirds that I never identified. They were enormous, dynamic animals, large chocolate-brown seabirds with yellow beaks. I think they were brown boobies, Harry Pidgeon's yellow bills—although this doesn't fit their range. I failed to capture them on my camera, but I remember them as gigantic. The birds sped across the steep seas, soaring across the early morning sun as it highlighted spindrift off the waves.

As I sailed along the coast, still under my storm jib alone, but now in the lee of the cliffs in calmer conditions, I navigated without incident but with one more hour of anxiety past a line of yellow buoys that presumably marked some sort of hazard. I couldn't find these buoys in my books, so I wasn't sure whether to leave them to port or starboard.

I managed to pass safely by, and then raised Cascais Marina on the radio, talking to someone who spoke English well. My engine had failed to even turn over. They agreed to tow me in. Just another Monday morning for them. I raised a reefed mainsail and short-tacked up for a couple of hours toward the mouth of the marina when, at approximately 1:40 p.m., two dashing Portuguese men zoomed out in their inflatable. In my memory they are both the soccer star Cristiano Ronaldo. The twin Ronaldos lashed me alongside their gray boat and zoomed me briskly behind the large breakwater and into the high-walled fortress of a harbor and pushed me into a slip, hurrying me along. The Ronaldos explained that I had to report immediately to customs. I stepped onto the dock. My knees wobbled. I was not only physically exhausted and exuberantly relieved, but under the sun of the suddenly still summer afternoon, now out of the wind, I was overheated, dizzy, and dehydrated. Behind the cement walls, it was as if I had walked into a sauna. The men did not give me a chance to change out of my wool sweater and my foul-weather overalls. We walked to see the customs officer, not talking, only the sound of my pants rubbing back and forth and the rubber bottoms of my scuba booties clinging to the asphalt.

The customs officer called me "Captain."

"How many crew?" he asked.

"None. I mean just me," I said.

He wrote down something, did not look up, and if he was impressed or even interested, he did not show it.

After phone calls and after falling asleep at a restaurant despite two cappuccinos and then dozing off again alone at a bar, I slept like the dead aboard *Fox*. I removed Sandy's wind vane, unrigged the lines to the tiller, and tilted him up out of the water, tied up—for good, as it would turn out, at least with me. *Fox* and I were safely laced up to the dock inside the walls, the wind whistling like werewolves through the tops of the masts of all the other boats at rest, the rope halyards softly clapping and jingling across the marina.

I was not necessarily in search of the miraculous, but I do want to make meaning out of my voyage across the Atlantic: the motivation to make it happen, the friends who helped me get off the dock, the start in the fog, the seabirds, the thirty-foot great white shark I fought off with a boat hook, the sea turtle, the dolphins, the gales, the mental strain of it all. I was granted more time on Earth by some larger power, by the spiritual hand of a good person. Or maybe by the precise lucky coincidence of angles that cut the wind, or maybe a vigilant watch officer on the containership, or even by Sandy itself, himself, a mechanical, wondrous little God-like geared machine, a functional work of art made out of stainless steel that for this one moment behaved entirely out of character.

One of the larger metaphors here is along the lines of a Joshua Slocum, a man nostalgic for the age of sail, steeped in wooden boatbuilding and celestial navigation, who was likely run down at sea by a steamship, "murdered by modernity." Here I was, over a century later, a far smaller and far less-accomplished character, with no claim to any legacy, sailing far distantly in his wake of precedent, but with updated paper charts, GPS, radar, a fiberglass boat, comfortable clothing, an engine (sort of), wind-driven and electric self-steering mechanisms, a satellite phone, an EPIRB, and I too was almost killed by not only a steamship, but more significantly by a containership, arguably the twenty-first century's greatest symbol of capitalism, over-consumption, and the linear economy. Could we extrapolate, as literary types are wont to do, that I was a wee symbol of Western culture and so far it has been a near miss, to be killed by our own products, our own emissions, but we have been granted a bit more time to do something with the life we've been left?

The heroes of this history of solo sailing for me are Bernard Moitessier and Bill Pinkney and Ellen MacArthur, not only for their sheer jaw-dropping seamanship and endurance as mariners at sea, but in their devotion on their return home to do more for others. Moitessier wanted a kinder, greener Earth and he sincerely wished to make lasting and meaningful art. Pinkney returned as a pioneer and activist for the African American community, for the teaching of American history and for empowering children. MacArthur dropped the extreme sport of ocean racing, a profitable endeavor in which she was transcendent and among the greatest ever to have lived, in order to work toward a more sustainable human future on Earth.

Back in 1952 when Ann Davison completed her trans-Atlantic crossing, she did not know what to do with herself. She did not want to continue being a solo sailor. "I still liked the *idea*, but not, as yet, the practical application of it. Being at sea was a lonely, uncomfortable business and very frightening." She knew she wanted to write her book, but after that, what? She did not want to be a ship's captain and being a solo sailor for her own satisfaction seemed useless. She concluded that a life's work must have some benefit for others.

Davison wrote at the end of *My Ship Is So Small* that

courage is the key to living. A more careful reading reveals that she did not mean this to be the need to do or overcome scary things, or even to go on physical solitary adventures: "Then what is courage?" she wrote. "An understanding and acceptance; but an acceptance without resignation, mark you, for courage is a fighting quality. It is the ability to make mistakes and profit by them, to fail and start again, to take heartaches, setbacks and disappointments in your stride, to face every day of your life and every humdrum, trivial little detail of it and realize you don't amount to much, and accept the fact with equanimity, and not let it deter your efforts."

I wonder if maybe it is not the right time in my life for me to try to sail to Hawai'i. I already have a similar adventure in my pocket. I have a child to help raise. And I want to give more somehow to where I live.

And yet—and yet, I still would love to have *Fox* back. If even just sitting in a yard on poppets for now. I could visit and varnish and paint. Change the home port on the stern. I still believe in the lessons of the little sailboat: of self-reliance, of patience, of long observation, and of deep appreciation for the diverse and awe-inspiring beauty of this rare, rapidly changing Earth. I do love being at sea, living simply, with a horizon of only ocean and clouds and storm-petrels and stars, a path toward a moment of ecstasy so pure: after the long night to be still awake by the grace of something or someone, watching the gray dawn breaking, the sunrise brushing pink the back of the sail as you ponder for the eight-billionth time: how am I to live this life?

# Dramatis personae

*Below are the major solo-sailing characters mentioned in this book, organized chronologically by their voyages and narratives.*

c. 3,000 BCE–1200 CE EARLY SOUTHEAST ASIAN AND PACIFIC PEOPLES sail the entirety of the central and south Pacific Ocean, deliberately settling over time Tahiti, Hawai'i, Rapa Nui Easter Island, and then finally Aotearoa New Zealand.

c. 520 BRENDAN THE NAVIGATOR and other IRISH MONKS perhaps sail on solitary voyages into the Atlantic.

c. 1300s IPO sails alone from Pitcairn to most likely Mangareva.

1728 INUIT KAYAKER arrives alone in Aberdeen.

c. 1787 JOSIAH SHACKFORD probably sails the Atlantic alone from France to Surinam.

1867 JOHN "ROB ROY" MACGREGOR sails alone across the English Channel in a custom-built little boat, then writes and illustrates *The Voyage Alone in the Yawl Rob Roy* (1867).

1869 E.E. MIDDLETON sails alone around Britain, then writes *The Cruise of "The Kate"* (1870).

1876 ALFRED "CENTENNIAL" JOHNSON sails alone across the Atlantic.

1882 BERNARD GILBOY sails alone from California and nearly reaches Australia, then writes *Voyage of the Boat 'Pacific' from San Francisco to Australia* (1883).

1892 JOSIAH "SI" LAWLOR disappears without a trace during a small-boat single-handed trans-Atlantic crossing, which he had previously accomplished twice before; WILLIAM ANDREWS, after being rescued on two previous attempts, finally makes it across alone in this race against Lawlor, after which Andrews writes *Columbus Outdone* (1893).

1898 JOSHUA SLOCUM completes the first known solo circumnavigation, then writes *Sailing Alone Around the World* (1900).

1899 HOWARD BLACKBURN, with no fingers, completes his first of two solo trans-Atlantic crossings.

1925 HARRY PIDGEON returns to Los Angeles following the first of his two single-handed circumnavigations, then writes *Around the World Single-Handed* (1928).

1929 ALAIN GERBAULT completes a solo circumnavigation, then writes *In Quest of the Sun* (1929).

1931 FRED REBELL (formerly Paul Sproge) sails from Australia to Los Angeles. Eight years later he writes *Escape to the Sea* (1939).

1934 ALFON HANSEN sails alone across the Atlantic and around Cape Horn in a small boat, the first known person to do so, but soon dies off Chile.

1936 J. W. "JOHNNY" WRAY cruises the South Pacific alone out of Auckland, then writes *South Sea Vagabonds* (1939).

1943 VITO DUMAS returns to Buenos Aires alone after a circumnavigation around the Southern Ocean with three stops, then writes *Alone Through the Roaring Forties* (1944).

1949 EDWARD ALLCARD crosses the North Atlantic alone, then writes *Single-Handed Passage* (1951), starting a long sailing and writing career.

1952 ALAIN BOMBARD crosses the North Atlantic in a survival raft, then writes *Story of a Voluntary Castaway* (1953).

1953 ANN DAVISON completes her crossing of the North Atlantic, becoming the first woman known to sail an ocean single-handed, then writes *My Ship Is So Small* (1956).

1956 FLORENTINO DAS completes a crossing of the western Pacific Ocean alone from Hawai'i to the Philippines, then writes articles for the *Honolulu Star-Bulletin*.

1960 BRIAN PLATT sails alone across the North Pacific from Japan to California.

1960 BLONDIE HASLER organizes the first trans-Atlantic race of the modern era (OSTAR), which includes himself, FRANCIS CHICHESTER, DAVID LEWIS, VAL HOWELLS, and JEAN LACOMBE.

1962 KENICHI HORIE crosses the North Pacific from Osaka to San Francisco, then writes *Kodoku* (English trans., 1964); he goes on to complete several more single-handed voyages across all oceans in a variety of vessels, including environmentally friendly experimental craft.

1965 ROBERT MANRY sails across the Atlantic in his 13.5-foot wooden boat, then publishes *Tinkerbelle* (1966).

1967 FRANCIS CHICHESTER finishes his one-stop single-handed circumnavigation, then writes *Gipsy Moth Circles the World* (1967).

1968 EDITH BAUMANN is the first woman to enter the OSTAR.

1969 After nearly finishing the Golden Globe race, BERNARD MOITESSIER publicly decides to stop competing, continuing on to sail one and a half times around the world alone, then writes and illustrates *The Long Way* (1971).

1969 ROBIN KNOX-JOHNSTON wins the Golden Globe race, becoming the first person to sail solo non-stop around the Earth, then writes *A World of My Own* (1969).

1969 DONALD CROWHURST, the last entrant in the Golden Globe race, fakes the route of his voyage, then almost certainly commits suicide in the North Atlantic, about which Nicholas Tomalin and Ron Hall write *The Strange Last Voyage of Donald Crowhurst* (1970).

1969 SHARON SITES ADAMS sails alone from Japan to California, then nearly forty years later publishes her narrative *Pacific Lady* (2008).

1970 INGEBORG VON HEISTER from Germany sails alone across the Atlantic and back.

1970 TEVAKE OF PILENI leaves, presumably on an intentional solo voyage of no return; he was one of the last traditional navigators of his generation in the region and gave some of his knowledge to David Lewis.

1970 ROBIN LEE GRAHAM completes his five-year circumnavigation (the youngest at the time at twenty-one), then writes *Dove* (1972).

1971 NICOLETTE MILNES WALKER sails across the Atlantic alone westbound, then writes *When I Put Out to Sea* (1972).

1972 DAVID LEWIS publishes *We, the Navigators*, and also this year is the first to sail alone to the Antarctic Peninsula, about which he writes *Ice Bird* (1975).

1976 CLARE FRANCIS crosses the Atlantic alone in the OSTAR, then writes *Woman Alone: Sailing Solo Across the Atlantic* (1977).

1978 NAOMI JAMES sails solo around the world via Cape Horn with two stops, then writes *Alone Around the World* (1979).

1982 JONATHAN RABAN sails alone around Britain, then writes *Coasting: A Private Voyage* (1986); he will later write *Passage to Juneau* (1999) about solo sailing up to Alaska from Seattle.

1987 TEDDY SEYMOUR circumnavigates the world via the Panama and Suez Canals, the first Black person to do so; a few of his onboard journals are later transcribed and posted online as "No Frills Circumnavigation."

1987 TANIA AEBI circumnavigates the world via the Panama and Suez Canals, then writes *Maiden Voyage* (1989).

1988 KAY COTTEE completes a single-handed non-stop circumnavigation, the first woman to do so, then publishes *First Lady* (1989).

1992 BILL PINKNEY completes a circumnavigation alone via the Southern Ocean, then later publishes *As Long As It Takes* (2006).

1995 PETER NICHOLS must abandon his boat only days from completing a solo trans-Atlantic crossing, then writes *Sea Change: Alone Across the Atlantic in a Wooden Boat* (1997).

1999 NEAL PETERSEN becomes the first Black person to complete an international solo circumnavigation race, then writes *Journey of a Hope Merchant* (2007).

2001 ELLEN MACARTHUR finishes second in the Vendée Globe, after which she writes *Taking on the World* (2003); in 2005 she set a new solo circumnavigation record of 71 days, then wrote *Race Against Time* (2005).

2010 JESSICA WATSON completes the youngest solo non-stop circumnavigation at sixteen, then writes *True Spirit* (2010).

2010 ABBY SUNDERLAND sails solo around Cape Horn and the Cape of Good Hope at sixteen, but her boat is dismasted, and she is rescued in the Indian Ocean, after which she writes *Unsinkable* (2011).

2012 LAURA DEKKER completes the youngest-ever circumnavigation at sixteen years and 123 days old, then writes *One Girl One Dream* (2013).

2017 FRANÇOIS GABART sets the new solo-circumnavigation record of forty-two days.

2021 At eighty-one years old JON SANDERS completes his eleventh solo circumnavigation.

2022 LISA BLAIR aboard *Climate Action Now* circumnavigates Antarctica non-stop, the fastest ever to do so; she wrote *Facing Fear* (2020) about her first attempt.

2023 KRISTEN NEUSCHÄFER of South Africa, after rescuing another competitor in the Indian Ocean, wins the Golden Globe race; only three of sixteen entrants finish the circumnavigation nonstop, during which no modern electronics for navigation or weather routing are allowed.

# Notes

### *1. Ann Davison and the Meaning of Life*

Ann Davison's *My Ship Is So Small* has been printed with an additional Part Four, with chapters describing her passage from Nassau up north to New York City. This includes a meeting with Edward Allcard. You can find this additional part in *Great Voyages in Small Boats: Solo Transatlantic*, pp. 227–85. Her foundational *why-go* quotation is from the William Sloane edition, pp. 13–15 (which does not have that fourth part); all other quotations from Davison unless specified are also from this edition. Robert Manry's line about art is from *Tinkerbelle*, p. 59. Tania Aebi's comment on returning to write the book is from her foreword to Laura Dekker's *One Girl One Dream*, p. 13. John Rousmaniere's quotation about "public confession" is from his foreword to Richard Henderson's *Singlehanded Sailing*, p. v. Henderson's book is a superb and careful book on many levels, including his own synthesis research about *why-go* and single-hander psychology. Bruce Ansley cited Harold Kidd on "sea gypsy culture" in his introduction to J. W. Wray's *South Sea Vagabonds*, p. 5; on this period of escapism to small boats see also D. H. Clarke's inciteful and hilarious *Blue Water Dream*, pp. 25–30. Clarke comically examines the *why-go*. For more on the setting of the 1940s and 1950s, including primitivism, see Gary Kroll's *America's Ocean Wilderness* and Susan Beegel's "Thor Heyerdahl's *Kon-Tiki* and Hemingway's Return to Primitivism in *The Old Man and the Sea*." J. R. L. Anderson's *The Ulysses Factor* makes an argument for the *why-go* in the context of historical exploration and physical challenge. With a scholarly eye, Richard Hutch's *Lone*

*Sailors and Spiritual Insights* digs deeply into the philosophy of single-handers and their narratives.


## 2. Seabirds

Seabird taxonomy, distribution, and ecology throughout is drawn from the Cornell Lab of Ornithology's "Birds of the World" (birdsoftheworld.org), with special thanks to Hugh Powell for a range of large and small questions over the years. Bill Pinkney wrote of this albatross in *As Long As It Takes*, pp. 133–34. One of the first seabird-specific field guides that single-handers could have packed aboard was W.B. Alexander's *Birds of the Ocean* first published in 1928, then revised in several editions. Robin Knox-Johnston had a copy aboard during his solo non-stop circumnavigation in 1968–69. My storm-petrel sightings were from about 66° 30' to 45° 00' West longitude.


## 3. Shackford, "Rob Roy," and "Centennial" Set the Stage

D. H. Clarke's claim about Inuit people is in his *An Evolution of Singlehanders*, p. 50. Sir Peter Buck wrote about Ipo in *Vikings of the Pacific*, p. 226. A good place to start for an overview of the earliest human voyaging on oceans is Brian Fagan's *Beyond the Blue Horizons*. For information on Pytheas, I turned to Barry Cunliffe's *The Extraordinary Voyage of Pytheas the Greek*. For more on St Brendan, for example, see W.H. Babcock, pp. 37–46, and D. H. Clarke, *An Evolution of Singlehanders*, pp. 19–26, and for a start to research on "The Wondrous Sea Voyage of Dionysus" painting, see Richard Hutch's *Lone Sailors and Spiritual Insights*, p. v. For the story of Patrick Watkins, see David D. Porter, *Memoir of Commodore David*

*Porter of the United States Navy*, pp. 129–33. On the history of Pacific Island voyaging, I recommend beginning with the resources provided by the Pacific Voyaging Society and *Hōkūle'a* (hokulea.com); Peter Buck's *Vikings of the Pacific* [*Vikings of the Sunrise*]; and a more recent linguistic, ecological, and anthropological synthesis by Andrew Crowe in his *Pathway of the Birds*.

There is a fun scholarly essay to be written about the story of the story of Josiah Shackford. As a sampling of how the account moved through the years in newspapers and journals, picking up on the way more details, sometimes contradictory, you can start with the original 1787 story of Shackford's voyage, for example, as it appeared in *The Essex Journal & New Hampshire Packet*, p. 3. From there a retelling in 1823 in the *New-Hampshire Gazette* (via the *New York Gazette*), "Miscellany," p. 1, and then in 1832 the surely fictional story involving Sir Joseph Banks in "Yankee's Visit," in *The Sailor's Magazine*, pp. 111–12. A generation later comes Charles Brewster's account, which is published in his 1869 collected *Rambles About Portsmouth*, series 2, pp. 219–23 (although it was probably first published in the *Portsmouth Journal*, Brewster's paper, c. 1860–61, since the *Gloucester Telegraph* reprinted it in part in February 1861). Continue this on to a chapter, "Josiah Shackford" in *Legends of Portsmouth, New Hampshire*, pp. 8–16, a pamphlet held at the Portsmouth Athenaeum (c. 1920s?); in this last story Shackford's dog is now named "Bruno." For Shackford's "disordered melancholy state" see "Notice," *New-Hampshire Gazette* (1805). I am grateful to the help of Robin Potter with this research. You can read her article on Shackford in *Maine Boats, Homes, and Harbors* (2023). Robin Silva at the Portsmouth Athenaeum and Trenton Carls at the Cape Ann Museum provided guidance and several helpful documents.

Henderson compiled an excellent general summary of the small-boat voyages before Slocum in *Singlehanded Sailing*, and he was the editor of a superb edition of William Andrews' logbooks, titled *The Dangerous Voyages of William Andrews*. Irving Anthony wrote about many of these early voyages in greater detail in *Voyagers Unafraid*, but with few citations for the historian. The narrative of Bernard Gilboy makes especially good reading, being well annotated in an edition by John Barr Tompkins with maps, illustrations, and photographs. This includes the 1883 poem from *Sydney Punch*, p. 16. Howard Blackburn's first-person accounts are included in the must-read *Lone Voyager*, in which historian Joseph Garland details their provenance, pp. 327–28. Arthur Ransome's 1954 introduction is published in the Dover edition of *The Voyage Alone in the Yawl Rob Roy*, pp. xi–xxv.

If you cannot visit the *Centennial* in person, the Cape Ann Museum website has more information. See www.capeannmuseum.org/collections/objects/johnson-dory.

## 4. Wind, Ships, Sleep, Engines, Wind

Naomi James expressed a similar feeling about how solo sailing provides the freedom to make your own mistakes in *Alone Around the World*, p. 45. The quotation from Dodge Morgan and Henderson is in the latter's *Singlehanded Sailing*, p. 71. Most of Johnny Wray's sailing was with small crews, but he is worth including here since his early influence was so wide in the region. The "Hansen sea-cow" is another similarly personified and hilarious outboard motor character as written by John Steinbeck and Ed Ricketts in their *The Log from the Sea of Cortez* (1941). Davison and Pidgeon's quotations here are from their published narratives, pp. 51, 232, and from p. 10 respectively, as is Slocum's from his *Sailing Alone Around the World*, p. 128.

## 5. The First Solo Circumnavigator: Joshua Slocum

This version of Masefield's "Sea-Fever" is from *The Oxford Book of the Sea*, p. 326. Charles Darwin's actual line from *The Voyage of the Beagle*, p. 204, was: "One sight of such a coast [the Milky Way] is enough to make a landsman dream for a week about shipwreck, peril, and death."

In terms of celestial navigation, Slocum had also mastered the lunar-distance method, which is a means to find longitude by measuring relative angles of the moon and another celestial body. The lunar-distance method is mathematically challenging but does not require an accurate timepiece. Slocum at one point says he even found an error in one of his tables. He wrote to a friend from the Indian Ocean, however, that he had only once found his longitude with this method during the whole voyage so far. See Teller, *Joshua Slocum*, p. 148.

All of the Slocum biographies make complementary reading and build on each other, including information and theories that have come up about the timing and events leading up to Slocum's death, which includes a debate about whether he left in 1908 or 1909. Teller did all the original baseline archival research and includes the Theodore Roosevelt letter, p. 223, and quotations from Slocum's children on the loss of Virginia, e.g. pp. 32, 34. Ann Spencer in *Alone at Sea* added a great deal in terms of Canadian history. Geoffrey Wolff in *The Hard Way Around* gave more of a maritime history and literary background. Stan Grayson in *The Man for All Oceans* seems to update this all and puts the voyage in a further context of boating history and includes a thoughtful analysis comparing Thoreau and Slocum. A sampling of some of the best photographs and a lovely synopsis of Slocum's career is in Grayson's article in *WoodenBoat* in 2020. Grayson helped me with a few facts in this chapter. In *The Man for*

*All Oceans* he summarizes arguments on the date of Slocum's death and when exactly he moved down to Fairhaven to work on *Spray*. I also learned a great deal from Bert Bender's literary analysis in his "Joshua Slocum and the Reality of Solitude."

## 6. Sharks

Shark biology and information about the largest recorded great white is from Ebert, Fowler, and Dando, *A Pocket Guide to Sharks of the World*, and from personal communication with David Ebert on 28 June 2018. One of the best photographs of a following shark is in Alain Bombard's *The Bombard Story*, p. 125. In D. H. Clarke's *An Evolution of Singlehanders*, p. 102, is a photograph of the German solo circumnavigator Walter Koenig with a shark hoisted on deck that he presumably captured. For the story on John Deer see the *60 Minutes Australia* "Fall Guy" (2022) episode.

I found the account of "Centennial" Johnson's brush with a shark as published with the lead "A Frail Craft" in *The New York Herald* versus the *St Louis Daily Globe-Democrat*, p. 2. Lawlor's story is in Richard Henderson's *Singlehanded Sailing*, p. 8. Slocum's thoughts and experiences with sharks cited here are from the *Liberdade*, p. 83, and *Destroyer*, pp. 182–85, narratives that are collected in *The Voyage of Joshua Slocum*, edited by Teller, as well as in *Sailing Alone Around the World*, pp. 127, 153. Stan Grayson's biography, p. 44, also helped my understanding on these details.

## 7. Just Cruisin' with Harry Pidgeon

For more on Dumas, see the excellent introduction by Jonathan Raban to a 2001 edition, as well as a recent biography by Ben

Lowings, *The Sun of May*. Not only do I give Dumas and Gerbault a small role here, but many early twentieth-century single-handers and other mariners of small boats with small crews on board, who also came home to write iconic books, do not even get on the stage at all here in this book, which will bring about the gnashing of teeth and the raising of palms from certain readers. I can only apologize and offer my own disappointment that I wasn't able here to include further stories about, say, Thomas Fleming Day, the founding editor of *The Rudder*, who many credit as being the most important driving force to growing interest in recreational sailing in the US in the early twentieth century. I urge unfamiliar readers also to see the works, among others, of John C. Voss in the early 2000s; of F. B. Cook, beginning in 1919; Eric and Susan Hiscock beginning in 1939; and Miles and Beryl Smeeton, John Guzwell, and Jean Gau in the 1950s.

In *Around the World Single-Handed*, Pidgeon published dozens of his photographs and still more in his *National Geographic* article in February 1928. Some of Pidgeon's photographs are held and viewable online at the California Museum of Photography and the Special Collections Library at Fresno State University.

Hansen and Dumas took a famous photograph together, with Hansen's pet dog and cat, which was published on the cover of the 10 March 1934 edition of *El Gráfico* (see https//commons. wikimedia.org). For more on Hansen, see Charles Borden, *Sea Quest*, pp. 273–75.

Professor emeritus Steve Jones, author of *Backwaters* (1979), among other narratives and maritime histories, shared with me in person and over correspondence from summer 2021 to winter 2022 his experience as a child being rowed out to meet Harry Pidgeon, as well as the importance of Pidgeon (and *The Rudder* and Thomas Fleming Day) and his influence on the yachting community of Long Island Sound.

John Vigor in *The Seaworthy Offshore Sailboat: A Guide to Essential Features, Gear, and Handling* was an invaluable book for me to get *Fox* ready for my own crossing. Throughout, Vigor has wise things to say about accidents and experience, using Pidgeon's grounding, p. 215, in South Africa as an example.

## 8. Sea Turtles, Fish, Squid

General open-water natural history and ecology about fish is from Julian Pepperell's *Fishes of the Open Ocean*. For the range and behavior of loggerheads, see NOAA Fisheries (fisheries.noaa. gov). My two sea-turtle sightings were on 28 July 2007 (~42°55' N x 48° 06' W) and 1 August 2007 (~41° 37' N x 41° 26' W). Gerbault's bonito is from *In Quest of the Sun*, p. 51, and his observations of fish are worth examining in each of his works, both compiled in English translation in *Firecrest Around the World*. Allcard's observations are from *Single-Handed Passage*, pp. 95, 119–20, 127, 145, and 161–62. On the history of Western understanding of the El Niño Southern Oscillation, I turned to Chunzai Wang and Paul C. Fiedler, "ENSO Variability and the Eastern Tropical Pacific: A Review," pp. 239–47. On 1925 as a La Niña year with enhanced upwelling, see Luc Beaufort and Michaël Grelaud. "A 2700-Year Record of ENSO and PDO Variability from the California Margin Based on Coccolithophore Assemblages and Calcification," p. 6, and NOAA's "Past Events." Thank you to Lisa Gilbert for assistance here. For eastern Pacific historical abundance, I read pp. 253–57 of Callum Roberts' *The Unnatural History of the Sea*, a foundational book of marine environmental history.

## 9. Florentino Das: For Family

Excerpts from Florentino Das' journal as published in the *Honolulu-Star Bulletin* in 1956 are cited from *Bold Dream, Uncommon Valor*, pp. 87–100. Peter Belmi's comments were on the *Invisibilia* podcast (2022). I primarily learned of events of the voyage and Das' life from *Bold Dream, Uncommon Valor* and from Quijano de Manila (Nick Joaquin)'s story, "Florentino Das: The Long Voyage Home," which includes the lines about the sharks, p. 52. The quotation from the Coast Guard official is in *Bold Dream, Uncommon Valor*, p. 38. The meeting of Das and de Bisschop is from Galit de la Cruz (2018) and alluded to in Manila's story. The quotation from the Coast Guard official is in *Bold Dream, Uncommon Valor*, p. 38. The French sailor Éric de Bisschop's career at sea in the 1930s through the 1960s and his books about his trips on traditional craft, usually with just his partner aboard, are worth their own attention, such as *The Voyage of the* Kaimiloa (1939).

Larry Raigetal's comment on community was during an online seminar given to the One People One Reef organization out of Santa Cruz, CA, on 4 March 2022. Information about the hero's journey and quotations are from Joseph Campbell's *The Hero with a Thousand Faces*, while specific quotations, including this book's epigraph, are from his *The Power of Myth*, pp. 123–39.

## 10. Pets, Companionship over the Rail

Ann Davison's comment on wanting something furry to stroke is in the additional Part Four of *My Ship Is So Small* in *Great Voyages*, p. 246. Slocum's story of the goat in *Sailing Alone Around the World* is on pp. 223–26, while Adams' story of her turtle is in *Pacific*

*Lady*, p. 46. The story of David Clark and his dog is in Herb McCormick, "A Single-Minded Sailor Conquers the Sea Solo," p. 8. For the quote from Robin Lee Graham on the loneliness brought about by losing his pet cat, see *Dove*, p. 50. For Aebi's cats on *Maiden Voyage*, see e.g. pp. 174 and 303. For another sad story, among others, of a cat overboard, see Naomi James, *Alone Around the World*, pp. 88–92. Citations from Dumas about the cape pigeons and the fly are from *Alone Through the Roaring Forties*, e.g. pp. 262 and 268. Petersen's relationship with "Cockie" is in *Journey of a Hope Merchant*, p. 172, and the documentary *No Barriers—The Neal Petersen Story*.

One of the most curious of pet stories is that of a young bear that sailed aboard the small boat of William Albert Robinson in 1928, although he was not sailing alone at the time. He carried the pet bear from Panama to the Galápagos, then left him with a new friend there, concluding that a small boat was no place for a pet, let alone a bear.

On companionship from sea life, citations are from Slocum, *Sailing Alone Around the World*, p. 219; Hemingway, *The Old Man and the Sea*, p. 61; and Aebi, *Cruising the World*, p. 67. Aebi's observation of the "sapphire-blue seaway" and the flying fish and the sea turtle is from *Maiden Voyage*, p. 103.

## *11. Kenichi Horie Against the North Pacific*

For more on Brian Platt see Stephen Davies, "How Briton Sailed a Junk Single-handed from Hong Kong to the US", and Charles Borden, *Sea Quest*, p. 227.

I am grateful to Kenichi Horie for meeting with me. Douglas Brooks and Kazuhiro Nishimura put in a great deal of time, several weeks in advance, to arrange this. Through the skilled

interpretation of Sayuri Norish, the flexible staff of Day Translations, and the generosity of the San Francisco Yacht Club, I
interviewed Horie on 17 March 2022. He took this time with Sayuri and me even as he was in the final days of preparing for the
voyage. Information and quotations in this chapter and throughout is also from his public talk given that same evening. The story
of Horie's first voyage was compiled primarily from the English
translation of his narrative *Kodoku*. In *Kodoku* is his photograph
of the albatross and shark. I suspect the albatross more likely
found the shark recently dead, but I'm hesitant to dismiss his
account, since albatrosses are big, tough birds.

The San Francisco Maritime Museum has *Mermaid* on display
as well as the premier collection in the US of artifacts and documents related to Kenichi Horie, many of which were donated by
Horie. The Japanese trailer for *Alone Across the Pacific* is viewable on
YouTube. Information on Starfish Prime is from Gilbert King,
"Going Nuclear over the Pacific," among other sources. For more
on Horie's later voyages, such as his wave-powered catamaran
among so many others, see "Making Waves with Green Pacific
Passage" in *Soundings* (2008). Hannes Lindemann in *Alone at Sea*,
p. 611, is one of the few solo sailors of whom I know that wrote
briefly about the post-voyage airplane experience.


## 12. *Extrasensory Perception*

Many of these quotations about extrasensory perception are
from Henderson, *Singlehanded Sailing*, pp. 71–72, 255–56. H. E.
Ross shared that moment about the tug with me by email on 14
January 2023. For more on the long and salty life of veteran
single-hander Michael Richey, see the obituary by Jim Flannery,
"Gentleman Sailor, Master Navigator." William King talks about

his ESP in his memoir *Adventure in Depth*, pp. 94, 165, and 212–13; and Stuart Woods witnessed King's ESP in action in *Blue Water, Green Skipper*, pp. 134–35. Slocum recorded his own moment in *Sailing Alone Around the World*, p. 74.

### 13. Sharon Sites Adams Had the Right to Sail Alone

Due to kind introductions from Karen Coates and Carol Baker, I was able to speak directly by phone on a couple occasions in 2022 and early 2023 with Sharon Sites Adams, whose generosity with her time and wisdom are inspiring. Quotations and information in this chapter are from these conversations and her *Pacific Lady*. I interviewed her friend and solo sailor Carol Baker on 8 March 2021. On the finding of *Sea Sharp II*, see Ramona McCallister's article "Retrieving a Treasure" and A.J. McCord's "Oregon's 'Pacific Lady' and a Friendship Forged at Sea," which includes a must-watch two-part video story about Adams, with historic clips, photography, video from her time at sea, interviews, and the delivery of the wheel.

The quotation from Ingeborg Von Heister was translated from Wilfried Erdmann's "Auf Drei Rümpfen [On Three Hulls]," pp. 52–53, which includes a summary of her achievements. Thank you to Susan Schnur for help with the translation. For a full account of Von Heister, see the biography by Erdmann titled *Ingeborg Und Das Meer*. Citations from Nicolette Milnes Walker are in *When I Put Out to Sea*, pp. 66, 74, 164, and 174.

### 14. Self-Steering

Among websites and explanations of self-steering systems, including in Richard Henderson, *Singlehanded Sailing*, pp. 148–61, and John Vigor, *The Seaworthy Offshore Sailboat*, pp. 154–58, there is an excellent animated video explanation created by Sailing Tutorials, "Wind Vane Self-Steering Systems" (2020), and Jessica Watson's video diary for 9 February 2010, "Sunset and Parker on *Ella's Pink Lady*," shows her wind vane "Parker" at work from the view of the cockpit. My wind vane was made by Norvane. On the history of self-steering, see Henderson, *Singlehanded Sailing*, pp. 147–70; and Yves Gelinas, "Yves Gélinas on Self-Steering." I learned of Hasube's scary story in Vigor, p. 216. Horie's steering snafu is in Kenichi Horie, *Kodoku*, p. 134. The Yves Gélinas interview was recorded by Andy Schell and Ryan Briggs for the *On the Wind* podcast.

## 15. Bernard Moitessier and a Sea of Spiritual Solitude

I learned a great deal about the national mood of Britain in the 1960s, primed to embrace Chichester, from Simon Winder's *The Man Who Saved Britain: A Personal Journey into the Disturbing World of James Bond*, pp. 86–97. Chichester on Cape Horn and his *why-go* is in his *Gipsy Moth Circles the World*, pp. 2–3. The history of the OSTAR and all the characters involved is well told up into the early 1970s by Frank Page in his *Sailing Solo to America*. Entering into the second half of the twentieth century are dozens of single-handers who have received very little mention or none at all here in this project, regrettably, especially those early and profoundly influential French single-handed racers such as Eric Tabarly and Alain Colas, many of whom were writers themselves.

The Golden Globe race of 1968–69 was huge news then and continues to fascinate. Journalists Nicholas Tomalin and Ron Hall did the exhaustive research to put together the events involving Crowhurst, publishing the compelling and well-written *The Strange*

*Last Voyage of Donald Crowhurst*, which was my source for most information on Crowhurst. For a closer look at Crowhurst's madness, for example, see e.g. 105–06, 234, 265–75. The 2006 documentary *Deep Water* is also a fascinating source. The ripples of the Crowhurst story can be found in Robert Stone's moving and brilliant novel *Outerbridge Reach* (1992) about an American single-hander who fakes his route in a circumnavigation race and copes with madness. Two feature films focused on Crowhurst were created around the time of the 50th anniversary of the Golden Globe, *Crowhurst* (2017), directed by Simon Rumbley, and *The Mercy* (2017), directed by James Marsh.

Peter Nichols' *A Voyage for Madmen* is phenomenal reading and was my entry to the race overall, sending me to the individual sources. My telling of the story of Moitessier's voyage was put together from *The Long Way* and from Nichols, as well as the biography by Moitessier's friend Jean-Michel Barrault, titled *Moitessier*, and from Moitessier's three other books. The quotation about seeing his non-stop voyage as a third book is in *Tamata and the Alliance*, p. 190. For more on Tetley's death, see Chris Eakin's *A Race Too Far*, pp. 266–77. On Bill King's views on loneliness and a short account of what happened to him during the Golden Globe, see his narrative *Adventure in Depth*, as well as a lovely short video featuring him, directed by Osmond and Rothwell.

Robin Knox-Johnston is woefully under-represented in this project, not only because of his extraordinary seamanship and endurance that he summoned to accomplish what he did, but in his long career's impact on sailing around the world since then, both in terms of racing and cruising. His *A World of My Own* is a classic. For his iconic scenes of repairing his boat underwater with sharks nearby and the battery acid in the eye for England, see pp. 44–45 and 75–76; on selfishly enjoying himself, pp. 142–43.

Nichols' writerly candor in *Sea Change* is on p. 214. Information on Bas Jan Ader is from two illuminating documentaries, *Bas Jan Ader: In Search of the Miraculous* (2010), directed by Soo Jin Jeong and the feature-length film, *Here Is Always Somewhere Else* (2008), directed by Rene Daalder; as well as the book-length biography by Alexander Dumbadze, titled *Bas Jan Ader: Death Is Elsewhere* (2015); and an essay by Tiernan Morgan in 2016, from which I sourced Dumbadze's quotation about Ader wanting desperately to make a masterpiece. Baricco's trackless sea line is in his *Ocean Sea*, p. 49. Thank you to Alison Glassie for the quote from Gabriel García Márquez, cited in Steven Price's *Little Black Book of Writer's Wisdom*, p. 115.

## 16. Landlessness, Loneliness, Death Wish

Adams wrote of her stress-induced suicidal thoughts in *Pacific Lady*, p. 51. On the stress of missed communications and single-hander dependency on these, citations are from Graham in *Dove*, p. 126; James in *Alone Around the World*, p. 142; and Petersen in *Journey of a Hope Merchant*, p. 152. Horie on drinking to pause loneliness is in *Kodoku*, p. 115. For the story of the sailor who burned himself with his small stove, see Max Campbell's "Life-Changing Voyage." Tristan Jones wrote several books about single-handing and was a fine storyteller. His thoughts on loneliness here are from *One Hand for Yourself, One Hand for the Ship*, p. 22. Moitessier on radio contact is from *The Long Way*, p. 5.

Teller connected Slocum's vision of the pilot, pp. 45–47 in *Sailing Alone Around the World*, to Slocum's reading of the Columbus biography in *The Search for Captain Slocum*, p. 103. On talking to themselves, others' voices, and full hallucinations, see Slocum in *Sailing Alone Around the World*, p. 25; Garland on Blackburn in *Lone*

*Voyager*, pp. 147–48; Dumas in *Alone Through the Roaring Forties*, pp. 254–55; Horie in *Kodoku*, pp. 111 and 116; Moitessier in *The Long Way*, pp. 40–41, 55–56; Graham in *Dove*, p. 19; Adams in *Pacific Lady*, p. 58, and pers. comm.; Davison in *My Ship Is So Small*, 92; Petersen in *Journey of a Hope Merchant*, pp. 138 and 170; and Manry in *Tinkerbelle*, pp. 76–80 and 104–09.

The OSTAR psychology forms are included in the appendix to David Lewis' *The Ship Would Not Travel Due West*, pp. 453–57. Walker wrote of her dreams in *When I Put Out to Sea*, pp. 71–72 and 108–09. Alain Bombard was not the only trans-Atlantic small-boat sailor whose *why-go* centered around research on open-ocean survival. In the mid-1950s, Hannes Lindemann went across in a dugout canoe and then again in a folding boat, on each voyage thinking about castaways. He concluded that morale was the single most important factor. See his *Alone at Sea* in the *Great Voyages in Small Boats: Solo Transatlantic* volume. John C. Lilly's quotation is from "Effects of Physical Restraint and of Reduction of Ordinary Levels of Physical Stimuli on Intact Healthy Persons," p. 4. Correspondence with Herb McCormick was on 10 November 2022.

## 17. Tevake and the Voyage of No Return

The review in *Cruising World* of *The Voyaging Stars* was by Ted Squier, p. 116. David Lewis was on board the first voyage of the *Hōkūle'a*; he incorporated Piailug's teachings into the revised edition of his scholarly book *We, the Navigators*. The story and correspondence related to Tevake's "voyage of no return" is in Lewis' *We, the Navigators*, pp. 355–56, and in *The Voyaging Stars*, p. 52.

## 18. Animism, the Boat

James Baldwin, two-time circumnavigator aboard his Pearson Triton, *Atom*, has a website (atomvoyages.com) with expert restoration and compelling story videos, and he has written four books about his voyages and travels, the first one titled *Across Islands and Oceans* (2012). We corresponded a bit in 2007, and he gave me excellent practical advice. Richard Hutch's thoughts on the boat as oyster are in *Lone Sailors and Spiritual Insights*, p. 353, as well as other spots in the book. Dumas' lines about his boat are translated in *Great Voyages*, pp. 299, 311, with thanks to Ben Lowings, pers. comm., and in his "Preface" to *Sun of May*, pointing out the masculine pronoun in Spanish. San Francisco Maritime Museum staff and boatbuilder Alana McGillis showed me around and shared her thoughts on *Mermaid* on 25 September 2022. Manry's words on the importance of the boat are in *Tinkerbelle*, p. 65.

## 19. Sailing While Black: Teddy Seymour
### Plays His Love Song

The early years of containerization is well-summarized in Benjamin Labaree, et al., *America and the Sea: A Maritime History*, pp. 599–610. According to the National Sailing Hall of Fame (via H. E. Ross), Teddy Seymour was the 161st person to sail solo around the world in 1987; solocircumnavigation.com has Seymour as the 132nd. The numbers of solo non-stop circumnavigators was accessed in February 2023 from the International Association of Cape Horners website. Hansen's speech and the context is in *The Global Warming Reader*, pp. 46–53. On discharge from ships, see the International Maritime Organization, "International Convention for the Prevention of Pollution from Ships (MARPOL)."

Public resources on Seymour's life and voyages are slim. He did not trust writers and journalists. His undated journal titled "No Frills Circumnavigation" is published only on a website titled "Blue Moment." A short note by Wallace Williams on 5 February 2005, in his *Your Library—What's In It For You* column, archived on the Digital Library of the Caribbean (https://www.dloc.com/AA00080862/00001/pdf), suggested these journal entries were intended to be a book. He wrote the supplemental outline to this in the fall of 2022, which was generously shared with me by his daughter Maya Gates-Seymour. I gathered information for my version of Seymour's story from "No Frills Circumnavigation"; the supplemental outline; the entry "Sailing Around the World" in the expansive and scholarly blog by H. E. Ross, "Atlantic Creole: Black Folk Don't Sail"; the interview Seymour gave to Yawu Miller for the *Bay State Banner* (1992) with the quotation about the police in LA; Wallace Williams' 2019 op-ed in *The St. Thomas Source*; and the entry on Seymour in *Contemporary Black Biography* (2013), which has Seymour's quotation about planning the trip with different women before he left. I learned so much from my correspondence and conversation with Maya Gates-Seymour in April, 2023. She read this chapter and felt her father would have approved.

I learned a great deal, too, from the 2011 interview with H. E. Ross on *BEAT Ahoy!* and was fortunate to speak with him in January 2023, during which he provided further information and perspective. Sendak's prose is from *Where the Wild Things Are*, pp. 13, 15. For a post-colonial reading of this children's book, see John Clement Ball's "Max's Colonial Fantasy: Rereading Sendak's 'Where the Wild Things Are'."

## 20. Dolphins, Whales

The Thomas Traherne quotation is taken from *Happiness and Holiness*, p. 125. Slocum wrote of dolphins in *Sailing Around the World*, pp. 25, 29, and 218. You will find some early "gamboling" dolphins in George Shaw, "Mammalia" (1801), p. 505. Pidgeon's and Allcard's gamboling dolphins are on pp. 32 and 64–65 respectively. Graham's dolphins in *Dove* appear often, e.g., pp. 27, 39, 77, 91, 161–62. Petersen recorded helpful dolphins at just the right time in *The Journey of a Hope Merchant*, p. 50.

Moitessier wrote of his marine mammal miracle in *The Long Way*, pp. 100–05. William Rodarmor translated Moitessier as writing "porpoises" throughout *The Long Way*, but I've changed the word to "dolphins" here because there are no true porpoises in the biological sense in that part of the world, and Moitessier throughout the book would not have meant porpoises literally since he often described species in the deep open ocean (where porpoises do not live). In addition, René Hague, in his translation of *Sailing to the Reefs*, has Moitessier using the word "dolphins." Single-hander and historian H. E. Ross shared with me a similar experience he had off the coast of Mexico, twice. He was sailing along when a dolphin seemed to urge him to go into a harbor. He followed the animal each time and put down his anchor to rest—just before a storm blew through. This happened once on the Pacific side and then another time on the Caribbean side, he wrote to me on 21 February 2023, "around Punto Herrero in Quintana Roo [I was led] by another stubborn dolphin who had a lot of scars and I think probably hung out around there to see what other mariners would be stupidly sailing around when a storm was brewing. Bless them both."

Seymour wrote of the orca interaction in "No Frills Circumnavigation," p. 11. In Bill King's *Adventure in Depth* there are suggestions it was a killer whale instead of a shark. For William Andrews' account see *Dangerous Voyages,* pp. 138–39. Slocum's whales are in *Sailing Alone Around the World,* pp. 53 and 132. For Dumas on whales see, e.g., pp. 268, 286, and 293. Clare Francis' quotation on killer whales in *Woman Alone* is on pp. 85–86, and on seeing them when approaching the coast, p. 156.

Recent orca-boat interactions off the Iberian Peninsula are discussed in Ruth Esteban et al., "Killer Whales of the Strait of Gibraltar"; Lydia Mullan's "Orca Encounters on the Rise" in *SAIL* magazine in 2021; and Scott Neuman's story on National Public Radio on 20 August 2022. Dougal Robertson recorded his family's experience of losing their boat to killer whales in *Survive the Savage Sea,* beginning on p. 23. Alan Eddy, one of the early solo sailors in a fiberglass boat, was also hit by pilot whales, but his vessel was not sunk. Henderson in *Singlehanded Sailing* compiled a summary of events, pp. 260–61. Steven Callahan's story of hitting what he thought was a whale is in *Adrift,* pp. 29–30 and 67–70. See also a whale interaction in Jesse Martin's *Lionheart,* pp. 150–51. Pinkney's moment with the pilot whales as he is leaving Boston is in *As Long As It Takes,* p. 19.

### 21. Bill Pinkney and Neal Petersen: For the Children

The story of Bill Pinkney was compiled from his memoir *As Long As It Takes* and from his documentary *The Incredible Voyage of Bill Pinkney* (1992) which includes priceless video of his life out at sea, arriving in South Africa flying the spinnaker with Black Liberation colors, and speaking to children at the end of the voyage in Boston. He kindly gave up his time for a phone interview with me on 26 January 2023, and then later corresponded by email. Several other sources reveal his life since the circumnavigation, including:

a podcast with Emma Garschagen in 2022, which has the quotation beginning "Six feet off the water"; an interview with Wendy Whitman Clarke in 2021; and with Tony Smith and ABC-7 Chicago in 2022.

Neal Petersen's story was compiled from his narrative *Journey of a Hope Merchant*; the documentary *No Barriers—The Neal Petersen Story* (1999); his TEDx Talk in 2014; "Interview with the Author" on his website; and the two interviews he filmed with Bill Pinkney.

Among other sailors who have expanded the representation of mariners in single-handed sailing is Dilipe Donde, who in 2010 was the first person from India to sail solo around the world. Donde then mentored Abhilash Tomy, another former officer from the Indian Navy, who between 2012 and 2013 became the first Indian to sail alone non-stop around the world. You can read more about Tomy and see him on video on the Golden Globe Race website.

## 22. Ships Again, Rescue

Seymour's quotation is from his unpublished journal, p. 14. Chris Nolan helped with my understanding of the rules of the road. For more on the loss of McMullen and Colas see full chapters in Nicholas Gray's *Last Voyages*. Letcher's story of the near miss is from Henderson, *Singlehanded Sailing*, pp. 254–55. Hasler's quotations on rescue are from Stuart Woods, *Blue Water, Green Skipper*, p. 84 (a similar version in Page, p. 15), and David Lewis, *The Ship Would Not Travel Due West*, p. 357. The disastrous rescue of Chichester in 1972 is from Page, pp. 58–59, and Joachim Schult's *Mayday! Yachts in Distress*, pp. 144–46.

The loss of Plant and the British solo sailor Nigel Burgess right before the 1992–93 Vendée Globe was reported by UPI in "Two Sailors Dead, But Race Pushes On." For more on Plant's end see the excellent documentary *Coyote: The Mike Plant Story* (2017). Plant is another single-hander who does not even step on the stage of this study, but is deserving of more attention as a mariner and an adventurer. His sister Julia Plant wrote a biography, *Coyote Lost at Sea* (2013). For the full, fascinating story of William Willis, who was a favorite of Bernard Moitessier, see T. R. Pearson's *Seaworthy*. For the story of the 2017 OSTAR rescues, see Helen Fretter "Surviving the OSTAR's Perfect Storm—The Full Story of the Racers Rescued in Force 11 Summer Gale," which includes a video shot of the sea condition from which Mervyn Wheatley was rescued. James wrote of the thought of rescue in her *Alone Around the World*, p. 137.

## 23. The Case of Youth: Laura Dekker, Jessica Watson, and Abby Sunderland

I learned a great deal about the setting of Dekker's voyage and the government's thinking in a fascinating scholarly essay by Joel Anderson and Rutger Claassen, "Sailing Alone: Teenage Autonomy and Regimes of Childhood," from which I quote about the court-appointed psychologist, p. 499. Also compelling and helpful about social views of risks, teenage solo sailors, and gender is Mike Brown and Dawn Penney's "Solo Sailing: An 'Ordinary Girl,' Voluntary Risk-Taking and (Ir)responsibility," from which I quote, p. 273.

Unique to any other solo-sailing narrative of which I'm aware, Jessica Watson's narrative *True Spirit* has QR codes that you scan to watch her video diary entries. These are also available on her YouTube channel "JessicaWatsonVideo." On this channel is the video footage of Watson's return home to Sydney and her words at the Sydney Opera House. Sir Richard Branson narrated the

2010 documentary *210 Days: Around the World with Jessica Watson*, and a recent fictionalized film about her voyage, *True Spirit*, was released in 2023. The Australian Transport Safety Bureau report on the collision between Watson's boat and the *Silver Yang* is both clearly written and hugely useful to small-boat sailors.

In addition to her narrative *One Girl One Dream*, Laura Dekker created an eight-part set of film footage that she shot over the course of her circumnavigation. These are available on her You-Tube channel for Laura Dekker World Sailing Foundation. Part 4 has the scene with the tropicbird "Messy" on board. In 2013 a feature-length documentary was produced, titled *Maidentrip*, directed by Jillian Schlesinger. Tania Aebi's "Foreword" to Laura Dekker's *One Girl One Dream*, pp. 9–14, is exceptionally insightful and brings together many themes, since Aebi had lived such a similar experience to Dekker and now had the experience of hindsight after raising her own children. Aebi reflects further on her own experience in a short 2017 video with David Lyman.

The documentary about Abby Sunderland's trip is titled *Wild Eyes: The Abby Sunderland Story* (2011), directed by her father Laurence Sunderland, which I used to tell her story, along with her narrative *Unsinkable*. On the finding of *Wild Eyes* in December 2018, see Bill Chappell, "Sailboat From U.S. Teen's Doomed Round-The-World Attempt Found Drifting Off Australia."

## 24. Storms, Waves

Don Treworgy's email to me was on 15 July 2007. For Raban's perceptive observations about shifts in storm writing see his "Introduction" in *The Oxford Book of the Sea*, pp. 31–33. Lewis' description of an Antarctic storm is in *Ice Bird*, pp. 57–59. Although I write far too little about Kay Cottee here, her accomplishment and her influence are significant, as evidenced by Jessica Watson's story *True Spirit* and Richard Hutch's scholarship in *Lone Sailors and Spiritual Insights*. Her observation of the sun through the big seas is on p. 72 of *First Lady*. For information about rogue waves research and the wreck of the German containership *MS München*, see Gary Griggs, *The Ominous Ocean*, pp. 70–81.

### 25. The Environmental Epiphany of Ellen MacArthur

Henderson's lists are at the back of his *Singlehanded Sailing*. The 2021 numbers of solo circumnavigators was accessed in February, 2023, from the International Cape Horners Association website at these pages: http://covarimail.com/IACH/solo_non-stop.lasso and http:// .../solo_withstops.lasso.

Jon Sanders' most recent circumnavigation and its mission about plastic waste was reported by Narelle Towie in *The Guardian* (2021), and Andy Schell recorded an illuminating interview with Sanders that same year on his *On the Wind* podcast. On Isabelle Autissier, who is highly deserving of more attention than her story receives here, especially in terms of her pioneering sailing beginning in the early 1990s, her stories of rescues, and her own writing. For brief introductions to Autissier see her page on WeAre-Minds.com, which has a link to her 2001 Tedx Talk; a 2020 interview in *BoatsNews*, which includes her carbon-footprint proposal; and a 2023 interview in the *Financial Times* by Victor Mallet.

Oliver Heer's research plan and science partnership for the 2024 Vendée Globe is introduced by Michael Wegner in the *Polar Journal* (2022). Gabart's remarks about ice and global warming in the Southern Ocean are from Brian Hancock's article in *SAIL* (2018). Lisa Blair's second Antarctic circumnavigation was reported by Carolyn Grant in *Sail-World* (2022). Bill McKibben's article "We're Hot As Hell and We're Not Going to Take It Any More" originally appeared in *Grist* on 5 August 2010, then was anthologized in *The Global Warming Reader*.

Ellen MacArthur's story was put together from her three books, especially her first one, *Taking on the World*, as well as the documentary about her Vendée Globe performance, titled *Ellen MacArthur: Taking on the World: The Official Story* (2001), and her TED Talk in British Columbia in 2015.

### 26. The Solo Sailor Survives and Tries to Find Meaning

The number of ships in the region is from a study the following year, in 2008, by P. Silveira, A. P. Texeira, and C. Guedes Soares, pp. 37–38. To my surprise, I learned that Richard Hutch had already thought about solo sailing in relationship to literary *deux ex machina* in his article in *Sailing: Philosophy for Everyone*, pp. 44–45. I tried to refine my thinking based on his work. See also Abrams for the literary definition, p. 42. I learned of Cal Currier's crossing in Monica Grant's story in the September 2022 issue of *Latitude 38*. My email correspondence with Sandy Van Zandt was on 28 September 2022.

# Selected Bibliography

*Solo Sailing Histories*

Anderson, J. R. L. *The Ulysses Factor: The Exploring Instinct in Man*. New York: Harcourt Brace Jovanovich, Inc., 1970.

Anthony, Irvin. *Voyagers Unafraid*. Philadelphia: Macrae, Smith, Co., 1930.

Borden, Charles A. *Sea Quest: Small Craft Adventures from Magellan to Chichester*. London: Robert Hale, 1967.

Clarke, D. H. *An Evolution of Singlehanders*. London: Stanford Maritime, 1976.

Clarke, D. H. *Blue Water Dream: The Escape to Sea Syndrome, A Practical Guide to the Joys and Terrors of Sailing Big Seas in Small Boats*. New York: David McKay Co., 1981.

Compton, Nic. *Sailing Solo: The Legendary Sailors and Great Races*. London: Mitchell Beazley, 2003.

Harris, MacDonald. *They Sailed Alone: The Story of the Single-Handers*. Boston: Houghton Mifflin, Co., 1972.

Heatter, Basil. *The Sea Dreamers*. New York: Farrar, Straus, and Giroux, 1968.

Henderson, Richard. *Singlehanded Sailing: The Experiences and Techniques of the Lone Voyagers*, 2nd ed. Camden, ME: International Marine, 1988.

Hutch, Richard. *Lone Sailors and Spiritual Insights: Cases of Sport and Peril at Sea*. Lewiston, NY: Edwin Mellen Press, 2005.

Hutch, Richard. "Solo Sailing as Spiritual Practice: A Phenomenology of Mastery and Failure at Sea." In *Sailing: Philosophy for*

*Everyone,* edited by Patrick Goold, 36–46. West Sussex: Wiley Blackwell, 2012.

## Solo-Sailor Narratives

Adams, Sharon Sites, with Karen J. Coates. *Pacific Lady: The First Woman to Sail Solo Across the World's Largest Ocean.* Lincoln: University of Nebraska Press, 2008.

Aebi, Tania, with Bernadette Brennan. *Maiden Voyage.* New York: Simon and Schuster, 1989.

Aebi, Tania. "When Solitaire's the Only Game in Town." *Cruising World* 13, no. 11 (November 1987): 64–9.

Allcard, Edward. *Single-Handed Passage.* London: Putnam, 1951.

Andrews, William. *The Dangerous Voyages of Captain William Andrews.* Edited by Richard Henderson. New York: Abercrombie & Fitch, 1966.

Baldwin, James. *Across Islands and Oceans: A Journey Alone Around the World by Sail and by Foot.* CreateSpace Independent Publishing Platform, 2012.

Blair, Lisa. *Facing Fear.* Sydney: Australian Geographic, 2020.

Bombard, Alain. *The Bombard Story (Naufragé Volontaire).* Translated by Brian Connell. London: André Deutsch, 1953.

Callahan, Steven. *Adrift: Seventy-Six Days Lost at Sea.* New York: Ballantine Books, 1987.

Campbell, Max. "Life-changing Voyage: Sailing Solo Across the Atlantic in a 22-foot Sloop." *Yachting World* (May 28, 2019): www.yachtingworld.com.

Chichester, Francis. *Along the Clipper Way.* London: Pan Books Ltd., 1974. [An anthology of various narratives, some of which are solo.]

Chichester, Francis. *Gipsy Moth Circles the World.* New York: Coward-McCann, 1967.

Cottee, Kay. *First Lady*: *A History-Making Solo Voyage Around the World*. South Melbourne: Macmillan Company of Australia, 1989.

Davison, Ann. "The Atlantic and I." *Life* 35, no. 5 (3 August 1953): 45–54.

Davison, Ann. *Last Voyage*. New York: William Sloane Associates, 1952.

Davison, Ann. *My Ship Is So Small*. New York: William Sloane Associates, 1956.

Dekker, Laura. *One Girl One Dream*. London: HarperCollins, 2016.

Dumas, Vito. *Alone Through the Roaring Forties*. In *Great Voyages in Small Boats: Solo Circumnavigations*. Clinton Corners, NY: John de Graff, Inc., 1976.

Francis, Clare. *Woman Alone: Sailing Solo Across the Atlantic*. New York: David McKay, 1977.

Gerbault, Alain. *Firecrest Around the World* [*The Fight of the Firecrest and In Quest of the Sun*]. New York: David McKay, Co., 1981.

Gilboy, Bernard. *A Voyage of Pleasure: The Log of Bernard Gilboy's Transpacific Cruise in the Boat "Pacific" 1882–1883*. Edited by John Barr Tomkins. Cambridge, MD: Cornell Maritime Press, 1956.

Graham, Robin Lee, and Derek L. T. Gill. *Dove*. New York: Bantam, 1974.

Horie, Kenichi. *Kodoku: Sailing Alone Across the Pacific*. Trans. by Takuichi Ito and Kaoru Ogimi. Rutland, VT: Charles E. Tuttle, 1964.

James, Naomi. *Alone Around the World: The First Woman to Sail Single-Handedly Around the World*. New York: Coward, McCann & Geoghegan, 1979.

Jones, Tristan. *One Hand for Yourself, One Hand for the Ship: The Essentials of Single-Handed Sailing*. Dobbs Ferry, NY: Sheridan House, 1996.

King, William. *Adventure in Depth*. New York: G.P. Putnam's Sons, 1975.

Knox-Johnston, Robin. *A World of My Own*. London: Adlard Coles, 2004.

Lewis, David. *Icebird*. Dobbs Ferry, NY: Sheridan House, 2002.

Lewis, David. *The Ship Would Not Travel Due West*. In *Great Voyages in Small Boats: Solo Transatlantic*. Clinton Corners, NY: John de Graff, Inc., 1982.

Lindemann, Hannes. *Alone at Sea*. In *Great Voyages in Small Boats: Solo Transatlantic*. Clinton Corners, NY: John de Graff, Inc., 1982.

Long, Dwight. *Sailing All Seas in the Idle Hour*. London: Rupert Hart-Davis, 1957.

Martin, Jesse, and Ed Gannon. *Lionheart: A Journey of the Human Spirit*. St Leonards, New South Wales: Sue Hines, 2000.

MacArthur, Ellen. *Full Circle: My Life and Journey*. London: Michael Joseph, 2010.

MacArthur, Ellen. *Race Against Time*. London: Penguin, 2006.

MacArthur, Ellen. *Taking on the World: A Sailor's Extraordinary Solo Race Around the Globe*. New York: International Marine/McGraw-Hill, 2005.

MacGregor, John. *The Voyage Alone in the Yawl "Rob Roy."* Mineola, NY: Dover, 2001.

Manry, Robert. *Tinkerbelle*. New York: Dell, 1966.

Middleton, E. E. *The Cruise of "The Kate."* London: Granada, 1984.

Moitessier, Bernard. *The Long Way*. Translated by William Rodarmor. Dobbs Ferry, NY: Sheridan House, 2003.

Moitessier, Bernard. *Sailing to the Reefs*. Translated by René Hague. Dobbs Ferry, NY: Sheridan House, 2001.

Moitessier, Bernard. *Tamata and the Alliance*. Translated by William Rodarmor. Shrewsbury: Waterline Books, 1995.

Nichols, Peter. *Sea Change: Alone Across the Atlantic in a Wooden Boat.* New York: Sheridan House, 2010.

Petersen, Neal, William P. Baldwin, and Patty Fulcher, *Journey of a Hope Merchant: From Apartheid to the Elite World of Solo Yacht Racing.* Charleston, SC: Elevate, 2007.

Pidgeon, Harry. "Around the World in the 'Islander'." *National Geographic Magazine* 53, no. 2 (February 1928): 141–205.

Pidgeon, Harry. *Around the World Single-Handed; The Cruise of the "Islander."* New York: D. Appleton and Co., 1932.

Pinkney, William. *As Long As It Takes: Meeting the Challenge.* Piermont, NH: Bunker Hill Publishing, 2006.

Rebell, Fred. *Escape to the Sea: The Log of a Homemade Sailor.* New York: Dodd, Mead, and Co., 1939.

Robinson, William Albert. *Deep Water and Shoal.* London: Jonathan Cape, 1943.

Seymour, Teddy. "No Frills Circumnavigation." Blue Moment, UK (n.d.): www.bluemoment.com/seymour.html.

Slocum, Joshua. *Sailing Alone Around the World.* Edited by Thomas Philbrick. New York: Penguin Books, 1999.

Slocum, Joshua. *The Voyage of the "Liberdade"* and *The Voyage of the "Destroyer."* In *The Voyages of Joshua Slocum.* Edited by Walter Magnes Teller, 39–123 and 171–95. Dobbs Ferry, NY: Sheridan House, 2002.

Sunderland, Abby, and Lynn Vincent. *Unsinkable: A Young Woman's Courageous Battle on the High Seas.* Dallas: Thomas Nelson, 2011.

Walker, Nicolette Milnes. *When I Put Out to Sea.* Briarcliff Manor, NY: Stein and Day, 1972.

Watson, Jessica. *True Spirit: The True Story of a 16-Year-Old Australian Who Sailed Solo, Nonstop, and Unassisted Around the World.* London: Atria, 2010.

Woods, Stuart. *Blue Water, Green Skipper: A Memoir of Sailing Alone Across the Atlantic.* New York: G.P. Putnam's Sons, 2012.

Wray, J. W. *South Sea Vagabonds.* Auckland: HarperCollins, 2014.


## Other Published Sources


Abrams, M. H. *A Glossary of Literary Terms.* 5th ed. Fort Worth: Holt, Rinehart, and Winston, Inc., 1988.

Aebi, Tania. "Foreword." In Laura Dekker. *One Girl One Dream*, 9–14. London: HarperCollins, 2016.

Alexander, W. B. *Birds of the Ocean.* New, revised edition. New York: G.P. Putnam's Sons, 1963.

Anderson, Joel, and Rutger Claassen. "Sailing Alone: Teenage Autonomy and Regimes of Childhood." *Law and Philosophy* 31 (September 2012): 495–522.

Australian Transport Safety Bureau. "Independent Investigation into the Collision Between the Australian Registered Yacht *Ella's Pink Lady* and the Hong Kong Registered Bulk Carrier *Silver Yang* off Point Lookout, Queensland, 9 September 2009." Marine Occurrence Investigation, No. 268 (Commonwealth of Australia, June 2010): i–37.

Babcock, W.H. "St Brendan's Explorations and Islands." *Geographical Review* 8, no. 1 (July 1919): 37–46.

Ball, John Clement. "Max's Colonial Fantasy: Rereading Sendak's 'Where the Wild Things Are." *ARIEL* 28, no. 1 (January 1997): 167–79.

Baricco, Alessandro. *Ocean Sea.* Translated by Alistair McEwen. New York: Vintage International, 2000.

Barrault, Jean-Michel. *Moitessier: A Sailing Legend.* Translated by Janine Simon. Dobbs Ferry, NY: Sheridan House, 2005.

Beaufort, Luc, and Michaël Grelaud. "A 2700-Year Record of ENSO and PDO Variability from the California Margin Based on Coccolithophore Assemblages and Calcification." *Progress in Earth and Planetary Science* 4, no. 5 (2017): 1–13.

Beegel, Susan F. "Thor Heyerdahl's *Kon-Tiki* and Hemingway's Return to Primitivism in *The Old Man and the Sea*." In *Hemingway: Eight Decades of Criticism*, edited by Linda Wagner-Martin, 513–51. East Lansing: Michigan State University Press, 2009.

Bender, Bert. "Joshua Slocum and the Reality of Solitude." *American Transcendental Quarterly* 6, no. 1 (1992): 59–71.

Berthold, Dennis A. "Introduction." In Joshua Slocum. *Sailing Alone Around the World*, pp. xiii–xxxvi. New York: Barnes & Noble Classics, 2005.

Brewster, Charles. *Rambles about Portsmouth*. Second series. Portsmouth, NH: Lewis W. Brewster, 1869.

Brown, Mike, and Dawn Penney. "Solo Sailing: An 'Ordinary Girl,' Voluntary Risk-Taking and (Ir)responsibility." *Sociology of Sport Journal* 31 (2014): 267–86.

Buck, Peter F. *Vikings of the Pacific* [*Vikings of the Sunrise*]. Chicago: University of Chicago Press, 1967.

Campbell, Joseph. *The Hero with a Thousand Faces*. London: Fontana Press, 1993.

Cape Ann Museum. "Alfred Johnson's *Centennial*" (accessed 2013): www.capeannmuseum.org/collections/objects/johnson-dory.

Castro, Alex. "Meet Florentino R. Das, the Filipino Sinbad Who Conquered the Pacific." *Esquire Philippines* (4 March 2019): www.esquiremag.ph.

Chappell, Bill. "Sailboat From U.S. Teen's Doomed Round-the-World Attempt Found Drifting Off Australia." National Public Radio (3 January 2019): npr.org/2019.

Clarke, Wendy Whitman. "Bill Pinkney Talks Solo Circumnavigation." *Soundings* (7 June 2021): www.soundingsonline.com.

Colmenares, Jr., Serafin P., Cecilia D. Noble, and Patricia E. Halagao. *Bold Dream, Uncommon Valor: The Florentino Das Story.* Aeia, HI: Congress of Visayan Organizations and the COVO Foundation, 2013.

Conrad, Joseph. "Typhoon." In *Great Short Works of Joseph Conrad*, 295–364. New York: Perennial Library, 1967.

Crowe, Andrew. *Pathway of the Birds: The Voyaging Achievements of Māori and their Polynesian Ancestors.* Auckland: David Bateman, 2018.

Cunliffe, Barry. *The Extraordinary Voyage of Pytheas the Greek.* New York: Walker and Co., 2002.

Darwin, Charles. *Voyage of the* Beagle. London: Penguin, 1989.

Davenport, William. "Notes on Santa Cruz Voyaging." *The Polynesian Society* 73, no. 2 (June 1964): 134–42.

Davies, Stephen. "How Briton Sailed a Junk Single-Handed from Hong Kong to the US" *South China Post*: *Post Magazine* (2 September 2017): scmp.com.

Dumbadze, Alexander. *Bas Jan Ader: Death Is Elsewhere.* Chicago: University of Chicago Press, 2015.

Eakin, Chris. *A Race Too Far: The Tragic Story of Donald Crowhurst and the 1968 Round-the-World Race.* London: Ebury Press, 2009.

Ebert, David A., Sarah Fowler, and Marc Dando. *A Pocket Guide to Sharks of the World.* Princeton: Princeton University Press, 2015.

Editors. "Gabart's Solo Achievement." *SAIL* (9 February 2018): www.sailmagazine.com.

Erdmann, Wilfried. "Auf Drei Rümpfen." In *50 Jahre Festschift.* Edited by Kirsten Panzer, 52–55. TransOcean EV (2018): www.trans-ocean.org/portals/0/media/download/50-Jahre-TO-Festschrift.pdf.

Esteban, Ruth, et al. "Killer Whales of the Strait of Gibraltar: An Endangered Subpopulation Showing a Disruptive Behavior." *Marine Mammal Science* (2022): 1–11.

Evans, Jeff. *Polynesian Navigation and the Discovery of New Zealand.* Auckland: Libro International, 2011.

Fagan, Brian. *Beyond the Blue Horizon: How the Earliest Mariners Unlocked the Secrets of the Oceans.* London: Bloomsbury Press, 2012.

Flannery, Jim. "Gentleman Sailor, Master Navigator [Michael Richey]." *Soundings* (4 March 2010): www.soundingsonline.com.

"A Frail Craft, Capt. Johnson's Perilous Transatlantic," *The New York Herald* via *St Louis Daily Globe-Democrat* (27 February 1877): 2.

Fretter, Helen. "Surviving the OSTAR's Perfect Storm—The Full Story of the Racers Rescued in Force 11 Summer Gale." *Yachting World* (10 August 2017): yachtingworld.com/news.

Fulloon, Gillian. "Fred Rebell (1886–1968)." *Australian Dictionary of Biography* 11 (1988, online 2006): https://adb.anu.edu.au/biography/rebell-fred-8171.

Galit de la Cruz, Mio. "Kin Honor Sailor's Feat, Unsinkable Dream." *Philippine Daily Inquirer* (6 May 2018): www.newsinfo.inquirer.net.

Garland, Joseph E. *Lone Voyager: The Extraordinary Adventures of Howard Blackburn, Hero Fisherman of Gloucester.* New York: Touchstone, 2000.

Gelinas, Yves. "Yves Gélinas on Self-Steering." *Sailing Canada* 50 (May 1988): caphorn.com/en/yves-gelinas-on-self-steering.

Grant, Carolyn. "Lisa Blair Sets New World Record on Solo Sail Around Antarctica." *Sail-World* (24 May 2022): sail-world.com/news.

Grant, Monica. "16-Year-Old's Solo Transatlantic Passage." *Latitude 38*, no. 543 (September 2022): 48–49.

Gray, Nicholas. *Last Voyages: The Lives and Tragic Loss of Remarkable Sailors Who Never Returned.* Leamington Spa: Fernhust Books, 2017.

Grayson, Stan. *The Man for All Oceans: Captain Joshua Slocum and the First Solo Voyage Around the World.* Thomaston, ME: Tilbury House and New Bedford Whaling Museum, 2017.

Grayson, Stan. "Slocum's Luck: A Life of Near Misses and Good Fortune." *WoodenBoat* 256 (May/June 2017): https://www.woodenboat.com.

Griggs, Gary. *The Ominous Ocean: Rogue Waves, Rip Currents and Other Dangers Along the Shoreline and in the Sea.* Guildford, CT: Sheridan House, 2022.

Hancock, Brian. "François Gabart Sets a New Singlehanded Round-the-World Record." *SAIL* (13 June 2018): sailmagazine.com.

Hemingway, Ernest. *The Old Man and the Sea.* New York: Scribner Classic, 1986.

Ihimaera, Witi. *The Whale Rider.* London: Penguin, 2010.

Ingersoll, Oliver Roland, et al. *Smallest Ship that Ever Crossed the Atlantic Ocean: The Log of the Ship-Rigged Ingersoll Metallic Life-Boat, "Red, White and Blue."* New York: Bunce and Co., 1870.

International Maritime Organization, "International Convention for the Prevention of Pollution from Ships (MARPOL)" (accessed 2023): www.imo.org.

Johnson, Clifton. "Captain Joshua Slocum—The Man Who Sailed Around the World in a Thirty-Seven-Foot Boat." *Outing* 41, no. 1 (October 1902): 35–39.

King, Gilbert. "Going Nuclear Over the Pacific." *Smithsonian* (15 August 2012): www.smithsonianmag.com.

Kroll, Gary. *America's Ocean Wilderness: A Cultural History of Twentieth-Century Exploration.* Lawrence: University Press of Kansas, 2008.

Labaree, Benjamin W. et al. *America and the Sea: A Maritime History*. Mystic, CT: Mystic Seaport, 1998.

Lewis, David. *The Voyaging Stars: Secrets of the Pacific Island Navigators*. Sydney: Fontana/Collins: 1980.

Lewis, David. *We, the Navigators: The Ancient Art of Landfinding in the Pacific*. 2nd ed. Honolulu: University of Hawaii Press, 1994.

Lilly, John C. "Effects of Physical Restraint and of Reduction of Ordinary Levels of Physical Stimuli on Intact Healthy Persons." *Illustrative Strategies for Research on Psychopathy in Mental Health*, Symposium No. 2 (New York: Group for the Advancement of Psychiatry, 1956): 1–9.

"Loggerhead Turtle." NOAA Fisheries. www.fisheries.noaa.gov/species/loggerhead-turtle.

Lowings, Ben. *The Dolphin: The Life of David Lewis*. London: Lodestar Books, 2020.

Lowings, Ben. *The Sun of May: Vito Dumas, A Life*. Windsor: Serantes Press, 2022.

Luck, Richard. "The Mystery of the Inuit Who Arrived in Scotland." *The New European* (31 May 2021): www.theneweuropean.co.uk.

Mack, John. *The Sea: A Cultural History*. London: Reaktion: 2011.

Mallet, Victor. "Sailor Isabelle Autissier: 'The Ocean Is The Axis Around Which My Life Has Turned'." *Financial Times* (20 January 2023): www.ft.com/content.

Manila, Quijano de [Nick Joaquin]. "Florentino Das: The Long Voyage Home." In *Ronnie Poe and Other Silhouettes* (Manila: National Book Store, 1977): 35–54.

McCallister, Ramona. "Retrieving a Treasure." *Central Oregonian* (18 August 2020): www.centraloregonian.com.

McCord, A. J. "Oregon's 'Pacific Lady' and a Friendship Forged at Sea." *KOIN 6 News* (20 May, rev. 4 June 2021): www.koin.com/news.

McCormick, Herb. "A Single-Minded Sailor Conquers the Sea Solo." *New York Times* (16 December 2001): 8.

McKibben, Bill, ed. *The Global Warming Reader: A Century of Writing About Climate Change.* New York: Penguin, 2012.

Miller, Yawu. "Pair of Black Sailors Recall Trials of Solo Sea Voyages." *Bay State Banner* (18 June 1992): 1.

Miranda, Jonas Robert L. "The Narratives of a Forgotten Filipino Conqueror of the Pacific: A Florentino Das Solo Voyage from Hawaii to the Philippines." Presentation at the DLSU Research Congress, De La Salle University, Manila (6–8 March 2014): 1–7.

"Miscellany" [via the *NY Gazette*]. *New-Hampshire Gazette* 68 (10 March 1823): 1.

Morgan, Tiernan. "In Search of Bas Jan Ader, the Artist Who Disappeared at Sea." *Hyperallergic* (30 November 2016): https://hyperallergic.com.

Mullan, Lydia. "Orca Encounters on the Rise." *SAIL* (9 September 2021): www.sailmagazine.com.

Neuman, Scott. "Killer Whales Are 'Attacking' Sailboats Near Europe's Coast. Scientists Don't Know Why." National Public Radio (20 August 2022): www.npr.org.

"Newburyport, May 2." *The Essex Journal & New-Hampshire Packet* 148 (2 May 1787): 3.

Nichols, Peter. *A Voyage for Madmen.* New York: Perennial, 2002.

"Notice, To All Whom It May Concern. Deborah Shackford . . ." *New-Hampshire Gazette* (5 November 1805): 3.

"Other Kinds of Sailing Records." World Sailing Speed Record Council (accessed 2 December 2022): www.sailspeedrecords.com.

Page, Frank. *Sailing Solo to America.* New York: Quadrangle Books, 1972.

"Past [ENSO] Events." NOAA Physical Science Laboratory (accessed January 2023): https://psl.noaa.gov/enso/past_events.html.

Pearson, T. R. *Seaworthy: Adrift with William Willis in the Golden Age of Rafting*. New York: Three Rivers Press, 2006.

Pepperell, Julian. *Fishes of the Open Ocean: A Natural History and Illustrated* Guide. Chicago: University of Chicago Press, 2010.

Petersen, Neal. "Interview with the Author" (n.d.): http://neal petersen.com/neal-petersen-author/interview-with-author.

Porter, David D. *Memoir of Commodore David Porter of the United States Navy*. Albany: J. Munsell, 1875.

Potter, Robin. "The First Solo Transatlantic Sailor Josiah Shackford." *Maine Boats, Homes, and Harbors* (July/Aug 2023): pp. 39–42.

Price, Steven D., editor. *The Little Black Book of Writer's Wisdom*. New York: Skyhorse, 2013.

Raban, Jonathan. "Introduction." In *The Oxford Book of the Sea*. Edited by Jonathan Raban, pp. 1–34. Oxford: Oxford University Press, 1993.

Raban, Jonathan. "Introduction." In *Alone Through the Roaring Forties*, by Vito Dumas, pp. xiii–xxii. Camden, ME: International Marine, 2001.

Roberts, Callum. *The Unnatural History of the Sea*. London: Shearwater Books, 2007.

Robertson, Dougal. *Survive the Savage Sea*. Dobbs Ferry, NY: Sheridan House, 2002.

Ross, H. E. (Herman). "Sailing Around the World [Teddy Seymour, et al.]." Atlantic Creole: Black Folk Don't Sail Blog (13 May 2014): http://herossea.blogspot.com.

Rousmaniere, John. *After the Storm: True Stories of Disaster and Recover at Sea*. Camden, ME: International Marine/McGraw Hill, 2004.

Sandomir, Richard. "Edward Allcard, Solo Sailor on the High Seas, Dies at 102." *The New York Times* (18 August 2017): www.nytimes.com.

Schult, Joachim. *Mayday! Yachts in Distress.* Translated by Detlef Jens. Dobbs Ferry, NY: Sheridan House, 1997.

Sendak, Maurice. *Where the Wild Things Are.* New York: Harper Collins, 2013.

Shaw, George. "Mammalia." In *General Zoology, or Systematic Natural History.* Part 2. London: G. Kearsley, 1801.

Silveira, P., A. P. Texeira, and C. Guedes Soares. "Analysis of Maritime Traffic off the Coast of Portugal." In *Maritime Engineering and Technology*, edited by Guedes Soares, et al., 35–41. London: Taylor & Francis, 2012.

Smith, Harrison. "Edward Allcard Obituary: Sailing's 'Dean of Loners' Survived Shark-Infested Waters, a Hurricane, and a 16-Year Journey at Sea." *Washington Post* (13 August 2017): www.washingtonpost.com.

Smith, Tony. "Chicago Native, Hall of Fame Sailor Writes New Children's Book." ABC-7 Chicago (7 June 2022): www.abc-7chicago.com.

Soundings Editors. "Making Waves with Green Pacific Passage." *Soundings* (3 June 2008): www.soundingsonline.com.

Spencer, Ann. *Alone at Sea.* Toronto: Doubleday Canada, 1998.

Sperry, Armstrong. *Call It Courage.* New York: Aladdin Books, 1990.

Springer, Haskell. "Joshua Slocum." Searchable Sea Literature (rev. 2021): https://sites.williams.edu/searchablesealit/s/slocum-joshua/.

Springfield Museums, "The Miniature Ship 'Red, White, and Blue.' On Her Voyage from New York to London," Currier & Ives (n.d.): www.springfieldmuseums.org.

Squier, Ted. "Book Review: *The Voyaging Stars.*" *Cruising World* 5, no. 3 (March 1979): 116–17.

Suedfeld, Peter. "The 'Sensed Presence' in Unusual Environments." *Environment and Behavior* 19, no. 1 (January 1987): 33–52.

"Teddy Seymour." *Contemporary Black Biography* 110 (Gale: 2013): go.gale.com.

"Teddy Seymour." National Sailing Hall of Fame (accessed 2023): nshof.org/nominees/seymour-teddy.

Teller, Walter Magnes. *Joshua Slocum [The Search for Captain Slocum]*. Rev. ed. New Brunswick: Rutgers University Press, 1971.

"That Dory Trip." *London Daily News* via *Milwaukee Daily Sentinel* (12 September 1876): 2.

Thompson, Nainoa. "Twenty-Five Years of Voyaging, 1975–2000." Hawaiian Voyaging Traditions and the Polynesian Voyaging Society (n.d.): https://archive.hokulea.com/holokai/nainoa_twenty_five_years.html.

Tomalin, Nicholas, and Ron Hall, *The Strange Last Voyage of Donald Crowhurst*. London: Adlard Coles Nautical, 1995.

Tourchon, Olivier. "Isabelle Autissier: 'Racing Has No More Impact Than Any Other Human Activity.'" *BoatsNews* 17 (November 2020): www.boatsnews.com.

Towie, Narelle. "Anything But Ordinary: The 81-Year-Old Who Has Sailed Around the World 11 Times." *The Guardian* (5 February 2021): theguardian.com.

Traherne, Thomas. *Happiness and Holiness: Thomas Traherne and His Writings*. Edited by Denise Inge. Norwich: Canterbury Press, 2008.

"Two Sailors Dead, But Race Pushes On." *UPI* (26 November 1992): upi.com/Archives.

Vibart, Eric. "In Search of Harry Pidgeon." *WoodenBoat* no. 206 (Jan/Feb 2009): 51–57.

Vigor, John. *The Seaworthy Offshore Sailboat: A Guide to Essential Features, Gear, and Handling*. Camden, ME: International Marine, 2001.

Wang, Chunzai and Paul C. Fiedler. "ENSO Variability and The Eastern Tropical Pacific: A Review." *Progress in Oceanography* 69 (2006): 239–66.

Wegner, Michael. "Swiss Researchers Obtain Southern Ocean Data from Racing Yacht." *Polar Journal* (15 September 2022): www.polarjournal.ch/en.

Williams, Wallace. "Op-ed: Capt. Teddy Seymour Was the First." *The St Thomas Source* (4 April 2019): https://stthomassource. com/content/2019/04/04/op-ed-capt-teddy-seymour-was-the-first/.

Winder, Simon. *The Man Who Saved Britain: A Personal Journey into the Disturbing World of James Bond.* New York: Picador, 2006.

"Yankee's Visit to Sir Joseph Banks, The." In *The Sailor's Magazine and Naval Journal,* vol. 5, December 1933, 111–12. New York: American Seaman's Friend Society, 1933.

### Websites, Films, Podcasts, and Other Multi-Media Sources

Aebi, Tania, and David Lyman. "Tania Aebi: Storyteller." Vimeo (6 December 2017): vimeo.com/246201626.

"*Alone Across the Pacific* Movie Trailer (1963)." www.youtube.com/ watch?v=jrsebQ6tmaQ.

Australian Sailing Hall of Fame. "Kay Cottee AO, video and photographs" (2023): https://sailinghalloffame.org.au/inductee/ kay-cottee-ao.

Brown, Lisa and Sheree Gibson, producers. "Fall Guy: How a Solo Sailor Survived Getting Stranded in Shark-Infested Waters." *60 Minutes Australia* (2022): www.youtube.com/watch?v=ditH W7qb2WA.

"Captain Bill Pinkney." www.captainbillpinkney.com.

Chandor, J. C. (director) and Robert Redford (sole actor). *All Is Lost* (2013).

"Chichester Arrival." British Pathé (1967): www.youtube.com/watch?v=DdEzSBPAdko.

"Chichester Knighted." British Pathé (1967): www.youtube.com/watch?v=vNWCcMGWG_I.

Cornell Lab of Ornithology. *Birds of the World* (2023): https://birdsoftheworld.org/bow/home.

Daalder, Rene. *Here Is Always Somewhere Else.* Directed by Rene Daalder (2008): www.youtube.com/watch?v=wW9PDCMI1iA.

Dekker, Laura. "A Few Excerpts of Sailing Footage from the Solo Around the World Voyage of Laura Dekker, Age 14–16, 2010–2012," 8 parts. Laura Dekker World Sailing Foundation (2010–2012): www.youtube.com/@lauradekkerworldsailingfou2133/videos.

Dekker, Laura. *Maidentrip* [documentary film]. Directed by Jillian Schlesinger (2013).

Gélinas, Yves, Andy Schell, and Ryan Briggs. "Yves Gélinas Recycled." *On the Wind* podcast 181 (2013/2017), www.59-north.com.

Golden Globe Race. Ocean Frontiers. https://goldengloberace.com.

Graham, Robin Lee, and Emma Garschagen. "Robin Lee Graham: Fifty Years Since Sailing *Dove*." *On The Wind* podcast 352 (5 April 2022): www.59-north.com.

"Harry Pidgeon Collection." California Museum of Photography. http://ucr.emuseum.com.

"Harry Pidgeon Photograph Collection." Fresno State Library. http://digitized.library.fresnostate.edu.

International Association of Cape Horners (IACH). https://www.capehorners.club/main/index.php.

"Isabelle Autissier." https://weareminds.com/en/talents/isabelle-autissier.

MacArthur, Ellen. *Ellen MacArthur: Taking on the World: The Official Story*. Produced and directed by Richard Simmonds and Andrew Preece (APP Production, 2001): www.youtube.com/watch?v=obxt-FzEsnA.

MacArthur, Ellen. TED Talk (Whistler, BC: March 2015): https://www.youtube.com/watch?v=ooIxHVXgLbc.

Media TV, "Sir Robin Knox-Johnston Sailing Legend." Clipper Ventures (2019): www.youtube.com/watch?v=WdIIYr1GdIs.

"Neal Petersen." www.nealpetersen.com.

Osmond, Louise, and Jerry Rothwell. *Bill King* (2006): vimeo.com/31019844.

Patrick Painter, Inc. *Bas Jan Ader: In Search of the Miraculous*. Directed by Soo Jin Jeong (2010): vimeo.com/11764389.

Petersen, Neal. "Bill Pinkney Conversation." (14 February 2014): www.youtube.com/watch?v=CsGOg_NqfE.

Petersen, Neal. "No Barriers." TEDx University of Nevada (1 February 2014): www.youtube.com/watch?v=QMK3RWzf7p Q&t=1059s.

Petersen, Neal and Bill Pinkney. "Neal Petersen and Bill Pinkney Inspirational Conservation." (9 April 2016): www.youtube.com/watch?v=7pkkAyRLo1w.

Petersen, Neal, et al., *No Barriers—The Neal Petersen Story*. Film documentary. No Barriers Education Foundation and the Charleston County School District Distance Education Learning Center (1999): www.youtube.com/watch?v=FgOy FWlwovU.

Pinkney, Bill. *The Incredible Voyage of Bill Pinkney* [documentary]. Directed by Lorie Conway. Narrated by Bill Cosby (1992): vimeo.com/444662476.

Pinkney, Bill, and Emma Garschagen. "Bill Pinkney: Solo Circumnavigator, Captain, and Author Returns to the Podcast." *On The Wind* podcast 361 (15 June 2022): www.59-north.com.

Polynesian Voyaging Society and *Hōkūle'a*. www.hokulea.com.

Raigetal, Larry. One People One Reef Seminar (4 March 2022): www.youtube.com/watch?v=iIusUqwvRW8.

"Robin Knox-Johnston's Return and Chichester's Comments." Compiled by Bud Taplin. Westsail Owners Association (posted 21 May 2011): www.youtube.com/watch?v=Glrkw_4-GhQ.

Ross, Herman. *Atlantic Creole: Black Folk Don't Sail* (2015): http://herossea.blogspot.com.

Ross, Herman. "Interview [video]." BEAT Ahoy! (25 May 2011): https://vimeo.com/37170017.

Rothwell, Jerry. *Deep Water: The Golden Globe Race and Donald Crowhurst* [feature-length documentary]. Directed by Louise Osmond and Jerry Rothwell (2006): https://www.youtube.com/watch?v=SiWv12EL4LE.

Rutherford, Matt. "Single-Handed Sailing Podcast." https://single-handedsailing.libsyn.com.

Sanders, Jon, and Andy Schell. "Jon Sanders/11-Time Circumnavigator." *On the Wind* podcast 323 (2021), www.59-north.com.

"Searchable Sea Literature." Edited by Richard King, Ned Schaumberg, and Alison Maas. Williams College (2023): https://sites.williams.edu/searchablesealit.

Searching for Coconuts, Sailing Tutorials. "Wind Vane Self-Steering Systems" (2020): www.youtube.com/watch?v=W8FyWojjgC8&t=10s.

Shaw, Yowei (host). "Power Tools," Invisiblia Podcast, National Public Radio (7 October 2022): www.npr.org/podcasts/510307/invisibilia.

Simmons, Thomas. *Coyote: The Mike Plant Story*. Produced by Ryan Lynch and Matthew Davis Walker (2017).

Sunderland, Abby, and Sachi Cunningham. "Abby Sunderland's Journey [short film documentary]." *Los Angeles Times* (2010): vimeo.com/246657360.

Sunderland, Abby. *Wild Eyes: The Abby Sunderland Story.* Directed by Laurence Sunderland (2011).

Watson, Jessica. *210 Days: Around the World with Jessica Watson* [documentary]. Narrated by Richard Branson. Sunstar Entertainment (2010).

Watson, Jessica. "Video Diary aboard *Ella's Pink Lady.*" Jessica-WatsonVideos, YouTube Channel (2009–2010): www.youtube.com/user/jessicawatsonvideo/videos.

Wystrach, Steve. The Robert Manry Project: https://www.robertmanryproject.com.

# Acknowledgments

Foremost thank you to Simon Winder at Penguin, who generously and enthusiastically believed in this project from the start, and to Wendy Wolf at Viking, who continued to tighten up the story with perfect experience and wit. Associate editors Eva Hodgkin and Paloma Ruiz provided careful, wise, and complementary feedback on the manuscript and so much help with other details, especially images. Thank you to production editor Anna Wilson and to the brilliant copyeditor Richard Mason. Thank you to Alice Gilbert-King for additional backmatter copy-editing. Thank you to my agent Russell Galen for taking me seriously and for his seemingly always correct advice.

My research benefitted from a collection of generous old and new friends, colleagues, and research assistants over three years, who read parts or all of the manuscript, fact-checked, and/or helped with a range of logistical matters and details at different stages of the project. A sincere thank you to Maya Anderson, Carol Baker, Gina Bardi, Dan Brayton, Douglas Brooks, Mike Brown, Trenton Carls, Karen Coates, Serafin "Jun" Colmenares, Alison Glassie, Stan Grayson, Patricia Halagao, Dixon Hollis, Kathi Kehmna, Ben Lowings, Herb McCormick, Alana McGillis, Jaja Martin, Kazuhiro Nishimura, Chris Nolan, Sayuri Norrish, Robin Potter, Hugh Powell, Elliot Rappaport, Matt Rigney, Polly Saltonstall, Susan Schnur, Gregg Selke, Robin Silva, Satomi Tsuboko-Ishii, and Dave Wiegel. Professors Steve Jones and Mike Brown each read a full draft and provided especially valuable feedback, enthusiasm, and knowledge. Captain H. E. Ross kindly offered important expert feedback on a few chapters, and author and editor Ben Lowings provided a brilliant and helpful reading in the final stages. Thank you to Alison O'Grady and the ILL staff at Williams College, to Paul O'Pecko and Maribeth Belinski at the Blunt White Library in Mystic, and to the English Department and library staff at the University of California Santa Cruz. I benefitted from collections, too, at the Filipino American Center at the San Francisco Public Library, Mystic-Noank Library, Connecticut College Library, Portsmouth Athenaeum, Middlebury College library in Monterey, and St Andrews University Library. The "On the Wind" podcast by Andy Schell and his colleagues has some important recent interviews, an oral history record, as does Matt Rutherford's "Singlehanded Sailing" podcast, the latter filled with his own insights as a solo mariner. I'm grateful to long-time colleagues and students at Williams College-Mystic Seaport and the Sea Education Association in Woods Hole, Massachusetts. Thank you to the anonymous people who built and maintain Google Books, HathiTrust, and Archive.org, opening the world of research to so many. I benefitted almost daily from their work in my research for this project. Mystic Seaport ran a fun seminar around Slocum and *Sailing Alone Around the World*, during which I learned a great deal from the participants—thank you to Arlene Marcionette for making this happen.

*Sailing Alone*, in an early form, along with my idea to cross the Atlantic by myself, began at the University of St Andrews in Scotland, where I was then in graduate school, surrounded by extraordinary writers and scholars who took time to share their expertise, notably Robert Crawford, Meaghan Delahunt, Douglass Dunn, Kathleen Jamie, and A. L. Kennedy.

In Anstruther I spent my most enjoyable days with the Scottish Fisheries Museum Boats Club; I thank all their members those many years ago for taking me in. I remain disappointed I was never able to bring *Fox* into the harbour there.

Thank you to single-handers Sharon Sites Adams, Kenichi Horie, Bill Pinkney, and H. E. Ross for taking their time to speak with me directly. It was an honor and privilege to learn from each of these four. Dame Naomi James, Robin Graham, Laura Dekker, and David's son Barry Lewis kindly corresponded with me and offered permission to use photographs. Thank you to Rita Gates and Maya Gates-Seymour for contacting me and so generously sharing more about Teddy's life.

Joel Smith in Noank sold me *Fox*, formerly *Sonar*. He gave me great advice. He was justly proud of his boat, he infused it with love, and he was pleased to see it travel far. Wes Maxwell helped enormously at the shipyard, and I'd have gone nowhere slowly—or perhaps never returned at all—if not for Sandy Van Zandt. Thank you to Rush Hambleton and the crew of *Catch It!*—Jon Mitchell, Lenny Bellet, and Munro Johnson—who joined me on the shakedown cruise and to whom I am so fortunate for their friendship. The tiller pilot, GPS, and radar were all impeccably set up for me by Dockside Electronics.

I've benefitted my whole life from endlessly supportive parents, Stephen and Essie King, and the Atlantic crossing would not have happened, nor would the time and space to write this, if not for my spouse Lisa Gilbert. Thank you to our child Alice Day, who gives the voyage meaning.

Richard King
Santa Cruz, California, May 2023

# Index

Adams, Sharon Sites, 169, 191, 192, 207, 264, 269, 338, 418; after solo sailing, 165–6, 172–7; before solo sailing, 171–2, 174; environmentalism, 170–73, 177; feminism, 174–5, 177; hallucination, 242; loneliness, 168, 172, 239–40; navigation, 166–7, 172; ocean/marine life relationship (general), 170–74; *Pacific Lady,* 165, 170; pet turtle, 138; reader/writer, 165, 167, 170, 174, 241; religious faith, 405; seabirds, 171; *Sea Sharp II,* 164, 166–7, 177; self-steering ("angel at the helm"), 164–5, 166, 168, 182, 186, 258, 405; shark, 171–2; suicidal thoughts, 232; trans-Pacific solo passages 163–5, 167–72; why go, 171–2, 174

Ader, Bas Jan, 211–12

Aebi, Tania, 221, 266, 267, 302, 325–6, 419; environmentalism, 375; marine life relationship, 142–3; pet cat, 139–41; reader/writer, 11, 344, 443

*Aenid,* 365

African American mariners (general), 161, 299, 419. *See also* Seymour, Pinkney, *et al.*

age and solo sailing, 94, 249, 325–7

airplane travel, 155–6

AIS (Automated Identification System), 316, 331–2, 401

Alacaluf people, 75

albatross, 24, 28, 29, 130–31, 157, 171, 199, 221, 304, 346, 431; MacArthur, 385–6; sooty, 385; wandering, 385, 388

alcohol at sea, 237, 238–9

Allcard, Edward, 12–13, 112–14, 116, 157, 285, 416, 421

*Alone Around the World. See* James, Naomi

*Alone Through the Roaring Forties. See* Dumas, Vito

Ancher, Michael, 40

Andersen, Mary Sue, 212

Anderson, J. R. L., 132

Andrews, Walter, 45

Andrews, William, 45, 47, 53, 70, 86, 192, 292–93, 416, 423–24

animism, 257–61, 339